ANSWERS TO QUESTIONS

Other works by F. F. Bruce

TRADITION OLD AND NEW
THIS IS THAT
THE SPREADING FLAME
ISRAEL AND THE NATIONS
AN EXPANDED PARAPHRASE OF THE EPISTLES OF PAUL
SECOND THOUGHTS ON THE DEAD SEA SCROLLS
THE TEACHER OF RIGHTEOUSNESS IN THE QUMRAN TEXTS
BIBLICAL EXEGESIS IN THE QUMRAN TEXTS
ST. MATTHEW
THE ACTS OF THE APOSTLES: GREEK TEXT WITH INTRODUCTION AND COMMENTARY
THE BOOK OF THE ACTS: ENGLISH TEXT WITH EXPOSITION AND NOTES
THE EPISTLE OF PAUL TO THE ROMANS: AN INTRODUCTION AND COMMENTARY
FIRST AND SECOND CORINTHIANS
THE EPISTLE TO THE EPHESIANS: A VERSE-BY-VERSE EXPOSITION
THE EPISTLE TO THE COLOSSIANS: ENGLISH TEXT WITH EXPOSITION AND NOTES
THE EPISTLE TO THE HEBREWS: ENGLISH TEXT WITH EXPOSITION AND NOTES
THE EPISTLES OF JOHN: INTRODUCTION, EXPOSITION AND NOTES
PAUL AND HIS CONVERTS
THE NEW TESTAMENT DOCUMENTS: ARE THEY RELIABLE?
THE APOSTOLIC DEFENCE OF THE GOSPEL
THE BOOKS AND THE PARCHMENTS
THE ENGLISH BIBLE
THE HITTITES AND THE OLD TESTAMENT
NEW TESTAMENT HISTORY

F. F. BRUCE

ANSWERS

TO

QUESTIONS

/5673

ZONDERVAN PUBLISHING HOUSE
A DIVISION OF THE ZONDERVAN CORPORATION
GRAND RAPIDS, MICHIGAN

TO
THE MEMBERS
OF
CRESCENT ROAD CHURCH
STOCKPORT
WHO ASK THEIR SHARE
OF QUESTIONS

ISBN: 0 85364 101 3
Copyright © 1972, The Paternoster Press

Library of Congress Catalog Card Number 72-95520
First Zondervan printing 1973

Reprinted by special arrangement with
The Paternoster Press

Printed in the United States of America

CONTENTS

PART I: ANSWERS ON BIBLICAL TEXTS

Old Testament

	page		page
The Pentateuch	2	The Poetical and Wisdom Books	21
The Historical Books	15	The Prophets	27

New Testament

The Synoptic Gospels	39	The Pauline Epistles	85
The Gospel of John	66	Hebrews and the "General" Epistles	120
The Acts of the Apostles	75	The Book of the Revelation	136

PART II: ANSWERS ON VARIOUS SUBJECTS

Ancient Literature and Archaeology	144	Evangelicalism	203
Antichrist	153	Excommunication	204
Apostasy	154	Faith	204
Apostolic Succession	154	Fate	205
Baptism	154	Federal Headship	205
Barth, Karl	155	Forgiveness	206
Belial	156	Fundamentalism	206
Biblical Criticism, Interpretation,		Gifts (Spiritual)	207
Texts, Versions, etc.	156	God the Father	207
Brethren History	163	Gospel	208
Calendars and Chronology	168	Harvest Festivals	209
Canon of Scripture	170	Healing	209
Catechumens	171	Heaven	210
Christ	171	Hebrew Words and Phrases	210
Church	180	Heresy	212
Confession	189	Holy Shroud	212
Covenant (New)	190	Holy Spirit	213
Creation	190	IHS	215
Creeds	190	Immortality	215
Crucifixion	191	Infant Dedication	215
Demon Possession	191	Inspiration	216
Dispensationalism	191	Jacob and Israel	218
Doctrine	192	Judas	218
Easter	194	Judgment	218
Ecumenism	194	Justification	219
Ekklesia	196	Kingdom of God/Heaven	221
Election	196	Laying on of Hands	222
Eschatology	198	Lord's Prayer	222
Eternity	202	Lord's Supper	223

	page		page
Marriage and Divorce	226	Salvation	238
Millennium	227	Sanctification	238
Ministry	228	Saul	239
Modernism	229	Science and Faith	240
Nazarenes	229	Sectarianism	240
Nebuchadnezzar	229	Sin	241
Open Brethren and Spiritual Liberty	230	Spirits	241
Parables	232	Sunday	242
Pentecostalism	232	Synagogue	243
Prayer	233	Tabernacle	243
Preaching	233	Tithing	243
Predestination	235	Typology	244
Regeneration	235	Universalism	246
Resurrection	236	Women and the Church's Ministry	247
Revival	236	Worship	247
Roman Catholicism	237	Writing	250
Sacrifices	237		

FOREWORD

IN THE MIDDLE OF 1952 I was invited by Dr. F. A. Tatford, Editor of *The Harvester*, a Christian periodical published by The Paternoster Press, to take over responsibility for the page headed "Answers to Questions." This page had previously been contributed by Harold P. Barker, a man with a highly original turn of thought and expression, who had impressed his own personality on it. When he died, no one could fill his incomparable shoes, but I accepted the editorial invitation and proceeded to deal with the page in my own way. From July 1952 to the present day I have endeavoured to answer over 1,800 questions in it month by month, with one intermission imposed by the British postal strike early in 1971.

Naturally enough, since the questions originated with readers of *The Harvester*, they reflect the background and interests of that readership. However, it will be seen that they range through a wide variety of subjects, and are not confined to any one confessional or connexional position. Their general context is the wider independent church order with which most readers of *The Harvester* would be familiar. Since they rise out of a strongly biblicist situation, most of them are biblically orientated and the authority of Scripture is the major premiss of questions and answers alike.

Perhaps it would be as well to remind readers of this volume that the questions answered in it are questions which have been sent to me, not questions which I myself might have originated. That is all to the good, since it can be expected that they reflect the majority interests of a worldwide constituency, and are therefore more likely to be of value to a greater number than if they had been the selection of an individual. The fact, for instance, that there are fewer questions asked about the great prophets of Israel than about various apocalyptic interpretations is not necessarily sinister; it simply reflects the concerns of those who asked the questions. Not only does this give a more varied character to the work; it does at the same time help to ensure that a large number of questions of general interest is included.

I have frequently been asked to answer questions in areas where I have no special competence. Since I have usually had readier access than my questioners to reliable sources of information, I have tried to give them the answers they sought, citing the appropriate authorities. But as the present work is my own responsibility, I have thought it unnecessary to reproduce such second-hand answers here.

Other questions have had to do with matters of taste and opinion. These I have usually declined to handle. On the few occasions when I have been less cautious, my temerity has at least led to an enlarging of my acquaintance with human nature. One recurrent theme of unanswered questions has been feminine dress. I have been invited to make pronouncements on many of its more interesting manifestations, ranging from hats in church to bikinis on the beach. There may be some theological professors who can speak with authority on such subjects, but I am not one of them. On one occasion, when I mildly observed that women's slacks could not be categorized as "that which pertaineth unto a man" within the meaning of Deut. 22:5, a thoughtful reader undertook to lighten my darkness by sending me a list of men's attire and women's. Unfortunately, it occurred to me that, if he was right, the kilt was a feminine garment, not masculine; and so palpably erroneous a conclusion constituted the *reductio ad absurdum* of his principle of classification. On another occasion, my answer to a questioner who doubted the propriety of administering communion to girls in miniskirts brought me the disapproval of some elder brethren and the award of the "*Buzz* Badge of Honour" for August 1968 from the magazine *Buzz*.

On a more serious level, my public answering of questions has from time to time brought me a number of private and personal questions and involved me in a ministry of pastoral counselling by post, for which I have no qualifications. Clearly some people will unburden themselves more readily to a complete stranger at a distance than to some more familiar figure close at hand; and however many readers are puzzled by the "spirits in prison" or by the fact that Jehoiachin's accession age is given as eighteen years in Kings and eight in Chronicles, their real problems lie elsewhere and are not susceptible of short and easy answers.

Both on the personal and on the general level, questions about divorce and remarriage have, regrettably but understandably, become more frequent with the passage of the years. My public answers to such questions have probably won me the reputation of a rigorist. But I should never dream of trying to lay down the law on matters of this kind—who would listen to me if I did? My policy has been regularly to give what seems to me to be the meaning of relevant scriptures. This is the only kind of service that I am really competent to render, and the bulk of this volume comprises what might be called occasional contributions to biblical exegesis.

Many of the answers that have appeared in the question page of *The Harvester* have been so ephemeral that they have properly passed into oblivion after a first reading. They might all have done so but for the interest of some friends in this and other countries who were anxious to give them a more enduring currency, and who pressed for their permanent publication in book form. Of these friends one in particular, the Rev. Clive L. Rawlins, was good enough to take upon himself the considerable labour not only of classifying the questions and answers according to biblical or topical sequence, but also of having them typed out suitably for my consideration. Had he not, of his own volition, undertaken this very considerable task, I doubt very much if I should have found time or inclination to undertake it myself. As it is, his compilation—severely pruned and edited so as to bring the whole within reasonable compass—has formed the basis of the following pages. In addition, he has relieved me of further labour by preparing the index. To him especially I express my gratitude, which must also be expressed to Mr. Arnold Pickering, who has given voluntary and valuable help with proof-correcting.

F.F.B.

PART I

Answers on Bible Texts

THE PENTATEUCH

Genesis 1:1. *Am I justified in preferring to understand Gen. 1:1 as meaning: "In the beginning God created the 'space' and the 'matter'"?*

Hardly. The word translated "heaven" in our common version includes the material of the heavenly bodies as well as the space in which they move; the word translated "earth" denotes our planet as distinct from the rest of the material universe. The two words together comprise the whole created universe of space and time.

Gen. 1:1. *What is the "beginning" of Gen. 1:1? Can it be understood as the beginning of God?*

No; from first to last the God of the Bible is revealed as the One who is from everlasting to everlasting and has neither beginning nor end. The "beginning" in which He created heaven and earth was the beginning of time; time (unlike eternity) is something which belongs to the created order. The material universe had a beginning then, and will in due course have an end.

Gen. 1:26. *In Gen. 1:26, when God says, "Let us make man", does the word "us" indicate the Holy Trinity?*

It is more probably to be treated as the "plural of majesty," or a plural denoting God as including within Himself all the powers of deity. See p. 208.

Please explain the words "in our image, after our likeness" in Gen. 1:26, and indicate the reason for the repetition.

I find it difficult to distinguish in sense between "image" and "likeness" here and suggest that the repetition is for emphasis

(cf. 1 Cor. 11:7, "he is the image and glory of God"). The words appear to denote man as a creature endowed with moral and intellectual responsibility with whom God can have fellowship and in whom He can see His own character reproduced.

Gen. 1:28. *Does the word "replenish" in Gen. 1:28 mean that there were people on earth before Adam? Is it the same word as is used to Noah in Gen. 9:1?*

The word used in both places is the ordinary Hebrew word meaning "fill"; it is so translated (rightly) in the R.S.V. and N.E.B. Of course, in Gen. 9:1 we know that the idea of replenishing is implied, for there were people on earth before Noah; but the Biblical record is silent on the presence of human beings before Adam (not to put it more categorically), and no such inference can be drawn from the language of Gen. 1:28.

Gen. 2:7. *In The Unfolding Drama of Redemption, Vol. 1, p. 55, Dr. W. Graham Scroggie writes with regard to Gen. 2:7, "The body and the spirit (breath . . .) constituted the soul. The soul is the middle term in which body and spirit meet in the unity of personality." This statement seems to imply that Body plus Spirit equals Soul. Is the writer advocating the dual nature of man? How would you deal with Gen. 2:7?*

The phrase translated "living soul" in Gen. 2:7 means "a living person"; i.e., the word "soul" (Heb. *nephesh*) here does not denote a component part of the living human being, but the whole. (The expression in Gen. 2:7 must not be confused with the formally identical expression used elsewhere with a collective force to denote

2

creatures of the animal world in the narrower sense, as, e.g., in Gen. 2:19, where it is rendered "living creature.)" That is to say, Gen. 2:7 does not teach that Body plus Spirit equals Soul (in the usual restricted sense of the word soul), but that Body plus Spirit equals Person. The man became a living person when God, having fashioned his body, breathed the breath of life into it. The difficulty lies partly in the fact that the Hebrew word *nephesh* has such a wide range of meaning (see p. 211), and partly in the fact that we tend to read later ideas back into the Old Testament. I doubt whether the familiar distinction between "soul" and "spirit" is clearly expressed in the Bible outside the Pauline writings; in fact, the terms seem at times to be used interchangeably. And even Paul, when he is not dealing explicitly with the soul-spirit tension, can use the terms in a more indefinite sense. The best discussion known to me of this whole subject in so far as it relates to the Old Testament is A. R. Johnson's *The Vitality of the Individual in the Thought of Ancient Israel* (Cardiff, 1949).

Gen. 3:1. *In his exposition of the Corinthian Epistles, the late Dr. G. Campbell Morgan writes (p. 173): "Again go back to the Garden of Eden, where Satan appeared as a bright and brilliant being. That is the story. The idea of the devil appearing as a snake is, of course, ridiculous. That is not the word at all. It is a shining one. Eve was beguiled by a brilliant appearance." Is there any support for this statement?*

There is none in the Biblical text. The Hebrew word is *nahash*, which is an ordinary word meaning "serpent"; the same is true of the Greek word *ophis*, which is used in the Septuagint of Genesis 3 and also in the New Testament references to the serpent, 2 Cor. 11:3 and Rev. 12:9, etc. I am not sure what the source of Dr. Campbell Morgan's statement was. There

is an old tradition, best known to us from Milton, which represents the serpent before the Fall as moving

... not with indented wave,
Prone on the ground, as since, but on his rear,
Circular base of rising folds, that towered
Fold above fold a surging maze, his head
Crested aloft, and carbuncle his eyes;
With burnished neck of verdant gold, erect
Amidst his circling spires, that on the grass
Floated redundant: pleasing was his shape,
And lovely, never since of serpent kind
Lovelier ...

Campbell Morgan's reference to "the word," however, suggests that he may have thought of the phrase *nahash saraph*, used for the fiery serpents of Num. 21:6; the word *saraph* ("burning") is also used for the seraphim of Isa. 6. But the serpent of Eden is not described as *saraph*, and there is nothing in the language of Gen. 3 that justifies the statement which you quote.

Gen. 3:15. *Can Gen. 3:15 be properly taken as referring to the suffering and death of our virgin-born Lord, and not rather to the strife and enmity which have marred creation ever since the fall? Surely the serpent had no power to bruise our Lord's heel, whereas His destroying of the one who had the power of death would be inadequately described as bruising the serpent's head.*

We can interpret Gen. 3:14f., where doom is pronounced on the serpent, on two planes. On the one plane we are to think of the literal serpent, crawling on its belly, eating the dust of the earth with its food, and having its head crushed by man's heel, which it can bite in retaliation. This natural hostility between human beings and serpents may certainly be regarded as a sample of the strife and enmity which mar creation. But the plenary Christian sense is expressed in Rev. 12:9, where "the old serpent" of Eden is identified with "the devil and Satan, the deceiver of the whole world." It is true, as you suggest, that men

3

of God have waged spiritual warfare against him throughout the generations, and in the measure in which they have gained the victory over him we may fairly see a fulfilment of Gen. 3:15 on a higher plane. (In the phrase "the seed of the woman" it is Eve and not Mary who if referred to as "the woman".) But their victory over him is effective only as it is caught up into the decisive victory of Christ. When He said to the men who arrested Him in Gethsemane, "This is your hour, and the power of darkness" (Luke 22:53), His words implied that the prince of darkness now had his moment of opportunity against Him, and this might well be described pictorially as the bruising of His heel by the serpent. But in the process the serpent had his head crushed—no inadequate figure for his being "destroyed" or brought to nought (Heb. 2:14). This does not conflict with our Lord's claim that He laid down His life of His own accord (John 10:18). In the history of the exegesis of Gen. 3:15 it is a matter of some interest that while Roman Catholic and Lutheran interpreters have, almost exclusively, taken "the seed of the woman" to refer to Christ alone, Calvinists for the most part have understood the phrase of mankind (or at least redeemed mankind), which is one day to triumph in Christ over the infernal serpent (cf. Rom. 16:20). So John Calvin himself: "I explain, therefore, the seed to mean the posterity of the woman generally. But since experience teaches that not all the sons of Adam by far arise as conquerors of the devil, we must necessarily come to one head, that we may find to whom the victory belongs."

Gen. 4:7. *In the Septuagint of Gen. 4:7 God is represented as saying to Cain, "If thou offerest rightly but dost not divide rightly, hast thou not sinned? Hold thy peace." Does this represent the force of the original text?*

The Septuagint of this verse deviates considerably from the Hebrew. To begin with, it seems to make Cain's doing well or not well depend on the correctness of his sacrificial procedure. (This reminds us of the argument sometimes heard that our Lord's words of institution, "This do in remembrance of me," really mean "This sacrifice in remembrance of me.") Then it obscures the reference to sin couching at the door, by translating the word rendered "coucheth" (R.V.) as if it were an imperative and applying it to Cain. The Hebrew text of the verse may be rendered thus: "If thou doest well, shall there not be lifting up (i.e. of thy fallen countenance)? And if thou doest not well, sin is a couching beast at the door and its desire is towards thee, but thou shouldest have it under thy control" (cf. R.S.V.).

Gen. 4:26. *In Gen. 4:26 ("then began men to call upon the name of the* LORD*") does the word "men" represent "Adam" in Hebrew? If so, might it point to Adam's personal salvation at this time?*

There is no word for "men" in the original. In Hebrew the verb "began" appears here in which might be called an impersonal passive form, literally translated: "then it was begun to call . . ." (i.e. "then people began . . ."). The reference is probably to the beginning of the use of the name Yahweh (Jehovah) for God.

Gen. 6:2. *If, as the Scofield Bible suggests, the "sons of God" in Gen. 6:2 are the "godly line of Seth" who intermarried with the "godless line of Cain," how can this be applied to Job 1:6 where (again according to the Scofield Bible) the "scene is in heaven"?*

Whoever the "sons of God" may be in Gen. 6:2 (and the view expressed in the Scofield Bible is itself not free from difficulties), it is certain that the beings so called in Job 1:6 are angels, members of the "council of Jehovah," of which we read also in 1 Kings 22:19; Ps. 82:1, and Jer. 23:18, 22. In this heavenly court Satan appears as official prosecutor; in

4

other words, he fills the role that his name suggests, for "Satan" means "adversary" (cf. Rev. 12:10). In Gen. 6:2 the reference may be to beings of angelic nature, as their nature seems to be contrasted with that of the wives whom they chose; the latter are described as "the daughters of Adam"—i.e. women of the human race. The Septuagint reads "angels of God" for "sons of God" in this verse. The analogy of other early folk-movements suggests that a conquering race of men with a higher culture might be designated "sons of God" by contrast with an "inferior" race of "mere" human beings. But that men's recognition of the beauty of "daughters of Adam" (i.e. women in general), and their choosing wives from them, should be commented on as something noteworthy (not to say reprehensible) seems rather improbable. The "daughters" of verse 2 and 4 are those of verse 1, and cannot be restricted to one particular family (e.g. the line of Cain, as some commentators have suggested). My own judgment is that the "sons of God" in Gen. 6 are angelic beings, just as they are in Job—that they are, in fact, the angels of Jude 6, who "did not keep their own position but left their proper dwelling".

Gen. 6:3. *In Gen. 6:3 A.V. and R.V. text render "strive with men", R.V. margin gives "rule in man" or "abide in man", R.S.V. has "abide in man" and N.E.B. "remain in man". Which is the best translation? And is the subject of the verb the Holy Spirit or the breath of life?*

The diversity of translation reflects the difficulty in understanding the Hebrew text as it has come down to us, and complete certainty in its interpretation is unattainable. An expansive paraphrase of the verse might run like this: "And the LORD said; The spirit of life which I have breathed into man shall not prevail in him indefinitely, for after all he is but mortal flesh; his days shall be restricted to 120 years."

Gen. 8:3. *In Gen. 8:3 we read that "the water returned from off the earth continually" (A.V. margin, "in going and returning"). Where did the waters return to?*

The reference no doubt is to the process of evaporation; if so, it was to the atmosphere that the waters "returned." The marginal reading gives a literal rendering of the Hebrew, which is translated more idiomatically and intelligibly in the text (cf. N.E.B.: "The water gradually receded").

With further reference to the last question, it is doubtful whether evaporation alone could account for the disappearance of such a volume of water so quickly. May not the "going and returning" (A.V. mg.) denote the flow and ebb of tidal motion (cf. "going and decreasing" in v. 5, A.V. mg.)?

It may. According to Gen. 7:11, the flood was due not only to heavy rain ("the windows of the heavens were opened"), but also to an immense tidal wave, resulting perhaps from a convulsion of the sea-bed ("all the fountains of the great deep burst forth"). The abating of the flood-water would therefore be due to a corresponding tidal recession as well as to evaporation.

Gen. 9:3. *In Gen. 9:3 Noah and his family are permitted to eat "every moving thing that lives." Is this to be taken in the same unrestricted sense as 1 Tim. 4:4, and if so, did the distinction between clean and unclean animals not obtain in Noah's time?*

The principle laid down in 1 Tim. 4:4 emphasizes that in Christianity there is no religious distinction made between eating one kind of animal flesh and another, and (more particularly) that there is no ban on eating animal flesh as such (as some Gnostic teachers maintained). A distinction between clean and unclean animals is made in certain parts of the story of Noah (e.g. Gen. 7:2), but not in the food-law of Gen. 9:3f.; the important restriction there relates to the eating of blood. We may be intended to gather that the distinction between clean and unclean animals as regards their use for food was not insisted on before the Levitical law (Lev. 11: 1-47; cf. Deut. 14: 3-20); this distinction was to be a mark of differentiation between Israel and the other nations.

Gen. 9:25, 26. *Has Gen. 9:25, 26 any relation to the colour question?*

No; it relates to the Canaanites' servitude to the Israelites, as in Josh. 9:23; Judg. 1:28, etc.

Gen. 11: 1-9. *What was the purpose of the tower of Babel?*

All that the Biblical narrative tells us about this is that the builders said: "Come, let us build ourselves a city, and a tower with its top in the heavens, and let us make a name for ourselves, lest we be scattered abroad upon the face of the whole earth" (Gen. 11:4). This indicates that, so far at least as the city was concerned, their purpose was to promote concentration and avoid dispersal—a purpose which was divinely reversed by means of the confusion of tongues. Apart from that, we can but draw our own inferences. (And be it borne in mind that, just as it is unwarranted to make another man responsible for the inferences which we draw from what he says, so it is unwarranted to suppose that our inferences from Holy Writ share the authority of Holy Writ.) Some commentators have supposed that the purpose of so high a tower was to serve as a place of refuge if another flood should come; I should prefer to link the words "a tower with its top in the heavens" with the name of the temple-tower of Babylon, E-temen-an-ki, "house of the foundation-platform of heaven and earth." An interesting discussion of the subject in the light of archaeology is available in the

little book entitled *The Tower of Babel*, by André Parrot (1955); he suggests that this tower, like other ziggurats in Babylonia, was envisaged as a stairway by which the deity who resided in the temple on its summit might descend to visit the earth and return home again. In the attempt to reach heaven he sees "not a clenched fist, but an outstretched hand", not defiance but entreaty. "It was," he concludes, "a strange and moving anticipation of Isaiah's cry: 'Oh that thou wouldest rend the heavens, that thou wouldest come down!' (Isa. 64:1). We know how, on Christmas night, God did come down."

Gen. 14:18-20. *In the light of Heb. 7: 1-10 should we regard the appearance of Melchizedek in Gen. 14: 18-20 as a Christophany, or was he an historical individual?*

In the light of Heb. 7:3, "resembling the Son of God," we can rule out the idea of a Christophany. The Son of God could not be "made like" Himself. We should recognize Melchizedek as a historical character, living in the earlier part of the second millennium B.C., king of Salem, a city of Canaan, and priest of God Most High (the designation under which the Creator was worshipped there), to whose priesthood the house of David succeeded (cf. Ps. 110:4). His record, as viewed by the writer to the Hebrews, is so controlled (as regards both what is said of him and what is not said) that it presents at a whole series of points a parallel with our Lord. See p. 122.

Gen. 30:37-42. *It is commonly said that the narrative of Gen. 30:37-42 reflects a form of genetic superstition. For example, A. Rendle Short in* The Bible and Modern Medicine *(p. 84) deals with it under the heading "Medical Folklore" and refers to Jacob's idea as superstition—the implication being that the large number of striped, speckled and spotted lambs and kids was due not to Jacob's stratagem* *(although Jacob no doubt thought it was) but to God's overruling. But does the word "so" in verse 42 ("so the feebler were Laban's") indicate that the narrator himself ascribes their large number to Jacob's stratagem?*

The word "so" in Gen. 30:42 is the ordinary Hebrew conjunction meaning "and"; it might imply, but does not assert, a causal connection between Jacob's stratagem and the fact that Jacob acquired the stronger animals and Laban the weaker. As Professor Rendle Short pointed out, Jacob himself ascribed his enrichment to God (even if he supposed that his own stratagem was the means which God used): "Thus," he said to his wives, "God has taken away the cattle of your father and given them to me" (Gen. 31:9).

Gen. 49:10. *What is the meaning of Shiloh in Gen. 49:10? Has the word anything to do with the place-name Shiloh (1 Sam. 1:3, etc.)?*

It would be very difficult to see any sense in Gen. 49:10 if Shiloh meant the place of that name, which lay in the tribal territory of Ephraim. One suggestion is to relate the word to a Babylonian word meaning "prince"; the Messianic reference would become quite clear if we read "until the Prince comes." But more probably we should read the word as *shello* ("whose it is") and render as in R.S.V., "until he comes to whom it belongs." Ezekiel was probably referring to this very prophecy when he said in God's name concerning the crown of Judah: "this also shall be no more, until he come whose right it is; and I will give it him" (Ezek. 21:27). The Messianic reference thus becomes even more unmistakable.

Exodus 3:18. *Did God encourage Moses to tell a "white lie" by seeking Pharaoh's permission for the Israelites who were in Egypt to go "three days' journey into the wilderness" to sacrifice to God (Ex. 3:18; 5:3; 8:27)?*

It may be that the expression "a three days' journey" was a current expression for a short journey. The journey referred to was to take them to Horeb (cf. Ex. 3:12, "you shall serve God upon this mountain"), which was much more than three days' journey away (in the event, as Ch. 19:1 shows, it was in the third month after their departure from Egypt that the Israelites arrived there). It should be noticed, however, that Pharaoh's willingness to obey God was tested first on a small scale. Had Pharaoh granted this moderate request, he would not have refused larger requests when they came, and would have reaped blessing and not loss by his obedience; as it was, his rejection of the small request which was made of him at first indicated that obstinacy at the core of his being which became increasingly intractable until at last it landed him in disaster.

Ex. 7-12. *It has been suggested that in the plagues of Egypt, or at least in many of them, one can trace a natural sequence, in which the features of one visitation can be viewed as the result of a preceding one. If this is so does it detract from the miraculous character of the plagues, which the Biblical record consistently characterizes as acts of God?*

A cause-and-effect connexion has indeed been traced between a number of the plagues; for the way in which this can be done reference could be made to Kenneth Kitchen's article "Plagues of Egypt" in the I.V.F. *New Bible Dictionary*, where he acknowledges his indebtedness to a study by Greta Hort. Not all the plagues lend themselves to this diagnosis; the tenth plague in particular, with its fearful selectivity, cannot be reduced to the operation of natural law. The point throughout the whole narrative is that God was at work on His people's behalf, now using the more familiar processes of nature, and now acting supernaturally. Whether He chose to use for His purpose

7

the laws of His own creation, or to transcend those laws, the action was equally His: even the Egyptian wizards had to acknowledge "the finger of God" in the course of events. The timing of the whole sequence of plagues, the circumstances in which each one started and finished, and the purpose which was accomplished by their means, alike attested the power of God exerting itself in judgment and deliverance.

Ex. 12:13. *What is the precise meaning of the verb "pass over" in Exodus 12:13, 23, 27?*

It means probably that the Lord would step across the threshold of each house that was marked with the blood of the passover lamb, and stand guard over the household within, so that the destroying angel would be prevented from entering.

Ex. 12:15. *What was involved in the sentence of being "cut off from Israel" in Ex. 12:15 and many other places?*

Sometimes execution (by stoning) is plainly indicated, as in Ex. 31:14, where the sabbath-breaker "shall be cut off from among his people" (compare verse 15, where "he shall surely be put to death"). This is probably the sense of most occurrences of the phrase. On some occasions outlawry rather than execution may be indicated, and in one or two instances the offence might be such as God alone would know, in which case He Himself might be expected to act in appropriate judgment.

Ex. 12:22. *A speaker, referring to the slaying of the paschal lamb in Exodus 12, said that the "bason" of verse 22 was really the threshold of the door. Is this right?*

It is very probably right. The Hebrew word which is here translated "bason" (A.V.) is *saph*. But *saph* is also the spelling of the Hebrew word for "threshold." The threshold, hollowed out as it was by the constant treading of feet, would in any case form a convenient receptacle for the blood of the passover lamb when it was slaughtered (so N.E.B. margin). Then, when some of the blood was put on the lintel and the side-posts of the door, the entrance to the house was protected on all four sides.

Ex. 12:33-15:19. *Are there any secular historians who record the fact of the Exodus?*

Yes, but the accounts given by secular historians are garbled and vitiated by anti-Jewish prejudice. For example, about 270 B.C. Manetho, an Egyptian priest, wrote a *History of Egypt* in Greek, on the basis of Egyptian records accessible to him. Many of his statements, when checked by inscriptions relating to the times with which he deals, prove to be remarkably correct. In the course of his narrative of the Nineteenth Dynasty he tells how a large body of lepers, who had been compelled to labour in the royal quarries, revolted against their Egyptian masters under the leadership of a priest named Osarsiph (whose name was changed to Moses), but were ultimately driven from Egypt by a king named Amenophis (the king now identified as Merenptah (c. 1230 B.C.). Josephus, the Jewish historian of the first century A.D., records this extract from Manetho, but refuses to believe that the expulsion of the lepers had anything to do with the Exodus. He prefers to identify the Exodus with the expulsion of the Hyksos, the Asian conquerors of Egypt, at the beginning of the Eighteenth Dynasty (c. 1560 B.C.). But Manetho knew what he was about; the account he gives is such an account as might be expected from a patriotic Egyptian historian. A similar account of the Exodus is given by the Roman historian Tacitus at the beginning of the second century A.D.; he says that many authors agree in this presentation of the matter. The author to whom he was chiefly indebted seems to have been Lysimachus of Alexandria, of the second century B.C., whose account is also quoted by Josephus. It is just barely possible that a contemporary reference to the Exodus is found in Egyptian records. The well-known victory stela of Pharaoh Merenptah contains the claim, "Israel is desolate; it has no seed"—where the form given to the word "Israel" indicates that Israel was not yet a settled community. It could conceivably be that the Exodus is here represented as a great Egyptian victory, resulting in the wiping out of the Israelites, although Merenptah more probably refers to them as having by now entered Canaan.

Ex. 12:37. *Mr. David Ben-Gurion has been reported as stating in the Israeli parliament at Jerusalem only about 600 Israelites left Egypt. In M.A. Beek's* A Journey through the Old Testament *it is stated: "If the Biblical account were taken literally, and if we assume an army marching in columns of four, one yard between each column, the front line of this army would have reached Damascus by the time the rear was still crossing the the Egyptian border. This is clearly an impossible exaggeration" (p. 66). Please comment on this.*

You may consult someone who has practical experience of the marshalling and moving of large bodies of men, and he will tell you how long it would take to move "six hundred thousand men on foot, besides women and children" (Ex. 12:37) and what the length of the column of march would be. But simply to delete three noughts, as Mr. Ben-Gurion evidently did, is an unsatisfactory way of dealing with the problem. A more serious suggestion is that in the course of transmission one meaning of the Hebrew word *'eleph*, "tent group" has been replaced by another meaning of the same word, "thousand." This was worked out in detail in Flinders Petrie's *Egypt and Israel* pp. 40ff.; he concluded that some 20,000 left Egypt. You will find an interesting discussion of the whole question in the *Journal of Transactions of the Victoria Institute* for 1955 (Vol. 87, pp. 82ff., 145ff.), arising out of a paper by Dr. R. E. D. Clark on "The Large Numbers of the Old Testament—Especially in Connexion with the Exodus."

Ex. 14:1ff.; 20:7. *It was reported some time ago that a new Jewish version of the Old Testament "says that Moses did not really cross the Red Sea, and revises the Third Commandment to condemn perjury, not profanity of God's name." Have you any comment on this?*

It is well known that the "sea" which the Israelites crossed at the Exodus was not the Red Sea as we know it today, but the *Yam Suf* or "sea of reeds"—perhaps a northerly extension of the Gulf of Suez or a sheet of water in the neighbourhood of the Bitter Lakes. I presume that the version in question makes this plain. As for the Third Commandment, it is quite true that what is primarily prohibited is swearing falsely in the Lord's name (perjury); although a principle is enshrined in the Commandment which "requireth the holy and reverent use of God's names, titles, attributes, ordinances, word and works", and "forbiddeth all profaning or abusing of any thing whereby God maketh himself known" (*Westminster Shorter Catechism*). And in the light of Matt. 5:33ff. it might be said that there are even certain kinds of swearing *truly* in the Lord's name which might come near to violating the spirit of the Third Commandment. But as regards the primary sense of the words I have no doubt that this Jewish version is right.

Ex. 14-15. *In* The Coming Prince, *p. 118, Sir Robert Anderson states that the children of Israel crossed the Red Sea on Nisan 17. Is there any evidence for this?*

I don't think the day—or rather the night—of the crossing can be determined so exactly. They set out on Nisan 15, "the morrow after the passover" (Num. 33:3); if the subsequent stages represent the places where they encamped each successive night, then they pitched in Succoth on Nisan 16 (which began at sunset on what we should still call Nisan 15), in Etham on Nisan 17, before Migdol on Nisan 18; the crossing of the sea would take place either on Nisan 18 or (more probably) after sunset which marked the beginning of Nisan 19. But these calculations have an element of uncertainty in them, and nothing can be built on them.

Ex. 22:2, 3. *In our Bible readings in Exodus we have found some difficulty in obtaining a clear meaning in verses 2 and 3 of Chapter 22. Can you give some help on this passage?*

The difficulty is due to the fact that in the text as it has been handed down to us verse 2 and the first half of verse 3 are inserted as a parenthesis into what is without them a coherent statement. The readjustment has been made in the R.S.V., which runs: "If a man steals an ox or a sheep, and kills it or sells it, he shall pay five oxen for an ox, and four sheep for a sheep. He shall make restitution; if he has nothing, then he shall be sold for his theft." There the second half of verse 3 follows immediately on verse 1, and is followed in its turn by verse 4. Thus the law about ox or sheep stealing (verses 1, 3b, 4) is stated as a coherent whole. (In this respect the law of Moses is more humane than the law of England was a few generations ago, when sheep-stealing was a capital offence.) Then, after verse 4, the parenthesis, dealing with house-breaking, appears as a separate unit. Killing a housebreaker by night ranks as justifiable homicide; but it is not justifiable by daylight, presumably because "if the sun be risen upon him" he can be identified and reported to the authorities.

Ex. 31:3. *Was Bezalel "filled with the Spirit of God" in the sense in which*

believers experience His indwelling today (Ex. 31:3; 35:31)?

No; Bezalel's filling with the Spirit took the form of the impartation of wisdom and skill for the work which he undertook in connexion with the house of God. Similar language is used of those who made the high-priestly vestments for Aaron (Ex. 28:3). We may say, indeed, that all true wisdom comes from "the Spirit of wisdom and understanding" (Isa. 11:2). But the indwelling and filling of the Spirit in the sense in which believers have experienced them from the first Christian Pentecost onwards could not have been known before the ascension of Christ (John 7:39; Acts 2:33).

Ex. 32:4. *Why should Israel, first under Aaron and again under Jeroboam, defect to the worship of a golden calf?*

They had Egyptian and Canaanite examples to seduce them into this form of idolatry. Calf-worship was practised in Egypt (we may think in particular of the cult of the bull-calf Apis) and in Canaan a bull-calf was sometimes depicted as the pedestal on which a god stood, if not indeed as a manifestation of the god.

Ex. 32:4, 5. *In Ex. 32:4-5 is Aaron saying that some god other than Jehovah brought them up from Egypt, or is he saying that the object before them was a representation of Jehovah?*

The words of Aaron at the end of v. 5 make it fairly clear that his intention was to represent Jehovah by this means, whether the calf was supposed (after the Egyptian model) to represent Him directly or (after the Canaanite model) to serve as the visible pedestal for His invisible presence. The latter is more probable. But whatever the intention of Aaron was, the narrative implies that it was to the calf itself that the people offered worship.

Leviticus 1-3. *The burnt-offering, meal-offering and peace-offering of Lev. 1-3* *not only appear to be voluntary, but no occasions are specified for their presentation. Was it left to the spiritual sensibility of the individual worshipper to decide which offering to bring, and when?*

The answer seems to be "Yes." We may contrast the detailed prescriptions given for the public sacrifices (most fully in Num. 28-29). The festal seasons, when so many Israelites congregated in Jerusalem, would provide specially convenient occasions for presenting these offerings, but they might be brought at any time that seemed good to the worshipper.

Lev. 4:2, 5:17. *Is there any difference between Lev. 4:2 and 5:17? Sins of ignorance appear to be contemplated in both places.*

That there is some difference appears from the fact that the former occurrence falls within the category of sin-offerings, the latter within that of guilt-offerings or reparation-offerings (A.V., "trespass offerings"). The comment of a German exegete on Lev. 5:17 may be helpful: "A second case appears when someone feels an obscure sense of guilt weighing upon him through the unintentional transgression of a divine commandment, without being able to give a more exact account of the matter: in this case too he is to bring a guilt-offering, because the transgression might conceivably consist of a 'breach of faith' or 'trespass' (of the kind mentioned in v. 15); but as the extent of the trespass cannot be gauged, there can naturally be no question of making restitution in the proportion of six parts to five."

Lev. 4:22ff. *In the prescriptions for the sin-offering in Lev. 4, where various animal sacrifices are prescribed in accordance with the rank of the offerer, why is no such provision made for the poor or the very poor as is made in Lev. 5:7-13? (It seems, too, that no one, whatever his social status, was to bring more than a female kid or ewe-lamb for the sins of*

Lev. 5:1-13.) Also, since in Lev. 5:14-6:7 a ram is uniformly prescribed as a trespass offering or guilt offering, how did the poor and very poor fare in such a case?

It is reasonable reading of the regulations to infer that the concessions of Lev. 5:7-13 applied to the general situation of unwitting sin committed by one of the common people in Lev. 4:27-35 as well as to the particular cases mentioned in Lev. 5:1-6. The ram prescribed as a guilt-offering in Lev. 5:14-6:17 seems to be viewed more definitely as a fine to be paid for a "breach of faith" (see R.S.V. of 5:14; 6:1), over and above the requirement of restitution with twenty per cent interest. The same fine is prescribed for all; whether in practice there was some mitigation or composition for anyone who could not afford a ram is not stated.

Lev. 11:6. *Is the Scofield Bible right in its statement on Lev. 11:6 that Heb. 'arnebeth is "certainly not a hare"? If not, what animal is it?*

It is usually supposed that the animal in question *is* a hare—the *Lepus syriacus*—which is some two inches shorter than the European hare and has slightly shorter ears. But the statement that it "chews the cud" does not mean that it is a ruminant, but refers to "refection" or pseudo-rumination, a physiological phenomenon recorded in rabbits and hares.

Lev. 16. *What is the significance of the two goats which figure in the ritual for the Day of Atonement in Lev. 16—especially of the second goat which was sent into the wilderness?*

Aaron was to cast lots between two he-goats selected for a sin-offering, and according to the lots one goat was assigned to Jehovah and one to Azazel (Lev. 16:8, R.V.). The goat for Jehovah was sacrificed as a sin-offering and its blood was brought into the Holy of Holies and sprinkled on the mercy-seat and in front of it to make atonement for Israel; the goat for Azazel (the "scape-goat," as A.V. has it) had the sins of the people symbolically laid upon its head and was then led into the wilderness and let loose in a solitary place. The anti-typical significance of the sacrifice of the former goat is expounded in the Epistle to the Hebrews: what it represented in a shadowy manner has been perfectly accomplished by Christ, who "through his own blood entered in once for all into the holy place, having obtained eternal redemption" (Heb. 9:12). The ritual associated with the other goat has been applied as a reminder to us that the Bearer of our sins has also removed them right out of the way; it is, however, not referred to in the Epistle to the Hebrews. The two phases of ritual are complementary. Whether Azazel is the name of a wilderness-spirit, or means "the Precipice" (N.E.B.) or "removal," the force of the phrase "the goat for Azazel" is that this goat symbolically removed the people's sins far from them by carrying them away into the wilderness.

Lev. 16. *Can you give a complete list of garments worn by the high priest whilst in the holy place (Lev. 16)?*

The garments to be worn in "the holy place within the veil" (Lev. 16:2) are enumerated in Lev. 16:4; they comprised the holy linen coat, the linen breeches, the linen girdle and the linen mitre. It will prevent confusion if it is noticed that in this chapter, which prescribes the ritual for the annual day of atonement, the inner sanctuary (elsewhere called "the most holy place" or "the holy of holies") is referred to simply as "the holy place"; the outer sanctuary (elsewhere called "the holy place") is referred to more generally as "the tent of meeting." Perhaps the question you have in mind is whether the ephod, with the shoulder-pieces and breastplate, was worn on this occasion. Since there is no mention of it among the specific directions of Lev. 16, we may conclude that it was not worn on the day of atonement. And the reason is not far to seek. "The ephod, with its shoulder-

stones and breastplate, formed peculiarly the *prophetic* dress of the high priest" (H. W. Soltau), and his ministry on that day was not a *prophetic* one. Neither is there any mention here of the bells and pomegranates; these were attached to the blue "robe of the ephod" (Ex. 28:31-35). On the day of atonement the high priest wore nothing but white linen because he then appeared "as bearing in his official capacity the emblem of that perfect purity which was sought by the expiations of that day" (A. Edersheim).

Numbers 19:19. *To whom do the words "bathe himself in water" refer in Num. 19:19? To the unclean person who has the water of purification sprinkled on him, or to the clean person who performs the sprinkling?*

It is really quite uncertain. There is nothing in the verse to indicate a change of subject half-way through, so that we might think of the clean person as having (after he has completed the ceremony for the unclean person) to wash his clothes and bathe himself in water. In that case the words are an anticipation of verse 21, except that there only the washing of the clothes, and not the bathing of the person, is mentioned. It is an interesting feature of the water of purification that while it cleansed the person suffering from ceremonial uncleanness, it rendered a clean person who touched it ceremonially unclean until sundown. On the other hand, a change of subject in the middle of a sentence is not always expressly indicated in Hebrew, and on the whole I am inclined to see a change of subject in verse 19. In that case the person for whom the week-long ceremony has been completed has nothing more to do after that than to wash his clothes; then at sundown he will return to a status of ceremonial purity.

Num. 32:33, etc. *In view of frequent references to the "half-tribe of Manasseh", can you say when and for what reason this tribe was divided?*

The tribal territory of Manasseh extended on both sides of Jordan, west and east. The part west of the Jordan was reckoned as one half, and the part in Transjordan as the other half. In the narrative of Num. 32 half the tribe of Manasseh, together with the tribes of Reuben and Gad, sought and received permission to settle in the area of Transjordan which the Israelites had just conquered from Sihon and Og. Josh. 22 records how these two and a half tribes entered into possession of their allotted territory. The territory given to the eastern half of the tribe of Manasseh (the descendants of Manasseh's sons Jair and Machir) was the former kingdom of Og, according to Deut. 3:13-15. The sons of Manasseh from whom the western half of the tribe traced their descent are listed in Josh. 17:2.

In reference to the foregoing question, is not Manasseh's double territory to be explained in terms of his double portion as Joseph's first-born (Deut. 21:17)?

It is hardly likely, because, although Manasseh was actually the first-born, Jacob deliberately bestowed the blessing of the first-born upon Ephraim (Gen. 48:14f.). The fact that Joseph is represented among the tribes of Israel by *two* tribes (Manasseh and Ephraim) is explained by the fact that he, although not Jacob's actual first-born, received the first-born blessing which Reuben forfeited (cf. Gen. 48:5, 22; 1 Chron. 5:1).

Deuteronomy 11:14. *What is meant by the "former rain" and the "latter rain" in Deut. 11:14 and other O.T. passages? Some say that the "latter rain" has been restored in Palestine since the beginning of Jewish immigration in recent days; others say that it points to a time of spiritual refreshment or revival in the "latter days", before the Lord's return. Which is right?*

The "former rain" is the rain of autumn, which follows the drought of summer and prepares the ground for ploughing and sowing; the "latter rain" is the rain of spring, which concludes the rainy season and is necessary for a good harvest. The sending of the former and latter rains, producing fertile soil and a good harvest, was an act of blessing on God's part; the withholding of them was an act of judgment. The idea that from the second half of the nineteenth century onward there has been a marked increase in the incidence of the "latter rain" in Palestine seems to be devoid of any sound basis in fact. A concise account of Palestinian rainfall given in the *Palestine Exploration Quarterly* for July, 1941, makes it plain that there has been no radical change in the rainfall of the land within human record. What may have given rise to the belief towards the end of last century, however, is the fact that (as a graph of the five-yearly mean rainfalls from 1861 onward would show) there was a thirty years zig-zag rise to a maximum about 1893, followed by a zig-zag fall. But there is nothing unusual in such cycles of greater and lesser rainfall.

As for the other matter, rainfall is used in Scripture as a figure of spiritual refreshing, as, for. example, in Hos. 6:3, where God is expected to visit His people "as the rain, as the latter rain that waters the earth." But there is no necessary connexion between the "latter rain" and the "latter days." While the first and second comings of Christ are peak-moments of divine blessing, the people of God may at all times pray for a revival of His work "in the midst of the years" (Hab. 3:2).

Deut. 23:1-3. *What was the situation before God of those persons mentioned in Deut. 23:1-3 as being excluded from "the congregation of the LORD" and therefore unable to offer sacrifices for their sins? Did they remain unforgiven?*

No, because happily forgiveness does not depend on animal sacrifices—"for it is impossible that the blood of bulls and goats should take away sins" (Heb. 10:4)—but on the grace of God. It follows then that in Old Testament times forgiveness was available even when no sacrifices were offered, just as the offering of sacrifice did not guarantee forgiveness, unless it was accompanied by true penitence of heart. The penitent psalmist of Ps. 51 says to God, "Thou delightest not in sacrifice, else would I give it" (verse 16); he enjoyed restoration of the joy of God's salvation through God's grace. And the people specified in Deut. 23:1-3, together with others who were deprived of access to the earthly sanctuary, might equally experience God's forgiveness if they brought Him the sacrifice of a broken and contrite heart, assured that He would not despise it (Psa. 51:17).

Deut. 32:8. *What is the significance of the change of reading at the end of Deut. 32:8 in the R.S.V.: "he fixed the bounds of the peoples according to the number of the sons of God" (similarly N.E.B.)?*

This reading, based on the Greek Septuagint, has recently been found in a Hebrew fragment of the passage among the Dead Sea manuscripts. The Massoretic reading "children of Israel" may suggest that God arranged the frontiers and destinies of other nations in relation to the central place occupied in His purpose by the nation of Israel. The traditional Jewish interpretation was that the seventy Gentile nations (so calculated from Gen. 10) were made to correspond in number with the seventy descendants of Jacob who went down to Egypt (Gen. 46:27). But the reading "sons of God" in this context suggests that while God appointed various angels to preside over the fortunes of other nations (cf. later Dan. 10:13, 20), He reserved Israel as His own heritage (Deut. 32:9).

THE HISTORICAL BOOKS

Joshua 6:20. *Could you comment on the word (or words) used for the "shout" of Josh. 6:20, in relation to the language used in connexion with our Lord's return in 1 Thess. 4:16?*

The Hebrew word translated "shout" in Josh. 6:20 is *teru'ah*, which in a military context like this means a war-cry or triumph-shout. Sometimes it denotes the signal to march, as in Num. 10:7, 9 (but there it is a trumpet-blast, not a human shout, that is indicated). In the Hebrew translations of the New Testament by Delitzsch and Salkinson *teru'ah* is used in 1 Thess. 4:16 to denote the "shout" with which the Lord descends from heaven. However, in the Septuagint of Josh 6:20 the Greek word used to render *teru'ah* is not *keleusma* ("word of command") which is used in 1 Thess. 4:16, but *alalagmos*, a more general term for a loud cry. It is interesting that both in Josh. 6:20 and 1 Thess. 4:16 we have the combination of the shout and the trumpet-blast, but I doubt if the Old Testament passage throws any light on the exegesis of the New Testament passage.

Josh. 7:24f. *Were the members of Achan's family mentioned in Josh. 7:24 present only as witnesses, or were they stoned along with him?*

The natural sense of verse 25 suggests that they shared Achan's fate, unless we simplify the text as N.E.B. does. This is not the only place in the Old Testament where we find a similar corporate responsibility and corporate punishment implied.

Josh. 24:2f. *According to Josh. 24:2, 3, Abraham and his family dwelt on "the other side of the flood", which we understand means the Euphrates. Is the reference to Ur or to Haran? The question is asked because while Haran lies on the other side of the Euphrates from Canaan, Ur lies to the west of the Euphrates.*

It is true that Ur now lies some nine miles west of the Euphrates. But the river has changed its course, and in ancient times it ran about a mile to the west of Ur. The reference in Josh. 24:2, 3, is probably therefore to the residence of Abraham and his family in Ur.

Judges 11:31. *Is there any significance in the use of the conjunction "or" in Judg. 11:31 in Robert Young's Literal Translation of the Bible: "it hath been to Jehovah, or I have offered up for it—a burnt offering"?*

The Hebrew form here translated "or" by Dr. Young is the very common particle usually translated "and", which he translates by "and" in a hundred or so other places where it appears in this chapter. There is nothing in the Hebrew which could have moved him to adopt another rendering in this one place; his decision to do so must have been based on non-linguistic considerations, and the same applies to his insertion of the preposition "for", which has no warrant in the original text.

Judg. 11:39. *It has been stated that Jephthah's daughter did not die in consequence of her father's vow, that a substitute was provided, and that she herself remained in solitude and meditation in the mountains. Is this correct?*

The view that Jephthah commuted his daughter's fate from burnt-offering to perpetual virginity is hardly warranted by the narrative. The plain and restrained statement that he "did with her according to his vow which he had vowed" (Judg. 11:39) is best taken as implying her actual sacrifice. Although human sacrifice was forbidden to Israelites, we need not be surprised that a man of Jephthah's half-Canaanite antecedents should follow Canaanite practice in this matter. Her two months' respite allowed her and her companions to bewail her untimely death, before she could marry and leave children to perpetuate her memory; and this period of mourning was thereafter recalled during the four days when "the daughters of Israel went yearly to celebrate the daughter of Jephthah the Gileadite" (verse 40).

Judg. 11:40. *Is there any basis for the suggestion that the daughters of Israel went yearly to "talk to" Jepthah's daughter, as Young's translation and the A.V. margin have it in Judd. 11:40?*

I know of no place where the Hebrew verb has this sense. It means "celebrate" (R.V.) or "commemorate" (N.E.B.) as also in Judg. 5:11 (R.V. "rehearse")—there with joy, here with sorrow (whence some versions, such as A.V., R.S.V. and *The Jerusalem Bible*, have "lament" here). The same verb has been discerned in Psa. 8:1: "thy glory is celebrated (R.S.V. 'chanted') above the heavens."

Ruth 4:6. *In what way would it have marred the inheritance of the nearer kinsman if he had married Ruth (Ruth 4:6)?*

He would have had to devote part of his time and energy to looking after Ruth's land, for the benefit of her family and descendants. He would thus have been obliged to pay less attention to his own land, and he might have feared that his family and heirs would be the losers thereby.

1 Samuel 3. *Would Samuel be 12 years old, or more, in the account of 1 Sam. 3?*

His age is quite uncertain. The Hebrew word *na'ar*, translated "child" in the A.V. of 1 Sam. 3:1, can cover anything from a newly born infant (like Ichabod in 1 Sam. 4:21) to someone of the age of Absalom (2 Sam. 18:5, 29, 32) or Zadok, "a young man mighty in valour" (1 Chron. 12:28). The general impression of the narrative of 1 Sam. 3 is that Samuel was quite young at the time, perhaps in his early teens. But one cannot base anything on a general impression.

1 Sam. 13:21. *When the Revised Standard Version says in 1 Sam. 13:21 "the charge was a pim for the plowshares and for the mattocks," what does it mean by the word "pim"?*

This is an example of the way in which archaeological discovery at times simplifies the understanding of formerly obscure passages of Scripture. A "pim" was "two-thirds of a shekel" (which is the N.E.B. rendering); specimens of such weights have actually been found in Palestine with the word "pim" inscribed on them. In the present instance what is meant is a "pim" of silver; this was the charge for sharpening the larger implements; as regards the smaller ones, the charge (as the R.S.V. goes on to state) was "a third of a shekel for sharpening the axes and for setting the goads." A shekel was about two-fifths of an ounce.

1 Sam. 16:10ff. *How many sons had Jesse? From 1 Sam. 16:10-12 we should gather that seven sons, and then David in addition, making eight in all, passed before Samuel. Similarly 1 Sam. 17:12 states that he had eight sons. But according to 1 Chron. 2:13-15 he appears to have had only seven, David being the seventh.*

There is no certain solution of this numerical problem. One of the eight sons may have died without leaving any children and so his name was not retained in the genealogical register which the Chronicler has preserved for us. Some suggest that Elihu, "one of the brethren of David" (1 Chron. 27:18) should be added to the seven of 1 Chron. 2:13-15; but this may simply be a variant spelling of Eliab's name. In default of fuller information, the first explanation seems to be a reasonably probable one.

1 Sam. 17:4. *Is there any reason to believe that Goliath and other giants killed by David and his men (1 Sam. 17:4; 2 Sam. 21:18-22; 1 Chron. 20:4-8) were the product of mixed marriages like the giants of Gen. 6:4?*

No; the word used of the Philistine giants is *rapha'*, whereas the giants of Gen. 6:4 were *nephilim* ("fallen ones"). Goliath and his kinsmen were possibly members of a family which suffered from an excessive secretion of pituitary growth hormone.

2 Sam. 3:33f. *In view of David's statement that Joab had "shed the blood of war in peace" (1 Kings 2:5), do you think that in 2 Sam. 3:33f. David was blaming Abner for not availing himself of the cities of refuge? How would you paraphrase David's lament to bring out what you believe to be the true meaning?*

The meaning of David's complaint against Joab in 1 Kings 2:5 is well brought out in the R.S.V., where Joab's murder of Abner and Amasa is described as "avenging in time of peace blood which had been shed in war." Abner had killed Joab's brother Asahel in the accepted conditions of war (2 Sam. 2:18-23); for Joab to take private vengeance for this after Abner had made his peace with David was contrary to the then recognized rules of civilized behaviour. The cities of refuge were not provided for the protection of men who killed their opponents in battle but for those who committed unintentional homicide in the circumstances of civil life. If the cities of refuge *had* been provided to cover a case like Abner's, then Abner should have been safe, for Hebron, where he was killed (2 Sam. 3:27; 4:1), was one of those cities (Josh. 20:7). But Abner had come to Hebron not because it was a city of refuge but because it was David's

residence. In David's lament there is no hint of blaming Abner; the question "Should Abner die as a fool dies?" (2 Sam. 3:33, R.S.V.) is a question expecting the answer "No." "Abner, David laments, has experienced a death that was undeserved: he has died the death of a *nabal*, a reprobate, godless person, whom an untimely end might be expected to overtake. There was nothing to prevent Abner from defending himself, had he suspected Joab's treachery (34a); as it was (34b), he had succumbed to the treacherous blow of an assassin" (S. R. Driver, *Notes on the Hebrew Text of Samuel*, p. 251).

2 Sam. 14:21ff. *On David's half-hearted forgiveness of Absalom in 2 Sam. 14:21ff., the Scofield Bible says: "Not so had God taught David to forgive. Legalists have thought Absalom's wilfulness to have been due to over-indulgence on the part of David. There is no such intimation in Scripture. Rather it would seem that had David at this time taken Absalom into intimacy, the rebellion might have been averted." Do you agree with this reading of the situation?*

No. David was torn between his duty as king to maintain righteousness in his realm and show his subjects a good example of regard for the law, and his inclination as a father to welcome his erring son. But there could be no true reconciliation because there was no repentance or confession on Absalom's part. The paternal kiss of 2 Sam. 14:33 would have had more lasting results if this prodigal son, like the one in the New Testament, had come home saying: "I have sinned . . . and am no more worthy to be called thy son." In that case the royal prerogative of clemency might have been fittingly exercised.

1 Kings 2:27. *In 1 Kings 2:27 Abiathar is "expelled . . . from being priest to the LORD" because of his support of Adonijah;*

17

yet in 1 Kings 4:4 he is linked with Zadok as priest. Does this indicate that he was an assistant to Zadok and thus demoted without being dismissed altogether?

While Abiathar was dismissed from the exercise of his priestly *function* in Jerusalem, where he shared with Zadok the principal charge of the tent-shrine which David erected for the ark, Solomon could not deprive him of his priestly *status*. In what is a formal list (1 Kings 4:2-19) his name is therefore included, in what may be called an *emeritus* capacity, alongside Zadok's. The I.V.F. *New Bible Commentary* (1953) ascribes the inclusion of Abiathar's name to "a piece of mechanical scribal writing," adding: "However early in the reign we place this list, we cannot justify Abiathar's name, for he and Joab lost their office at the same time." There are two differences, however, between Joab and Abiathar which may explain why Joab's name is not included alongside Benaiah's as Abiathar's name is included alongside Zadok's: first, Joab had no permanent status which he could retain even after his deposition from office, and secondly, Joab was put to death soon after his deposition. Abiathar was allowed to live at his home in Anathoth (and it is highly probable that "the priests that were in Anathoth," to whom Jeremiah belonged, traced their descent from him).

1 Kings 4:7-19. *Is there any Scriptural basis for the idea that Solomon exempted the tribe of Judah from the forced service which he exacted from all the other tribes?*

This has been inferred from the fact that the twelve officers listed in the received text of 1 Kings 4:7-19 were appointed over various divisions of the land of Israel with the exception of Judah. But the last clause of verse 19, which makes no sense in the A.V. and R.V., should probably be read, "And there was one officer in the land of Judah" (so R.S.V. following LXX; the word "Judah" has fallen out of the Hebrew text here before the "Judah" at the beginning of the following sentence), Evidently then, Judah had to contribute to the royal maintenance as well as the tribes of Israel. (N.E.B. gives instead a conjectural emendation: "In addition, one governor over all the governors in the land"—which is less likely than the R.S.V. rendering.)

1 Kings 6:23; 12:28. *Why were golden cherubim sanctioned in the temple at Jerusalem when golden calves were condemned at Bethel and Dan?*

The cherubim, being symbolical figures, did not reproduce "any likeness of any thing that is in heaven above, or that is in the earth beneath, or that is in the water under the earth," in the terms of the Second Commandment. Nor were cherubim associated with Canaanite idolatry, as calves were (cf. p. 10). And there is no evidence that the cherubim in the holy of holies were ever regarded as anything but the supporters of the invisible presence of Israel's God.

1 Kings 7:13. *Was it Hiram king of Tyre or another Hiram that Solomon brought from Tyre to cast the two pillars for the temple porch?*

Not the king of Tyre but another man of the same name, whose father was a Tyrian bronze-worker and whose mother was an Israelite from one of the northern tribes. (King Hiram's father was king before him and bore the name of Abibaal.) According to 2 Chron. 2:7, 13ff., it was King Hiram who sent the craftsman Hiram to Jerusalem in response to Solomon's request. In 2 Chron. 2:13 the craftsman's name is given as Huramabi (see R.S.V.); a corrupted form of this name ("Hiram-Abiff") survives in Masonic lore.

1 Kings 10:19. *What authority has the Revised Standard Version for the rendering "at the back of the throne was a calf's head" in 1 Kings 10:19, where R.V. has "the top of the throne was round behind"?*

The R.S.V. and N.E.B. here follow the Septuagint in treating Heb. *'agol* as a variant of *'egel* ("calf") instead of translating it "round", which is its meaning elsewhere. The order and construction of the Hebrew clause give some support to the LXX, R.S.V. and N.E.B.

2 Kings 3:4ff. *The narrative of 2 Kings 3:4ff states that Moab rebelled against the oppression of Israel after Ahab's death (cf. 1:1), while the Moabite Stone clearly states that the rebellion took place in the latter years of Ahab's reign. Can we account for this discrepancy?*

Apart from the mention of Mesha's throwing off the yoke of Israel, the Hebrew and Moabite accounts have but little in common; the Hebrew account does not record the incidents mentioned on the Moabite Stone. It is conceivable that Mesha describes an earlier revolt against Israel which succeeded for a time but was ultimately crushed by Ahab. However, I am more inclined to think that the son of Omri under whom Mesha says he rebelled was Omri's grandson Jehoram, not his son Ahab. If an Assyrian king can describe Jehu, the exterminator of the house of Omri, as "the son of Omri," how much more might not a Moabite king describe Omri's own grandson as his "son"? Again, Mesha gives the years of Israel's oppression of Moab as "forty years". But even if we regard this as a round number, the days of Omri and half the days of his son (during which Mesha says Israel occupied Moab) would amount to barely twenty years if Omri's son here is Ahab (for it is hardly conceivable that Omri could have taken time off to conquer Moab so long as his rival Tibni was

around). If, however, Mesha's revolt took place half way through the reign of Jehoram, we should be getting nearer his figure of forty years. In any case, some of Mesha's claims must be taken with a grain of salt; his statement, for example, that "Israel utterly perished for ever" is something of an exaggeration.

2 Kings 24:8. *Why, if Jehoiachin was eighteen years old when he began to reign, as 2 Kings 24:8 says, do we read in 2 Chron. 36:9 that he was eight years old at the time?*

"Eighteen" is certainly the right reading, since when he was deported to Babylon three months later his wives were deported with him (2 Kings 24:15), and we know from a Babylonian document that five years later he had five sons. The simplest course is to read "eighteen" instead of "eight" in 2 Chron. 36:9, with the support of a marginal note in one Hebrew manuscript, and the text of an important Septuagint manuscript and the Syriac version. In these authorities the reading "eighteen" may be a correction, but it is a sound correction. (Another suggestion that has been made is that Jehoiachin was associated in the kingship with his father at the age of eight, ten years before his father's death, but this is not the natural sense of 2 Chron. 36:9.)

1 Chronicles 28:19. *What is intended by the words: "the LORD made me understand in writing by his hand upon me" (1 Chron. 28:19)?*

The R.V. varies the wording slightly: "All this . . . have I been made to understand in writing from the hand of the LORD." The "hand" of the Lord is a figure used several times in the Bible for the power, or Spirit, of the Lord (cf. Ezek. 1:3; Luke 1:66). And it is evident that this is the meaning of the expression in the passage you quote, for reference is made a little earlier to "the pattern of all that he had by the spirit" (verse 12, R.V.). The implication might be that the inspiration came upon David as he sat pen in hand, and guided the words that he wrote. Alternatively, as H. L. Ellison suggests in the I.V.F. *New Bible Commentary*, "David described to Solomon the vision that he had had by inspiration ... If this is correct, then the writing in verse 19 is the account in Exodus of the tabernacle, the necessary modifications of which to suit the temple David was caused to understand by inspiration."

2 Chron. 15:1-8. *In 2 Chron. 15 it would seem, on the face of it, that there is a confusion between Azariah (v. 1) and Oded (v. 8) as the mouthpiece of the prophecy of vv. 2-7. Can this apparent inconsistency be reasonably explained?*

The Revised Standard Version removes the inconsistency by translating verse 8 "When Asa heard these words, the prophecy of Azariah the son of Oded ...". This reading, which maintains agreement with verse 1, is based (as the R.S.V. footnote says) on the Syriac and Latin Vulgate texts; it is probable that one or two words, including the name "Azariah", have fallen out of the Hebrew text of verse 8 in the course of copying.

Job 1:11; 2:5, 9. *Why is the Hebrew word which normally means "bless" translated as "curse" in Job 1 and 2?*

Because the context obviously demands it. In Job 1:11 Satan plainly does not mean that Job will bless God if he loses all his property. The same phenomenon appears in 1 Kings 21:10, 13. It is the result of a curious principle of polarity found particularly in the Semitic languages, by which a word sometimes takes the opposite meaning to its normal one. The resemblance to the euphemistic use of the adjective "blessed" in English when what is really meant is "cursed" is only superficial; this is a mere vulgarism and not a recognized literary usage, as the Hebrew idiom in question is.

Job 27: 13ff. *How would you reconcile Job 27:13-23 with Job's resistance elsewhere to such a charge by his three friends? (i) Is Job at last accepting such an argument? Or (ii) is he summarizing the arguments of his friends as a sample of the vanity with which he has charged them in verse 12, without accepting them? Or (iii) is he, following his own argument in verses 1-12 and as a lead-up to Ch. 28, quoting his three friends in a rebuking or aggrieved spirit? Or (iv) would these eleven verses and perhaps Ch. 28 be in fact the words of one of his three friends, an opening statement to that effect ("Then answered ... and said, 'This is the portion ...'") having been lost in the course of transmission?*

I am sure that the first solution must be ruled out. As in 27:5, 6, Job maintains his integrity to the end of the argument (cf. Ch. 31). As for the second and third solutions, they imply a capacity for sustained sarcasm unparalleled elsewhere in the book and unsupported by the context. The fourth solution is probably nearest the truth of the matter, although perhaps not only an opening statement ("Then answered ... and said") but something more has been lost at this point in the course of transmission; H. L. Ellison suggests "loss of a section owing to the breaking of the papyrus roll" (*From Tragedy to Triumph*, p. 21). In his treatment of Ch. 27, Mr. Ellison describes the passage about which you ask as "an affirmation of all [that] the three friends have been proclaiming and a flat contradiction of Job's own views. We shall probably do best to see Zophar speaking here, making dogmatism take the place of evidence and vehemence that of proof. It may be that Job's answer is lost, or more probably he looks on such statements as unworthy of being refuted again and deals with them by implication in his summing up" (p. 88). Chapter 28 is probably a meditative interlude by the author of the book.

Psalm Titles. *In the Revised Standard Version, why do the titles of the Psalms precede the Psalm-numbers?*

Possibly because in a number of instances the title, especially where it is a musical direction, should be attached as a colophon to the preceding Psalm.

What feature of the N.E.B. Old Testament do you regard as most open to criticism?

The omission of the titles to the Psalms. Despite the reasons given for their omission in the introduction to the Old Testament in the N.E.B., they do form part of the Massoretic text which (in Kittel's third edition) is acknowledged to be the basis of the new version. Moreover, they antedate the Massoretic age by centuries, for we find them in the pre-Christian Psalms scroll from Cave 11 at Qumran, and still earlier in the Septuagint. It would have been of great interest to many readers of the N.E.B. to know what the translators, with their unsurpassed apparatus of philological scholarship, made of some of the Psalm titles.

Psalm 2:11. *Why does the Revised Standard Version render "with trembling kiss his feet" in Psa. 2:11 instead of "and rejoice with trembling. Kiss the son" (R.V.)?*

The R.S.V. rendering represents a shift in the consonants of the Hebrew text. (The Hebrew text in its original form consists of consonants only.) Instead of the Massoretic consonants, which may be indicated *wgylw br'dh nšqw br*, the R.S.V. presupposes the order *wbr'dh nšqw brglyw*. The main reason for the change is that it is strange to find the Aramaic word for "son" (*bar*) here after the ordinary Hebrew word (*ben*) has been used in v. 7. The Septuagint renders the opening words of v. 12 "Lay hold of instruction," the Latin Vulgate says "Worship in purity," the Syriac alone of the ancient versions has "Kiss the son;" N.E.B. renders "kiss the king." This diversity suggests that the R.S.V. footnote is right in saying that the Hebrew is uncertain. But the divine sonship of Messiah is not put in question by R.S.V., since it is plainly stated in v. 7.

Psalm 16:10. *Is there definite evidence to show whether Sheol in Psa. 16:10 refers to the grave or to the place of departed spirits?*

Sheol is regularly the general assembly-place of the dead, where they continued in a shadowy existence, and not the grave in which the body was laid. In the Septuagint it is translated by Hades, and, as the quotation and application of that version of the psalm in Acts 2:25-31 makes plain, a distinction is there drawn between the tomb in which a man's body was laid and "saw corruption" and Hades, to which his "soul" passed at death. (In the Hebrew text Sheol and "the Pit" are in synonymous parallelism.)

Psalm 19:1. *When the Psalmist says, "The heavens declare the glory of God" (Psa. 19:1), does he refer to God's glory as Creator or to His glory as Redeemer as well?*

To His glory as Creator. It is, as Paul says in Rom. 1:20, "his everlasting power and divinity" that are revealed there; the glory of His redeeming grace is revealed in Christ and proclaimed in the Scriptures. Paul does, indeed quote Psa. 19:4 in Rom. 10:18, but the context shows that he applies the words there to the fact that by A.D. 57 the gospel had been preached in every part of the world where there were Jewish communities.

Psalm 23:6. *J. N. Darby translates Psa. 23:6 "I will dwell in the house of Jehovah for the length of the days." Is this right? If so, may it not refer to the period preceding the Second Advent (cf. 1 Peter 4:7) rather than to the Christian's eternal abode in the Father's house (cf. John 14:2f?*

Darby's version is a literal rendering of the Hebrew (cf. R.V. mg.; also N.E.B. "my whole life long"). The two clauses of verse 6 are in synonymous parallelism. Before Christ brought life and immortality to light through the gospel, the people of God generally had much less definite appreciation of their eternal hope than they had later. When Christians use the language of the Psalmist to express their faith, it has a fuller meaning for them than it could have had for him. He used an expression denoting indefinite duration, but the common English version does not do violence to the sense by rendering that expression by the phrase "for ever." For when the Christian takes the language of the Psalm on his lips, he knows with complete assurance that not death, nor yet the Second Advent, will bring an end to the "length of days" during which he will "dwell in the house of the LORD."

Psalm 45. *Can we be sure when the bride-groom is being addressed in Psalm 45 and when the bride?*

Yes, because of the happy feature in the Hebrew language of having different forms for the second person according as the person addressed is masculine or feminine. The Hebrew text thus makes it clear that from verse 2 to verse 9 the royal bridegroom is addressed, from verse 10 to verse 15 the bride, and in verses 16 and 17 the bridegroom again. If one were to reply on the English alone (or the Latin Vulgate or Greek Septuagint for that matter), it might be thought that the bride is addressed from verse 10 to the end of the Psalm; and this, in fact, has been assumed by a number of writers, such as W. Graham Scroggie. (*The Psalms*, Vol. I, pp. 259f) and C. S. Lewis (*Reflections on the Psalms*, Fontana edition, p. 109). But the Hebrew is unambiguous; it is the king, not the queen, who is told: "Instead of your fathers shall be your sons . . .".

Psalm 51:5. *When the Psalmist said, "Behold, I was shapen in iniquity, and in sin did my mother conceive me" (Psa. 51:5), did he mean that there was some-thing specially sinful about the circum-stances of his own begetting, or that there is something inherently sinful about all human conception and birth?*

Neither: he meant that he was born a sinner, that he inherited a sinful nature from his parents—which, of course, is true of us all.

Psalm 68:13. *What is the meaning of Psalm 68:13, "Though ye have lien among the pots, yet shall ye be as the wings of a dove covered with silver, and her feathers with yellow gold" (A.V.)?*

I do not know the precise meaning of this verse, nor do I know anyone else who does. First of all, we should note (i) that the R.V., R.S.V. and N.E.B. render "sheep-folds" instead of "pots", and

(ii) that the words "yet shall ye be as" are italicized in the A.V., because they have no equivalent in the Hebrew but are added by the translators to make some sort of sense. The literal translation of the verse would be: "Though (or 'if') you lie among the sheepfolds. Wings of a dove (that is) covered with silver, and its pinions with yellow (or 'gleaming') gold." If we look at the context, it is concerned with a victory won by some tribes of Israel over their enemies in Transjordan. When the victory is won, the joyful news is spread among the other tribes: "The Lord gives the message; the bearers (fem.) of glad tidings are a great host" (v. 11). The following verses may then give the content of the message which is thus spread abroad: "Kings of armies flee, they flee, and the housewife divides the spoil, even though *you* (the recipients of the message, who did not go out to take part in the fighting) remain among the sheepfolds" (compare Judges 5:16). So far the meaning is fairly clear; but the reference to the doves remains a problem. We may, I think, dismiss B. D. Eerdmans' idea that they were carrier pigeons which carried the news of the victory home. We are then left with a choice among these possibili-ties: (i) that the words describe the women at home dividing the spoil (so R.S.V., which also, with doubtful justifica-tion, refers the remaining among the sheep-folds to these women); (ii) that the words describe part of the spoil which they are dividing (so, apparently, R. K. Harrison in his translation of the Psalms appended to Norlie's *Simplified New Testament*); (iii) that the words describe the victory celebrations; (iv) that the words describe the non-combatants who stayed at home among the sheepfolds, sleekly basking in indolence and ease, while their brethren were fighting the national enemies (S. R. Driver); (v) that the words go closely with the following verse, the general sense being that when God manifested Himself in His people's defence, the splendour of His glory made the clouds appear like doves in gold and silver sheen, and the battlefield like an expanse of snow (A. Weiser); (vi) that the words are an ancient rubric in the text whose significance is no longer attainable. My own preference would be for the third of these; that the release of doves with gilded or silvered wings formed part of the victory celebrations is argued by B. S. J. Isserlin in the *Palestine Exploration Quarterly*, January-June 1971. In spite of those who preferred slothful ease, Israel again enjoys the blessing of peace and prosperity because of those who hazarded their lives in battle. But the connexion is so obscure that there can be no positive assurance about the original sense.

Psalm 78:9. *It has been said that the R.S.V. in Psa. 78:9, in rendering Heb. nôsheqê rômê qasheth by "armed with the bow" (as against A.V. and R.V. "being armed and carrying bows"), has failed to translate the word rômê. Is this a fair criticism?*

The literal sense of the Hebrew phrase is something like "equipped with, shooting the bow." But competent Hebraists acknowledge that the expression is a difficult one, and there cannot be complete certainty about the translation, although the general sense is plain. The R.S.V. gives the general sense in the text, but points out in the footnote that "armed with" is literally "armed with shooting." N.E.B. gives a completely adequate rendering: "bowmen all and marksmen."

Psalm 137:5. *Why does the R.S.V. of Psa. 137:5 read "let my right hand wither" (N.E.B. "wither away")?*

This reading represents Heb. *tikḥash* ("let her wither") instead of *tishkaḥ* ("let her forget"). A.V. and R.V. have to add "her cunning" in order to make sense of the latter reading. The Septuagint and Jerome's Latin version have "let my right hand be forgotten."

Proverbs 8:22ff. *Do passages such as Prov. 8:24-25 ("I was brought forth"); John 1:14, 18; 3:16, 18; Heb. 1:6; 11:17; and 1 John 4:9 imply that our Lord came into existence for the first time at an epoch before the creation of the universe? If not, why is the metaphor of birth used? Is the distinction expressed in the credal phrase "begotten, not created" a Scriptural one?*

In Prov. 8:22-36 the words are those of Divine Wisdom personified; she is, so to speak, portrayed as the eldest daughter of the Almighty (since "wisdom" is a feminine noun in Hebrew). Several New Testament writers draw largely upon the language of this passage to describe the cosmic role of Christ—appropriately so, since the New Testament presents Him as the Wisdom of God, not merely personified by a figure of speech (as in Proverbs), but really existent as such. Everything in Prov. 8:22ff. that is applicable to Him may therefore be applied to Him, but we cannot conclude without more ado that everything in these verses is in fact applicable to Him. This last idea caused considerable trouble to many of the Greek Fathers in the days of the Arian controversy, because they knew no Hebrew and read the passage in the Septuagint, where it begins: "The Lord *created* (Gk. *ktizō*) me . . .". Taking the passage as a straightforward utterance of the Son of God before His incarnation they were hard put to it to refute the Arian claim that the Son was a created being—that "there was once when He was not." We may see a deeper meaning in Prov. 8:22ff. in the light of New Testament Christology, but we should not base our Christology itself on these verses. As for the New Testament passages you refer to, those from John's Gospel and Epistles designate Jesus as the "only-begotten" Son of God. This word (Gk. *monogenēs*) is one of the Septuagint equivalents of Heb. *yāḥīd*, meaning "only" or "unique." This is the Hebrew word used, for example, in Gen. 22:2, where Abraham is commanded to take his "only son" and offer him up. The Septuagint there renders *yāḥîd* by *agapētos* ("beloved"), but the writer to the Hebrews in a passage to which you refer (Heb. 11:17) renders it by *monogenēs*, conventionally translated "only-begotten." Yet Isaac was not Abraham's only-begotten son, for he had others; Isaac, however, was his "unique" son in that he was the child of promise, and he was in a special sense his beloved son. In other words, when *monogenēs* is used in the Septuagint and the New Testament, the emphasis is on the first part of the compound rather than the second—on the "uniqueness" rather than the being begotten. In R.S.V. and N.E.B., accordingly, it is simply rendered "only." The other New Testament passage you refer to is Heb. 1:6, where Christ is called the "first-begotten" (A.V.) or "first-born" (R.V.). This title (Gk. *prōtotokos*) is applied to Him elsewhere in the New Testament—in Rom. 8:29; Col. 1:15, 18; Rev. 1:5. "The First-born" is a title of the Davidic King (Psa. 89:27), and these New Testament passages make use of it to denote not only our Lord's Messiahship but also His primacy and supremacy in relation to the created universe (Col. 1:15), to the resurrection of the dead (Col. 1:18; Rev. 1:5), and to His people who through Him become sons of God (Rom. 8:29). In none of these places is any emphasis laid upon His birth in Bethlehem, for that is not the basis of His primacy and supremacy in these various respects. As regards the credal expression "begotten, not created", we must remember that such affirmations were intended rather to exclude heresy than to express the full truth adequately. On such subjects we often have to choose between using inadequate language and saying nothing at all. That the Son of God already existed when creation took place in the beginning is clear from John 1:1 and elsewhere; that He through whom all things were created was Himself "not created" is Scripturally unexceptionable. Since then He was not created by God, what verb will best express His relation to God? He is the Son of God, and as Son He may fittingly be said to have been "begotten" by the Father. Indeed, this seems to be stated in 1 John 5:18, where the R.V. is to be preferred to A.V. "We know that whosoever is begotten of God (i.e., every believer) sinneth not; but he that was begotten of God (i.e., Christ) keepeth him . . ." (cf. R.S.V., N.E.B.). Of course if we go farther and ask, as the metaphysically-minded Greek Fathers did, "When was He begotten?", the answer can only "In eternity"; but the "eternal generation" of the Son, an expression first formulated by Origen, simply means that He is the Son of God eternally.

Prov. 11:30. *Can you explain the discrepancy between these renderings of the last clause of Prov. 11:30—"and he that winneth souls is wise" (A.V.; cf. "and he that is wise winneth souls", R.V.); "but lawlessness takes away lives" (R.S.V.; cf. "but violence means the taking away of life", N.E.B.)?*

The difficulty of deciding which is the true sense of this clause may be further indicated by quoting some other renderings: "the lives of the lawless are taken away before their time" (LXX); "grasping greed is death to men" (Moffatt); "violent behaviour takes away souls" (Basic); "the wise man's reward is living souls" (R. A. Knox, giving the sense of the Latin Vulgate). The R.S.V. and N.E.B. agree with the Septuagint and Peshitta (Syriac) in reading Heb. *ḥāmās* ("violence", "lawlessness") in place of *ḥākhām* ("wise") of the Massoretic text. But we can very well keep the Massoretic reading and translate "a wise man catches souls (*or* catches lives)"—just as, contrariwise, a fool (in the Biblical sense) is deadly to himself and to everyone else. How a wise man catches souls may be illustrated by our Lord's words to Peter in Luke 5:10, "henceforth you will be catching men" (lit. "catching men alive").

Ecclesiastes 8:10. *What is the meaning of Eccl. 8:10?*

The Revised Standard Version renders this verse: "Then I saw the wicked buried; they used to go in and out of the holy place, and were praised in the city where they had done such things. This also is vanity." The verse is a difficult one to translate; but the meaning seems to be that wicked men got a reputation for piety because they attended the temple or synagogue regularly, and at the end of their lives were given a splendid funeral. If this life were all, then such facts as these would suggest that there is no meaning in the whole business, that it is all "vanity", since the wicked fare as well as the righteous, perhaps even better.

Eccl. 12:1. *Is the word "Creator" plural in Eccl. 12:1? If so, what is the explanation?*

Hebrew manuscripts vary here, some reading the singular and some the plural. But the plural seems to be the better attested reading. It could be explained as being a "plural of majesty"—a construction found in other Hebrew designations for God, e.g. *'Elohim, 'Adonai*. But it would be a breach of idiomatic usage (as well as a theological error) to translate such words by an English plural.

Canticles. *D. S. Margoliouth (Lines of Defence of the Biblical Revelation, 3rd ed., 1903, pp. 30f.) argues that the language of the Song of Solomon is highly mystical, resembling certain Oriental literature, its love and wine, for example, standing for something very different from their usual significance; and that therefore to expect it to have a literal interpretation is unreasonable. This suggestion receives no mention in recent works on Old Testament Introduction. Has it been worked out, and if so, with what result?*

Like several other suggestions in Margoliouth's book, this one has not been worked out in recent times, because it has not found much acceptance. Margoliouth had in mind such compositions as the odes of the Islamic mystic Ibnu'l-Farid, in which the whole compendium of Sufic mystical theology is said to be conveyed by means of the imagery of love and wine. But this was Ibnu'l-Farid's intention from the outset, whereas (as Margoliouth himself agrees in his notes on the Song of Songs in the *New Commentary on Holy Scripture*, 1928) it is difficult to ascribe any such intention to the author of the Song of Songs. If Jewish and Christian readers have understood it mystically and thus derived devotional benefit from it, that is one thing; it is another thing to infer that the work bore such a meaning from its first conception.

THE PROPHETS

Isaiah 1:26. *The Scofield Bible, in its note on Isa. 1:26 ("I will restore thy judges as at the first, and thy counsellors as at the beginning"), links this passage with Matt. 19:28 ("in the regeneration . . . ye also shall sit upon twelve thrones, judging the twelve tribes of Israel"). Will the judges mentioned by Isaiah be the twelve apostles of Matt. 19:28, or are they another group of men who in the millennium will act as judges?*

It would not have occurred to me to connect these two passages. Isaiah, in the 8th century B.C., communicates a promise that when Jerusalem was cleansed from the iniquities which then polluted her (as cleansed she was in the crucible of exile), God would restore the former theocratic ideal, replacing her present unworthy princes by rulers who would be His representatives in deed as well as in name, and who would govern her in righteousness. We may think in this connexion of men like Zerubbabel and Jeshua, or Ezra and Nehemiah. In Matt. 19:28 (with which we must take Luke 22:30) we have our Lord's declaration of the apostolic authority which the Twelve were to exercise among the people of God in the new age.

Isa. 6:1. *Is it possible to date Isa. 6:1?*

"The year that King Uzziah died" would be around 740 B.C., with a variation of a few years on either side, according to the preferred reckoning of the regnal years of the books of Kings.

Isa. 7:14. *In An Introduction to the Revised Standard Version of the Old Testament, p. 30, Dr. H. M. Orlinsky says that when Aquila translated the Old Testament into Greek, he "rendered the Hebrew word ha-'almah in Isaiah 7:14 literally 'the young woman' in place of the word 'virgin' which the Christians had*

substituted for it." Can this charge of substitution be substantiated?

No, and it is astonishing that so eminent a Septuagint expert should have slipped up like this. There is no evidence that the Septuagint version of Isa. 7:14 ever had anything but *parthenos* ("virgin") as the rendering of *'almah* (as quoted in Matt. 1:23). The proselyte Aquila was the first, so far as we know, to render it here by *neanis* ("young woman") when he produced his official Jewish translation of the Old Testament into Greek early in the second century A.D.

Is there any difference in meaning between the Hebrew word 'almah, *used for "virgin" in Isa. 7:14, and* bethulah?

The difference is not great, if Old Testament usage is to guide us; it may be said that *'almah* normally implies virginity, like such English words as "maiden" and "damsel", while *bethulah* normally asserts it, like the English word "virgin." In Isa. 7:14 we have the echo of an ancient annunciation formula appearing elsewhere in the Semitic world. Its earliest known appearance is in a text from Ras Shamra, c. 1400 B.C., where it is expressed in two parallel clauses; to the Ugaritic equivalent of Heb. *'almah*, "young woman", in the first clause, the parallel in the second clause is the Ugaritic equivalent of *bethulah*, "virgin." In Israel this annunciation formula was associated with the birth of an expected Prince of the house of David, whose mother was also a figure of special expectation; cf. "she who is in travail" in Micah 5:3. In Isa. 7:14, where this expectation is incorporated in the oracle to King Ahaz, its fulfilment is characterized as a "sign." All this does not add up to a demonstration that "virgin" is the only correct rendering here, but it strongly suggests to me that the Septuagint translators had sound reasons for preferring *parthenos* to *neanis* in this verse. As it is, R.S.V. text and margin between them enable us to make the best of both renderings; whatever degree of immediate fulfilment the oracle had is satisfied by the rendering "young woman" in the text; the definitive fulfilment (Matt. 1:23) is satisfied by the marginal rendering "virgin."

Isa. 9:6. *Why is Christ called "Everlasting Father" in Isa. 9:6? How can the Son be the Father?*

The title "Father" in Isa. 9:6 has nothing to do with the mutual relationships of the Persons of the Godhead. A king ought to be a father to his people: the Divine King whose birth is announced in this prophecy will be "a father for ever" to those over whom He reigns.

In the R.S.V. of Isa. 9:6 the titles of the Coming Prince are given a punctuation differing from that in the A.V. and R.V. Which punctuation do you think is preferable?

The R.S.V. omits the comma between "Wonderful" and "Counsellor", thus adopting the alternative proffered in R.V. margin which makes the titles four in number instead of five. From the construction of the passage I have no doubt the R.S.V. is right; the first title is literally "wonder of a counsellor." To be wonderful in counsel is a divine attribute, as Isa. 28:29 makes plain.

Isa. 11:15. *What is the point of the drying up of the tongue of the Egyptian sea in Isa. 11:15?*

The same as the drying up or the reccession of the "sea of reeds" at the time of the Exodus—to let the Israelites in Egypt get across dryshod. The prophets repeatedly picture the return of Israel from exile or dispersion in terms of a second Exodus. In the present passage the division of the Euphrates into seven channels has the same purpose—to allow the exiled Israelites in Assyria to get across dryshod on their homeward journey. A further use for the uninterrupted highway thus established between Egypt and Assyria is indicated in Isa. 19:23-25, one of the high spots of the Old Testament.

Isa. 14:12ff. *Do you think there is a reference to Satan in Isa. 14:12ff?*

The whole passage proclaims the downfall of a tyrant, described as "king of Babylon." While he lived, all nations dreaded him, so mighty and oppressive was he; and he fancied himself the rival of God. But now he has died: his body is thrown out unburied (verses 19, 20), his posterity is cut off (verse 21), while the descent of his shade to Sheol arouses the surprised exclamation of those who are already there that one so apparently invincible should at last become weak in death like themselves. So great is the contrast between his former splendour and his present helpless plight that it is as if the morning star itself had fallen from the sky. It is difficult to find an allusion to the fall of Satan here.

Isa. 14:12. *Does the word translated "Lucifer" in Isa. 14:12 occur anywhere else in the Bible?*

This is the only Biblical occurrence of the Hebrew word (*helel*), which by derivation means "shining one" and is apparently a name for the morning star. The word used in the Septuagint (*heōsphoros*, "dawn-bringer") is used also in 1 Sam. 30:17 ("twilight"); Job 3:9; 41:18 (R.V. "eyelids of the morning"); 11:17 ("morning"); 38:12 ("day-spring"); 41:18 ("eyelids of the morning"); Psa. 110:3 ("morning").

Isa. 18:1. *What is the "land of the rustling wings" in Isa. 18:1?*

The land is part of the present-day Republic of Sudan; the rivers which divide it (verse 2) are probably the White, Blue and Black Niles, and the "whirring wings" of verse 1 may refer to its insect life. At this time Egypt was ruled by an Ethiopian dynasty with its capital at Napata near the fourth cataract. From Napata ambassadors were sent forth "by the Nile, in vessels of papyrus upon the waters" (verse 2). The point of the following words is obscured in A.V. and R.V. by the gratuitous and indeed mistaken addition of "*saying.*" The command, "Go, ye swift messengers . . ." is addressed by the prophet to the Ethiopian ambassadors, telling them to return to their own people and not try to entice the king of Judah into an anti-Assyrian alliance. The description of the Ethiopians as "a nation tall and smooth, a people feared near and far, a nation mighty and conquering" is particularly apt to their status during the sixty years from about 725 B.C. onwards, when they dominated north-east Africa as far as the Asian frontier and presented a challenge to the Assyrians (cf. the reference to Tirhakah king of Ethiopia in 2 Kings 19:9; Isa. 37:9).

Isa. 29:21. *Was there any Old Testament or Israelite ruling on age when the congregation deliberated in the market square (Isa. 29:21)?*

There was no express ruling, so far as I know, but age, maturity and experience counted for so much that no notice would normally be taken of anything said by a beardless youth. Elihu was probably a grown man when he intervened in the conversation between Job and his friends, but he realized his great daring in presuming to speak in the presence of men so much older than himself (Job 32:6ff.). In the story of Susanna (one of the Septuagintal additions to Daniel) the respect paid to Daniel's interposition in a public hearing, youth though he was, was quite exceptional, but the people recognized that he spoke by divine inspiration.

Isa. 34:6; 63:1. *To what occasion do Isaiah 34:6 and 63:1 refer? Is Bozrah identical with Petra?*

The reference in these and other passages to God's impending judgment on Edom is probably to the Edomites' expulsion from their homeland by invaders from the east and south during the post-exilic age, interpreted as divine vengeance on them for their unbrotherly treatment of Judah at the time of the Babylonian conquest. Bozrah is usually identified with El-Buseira, about 25 miles S.E. of the Dead Sea; Petra lies 50 miles south of the Dead Sea, in the neighbourhood of (if not identical with) the Old Testament Sela. The language of the two passages to which you refer is later applied to God's final dealing with His enemies in the day of visitation and deliverance, and is taken up, without local restriction, in Rev. 19:11ff. to portray a victory of a very different kind from that envisaged in the oracles against Edom.

Isa. 52:1. *To which Jerusalem does Isa. 52:1 refer?*

To the city which was sacked and depopulated by the Babylonians in 587 B.C.; its restoration in pursuance of the edict of Cyrus (cf. Isa. 44:28; 45:13) is here promised. The cleansing from foreign defilement which is described at the end of this verse was realized to a large extent through the reforms of Ezra and Nehemiah. In the New Testament, however, we have a reinterpretation of these chapters in terms of the gospel. Thus, in Rom. 10:15, the messengers of Isa. 52:7 who bring the good news of Zion's liberation become the preachers of the gospel of Christ, and the orphaned city of Isa. 54:1 becomes in Gal. 4:26f. "the Jerusalem that is above", the metropolis of the freeborn children of God. In this Christian interpretation the prophecy of Isa. 52:1 finds a fulfilment far greater both in scope and duration than was witnessed in the return from exile.

And if it be asked what is meant in this interpretation by the exclusion of the uncircumcized, Paul will give the answer again: "We are the circumcision, who worship by the Spirit of God, and glory in Christ Jesus" (Phil. 3:3).

Isa. 53. *Why do we find such variation in tenses in Isa. 53? E.g. "He shall grow up" (v. 2), "He is despised" (v. 3), "He hath borne our griefs" (v. 4), "He was wounded" (v. 5), and so on.*

These verses should be examined in the R.V., where there is much less variation of tense. For the most part the perfect tense is used in the Hebrew of these verses, translated properly by the R.V. "He grew up", etc. This use of the perfect might be regarded as the "prophetic perfect"; i.e. something which is still future is regarded as so certain of fulfilment that it is described as if it had already taken place. But when we consider this fourth "Servant Song" as a whole from 52:13 to 53:12, we find that the perfect tenses are set in a framework of imperfect tenses, translated properly by the English future, in the first three verses (52:13-15) and the last three (53:10-12). The perfect tenses of at least the first six verses of ch. 53 are spoken by those "many nations," with their rulers, to whom the Servant's true identity comes home; they describe something that they saw but did not understand at the time of their seeing it. But when at last their eyes are opened, "that which they had not heard shall they understand" (52:15), and their wondering response finds expression in the words that follow, which may be summarized: "Who would have believed the tidings which we heard? We saw his sufferings, but did not realize why he had to endure them; now we see that it was for *our* transgressions that he was wounded."

Isa. 53:10. *One version (the American Jewish) translates Isa. 53:10 thus: "Yet it pleased the* LORD *to crush him by disease; to see if his soul would offer itself in restitution." What would you say about its accuracy and interpretation?*

The first clause is a possible translation of the words rendered in R.V., "Yet it pleased the LORD to bruise him; he hath put him to grief"; it involves a minor but acceptable emendation of the Massoretic text. The phrase "he hath put him to grief" does in any case imply disease or sickness (cf. R.V. margin, "made him sick"); and one of the figures under which the Servant's suffering is pictured is that of someone afflicted by a loathsome disease. I do not care much for the second clause, for which I prefer the translation: "Truly he has given himself as a guilt-offering." N.E.B. has an attractive rendering: "Yet the LORD took thought for his tortured servant and healed him who had made himself a sacrifice for sin."

Isa. 53:12. *Who are "the strong" of Isa. 53:12 with whom the Servant of the Lord is to divide the spoil?*

"The strong" or "the mighty" is probably a generic expression for conquerors; the Servant, who triumphed through submission and suffering, emerges as the mightiest conqueror of all. There is, however, a variant rendering of the clause which runs "and numberless shall be his spoil" (so, e.g. C. R. North and H. L. Ellison), in which "the strong" as a category of people disappear.

Jeremiah 51:39, 57. *In Jer. 51:39, 57, we read of the rulers of Babylon as doomed to "sleep a perpetual sleep", from which they will never wake. How can one meet the arguments of Jehovah's Witnesses and others who say that this means that the wicked are already in Gehenna, the second death, and will have no resurrection?*

First of all, it must be emphasized that we do not go to the Old Testament for details of the doctrine of the life after

30

death, for very little was revealed on this subject within the Old Testament period. Therefore one should always suspect people who base their arguments on this subject mainly on passages from the Old Testament, whether from Jeremiah or Ecclesiastes. The Old Testament passages must be understood in the light of the plainer and fuller teaching of the New Testament, and not *vice versa*. In the second place, Jeremiah is referring here to the complete and irrevocable character of the sudden destruction which is to overtake Babylon; he is not thinking about the after-life of individual Babylonians. We ourselves commonly talk of death as the sleep from which there is no awakening, when we mean to contrast it with literal sleep; and such a form of speech is not intended to exclude the idea of resurrection.

Lamentations 3:4. *Do the words "he hath broken my bones" in Lam. 3:4 refer to our Lord, in view of the words "A bone of him shall not be broken" (John 19:36, citing Ex. 12:46)?*

No. The speaker in Lam. 3 is the personified community of Israel, accepting at God's hand the judgment that has been poured out in the Babylonian conquest and the destruction of Jerusalem and her temple. There is no good reason for applying these words to our Lord; that some of them have been so applied traditionally is due in part to the remarkable affinity which has been pointed out between some of the language of Lamentations and that in which the Suffering Servant is portrayed in the book of Isaiah.

Ezekiel 1:10. *In Ezek. 1:10 we have a description of the four faces of the living creatures mentioned in verse 5; in Ezek. 10:14 the four faces are described again but where formerly one of the faces was like that of an ox, here the corresponding face is like that of a cherub. Since Ezek. 10:15 makes it clear that the same living creatures are referred to in both places, why is there this change?*

The commonest answer today appears to be that in Ezek. 10:14 we should read "ox" instead of "cherub." Thus H. L. Ellison writes: "Already the rabbis wondered what had happened to the face of an ox in v. 14. Since no explanation is given what the face of a cherub is like, it seems obvious that we have to do with a careless scribal error" (*Ezekiel: The Man and his Message*, p. 45). If we do not accept this, we might consider H. A. Redpath's note on the verse in the "Westminster Commentaries" series: "A comparison of the two visions shews us what idea the word cherub conveyed to the prophet." He thinks Ezekiel had in his mind's eye the great human-faced bulls which guarded temple gateways in Babylonia and Assyria. The trouble is that though these colossi had the bodies of bulls or oxen they had *human* heads and faces, so that if "the face of the cherub" referred to these, it would be the face of a man and not of an ox. Walther Zimmerli suggests that the conception of a cherub with one face (cf. Ex. 25:20) has overlain that of a cherub with four faces. We may compare the four living creatures of Rev. 4:6ff., except that instead of each of them having four faces, each of them presents a different aspect from the three others; they resemble respectively the four creatures whose faces are worn by each one of Ezekiel's living creatures. G. R. Beasley-Murray, in his remarks on Ezek. 10:14 in the I.V.F. *New Bible Commentary*, quotes Rabbi Resh Lakish to the effect that "Ezekiel besought the Merciful One with regard to it (the ox face) and He changed it into a cherub"—but this will scarcely commend itself to present-day readers as a solution to the difficulty.

Ezek. 28:11ff. *Do you think there is a reference to Satan in Ezek. 28:11ff?*

The fall of the king of Tyre is described in these verses in terms of the expulsion from Eden of an angelic being by the very cherubim who formed his bodyguard. Perhaps the reference here is not simply to the human ruler Ethbaal II (who was king of Tyre at the time of Ezekiel's prophecy) but to the Tyrian deity Melkart (literally "king of the city"), whose priest and vicegerent Ethbaal was.

Ezek. 38:2. Is it possible to identify Gog, Magog, Rosh, Meshech and Tubal (cf. R.V., N.E.B.) with any degree of certainty?

Meshech and Tubal, mentioned previously in Ezekiel (27:13; 32:26), are the Moschi and Tibareni, known to the Assyrians as the Mushku and Tabalu; they lived in the north of Asia Minor, in a region where copper was mined, for they traded in this metal with the merchants of Tyre (Ezek. 27:13). Among their associates Gomer and Togarmah (Ezek. 38:6) are also readily identifiable; Gomer represents the Cimmerians, whom the Assyrians knew as the Gimirrai when they broke into the Fertile Crescent and Asia Minor from the north in Esarhaddon's reign (early in the 7th century B.C.), and Togarmah is Armenia. Gog is an Anatolian personal name (reproduced in Assyrian as Gugu, in Greek as Gyges), Magog is a place-name from the same root. As for Rosh, I am disposed to follow A.V. and R.S.V. ("the chief prince of Meshech and Tubal") in regarding it not as a proper noun at all, but the ordinary Hebrew word meaning "head" or "chief." Ezekiel envisages an invasion of Palestine from the mountainous areas north of the Fertile Crescent on much the same lines as the Scythian invasion which threatened the land two or three years before his own birth.

Would you agree that Gog (Ezek. 38:2) is to be identified with Gyges, king of Lydia about 685 B.C.—the identification favoured by the Westminster Dictionary of the Bible?

The *name* may very well be the same, but the *persons* can scarcely be identified: Ezekiel is not apostrophizing a man who flourished a century before his own time. What the *Westminster Dictionary of the Bible* says is: "The name may have been taken from Gyges." It makes it plain, however, that the Gog of Ezek. 38:2 "is prophetically described as invading the land of Israel in the last times, and being defeated on the mountains with immense slaughter.... He and his people and his allies serve the prophet as a type of heathenism contending against the Kingdom of God."

Ezek. 43ff. I should value help in the interpretation of Ezek. 43, 44 and 46 in the light of the Epistle to the Hebrews. Since Christ is the end of the law unto righteousness, how can we understand the reintroduction of Levitical conditions in Israel's future as envisaged in these three chapters?

Paul's statement that "Christ is the end of the law, that every one who has faith may be justified" (Rom. 10:4) is an abrogation of the law viewed as a basis of justification before God; the Epistle of the Hebrews is concerned rather with the abrogation of the law (more specifically, the priestly and sacrificial law) as a means of access to God. The interpretation of the closing chapters of Ezekiel has been a problem for Jewish and Christian exegetes for two thousand years. But if I find a line of interpretation leading me to the conclusion that animal sacrifices, which could never take away sin in themselves and which were in any case rendered obsolete by the self-sacrifice of Christ, will once again be accepted by God for the making of atonement, I shall immediately suspect that something has gone wrong along the line of reasoning which leads to so preposterous a conclusion (as I see it). It will not do to say that the sacrifices of Ezekiel's new commonwealth are only memorial in character; they are expressly said to be atoning or propitiatory (Ezek. 43:20, 26; 45:15, 17, 20). The Christian interpretation of the closing chapters of Ezekiel in terms of the gospel will be found in the last two chapters of Revelation; as for the sacrifices of Ezekiel's new commonwealth, their fulfilment is to be found in Christ just as the fulfilment of the Levitical sacrifices is to be found in Him.

Daniel 1:3, 7. *Is it to be inferred from Daniel 1 that Daniel was made a eunuch?*

This is not stated in so many words, but it could be inferred from the fact that he and his companions were placed in charge of "the chief of the eunuchs" (if this title is to be understood literally). In that case we should have a fulfilment here of Isaiah's prophecy to Hezekiah that some of his offspring would be "eunuchs in the palace of the king of Babylon" (2 Kings 20:18; Isa. 39:7).

Dan. 2:44; 9:27. *According to Archibald Hughes* (A New Heaven and a New Earth, *1958, p. 169), in his discussion of Dan. 9:27 ("and he shall confirm a covenant with many for one week"), the preposition "for" is not in the Hebrew text. Is this so? Also do you believe that "these kings" spoken of in Dan. 2:44 are future?*

It is true that there is no preposition before "one week" in the Hebrew text of Dan. 9:27, which reads literally: "And he will make strong (i.e. confirm, enforce, or validate) a covenant with the many one week ...". But if we leave out the word "for", does the omission make any difference to the sense? We could, of course, follow the Septuagint and make "one week" the subject of the clause ("and one week will enforce a covenant for many"), but does that make any better sense? I think not. The Revised Standard Version, which is certainly not prejudiced in favour of the interpretation which Archibald Hughes is opposing, renders,

"And he shall make a strong covenant with many for one week" (N.E.B. similarly has "for one week"). I am not convinced that "he" who is to "confirm the covenant" in Dan. 9:27 is, as Hughes maintains, the anointed prince of verse 25, although it is an ancient and widely held interpretation. As for "these kings" of Dan. 2:44, I regard them as past, believing as I do that the eternal kingdom foretold in that verse is the kingdom of God whose near advent was announced by our Lord at the beginning of the Galilaean ministry (Mark 1:15).

Dan. 7:17. *In Dan. 7:17 the four beasts of Daniel's vision are said to be "four kings, which shall arise out of the earth." Would it be right to infer from this that the emergence of all four was still future in Daniel's time, and that the first of the four could not therefore be Nebuchadnezzar?*

This conclusion must be established on other grounds than consideration of tense. The tense of the Aramaic verb translated "shall arise" is imperfect, and the Aramaic imperfect (like the Hebrew) denoted the fact that the action was incomplete, and not the time at which the action took place. Probably the present tense would be most satisfactory here in English: if we read that the four kings "arise out of the earth," then the question of their identification can be investigated without being prejudiced by the importation of a future emphasis which is not necessarily present in the original text.

Dan. 9:27. *Is the following a permissible rendering of the latter part of Dan. 9:27? "And upon the battlements shall be the idols of the desolator until the appointed consummation is poured upon the desolator."*

This would require two very slight emendations: the Hebrew text as it stands reads we'al kenaph shiqquṣim meshomem, "and on the wing (battlement) of abominations (idols) a desolator (will come)"; if we read *we'al kanaph shiqquṣê meshomem* we get the sense "and on the battlement (will be) the idols of the desolator." (The former of these two emendations involves only a change in the Massoretic vowel-points, not in the consonantal text.) The following clause, "until the appointed consummation is poured upon the desolator", is the probable meaning of the Hebrew text as it stands (cf. R.S.V.). The verse is a notorious crux; the earliest Greek translations represent more radical emendations of the text than that which your suggested version involves. If once the permissibility of emendation be conceded, this is a reasonable one; I should be disposed to emend slightly differently (*we'al kanaph shiqquṣ meshomem*) and translate "and upon the battlement (will be) a desolating abomination" (i.e., the idolatrous installation called the abomination of desolation in Dan. 11:31 and 12:11). (The word translated "battlement" means strictly "wing", then "pinnacle" or any extremity of a building or other object.)

What did the Christian writers of the earliest centuries A.D. teach regarding Daniel's seventieth week? The foreword to a book entitled Daniel's Seventieth Week: Is It Still Future? *says that "it gives the interpretation held by the Church for nearly two thousand years, an interpretation superseded only within the last seventy years by one school of interpreters."*

There is no unanimity among early Christian writers about the interpretation of Daniel's seventy weeks in general, or about the seventieth week in particular. The passage is not one which is expressly quoted and applied in the New Testament, although the period of time variously described in Rev. 11:2, 3; 12:14; 13:5 may reasonably be correlated with the "half of the week" in Dan. 9:27. (But even if the passage had been expressly quoted and applied in the New Testament,

experience teaches that this would not have ensured unanimity among Christian interpreters.) The "Epistle of Barnabas" (c. A.D. 100) refers the seventieth week to the present building of the new spiritual temple. Irenaeus (c. 180) and Hippolytus (c. 215) present a futurist view; Hippolytus, who treats the matter in greater detail, places the present gospel age between the sixty-ninth week and the seventieth. Clement of Alexandria (c. 180), followed by Origen (c. 230), envisages the whole period of seventy weeks as coming to an end with the events of A.D. 70. Tertullian (c. 200) says that if the Jewish nation had accepted Christ, the whole prophecy would have been fulfilled; as it was, by their rejection of Him they forfeited their title to the blessings which it promised and the only part which was left to be fulfilled to them was the destruction of the city and temple of Jerusalem, which took place in A.D. 70. The writer whom you quote therefore simplifies the issue unduly in suggesting that until recent years the Church maintained one uniform interpretation; in fact, the main varieties of interpretation current today were current already in the early Christian centuries.

Dan. 11:37. *Who or what is "the desire of women" in Dan. 11:37?*

"The one beloved by women" (R.S.V.) is probably the Syrian god Adonis or Tammuz, whose cult was specially attractive to women (cf. Ezek. 8:14). The point about the king here described is that instead of honouring any of the deities which had customarily been worshipped in his realm, he promotes the worship of "the god of fortresses . . . whom his fathers knew not", i.e. Jupiter Capitolinus, the Roman counterpart of Olympian Zeus, the Greek deity whose manifestation on earth Antiochus Epiphanes claimed to be.

Dan. 11:44. *What were the tidings out of the east and the north referred to in Daniel 11:44?*

If the king here is still Antiochus Epiphanes, as in the section of this chapter introduced by verse 21, then the reference is to rumours of threatened invasion by hostile neighbours (pre-eminently the Parthians) or of insurrection by rebellious subjects (e.g. the Armenians) on the eastern and northern frontiers of his empire. Indeed, something of the same sort would be intended if the king is not Antiochus but a later ruler in the same territory (even a ruler yet future, as held, e.g., by S. P. Tregelles and W. Kelly). Among rival interpretations, a particularly ingenious one is that of Philip Mauro, who identifies "the king" of verses 36-45 with Herod the Great, takes the "tidings out of the east" to be the wise men's announcement of the birth of a new King of the Jews (Matt. 2:1ff.), while the tidings from the north, he suggests, might be news from Rome (mentioned by Josephus) accusing certain members of his family of plotting against him. This interpretation, propounded in *The Seventy Weeks and the Great Tribulation* (1923), pp. 139ff., was anticipated in some respects, as Mauro acknowledges, by James Farquharson, *Daniel's Last Vision and Prophecy* (Aberdeen, 1838).

Amos 1:1. *When was the earthquake of Amos 1:1? Is there any Scriptural reference to it apart from Zech. 14:5?*

We may date it approximately around 750 B.C.; we have no more explicit evidence. There is no other Scriptural record of it apart from Zech. 14:5, unless those interpreters are right who see a reference to it in the first half of Amos 9:1 (the account of a vision which in that case would be dated two years later than Amos's inaugural oracle); but this interpretation of Amos 9:1 is quite precarious. Josephus makes the earthquake coincide with the incident of 2 Chron. 26:16ff., when Uzziah was smitten with leprosy (*Antiquities* ix. 225).

Amos 6:10. *Does Amos 6:10 encourage cremation or condemn it, and why does it say the name of the* LORD *may not be mentioned?*

The circumstances of this passage do not envisage the *normal* disposal of the dead, and so provide no guidance about cremation as a regular practice. Amos is foretelling the straits to which the inhabitants of Samaria were to be reduced during the long siege of their city by the Assyrians (2 Kings 17:5). If I may quote H. L. Ellison, "the final agonies of Israel are depicted in terms of starvation or plague. In a graphic picture a near relation (verse 10—'uncle' is too specific) comes to carry out the last rites and finds the dead man mere skin and bones. He cannot be buried, but must be burned, for the enemy are round about the city. As he calls out in the great, rich house, asking if there is yet someone alive, a weak, and it may well be dying, voice answers from a back room, 'Yes! but don't mention the name of Jehovah!' At last, but too late, the hand of God stretched out in judgment has been recognized" (*The Prophets of Israel*, 1969, pp. 89f.). They do not wish to hear the Lord's name, for it is by Him that this disaster has been sent, because they paid no heed to His message through the prophet.

Jonah. *It is commonly suggested that the story of Jonah is a parable of Israel's passing through the Babylonian captivity, and emerging from it to be God's messenger to the nations. Is this a valid interpretation?*

It is certainly a widely held interpretation, but, although it cannot be ruled out entirely, it must be said that there is very little in the book of Jonah to support it. The one event of which the experience of Jonah is said in Scripture to be a sign is the burial and resurrection of Christ (Matt. 12:40), and the prayer of Jonah in Ch. 2:2-9 is in conformity with this; the words "thou didst bring up my life from the pit" (Jonah 2:6) lend themselves as readily to Christ's resurrection as do the words of Psa. 16:10 quoted to this effect by Peter in Acts 2:27 and by Paul in Acts 13:35 (the same Hebrew word, *shaḥath*, is translated "pit" in Jonah 2:6 as is translated "pit" or "corruption" in Psa. 16:10).

Further to the preceding question, may not Jer. 51:34, where Zion complains that "Nebuchadnezzar the king of Babylon ... has swallowed me like a monster (Heb. tannin)," support the view that Jonah being swallowed by the sea monster is a figure of Israel being engulfed in the Babylonian exile?

Perhaps; but the difficulty I see in this view is that the prophets regard the exile as a divine judgment on Israel, "double for all her sins" (Isa. 40:2), whereas the sea monster was not sent as a judgment on Jonah but (as he himself acknowledged) as a means of delivering him from the mortal peril of the sea and conveying him safe back to dry land.

Micah 3:12. *When was Micah's prophecy, "Therefore shall Zion for your sake be plowed as a field" (Micah 3:12) fulfilled?*

It is unnecessary to look for a direct fulfilment of Micah's words. According to Jer. 26:15, 19, Micah's warning was heeded by the king and people of Judah, so that "the LORD repented of the evil which he had pronounced against them." In this respect Micah's words, like the words of Jonah pronounced against Nineveh, illustrate the conditional character of much Biblical prophecy, especially prophecy of judgment. In so far as a later lapse into rebellion by the people of Judah and Jerusalem incurred a renewal, on the lip of Jeremiah and other prophets, of the pronouncement of doom previously made by Micah, we need look no farther for a fulfilment than to the desolations of Jerusalem which followed its capture and

sack by Nebuchadnezzar's armies. If we press the language of this oracle of doom, it requires for its fulfilment a time when not only is Mount Zion plowed up like a field, but the whole of Jerusalem lies in ruins, and the "mountain of the house" (i.e. the Temple area) is "like a wooded height" (i.e. completely overgrown).

Micah 5:2. *In the R.S.V. of Micah 5:2 why does the plural word rendered "goings forth" in A.V. appear as "origin"? And is the phrase "ancient days" in the same verse an adequate rendering? I have been told that the literal rendering is "days of eternity."*

It would have been easy for the revisers to put the plural "origins" rather than the singular "origin" in Micah 5:2, but I do not think that this would have really met your point, since you regard the word as referring to "the activities or manifestations of the Lord in time and eternity past." Probably the revisers understood the language to refer to the antiquity of the promised King's human ancestry. As for "ancient days" ("days of *'olam*"), the word *'olam* implies indefinite duration, and may denote eternity where the context requires. The same phrase ("days of *'olam*") occurs in Micah 7:14, where both A.V. and R.S.V. properly translate "the days of old" (N.E.B. "days gone by") —the reference being to the period following Israel's settlement in Canaan, several centuries before Micah's time. The question illustrates an important point—that it is necessary to understand a passage before one can translate it, and where it is understood in different ways, the words chosen to translate it will differ.

Habakkuk 2:2ff. *Can we deduce from the verses that follow Hab. 2:2 what was the vision which the prophet was to write plainly?*

The "vision" (which, despite the primary meaning of the word, was, like many other prophetic visions, heard rather than seen) may very well have consisted of the words of verse 4. A short sentence in large letters is indicated, which the man who runs past it can take in at a glance, like Isaiah's Maher-shalal-hash-baz (Isa. 8:1). Verse 4 in Hebrew consists of nine words at most. This summarizes the essence of the "vision"; the message is spelt out in greater detail in the five "Woes" of verses 6b-19, which declare the oppressor's downfall and the vindication of God's cause.

Hab. 3:3. *When will God come from Teman and Mount Paran (Habakkuk 3:3)?*

He will not come; He came. Habakkuk describes a vision of God, a theophany, experienced by himself. In it he sees God coming from the direction from which, centuries before, He had led Israel up from the wilderness. We may compare the very similar language in which the blessing of Moses describes an earlier theophany (Deut. 33:2), and that in which the song of Deborah and Barak describes God's coming to the help of His people in the war against Sisera (Judges 5:4, 5).

Haggai 2:7. *It has been suggested that "the desire of all nations" in Hag. 2:7 (A.V.) refers to Christ. But the R.V. has "the desirable things of all nations", which obviously cannot refer to the Messiah. Which do you think is the correct version?*

The A.V. follows the Latin Vulgate, which treats the reference as personal: "He shall come who is desired by all the nations." Hence the phrase has made its way into Christian language as a title of the Messiah, as in Wesley's line, "Come, Desire of nations, come." The R.V. rendering, "the desirable things of all nations" follows the Septuagint (cf. R.S.V. "treasures"; N.E.B. "treasure"). The Hebrew noun simply means "that which is desired (*or* desirable)" and could have a personal or impersonal reference, accord-

to the context; the Hebrew verb "shall come" is unambiguously in the plural. Here the context seems to favour the R.V. rendering: for the language we may compare Rev. 21:26.

Zechariah 6:11. *Why was Joshua the high priest crowned in Zech. 6:11?*

It was certainly an unusual thing to crown the high priest. But at the time it would have been unsafe to crown Zerubbabel, the civil ruler, as the Persians would have interpreted that as a declaration of independence and an act of rebellion. To mark the restoration of national life and the resumption of the temple worship, therefore, the high priest was chosen as the figure to be crowned; the Persians would not have objected so much to this. The crown (singular, as in R.V. margin) was on this occasion a token of honour rather than of royalty.

Zech. 6:12. *Who is "the man whose name is the Branch" in Zech. 6:12?*

The reference is, in the first instance, to Zerubbabel, who is being pointed out to Joshua in this capacity. (Note that the second-last clause in verse 13 should be rendered "there shall be a priest beside his throne"; i.e. Joshua the high priest would stand by Zerubbabel the civil governor, and there would be concord between them.) Zerubbabel, of course, was not the man in whom "the holy and sure blessings" promised to David found their ultimate fulfilment. But the fact that after the return from the Babylonian exile a prince of the house of David was governor of Judah showed that Jeremiah's prophecy of "a righteous Branch" to be raised up "for David" (Jer. 23:5; 33:15) had not been nullified; Zerubbabel was the guarantee that the Messiah of David's line would indeed come; and in fact both the New Testament genealogies of our Lord show Zerubbabel as His ancestor (Matt. 1:12f.; Luke 3:27).

Zech. 12:7ff. *In Zech. 12:7 what do you think is indicated by God's purpose to "save the tents of Judah first"? Since Zechariah has distinguished "Judah" from "the inhabitants of Jerusalem", does he imply that Judah participates in the mourning (12:10-14) and the cleansing (13:1), said to be for "the inhabitants of Jerusalem"?*

The tents of Judah appear to be delivered first because their need is more urgent; the inhabitants of the undefended country districts are in greater danger than those within the city walls. Judah's participation in the mourning of Zech. 12:10-14 is probably implied, although not expressed; if members of the tribe of Levi share in it, we might all the more expect the tribe of Judah to do so, although the only members of that tribe actually mentioned are the house of David and of his son Nathan. (Compare the tracing of our Lord's genealogy back to David through Nathan in Luke 3:31.) Again, we need not exclude Judah from the cleansing provided in Zech. 13:1 for the house of David and the inhabitants of Jerusalem; the most prominent members of the tribe are mentioned, but they may be taken as representative of the whole tribe, and in fact verse 2 makes it plain that the *land* is to be cleansed (the land of Judah at the very least, and quite possibly the whole land of Israel).

Zech. 13:5. *In Zech. 13:5 A.V. renders the last clause "for man taught me to keep cattle from my youth", whereas R.V. has "for I have been made a bondman from my youth' and R.S.V. "for the land has been my possession since my youth."*

What is the reason for these variations?

The variation is due to uncertainty about the Hebrew word *hiqnani* in this clause; R.V. derives it from *qānāh*, "acquire" or "purchase"; A.V. connects it with *miqneh*, "flock" or "herd"; N.E.B. (following the Syriac version) relates it to the word translated "passion" (A.V., R.V., R.S.V. "jealousy") in Cant. 8:6, and gives an improbable rendering; R.S.V. emends or amplifies the Hebrew text, which it renders more literally in the margin "for man has caused me to possess (since my youth)." Whichever translation we adopt, the clause is an amplification of the preceding one ("I am a tiller of the ground") and means that the speaker is a simple agricultural labourer and no prophet.

Malachi 4:15. *Did the prophet Malachi regard the Messianic reign as the great and dreadful day of the* LORD *(Mal. 4:5)?*

Since Malachi does not explicitly mention the Messiah, it is difficult to give a completely confident answer to this question; but if he were asked, he might say that he regarded the great and terrible day of the LORD as inaugurating the Messianic reign. It seems probable that this is the same day as the day "burning like an oven" of Mal. 4:1 and possibly also the day of Mal. 3:2—"who can endure the day of his coming, and who can stand when he appeareth?" One time indication is clear enough: Elijah will come *before* the great and terrible day, and we have the New Testament interpretation of the Elijah prophecy in terms of John the Baptist (Matt. 11:14; 17:10-13), discussed below, pp. 49, 67, 153f.

THE SYNOPTIC GOSPELS[1]

Matthew 1:8. *Why are Ahaziah, Joash and Amaziah omitted from the genealogy in Matt. 1:8 between Joram and Uzziah? Jehoiakim's omission from verse 11 may be explained by his being blotted out of the book of life because of his treatment of the divine oracles (Jer. 36:23), but what reason can be given for the omission of those three earlier kings?*

It is no unprecedented thing for links in a genealogical chain to be omitted in Scripture. Whether any spiritual reason underlies the omission in Matt. 1:8 is uncertain. At one time it was commonly suggested that because of Joram's marriage to the Baal-devotee Athaliah, the daughter of Ahab and Jezebel, their progeny is passed over in this record "to the third and fourth generation." This is, at least, less improbable than the view that Matthew simply "cooked" the generations so that this middle section of his genealogy, like the other two, might yield a total of fourteen.

Matt. 1:15. *Is the Rahab of Matt. 1:15 the same as the Rahab of Joshua 2:1ff.?*

This is almost certainly what we are intended to understand, and there is considerable significance in the fact that of the women who are mentioned in the earlier part of our Lord's genealogy in Matt. 1 three at least, and possibly all four, were Gentiles by birth. Salmon was of the same generation as Rahab, for his father Nahshon was leader of the tribe of Judah in the earlier period of the wilderness wanderings.

Matt. 1:23. *Some years ago there was an animated correspondence in* The Times Literary Supplement, *arising out of reviews of the New English Bible New Testament (1961), but ultimately concentrating on the meaning of the Hebrew and Greek words translated "virgin" in the common version of Isa. 7:14 and Matt. 1:23. One of the writers has maintained that both the words (Heb. 'almah and Gk. parthenos) ought "always to be translated 'young woman', which is all that they in fact import." Would you comment on this?*

The Greek word *parthenos*, used in Matt. 1:23 (quoting the Septuagint of Isa. 7:14), quite definitely means "virgin," regardless of its etymology (to which appeal was made in the *T.L.S.* correspondence). There may be a few places where the context shows that it has a more general meaning, but these are merely the exceptions that prove the rule. Indeed, so completely does it convey the sense of virginity that on occasion it may be used even of male celibates, as in Rev. 14:4. The Athenians called their city's patron goddess Athene *Hē Parthenos*, that is to say, "The Virgin" *par excellence*; and the temple built in her honour on the Acropolis was called the Parthenon because it was "The Virgin's House." As for the Hebrew word, I am not competent to criticize the most distinguished Semitic philologist in the British Isles, but I have the impression that with the Hebrew, as with the Greek word, too much weight is given to the etymology in deciding the meaning. It is certainly helpful to know as much as we can about cognate words in other Semitic languages, but the most important consideration in determining the meaning of the Hebrew word is its actual usage in classical Hebrew literature (i.e. the Old Testament), where it is attested seven times. In the course of the correspondence to which you refer regret

---

[1] Questions on the Synoptic Gospels are arranged in the sequence of a tentative Gospel harmony.

was expressed that the word "virgin" was used in the N.E.B. at Matt. 1:23, because this has "the unfortunate result that the connexion with the Old Testament is obscured." It would, however, be possible to prevent any such obscuring of the connexion if the same word were used to render *'almah* in Isa. 7:14. I have argued elsewhere (see p. 27) for the view that a good case could be made out for the translation "virgin" in Isa. 7:14 quite apart from the Christological question. For the sake of clear thinking, however, let it be added that our Lord's virgin birth is not brought into question by these philological debates; this is plainly recorded as a fact in the nativity narratives of Matthew and Luke, whatever may be said about the quotation of Isa. 7:14.

Luke 2:7, 12. *Could the word translated "swaddling clothes" in Luke 2:7, 12, be translated as "rags"?*

No; the word is the proper term for "swaddling" or winding a new-born child round and round in the long strip or strips of cloth used for that purpose. We are perhaps given a misleading impression by the line of the carol which describes the infant Christ as "all *meanly* wrapped in swaddling bands", but there is no suggestion in the New Testament text that these swaddling bands differed at all from those in which new-born children were normally wrapped. Mary had probably brought them with her from Nazareth in readiness for the birth of her Child.

Luke 2:33. *In Luke 2:33 the R.V. reads "his father and his mother" where A.V. has "Joseph and his mother." Is the R.V. reading justified? If so, does not Luke here contradict what he has said earlier about our Lord's virgin birth?*

The R.V. rendering represents the more reliable text. But there is no inconsistency here with the fact of the virginal conception, clearly stated in Luke 1:26ff.

Although Joseph was not actually our Lord's father, he was so by repute and in law (cf. Luke 3:23; John 1:45); hence Luke can speak of "his parents" (2:41, 43) and Mary herself, who knew the facts better than anyone else, says "thy father and I" (2:48) when speaking to Jesus about Joseph and herself.

Luke 2:42. *Was the age of Israelite responsibility twelve years? This arises in the light of Luke 2:42.*

The earliest explicit statements that we have on this subject indicate that thirteen years was the age of responsibility—at least of responsibility to keep the commandments, as it is to this day in orthodox Judaism. This ruling is embodied in a saying ascribed to Rabbi Judah ben Tema (late 2nd century A.D.) but certainly did not originate with him. It is doubtful whether any significance of this kind should be attached to the age of Jesus at the time of the Jerusalem visit of Luke 2:41ff.

Luke 3:16; Matt. 3:11. *Do you agree with Godet that the absence of the preposition before "fire" in Luke 3:16 rules out the interpretation that the fire is the fire of judgment?*

The preposition "in" (Gk. *en*) preceding "Holy Spirit" may well go with "fire" also, but if not, the dative by itself can have instrumental force as easily as the dative preceded by *en*. It is difficult to dissociate the "fire" of verse 16 (cf. Matt. 3:11) from that of the following verse, where the Coming One will burn up the chaff "with unquenchable fire." The purifying activity of the Holy Spirit involves an element of judgment, just as fire refines the precious metal by consuming the dross.

Luke 3:23-38. *How can it be proved that the genealogy in Luke 3:23ff. is that of Mary?*

I don't think it can be proved. I suppose the view that it is Mary's genealogy is simply an inference from the fact that the genealogy of Matt. 1:2-16 is so obviously Joseph's. But there is another possibility—namely, that the genealogy in Matt. 1 is intended to give the line of succession to the throne of David (which did not always tally identically with the line of descent from father to son), while Luke 3 traces Joseph's actual descent from David by another branch of the family than that which produced the kings who followed David. The most satisfactory treatment of the problem known to me is that given by J. G. Machen in *The Virgin Birth of Christ;* he favours the possibility referred to in the foregoing sentence, adding: "There is nothing at all inherently improbable in such a solution. When a kingly line becomes extinct, the living member of a collateral line inherits the throne. So it may well have been in the present case" (p. 204). But whichever view one adopts, a number of unresolved difficulties are left, and one cannot be dogmatic; different students will make different assessments of the balance of probabilities.

Matt. 4:1-11; Luke 4:1-12. *What is the reason for the difference in order of the three temptations of our Lord, as recorded in Matt. 4:1-11 and Luke 4:1-12?*

Since we are not told the reason, we can but speculate. It is natural to suppose that each of the Evangelists regards the temptation narrative as reaching a climax with the third temptation; but the climax will be related to the dominant emphasis of the particular Gospel involved. In Matthew the tempter's offer of world dominion to Jesus makes a fitting climax, since this Gospel presents Jesus as the one to whom all authority is given. It is worth observing that Matthew explicitly mentions a mountain in connexion with this temptation, whereas Luke does not (although he implies something of the sort in the words "he led him up"); there

may be a suggested contrast between this mountain, on which Jesus refuses the dominion offered Him by Satan, and the mountain of Matt. 28:16ff., where He announces that universal dominion has been conferred upon Him (by His Father, of course, as in Matt. 11:27 and Luke 10:22). Luke, on the other hand, makes the climax of his temptation narrative our Lord's refusal to put God to the test and see whether He really meant what He said in the words He spoke at the baptism. This is in line with Luke's portrayal of our Lord as the obedient Son of Man, proceeding to discharge the ministry for which He had been so recently anointed and commissioned (compare His reading and application of Isa. 61:1f. in Luke 4:18ff.). Which was actually the chronological order of the temptations is another question, and one which cannot now be answered with certainty.

Matt. 4:6; Luke 4:10. *It is sometimes said that Satan deliberately omitted part of Psa. 91:11f. ("to keep thee in all thy ways") when he quoted it to our Lord (Matt. 4:6); but would not the addition of these words have strengthened his argument?*

If other people in the New Testament who quote the Old Testament were dealt with by the same severe standards as are applied to Satan here, the results would be surprising. According to Luke 4:10 Satan did at least quote the words "to keep thee." I have even heard preachers criticize him for adding "at any time" or "haply" after the word "lest"—not realizing that he was following respectable precedent by using the Septuagint. You are quite right; and the point is not that Satan *misquoted* the Scripture but that he *misapplied* it by inviting our Lord to put Himself gratuitously into a position of danger in which He could claim a promise which had no reference to actions of that kind. To pay heed to such a suggestion would indeed have been "tempting God", and that would have been a violation of Deut. 6:16—which our Lord quoted with the singular of the Septuagint ("Thou shalt not tempt...") and not with the plural of the Massoretic Hebrew ("Ye shall not tempt...").

Matt. 4:24. *Does the Greek of Matt. 4:24 imply that epilepsy (cf. R.V.) is a result of demon-possession?*

No; in this verse demon-possession, epilepsy and paralysis are mentioned as three distinct ailments which our Lord cured. In Matt. 17:14-18 however, epilepsy and demon-possession are found together in the same person, and in this instance the epilepsy is represented as resulting from the demon-possession.

Matt. 5-7; Luke 6: 17-49. *According to Hogg and Watson,* On the Sermon on the Mount *(3rd imp., p. 19), "the Sermon on the Mount is intended for the guidance of regenerate persons in an unregenerate world." Do you agree with this or do you think that the Sermon relates primarily to some other age or period, and if so which? Is it of any significance that it was addressed to the disciples (Matt. 5:1f.)?*

Yes, I think it is of significance that it was addressed to our Lord's disciples, even if it was heard (or overheard) by the multitudes of Matt. 7:28. I quite agree with the authors whom you quote. Naturally, while the principles laid down by our Lord are of abiding validity, the particular ways in which they are to be put into practice will differ from place to place and time to time; for example, the precept about going the second mile, in its literal sense (Matt. 5:41), had special reference to the conditions of life in occupied Palestine during our Lord's ministry; but it is not difficult to recognize the general principle underlying it. The Sermon is intended for followers of Christ in days when they are liable to be reproached on His account and persecuted for righteousness' sake.

Matt. 5-7; Luke 6:17-49. *Was the sermon of Matt. 5-7 the same as that of Luke 6:17-49?*

I believe so, although the Matthaean version is more comprehensive than the Lucan, including some material which Luke reproduces in other contexts. There is no inconsistency between the mountain of Matt. 5:1 and the level place of Luke 6:17, if W. M. Christie was right in identifying the spot with a level piece of ground on the ridge running parallel with the Lake of Galilee between Tell-Hum (? Capernaum) and Et-Tabgha. "There the twelve were chosen, and the Sermon was preached on the level a little way lower down. Matthew walked up with the crowd, and to him it was certainly a hill. Luke came over from Caesarea to view the scene he was to describe, and was impressed with the 'level place' on which he looked down from the Roman highway on the adjoining height" (*Palestine Calling*, 1939, p. 35).

Matt. 5:22. *If a Christian calls a fellow-believer a fool, does he come under the condemnation of Matt. 5:22?*

What our Lord is emphasizing here is that outward acts of evil should be checked at the source. National law penalizes the murderous attack, but the divine law condemns the angry thought, the insulting word, from which issues the train of hostility and hatred which can result in murder. It is in the light of this context that we must judge whether a particular expression comes within the scope of our Lord's words and incurs the judgment of the fiery valley. It has been suggested that the word used here (*mōre*) is not the vocative case of Gk. *mōros* ("fool"), but the term (Heb. *mōreh*) used by Moses and Aaron in Num. 20:10 ("Hear now, you *rebels...*"), with such severe consequences to themselves. Whether that be so or not, discourteous language is un-Christian language.

Matt. 5:32; 19:9. *What do you think of the exception "saving for the cause of fornication", in Matt. 5:32 (cf. Matt. 19:9)? Does the exception cover a case of adultery?*

I think the term *porneia* ("fornication") has the same sense here as in 1 Cor. 5:1 (and probably also in the apostolic decree of Acts 15:20, 29; 21:25); that is to say, it refers to marital unions within prohibited degrees, as laid down in Lev. 18, and not to adultery. Where such unions have been contracted, the separation of the parties concerned when they become Christians is permissible, if not indeed obligatory. You ask me what I *think*, and I have told you; but I would not assert this dogmatically. An alternative view relates the exceptive clause to the situation envisaged in Deut. 22:20f.

Matt. 5:34. *Since our Lord in Matt. 5:34 says to His disciples, "Swear not at all", does this mean that as Christians we are not to take the oath in a court of law?*

Our Lord wishes His followers to be known as men of their word, whose statements do not require to be reinforced by oaths to carry conviction to their hearers. And it is a fact that people like the Friends, who interpret our Lord's command with literal simplicity, command more credence by their unsupported word than most other people do when they bind themselves by the most solemn oaths. Certainly the circumstances of a law-court form a special case, and such well-known writers as C. F. Hogg and J. B. Watson (*The Sermon on the Mount*, p. 47f.) and G. H. Lang (*The Christian Relation to the State and to War*, p. 18ff.) give reasons for thinking that the oath of testimony does not fall within the scope of our Lord's prohibition, which is to be understood in the light of the instances which He mentions with disapproval. But, as the two writers first named point out, "happily it is now the right of every British subject to declare or affirm in lieu of taking the oath in a court of law, if his conscience forbids him to swear (Section 1, Oaths Act, 1888)." Plainly a solemn invocation of the name of one of the Persons in the Godhead, such as Paul utters in Rom. 1:9; 9:1; 2 Cor. 11:10f., 31; 12:19; Gal. 1:20, would not come under our Lord's ban. Neither, in my judgment, does the solemn form of words which an apprentice uses on becoming a freeman (concerning which you also ask); it is comparable rather to the *sponsio academica* which a student makes on admission to a university.

Matt. 6:10; Luke 11:2. *What is the kingdom in Matt. 6:10 and John 18:36?*

In Matt. 6:10 ("Thy kingdom come") our Lord points to the future consummation of the kingdom of God rather than its current inauguration by means of His ministry (for which see Matt. 12:28). This consummation of God's kingdom, as the neighbouring clauses in the Lord's Prayer suggest, will be marked by the hallowing of His name and the doing of His will on earth as in heaven. (The words "on earth as it is in heaven" probably refer to all three of the preceding petitions.)

In John 18:36 our Lord is being questioned by Pilate, before whom He has been accused of claiming to be a king (king of the Jews). Interrogated on this point, He replies in effect: "Yes, I am a king, but my kingship is not of a kind in which Roman law would be interested. If my kingship were of the ordinary secular and political kind, then my servants would fight to prevent my arrest. As it is, my kingship does not belong to this world-order; the kingdom of which I am king is the kingdom of truth. I came to bear witness to the truth, and those who belong to the kingdom of truth manifest that fact by paying heed to what I say and thus acknowledging my kingship." Pilate might dismiss all this talk of truth impatiently enough, but he realized that this harmless visionary (as he thought Him) constituted no threat to imperial law and order. The kingdom, then, of which our Lord speaks in this passage has as its citizens those who hear and obey Him, confessing that not only His teaching but He Himself is the truth.

Matt. 6:13; Luke 11:4. *How should we understand the petition "Lead us not into temptation" in the Lord's Prayer?*

I am inclined to favour C. C. Torrey's rendering "let us not yield to temptation" (*The Four Gospels*, pp. 12, 143); that is to say, "keep us from failing under trial." To fail under trial would be to give in to the evil one; to be kept from failing would be deliverance from him. Thus the clause about which you ask and the one immediately following explain each other. (There could be a special reference to the supreme test of faith in the distress of the end-time.) There is a similar passage in Matt. 26:41 and parallels: "Watch and pray that you may not enter into temptation." Here the sense appears to be: "Stay awake, and pray that you may not fail under trial." In Gethsemane the disciples were exposed to a very severe temptation; they could not avoid entering into it in the literal English sense of the words, but they might well pray for strength to stand their ground when the moment of testing came.

Matt. 8:17. *In the light of Isa. 53:4, 12, and the application of the former verse in Matt. 8:17, did Christ's sacrifice on the Cross atone for our sins and sicknesses? Please comment on the Hebrew and Greek terms translated "bear" in these verses.*

The quotation of Isa. 53:4 in Matt. 8:17 may be dealt with first. The Greek form of Matthew's quotation is quite different from the Septuagint; it represents an independent rendering of the Hebrew. The Hebrew says, "Surely our sicknesses he bore (*nāsā'*) and our pains he carried (*sābal*)." The verb *nāsā'* can mean either "bear" or "take away" according to the requirements of the context, and *sābal* stands in synonymous parallelism with it here, so that whatever meaning the former verb bears in this place is borne by the latter verb too. Matthew interprets the verbs in the sense "take away" when he renders "he himself took (*lambanō*) our infirmities and bore (*bastazō*) our sicknesses"; for he interprets the passage as a prophetic testimony of our Lord's healing ministry. When our Lord, in this context of Matthew, relieves Peter's mother-in-law of her fever, heals other people of their sicknesses and casts out demons from those who were possessed, Matthew does not mean that He took the fever, the other sicknesses and the demon-possession on Himself, enduring these things vicariously on behalf of those who had been afflicted by them; he means that He took them away. Like Heb. *nāsā'*, Greek *bastazō* can mean either "bear" or "take away" as the context may indicate; in Matt. 8:17 it means "take away." This is the only place in the New Testament where Isa. 53:4 is quoted. The force of the passage in its original context is, however, rather different: the speakers, who at one time had reckoned the Servant's sufferings to be the result of His incurring God's displeasure, now realize the truth and acknowledge that the sufferings endured by Him are those which they themselves had merited, but which He has borne in their place. As for Isa. 53:12, "he bore (*nāsā'*) the sin of many," this repeats the sense of the last clause of verse 11, "their iniquities he shall bear (*sābal*)," and its New Testament fulfilment is made clear by its quotation in Heb. 9:28, "Christ was once offered to bear the sins of many," and in 1 Pet. 2:24, "He himself bore our sins in his body on the tree." In both of these latter passages the Greek verb, as in the Septuagint of Isa. 53:12, is *anapherō*, a word repeatedly used in a sacrificial context. In His sacrifice our Lord both took His people's sins upon Himself, as these Scriptures state, and also took them away, as is stated in John 1:29 (where the verb is *airō*). Now to come back to your first question: it is nowhere stated, or implied, in Scripture, that by His sacrifice on the cross our Lord made atonement for His people's sicknesses as well as for their sins. The one New Testament passage, as we have seen, where Isa. 53 is applied to sicknesses has reference to His curing people of their diseases and afflictions in the course of His healing ministry. Moreover, sicknesses do not require to be atoned for; they require to be relieved and removed. Sin too requires to be removed, but it is removed by being atoned for; and it was by taking His people's sin on Himself and thus making atonement for it that our Lord removed it.

Matt. 8:28; Mark 5:1; Luke 8:26. *What is the difference between "Gergesenes" (Matt. 8:28) and "Gadarenes" (Mark 5:1; Luke 8:26)? How could the Gadarene swine be drowned in the Lake of Galilee, seeing that Gadara is seven miles away from the Lake, and separated from it by the deep gorge of the Yarmuk?*

There is very considerable confusion about the place-name in the textual transmission of the three Synoptic accounts. The incident probably took place in the neighbourhood of the modern village of Kersa (Kursi), east of the Lake. The name Kersa probably represents ancient Gergesa (whence "Gergesenes", Matt. 8:28, A.V., and Luke 8:26, R.V. margin). But the city of Gadara, we are told, owned some land around Kersa, so that the term "Gadarenes" (Matt. 8:28, R.V.; Mark 5:1 and Luke 8:26, A.V.) is not out of place. The reading "Gerasenes" (Mark 5:1 and Luke 8:26, R.V.) properly refers to the large and important city called Gerasa nearly 40 miles south-east of the Lake, but this city, the modern Jerash, has nothing to do with the Gospel narrative.

Matt. 9:9; Mark 2:14; Luke 5:27. *Was Matthew—called in Mark 2:14 "Levi the son of Alphaeus"—a brother of James the son of Alphaeus? Would Matthew have had to pay a year's taxes in advance in order to get his post?*

It is not known whether Alphaeus the father of Levi was identical with Alphaeus the father of James, or not. It was customary that a tax-collector should pay a lump sum for the privilege of collecting the taxes of a district for a year or a longer period. A minor official like Matthew would pay this sum to the chief tax-collector of Capernaum, and he in turn would buy the privilege from the ruler of Galilee (at this time, Herod Antipas). The collector would then endeavour to recoup himself by the taxes which he exacted, and the temptation was strong to exact as much more as he could.

Matt. 9:24; Mark 5:39; Luke 8:52. *Had Jairus's daughter actually died, or was she simply asleep (Mark 5:39)?*

Probably she would have been certified as dead by any doctor then or now. But our Lord knew what He was about, and treating the certainty of her restoration as a fact already accomplished, He said: "the child is not dead, but asleep." We may compare His words about Lazarus in John 11:11. It has been pointed out that while the verb there used for sleeping is *koimaomai*, here it is *katheudō*. It is true that *katheudō* is much less common as a metaphor for death than *koimaomai*, but there are a few examples of its use in this sense (cf. 1 Thess. 5:10), and it may be used here because there was such a short space of time since the girl's heart had ceased to beat. Such, at least, is my judgment, but it ill becomes us to dogmatize one way or the other; at this remote date we cannot have the confirmation which medical certification would supply.

Luke 8:53. *In the previous question it was asked if Jairus's daughter was really dead, or only asleep, as we normally use the term. Is not Luke's use of the verb*

45

"to know" a decisive consideration here: "And they laughed him to scorn, knowing that she was dead" (8:53)? Would not Luke have said "believing" or "supposing" if there had been any doubt?

Luke certainly had no doubt that she had really died. It might be argued that we should read implied quotation-marks around "knowing", as though Luke simply meant to convey to us that they said: "We *know* she's dead!" But if that had been his intention, he would have indicated it more clearly.

Matt. 9:38; Luke 10:2. *Who is the "Lord of the harvest" in Matt. 9:38 and Luke 10:2?*

He seems beyond question to be God the Father. In the interpretation of the Parable of the Tares (Matt. 13:37ff.) it is the Son of man who sows the good seed and commands the angel-harvester, but the Son of man has received authority from God both for gospel blessing and for the execution of final judgment.

Matt. 11:3; Luke 7:19. *In view of the signs which accompanied our Lord's baptism by John—the descent of the dove and the heavenly voice (Luke 3:21f.; John 1:32ff.) —why was it necessary for John to send his disciples to Jesus with the question, "Are you he who is to come, or shall we look for another?" (Matt. 11:3; Luke 7:19)?*

John, like his prototype Elijah and many another servant of God, had his hours of depression as well as his mountain-top experiences. As he lay in Herod's prison fortress and heard reports of Jesus' mighty works, he may well have considered that these were not the works of judgment which he had said the Coming One would perform (Matt. 3:12; Luke 3:17). And if Jesus was performing so many miracles, why did he not do something on John's behalf? Such reflections as these could lead him to wonder whether

he had been right after all in so confidently identifying Jesus with the Coming One. But the answer he received to his question was expressly designed to give him the fullest assurance and encouragement: he had made no mistake; Jesus was indeed the Coming One, for He was doing exactly those things that Isaiah and other prophets had said the Coming One would do, preeminently in His proclaiming good news to the poor (Isa. 61:1).

Matt. 11:11; Luke 7:28. *What did our Lord mean when He said that the least in the kingdom of heaven was greater than John the Baptist (Matt. 11:11)?*

He was not referring to personal character, or self-sacrificing devotion, for in those respects He bore witness to John as unsurpassed by any born of women. But while John stood on the threshold of the new age and announced its advent, those who by faith in Christ have entered into the kingdom of God in this life have great advantages over John—not by what they do for God, but by what God does for them. John "was the last and greatest of the heroes of faith, who looked for 'the city that hath foundations, whose builder and maker is God,' who died without receiving the promises" (T. W. Manson).

Matt. 12:31, 32; Mark 3:28, 29; Luke 12:10. *Could you distinguish between the two types of blasphemy mentioned in Matt. 12:31, 32, and explain how even the sacrifice of Christ is ineffective as an atonement for the sin of blasphemy against the Holy Ghost?*

If "the Son of man" in verse 32 means our Lord Himself, and not (as is widely supposed) "the son of man" in the generic sense of "mankind", then speaking against the Son of man might be due to a failure to recognize Him for what He is. So Paul recalls how in his pre-Christian days he thought it his duty to oppose the name of Jesus of Nazareth. But if, having seen the light on the Damascus road, he had deliberately closed his eyes to it and kicked out against the goad which was directing him into the true path, that would have been the sin against the Holy Spirit. The Holy Spirit persuades and enables men to accept Christ and enjoy the saving benefits of the gospel, but if anyone' refuses to submit to the Spirit's gracious constraint, preferring to call good evil and evil good, how can the gospel avail for him? The deliberate refusal of the grace of God is the one sin which by its very nature is irremediable.

Matt. 13:33; Luke 13:20f. *Is the leaven in the Parable of the Leaven a type of evil, as elsewhere?*

It is leaven in the wrong place (especially where its use is forbidden, as in Exod. 12:15) that is a symbol of evil, not leaven in itself. But our Lord in this parable is not speaking typologically; He is using an ordinary domestic action, such as any housewife would perform daily, to illustrate one aspect of the operation of the Kingdom. We may compare the "hiding" of the leaven in Matt. 13:33 and Luke 13:21 with the secret growing of the seed in the parable of Mark 4:26-29.

Matt. 13:45, 46. *In Matt. 13:45, 46, who is the merchant and who or what is the pearl of great price? Is Christ the merchant or is He the pearl?*

He is neither. We must beware of thinking that the separate details in a parable have each an allegorical meaning. In this parable the point of comparison consists in the whole situation rather than in any particular detail. The kingdom of heaven is a treasure of such surpassing worth that the wise man will be ready to sacrifice everything else in order to secure it. This I take, in brief, to be the point of the parable.

Matt. 13:55f.; Mark 6:3; Luke 8:19. *Is it true that in the original Greek the words used for our Lord's "brothers" and "sisters" in Mark 6:3; Luke 8:19, etc., can equally well mean "cousins" or other near relations? Are there any other biblical indications as to whether Mary in fact remained a virgin, apart from the verses referring to her "first-born" Son?*

When someone's mother, brothers and sisters are all mentioned together, as in Mark 6:3 and parallel passages, the natural inference is that the words are used in their ordinary sense, and the burden of proof rests on those who wish to understand them differently. In Greek, as in English, "brothers" and "sisters" can occasionally be used in a wider sense than the ordinary one, but when that is so, the context makes it plain. The perpetual virginity of Mary is an ecclesiastical dogma, not a Scriptural doctrine, and it is not the natural inference which one would draw from Matt. 1:25. The idea that the brothers and sisters mentioned were actually our Lord's cousins, sons and daughters of Mary's sister, appears to have been first propounded by Jerome. Another, rather earlier, theory was that they were children of Joseph by an earlier marriage (for which there is no evidence). If they were our Lord's cousins, there is no good reason why the ordinary Greek word for "cousin" should not have been used. The whole debate is really the product of the dogmatic exaltation of virginity above marriage; but unless evidence is forthcoming for taking the words "brothers" and "sisters" in an exceptional sense we may be content to understand them in the usual way.

Matt. 14:15-33; Mark 6:35-52; Luke 8:12-17; John 6:1-14. *What fundamental difference is there between the narratives of the feeding of the multitude in Matt. 14: 15-33 and John 6: 1-14?*

There is no fundamental difference; both passages record one and the same incident—the feeding of the five thousand, followed by a crossing of the lake. (The incident of Peter's attempt to walk on the water is recorded by Matthew alone among the evangelists.) But when we compare the accounts of this miracle in the Synoptic Gospels with that in John, we may discover one of the most characteristic features of John's Gospel. The Synoptic Gospels indicate quite plainly that' there was more in the miracle than met the eye, that there was a lesson in it which the disciples might have been expected to grasp (compare Mark 8:14-21). But John appends to his narrative of the feeding the report of a discourse by our Lord in which the spiritual import of the miracle is expressly brought out—namely, that our Lord Himself is the bread of life, the nourisher of the souls of men. John makes explicit what is implicit in the Synoptic account. The feeding of the five thousand lends itself especially to comparative treatment, because it is the one miracle of the ministry which is recorded both by John and by all three Synoptists.

Matt. 15:21-28; Mark 7:24-30. *I should like some help on the incident of the Syrophoenician woman (Mark 7:24-30). According to the margin at verse 26, she was a Gentile, and yet the Lord rewarded her faith. If the Lord at this time reached out to Gentiles, how do some regard the Cornelius episode of Acts 10 as marking the introduction of the Gentiles, while others find the definitive turning to the Gentiles in Acts 13:46?*

Expositors long ago saw that, in the section of the Gospel narrative which includes the incident of the Syrophoenician woman, our Lord is communicating Himself to the Gentiles. We may compare His response to the faith of the centurion of Capernaum (Matt. 8:5ff.; Luke 7:2ff.). Such incidents on the one hand continue the Old Testament tradition of blessing to individual Gentiles to which our Lord Himself drew attention in the synagogue of Nazareth (Luke 4:25-27); on the other hand they contain the promise of that abundant outpouring of blessing upon Gentiles of which we read in Acts, commencing with the Cornelius episode of Chapter 10. As for the turning to the Gentiles in Acts 13:46, there is nothing specially epoch-making there; it is but one instance of a pattern of events which reproduced itself in many cities to which Paul and his colleagues brought the Gospel; time after time the majority of the Jews to whom it was first offered refused it, while Gentiles eagerly embraced it (cf. Acts 28:28).

Matt. 16:18. *As we are told that in Matt. 16:18 the words "Peter" and "rock" are the same in Aramaic, should we lay so much stress on the fact that they are different in Greek* (Petros *and* petra)? *May we not understand the passage in the sense of Eph. 2:20, "built upon the foundation of the apostles and prophets"?*

It may well be that our Lord used the Aramaic word *kēphā* (the word which He gave as a surname to Peter, the "Cephas" of the English Bible) when He said "upon this rock." When He heard one of His disciples confess Him as Messiah and Son of God, He said in effect, "Now I can make a beginning with the building of my *ekklesia*." The words "Thou art Peter" point to the fact "that our Lord builds His Church by means of the testimony of those who know Him to be the Christ, and that to Peter was given the privilege of opening the testimony on the Day of Pentecost" (T. C. Hammond, *The One Hundred Texts*, p. 311). In Eph. 2:20 the apostles and prophets personally are the foundation-stones of the building, but not the rock on which the whole building rests.

Does the rendering of Matt. 16:18 in the New English Bible ("You are Peter, the Rock; and on this rock I will build my church . . .") suggest a leaning towards Roman doctrine on the part of the translators?

In view of the heavy Nonconformist element in the New Testament panel, a leaning towards Roman doctrine would in any case be unlikely (and equally unlikely, one should add, when the standpoint of the Anglican members of the panel is considered). In any case, the official Roman interpretation of these words is not so unambiguous as many suppose: the Council of Trent, for example, speaks of the historic creed of the whole Church as "that basic principle on which all who profess the faith of Christ necessarily agree, and the firm and sole foundation against which the gates of hell shall never prevail"—which suggests that Peter's confession, rather than Peter himself, is the "rock" in question. But all that the N.E.B. translators were concerned to do was to give a rendering which would bring out the significant juxtaposition of *Petros* ("Peter") and *petra* ("rock")— two words which in our Lord's Aramaic utterance would have been even more alike than they are in Greek, if both were represented by the identical form *kepha*.

In the light of Matt. 16:18 can we speak of Abraham as part of the church?

The church of Matt. 16:18 described by our Lord as "my church" is the community of those who, Peter-like, acknowledge Him as Messiah and Son of God. There is a vital continuity between the people of God before Christ came and the people of God after His coming, but after His coming the people of God underwent a fresh beginning by dying with Him and rising with Him to new life; hence the future tense "I will build." But Abraham is the first man called by God to leave his natural environment and become the founder of a new people—a new people consisting of all those, Jew and Gentile alike, who have faith in God as Abraham had. Abraham had the gospel preached to him (Gal. 3:8), he believed God and it was counted to him for righteousness (Gen. 15:6), he received the promises (Heb. 6:13, etc.), he saw the day of Christ and rejoiced (John 8:56). Abraham is thus the "rock" whence the people of God are hewn (Isa. 51:1f.), and if our definition of the church excludes Abraham, we should be well advised to look at our definition again and see what is wrong with it. B. W. Newton's indignant question is worth quoting: "Are we to say that Abraham hath '*the* promises', and yet that the chiefest results of those promises he hath *not*? Are we to say that Abraham belongs to that heavenly city whose maker and builder is God ... and yet that he hath not the blessings which pertain to that city?" (*The Old Testament Saints not to be Excluded from the Church in Glory*, 1887, p. 14).

Matt. 16:19. *Do you approve of the rendering of Matt. 16:19 in C. B. Williams's New Testament in the Language of the People: "Whatever you forbid on earth must be what is already forbidden in heaven..." (and similarly in Matt. 18:18)?*

No: it overlooks the characteristic force of the future–perfect tense in Greek, whether expressed periphrastically (as here) or by a simple form—the force of a specially emphatic future. Our Lord was not given to uttering banalities. On the other hand, anyone who wished to express the sense of A.V., R.V., R.S.V. and N.E.B. in these two verses as solemnly and emphatically as possible in Greek, could not have done so more explicitly than in the words of the existing Greek text. That is to say, when those to whom our Lord has given a specific commission act faithfully upon the terms of His commission, their decisions are assured of ratification in the heavenly court.

Matt. 16:19; Matt. 18:18; John 20:23. *How should we explain our Lord's statements in Matt. 16:19; 18:18, and John 20:23, bearing in mind the teaching about His sole mediatorship in 1 Tim. 2:5?*

We may well regard as fundamental the affirmation of 1 Tim. 2:5 that our Lord is the one Mediator between God and men, because, being both God and Man in His one person, He can (in Job's words) "lay his hand upon us both." But there are certain aspects of His authority which He can and does delegate to His servants to exercise in His name. These aspects of His authority include the "binding" and "loosing" of Matt. 16:19 and 18:18, and the "remitting" and "retaining" of sins in John 20:23. It is from such pronouncements as these that the servants of Christ derive authority to assure men and women that their sins are forgiven through faith in Christ, and also authority to administer church discipline. When Peter opened a door of faith to the Jews by his preaching in Jerusalem on the day of Pentecost, and to the Gentiles by his preaching in the house of Cornelius at Caesarea, he was using the keys of the kingdom which his Master promised to give him. When he acted as he did in the case of Ananias and Sapphira, he exercised the power of binding and loosing, as Paul also did in the case of one or more offenders in the Corinthian church (1 Cor. 5:3-5; 2 Cor. 2:5-11). When Paul proclaimed forgiveness of sins to believers at Pisidian Antioch, and uttered a solemn warning to those who repudiated the message and judged themselves unworthy of eternal life (Acts 13:38, 46), he was exercising his delegated authority to remit and to retain sins—to remit them in the case of those who repented and believed, to retain them in the case of the impenitent and unbelieving. When the apostolic council of Acts 15 issued its decisions in the latter of verses 23-29, this was a further exercise of the power of binding and loosing (forbidding and permitting). Such examples from the later books of the New Testament help us to understand the meaning of the Gospel passages to which you refer. See p. 73.

Matt. 16:28; Mark 9:1; Luke 9:27. *Am I correct in thinking that our Lord's statement in Matt. 16:28; Mark 9:1; Luke 9:27 means that unbelievers will not experience the second death until He comes again in power and glory?*

I should not have thought of understanding the expression "taste of death" in this passage as a reference to the second death; I doubt whether there was anything in the context which would have led our Lord's hearers to understand Him in this way. I should take the coming of the kingdom of God with power (Mark 9:1) quite simply to denote something which was to take place (and which did take place) within the lifetime of some who heard these words.

Matt. 17:12; Mark 9:13. *In Mark 9:13 ("But I say unto you, that Elijah is come, and they have also done unto him whatsoever they listed, even as it is written of him") are we to understand that the death of John the Baptist was foretold in the Old Testament? If so, where is it foretold?*

The meaning of our Lord's words may be that what the first Elijah's enemies wished ("listed") to do to him ("even as it is written of him" in 1 Kings 19:2, 10, 14) the second Elijah's enemies succeeded in doing to *him*.

Matt. 18:1-4. *What fundamental difference is there between our Lord's words in Matt. 18:1-4 and His words to Nicodemus in John 3:3, 5?*

Such difference as there may be is not fundamental; in Matt. 18:3 conversion—in the sense of becoming like little children—is necessary for entrance into the kingdom of heaven; in John 3:3, 5 the new birth is necessary for entrance into the kingdom of God. The kingdom of heaven in Matthew is identical with the kingdom of God in the other Gospels. One may wonder, however, whether being "converted" in Matt. 18:3 goes so far as the regeneration spoken of in John 3.

50

The conversion of Matt. 18:3 is not so much conversion in the modern evangelical sense as a complete change of mind and outlook—something that even the regenerate occasionally stand in need of. The disciples' question in verse 1 showed that their conception of the kingdom of heaven was so distorted that they would have to do a right-about-turn in their thinking about it if ever they were to get into it. Their ideas of greatness were based on the ordinary standards of the world, which were diametrically opposed to those of the kingdom of heaven. Matt. 20:25-28 elaborates the same lesson: humility and service were the qualities which carried with them greatness in the kingdom of heaven, and until the disciples learned this primary lesson they could not even enter that kingdom, far less achieve greatness in it.

Matt. 18:7-9; Mark 9:42-48; Luke 17:1, 2.

How are we to understand the warning ol Mark 9: 42-48 given in reply to John's words in verse 38? Were the apostles and disciples of Christ as yet not "saved" in the sense in which this term is used in the Epistles? Or has the term "hell" a secondary sense, other than its usual one? Were believers during Christ's ministry on earth in danger of not continuing in His word and thus not being made "free" (John 8:31, 32)?

Our Lord's words were intended to make His disciples think soberly about certain important issues. It was possible, on the one hand, for people who did not follow with them to be nevertheless on Christ's side. It was equally possible, on the other hand, for one who did follow with them to show his real quality in due course by playing the part of Judas. The fact is emphasized in the Gospels and Epistles alike that a true believer, a "disciple indeed", is one who continues in faith and discipleship. Continuance is one of the surest ways in which we can recognize whether a confession of faith is

genuine or not; it was the way in which a spectator could distinguish the seed sown on good ground from that sown on rocky ground. To begin with, there was no obvious difference; but the one continued and the other did not. It was as true during our Lord's earthly ministry as afterwards that those who came to Him were saved by faith. But it is the hour of testing that shows whether one's faith is real or not. There were many who said to Him "Lord, Lord", but would not do the things that He said. The word for "hell" in Mark 9:43, 45, 47, is "Gehenna", the strongest word that could be used. This does not detract at all from the security of those who place their trust simply and wholeheartedly in Christ; it does warn us, if ever we are tempted to presume upon our status as His followers, that in the day of Christ it is His assessment of us, and not our own, that will count.

Matt. 18:15. *What is your view of the external and internal evidence for the words "against you" in Matt. 18:15?*

The division of the evidence makes certainly impossible, but on balance I am inclined to approve their omission. They were absent from the Alexandrian text of the Gospels, and probably from the Caesarean too. Internally, their insertion could be explained from the analogy of verse 21, with which the next paragraph begins.

If, as you say in the answer to the foregoing question, the words "against you" should perhaps be omitted from Matt. 18:15 (in accordance with R.V. margin), does this mean that the offence in question is not a private one?

Even if the words "against you" were added later as a gloss, the context makes it plain that the sin is of a private nature. If it were a public sin, it could certainly not be put right by a private interview between the offender and one of his brethren. The words "If he listens to you, you have gained your brother" confirm the view that the trouble is a personal one.

Matt. 18:17. *What is the sense of "the church" in Matt. 18:17, seeing that the Christian Church had not yet come into being?*

Although the words were spoken before the death and resurrection of Christ, their validity is not restricted to that earlier period; they apply to the period following. The "church" in this verse is to be understood as the local church, the particular company of believers with which one is directly associated. The Aramaic word *kenishta* which probably lies behind Gk. *ekkēsia* here and in Matt. 16:18 was current in Palestine in a twofold sense: (*a*) the whole community of Israel; (*b*) a local community or synagogue of Jews. What we have in Matt. 18:17 is an extension of the latter usage to a particular community or "synagogue" of disciples of Jesus.

Luke 10:1, 17. *Luke 10:1, 17, in A.V., R.V. and R.S.V. says that the Lord sent out seventy, but in N.E.B. the number is given as seventy-two. Which rendering is correct?*

The difference goes back to the manuscripts and early versions, as the margins (or footnotes) of R.V., R.S.V. and N.E.B. indicate. It is not easy to say definitely which is correct, as the weight of the evidence is fairly evenly divided. Our oldest witnesses have "seventy-two." The Greek New Testament of the British and Foreign Bible Society (1958) reads "seventy-two"; so does the more recent edition (1966) published by the American Bible Society and four other Societies in various lands, but it indicates a measure of doubt by putting brackets round "two."

Luke 10:28. *Luke 10:28 ("do this, and you will live") seems to imply that a man could be saved by keeping the law. Does*

"live" here refer to eternal life, or to long life on earth? Could the lawyer possibly have obtained life by keeping the commandments, in spite of the sins of his past?

First of all, bear in mind that the lawyer did not simply ask his question out of a pure desire to learn the truth, but by way of "tempting" our Lord, i.e. to see if He would give an orthodox answer or not. Our Lord, knowing this, met him on his own familiar ground: "What is written in the law?" And when the lawyer summarized the law, our Lord went on to remind him that these were the commandments of God "which, if a man do, he shall live in them" (Lev. 18:5; Rom. 10:5). But the lawyer realized at once what Jesus meant by this reminder, and his conscience was touched; why else should he have wished "to justify himself"? While the primary reference in Lev. 18:5 may have been to long and prosperous life in the land, yet by New Testament times the deeper sense of "the life of the age to come" (eternal life) was generally discerned in such passages of Scripture; this interpretation is implied in the lawyer's question and confirmed by our Lord's answer. When the practical implications of the law's requirements were brought home to the lawyer by the parable of the good Samaritan, the attainment of life by keeping the law no longer seemed such a straightforward matter.

Luke 10:34. *I heard a preacher expound the parable of the Good Samaritan and say that the "inn" (Luke 10:34) represented "the Brethren's assembly." Is this so?*

If you had gone to another place, you might have heard a preacher say that the inn represents the Roman Catholic Church. The one interpretation is as true as the other. Both arise from the fundamental mistake of taking this narrative as an allegory, whose every detail must have a spiritual significance, instead of seeing it for what it really is—a parable told to drive home a practical lesson which our Lord states as explicitly as possible at the end of verse 37: "Go and do likewise."

Luke 11:13; Matt. 7:11. *Does Luke 11:13, with its reference to asking for the Holy Spirit, apply today, or is it simply intended for the period before Pentecost?*

It may be important to observe that there is no definite article before "Holy Spirit" (although our common English versions supply it). This could suggest that what is in view is not the Holy Spirit in person, but His gifts. This is rendered the more probable by a comparison of the parallel passage in Matt. 7:11, "how much more shall your Father who is in heaven give *good things* to them that ask him?" The good things are the gifts of the Spirit, and the command to ask for them applies today as much as when the words were spoken (cf. 1 Cor. 12:31; 14:1; Jas. 1:5f.). (One of our oldest witnesses, Papyrus 45, reads "a good gift" instead of "Holy Spirit" in Luke 11:13).

Luke 11:51; Matt. 23:35. *To which Zacharias was our Lord referring in Luke 11:51—to Zechariah son of Berechiah (Zech. 1:1; cf. Matt. 23:35) or to Zechariah son of Jehoiada (2 Chron. 24:20)?*

Our Lord was referring, I am sure, to Zechariah the son of Jehoiada, the last martyr mentioned in Hebrew Scripture according to its traditional order, in which the Books of Chronicles come at the end. Matt. 23:35 is no doubt parallel to Luke 11:51; "the son of Berechiah" in the former passage is probably a very early gloss (omitted, e.g., by the first hand in *Codex Sinaiticus*). The suggestions that the reference is to the Zechariah of Zech. 1:1, or of Isa. 8:2, or to Zacharias the son of Baruch mentioned by Josephus in the *Jewish War*, iv. 335-344, are less probable.

Luke 12:33. *Is Luke 12:33 applicable to Christians?*

The whole discourse was spoken by our Lord to His "disciples." Since the designation Christians was given to "the disciples" (Acts 11:26), it would seem that a short answer to your question would be "Yes." You are not the first to ask for whom this discourse was intended; Peter asked about this matter, with more particular reference to the parable with which the discourse ends (verse 41). And our Lord's answer to Peter confirms what we should in any case have gathered from His preceding words, that what He said had special application to those disciples who would be alive at the coming of the Son of Man. But since the time of that coming is unknown, each successive generation of His disciples should so live as if it were the generation which would witness the coming. The teaching of Luke 12:33, after all, is the same as that of Matt. 6:19-21. Do Christians lay up treasure on earth, or in heaven? The crucial question is where, and what, our real treasure is.

Luke 12:58, 59. *Can you enlighten me on the meaning of Luke 12:58, 59?*

These words come at the end of a paragraph addressed by our Lord to "the multitudes" (verse 54). While they embody a principle of wide application, their immediate reference is to the situation of the Jewish people in Palestine at that time. The course along which they were allowing themselves to be led could only result in a head-on collision with the Romans and consequent disaster. A complete change of policy, if adopted in time, could prevent this from happening. (Compare Luke 19:41-44, according to which Jerusalem might have avoided the calamity of A.D. 70 had she grasped the opportunity afforded by the Lord's visitation and recognized "the things that make for peace.") More generally, these verses teach us to take such steps in advance of a crisis as will preserve us from being overtaken by it unprepared and defenceless, and so being involved in ruin. "You are shortly to appear before the judge" (so the words have been paraphrased), "in danger of condemnation and imprisonment. At any moment you may be arrested: act at once while you are still at liberty, and settle the matter while it is still possible." There is a parallel passage in Matt. 5:25f., but the lesson taught there (to judge by the context) is the necessity and wisdom of reconciliation.

Luke 14:33. *Can you throw some light on Luke 14:33: "Whoever of you does not renounce all that he has cannot be my disciple"?*

If we find any difficulty in these words, it is of our own making; we should not like to think that to be a disciple of Christ is so costly a thing as they suggest. At the time when He spoke, it was necessary to make it clear that to follow Him, far from being a means of aggrandisement, meant losing friends, property, expectations, reputation, possibly even life itself. These words should be read alongside Luke 9:23-26. And even today there are places where it is just as costly as that to be a disciple of Christ. If we congratulate ourselves that we are able to combine His discipleship with the retention of much that we hold dear, let us at least ask ourselves which we should let go if we could no longer retain both. The true answer to that question will show whether we are real disciples or not.

Luke 16:9. *Does not the advice of our Lord in Luke 16:9 ("Make friends for yourselves by means of unrighteous mammon") contradict the teaching of the New Testament Epistles, according to which Christians are called to be crucified to the world (e.g. Gal. 6:14)?*

There is no contradiction: in Luke 16:9 our Lord teaches His disciples to use material and temporal opportunities not for momentary advantage, but with a view to the long-term issues of eternity. This is a principle which the parable of the unjust steward shares with the parables of the talents and the pounds, although each of the three parables applies the principle in its own way. Later in Luke 16 we have the account of a man who had plenty of this world's wealth ("the unrighteous mammon") but used it in such a way that when he died he had not one friend to receive him "into the eternal habitations." A man who constantly remembers that he will have to render an account of his stewardship of these things when he appears before the tribunal of Christ will be the less inclined to expend them in a worldly manner.

Matt. 19:9. *In Matt. 19:9 the clause "when she is put away" (R.V.) represents the Greek perfect participle* apolelymenēn, *treated as being in the passive voice. Could the participle be regarded as being the middle voice? It it so interpreted by the late Dr. Joseph Tracy of Boston, in an article on "The Bible Doctrine of Divorce" published in* Bibliotheca Sacra *for July 1866; his argument is that the reference is not to a woman who has been divorced by her husband, but to one who has taken the initiative in divorcing her husband.*

With Matt. 19:9 we must take Matt. 5:32, where the same form appears. It is, of course, true that in all tenses except the aorist and future the Greek forms of the middle and passive voices are identical. By itself, therefore, the participle mentioned in your question could be interpreted as either middle or passive. But if it were middle, in the sense which Dr. Tracy gives it, one would expect the object ("her husband") to follow, as it does in Mark 10:12. Moreover, in Mark 10:12, where the woman is envisaged as taking the initiative in divorce, the verb "put away" (in the aorist participle) is not in the middle voice but in the active, and it is the active voice that we should expect to find in Matt. 5:32 and 19:9 if Dr. Tracy's interpretation were right. It has been thought that the language of Mark 10:12 has special reference to Herodias's action with regard to her first husband—action impossible under Jewish law but permitted by Roman law. In the second part of Luke 16:18 the participial form used is identical with that in Matt. 5:32 and 19:9 and is almost certainly passive. If it be taken as middle in Luke 16:18, then the meaning can only be: "he who marries one who has put herself away from a husband"—which is much less satisfactory than R.V., "he that marrieth one that is put away from a husband." Two further points may be mentioned on Matt. 19:9. First, the R.V. rendering, "he that marrieth her when she is put away" (as also in 5:32), would strictly require the definite article in front of the participle (as Dr. Tracy is quick to point out); but this is taken care of if we modify the translation along the lines of Luke 16:18 so as to read: "he that marrieth one that is put away." And secondly, as R.V. margin at Matt. 19:9 tells us, the words from "and he that marrieth her when she is put away committeth adultery" are omitted by some ancient authorities for that verse; they are missing from the text of R.S.V. and N.E.B. and from the Greek Testament published by the British and Foreign Bible Society (1958). The longer text may be due to the influence of the parallel in Matt. 5:32. Lastly, it should be observed that the practical effect of our Lord's ruling was to redress an unequal balance which, as the law stood, put women at a serious disadvantage. Under Jewish law a husband could divorce his wife for a variety of reasons. These reasons varied according to the interpretation of "some unseemly thing" (Deut. 24:1) preferred by this school or that—the stricter school of Shammai, for example, limited it to evidence of premarital unchastity; the school of Hillel interpreted it much more liberally. But a wife could not initiate divorce proceedings against her husband, and had little redress

if he (for some reason that seemed good in his eyes) chose to divorce her. Jesus, therefore, by carrying the question back from the exegesis of the Mosaic concession to the Creator's declared purpose in instituting marriage, safeguarded her rights by making it as impossible for the husband to divorce his wife as it was for her to divorce him. He was *not* giving His disciples occasion for instituting a new legalism on the basis of His ruling, as some of them have tried to do. What He said about the sabbath law could be said of the marriage law: it was made for human beings, and not *vice versa*.

Matt. 19:24; Mark 10:25; Luke 18:25. *It has recently been stated that the passage about a camel going through the eye of a needle (Mark 10:25) has been mistranslated owing to a confusion between the Greek words* kamēlos *("camel") and* kamilos *("rope"), and that our Lord actually spoke of a* rope *going through the eye of a needle. Is this so?*

In Mark 10:25 the textual evidence seems to be unanimous in favour of *kamelos* ("camel"). As for the two Synoptic parallels, a handful of minuscules and the Armenian version attest *kamilos* ("rope") in Matt. 19:24, as do one late uncial and a few minuscules in Luke 18:25. In all three places the evidence is overwhelming for "camel"; and this is acknowledged by most translations. The only English version of which I can think at the moment which gives the rendering "rope" is *The Book of Books*, published in 1938. The few scribes or editors who replaced "camel" by "rope" may have been unconsciously influenced by a desire to make the entry of a rich man into the kingdom of God slightly less difficult than our Lord said it was. The same may be said of the idea that His words refer to a small postern gate in a large gateway, through which a camel might squeeze when the main gates was closed, provided that its pack were first removed. Our

Lord meant to rub in the impossibility of a rich man's entering the kingdom. If we saw a camel getting through the eye of a needle, we should say it was a miracle; and it is equally a miracle for a rich man to be saved. This is not my interpretation; it is our Lord's plain statement: "With men it is impossible, but not with God: for all things are possible with God" (Mark 10:27). One additional remark: in comparison with conditions in Palestine in our Lord's day most of us who enjoy the standards of living common throughout our western "affluent society" today would rank as "rich."

Mark 11:12-14, 20-24 (*see also* **Matt. 21:18-22**). *It has been suggested that it was unreasonable of our Lord to look for fruit on the fig tree, when "it was not the season of figs" (Mark 11:13). How should this suggestion be answered?*

Since, as Mark says, it was not time for figs, we may be sure that it was not figs that our Lord was looking for. In fact, the fully-formed fig would not appear for another six weeks or so. But we are told that when the fig-leaves appear about the end of March, they are accompanied by a crop of small knobs, called *taqsh* by the Arabs, which people sometimes pick and eat when they are hungry. These knobs drop off before the real fig is formed. But if the leaves appear unaccompanied by the knobs, it is a sign that there will be no figs that year.

Matt. 21:19; Mark 11:14. *What do you think of the rendering "for the age" instead of "for ever" in Matt. 21:19?*

I see no reason for departing here from the regular sense of *eis ton aiōna* ("for ever"). Whatever the parabolic significance of our Lord's sentence upon the fig-tree might be, His words are directed primarily to the tree. The absence of the *taqsh* showed that this was a hopeless, fruitless tree. And as it withered up soon afterwards, no one did in fact eat any fruit from

it *ever again*. This may have been intended as a parable of the fate of a city which had by this time ceased to produce any fruit for God. But that is not the lesson which our Lord Himself is said to have drawn from the incident; He used it to teach His disciples the power of faith in God.

Luke 17:37 (Matt. 24:28). *What is the meaning of Luke 17:37 ("Where the body is, thither will the eagles also be gathered together")?*

The meaning of the saying is that where there is a situation ripe for divine judgment, the executors of that judgment will unerringly find it out, just as vultures swoop from afar to prey on carrion. The word translated "body" here is *sōma*, but the parallel passage in Matt. 24:28 has the more explicit word *ptōma* (meaning "carcase," as in R.V.). It is, in my judgment, a grotesque travesty of exegesis to understand the "body" as a reference to Christ, to whom His people ("the eagles") gather together at His advent. The birds of prey which one would have expected to find mentioned in this saying are vultures (so the margins of R.V. and R.S.V. and the text of N.E.B.); if eagles (Gk. *aetoi*) are explicitly mentioned instead, this is probably because the judgment more particularly in view at the time was that of which the Romans, with their "eagles" (*aquilae*) or legionary standards, were to be the executioners.

Luke 19:8. *Do the words of Zacchaeus in Luke 19:8 relate to the past or the future? Is it possible that he was another such as Cornelius?*

If we took the first half of Luke 19:8 in isolation, we could regard it as a man's statement of his regular practice and compare him to Cornelius, who was eminent for his acts of charity (Acts 10:2). But wrongful exaction, such as is mentioned in the second half of the verse, is not the sort of thing that a man could commit unawares; and the whole tenor of the Zacchaeus story suggests rather that verse 8 is the statement of a new resolution, expressed in the present tense for vividness and emphasis. The system of tax-farming employed in the Roman Empire would not afford much scope for the practice of philanthropy.

Matt. 22:14. *Is it possible for the words, "Many are called, but few are chosen" (Matt. 20:16; 22:14), to be otherwise interpreted as "Many are called, but few are choice"? This latter interpretation would mean that few of the Lord's people rise above the low level in which most of us are found.*

It is very probable that "chosen" includes the idea of "choice", just as there is the easiest of transitions from "elect" to "élite." But the words you quote are absent from the best texts of Matt. 20:16 (cf. R.V.); we are thus confined to Matt. 22:14 in considering their meaning. Here, at the conclusion of the parable of the marriage feast, the words point the contrast between the leaders of Israel who first received Christ's invitation and rejected it with violent contumely, and the outcasts and Gentiles who subsequently received His invitation and eagerly responded to it. Not all who are invited accept. (The call here is much more general in its scope than that in Rom. 8:28-30, where "effectual calling" is obviously intended.)

Matt. 24:3; Mark 13:4; Luke 21:7. *There are three questions in Matt. 24:3, to which our Lord replies in the following verses, but it is difficult to see which verses to this or that question. Can you give any help on this?*

It would, I think, be more accurate to speak of two questions, since what you regard as the second and third are essentially one. The two questions are these: (i) "When shall these things be?" (referring to the things mentioned in the preceding verse, the destruction of the Jerusalem temple), and (ii) "What shall be the sign

of thy coming (*parousia*) and consummation of the age?" (Since the definite article is not repeated before "consummation", the implication in the questioners' minds is that the consummation of the age coincides with the *parousia*.) You will have observed that the second question in Matthew is much more explicit than its parallels in Mark (13:4) and Luke (21:7). Answers are given to the two Matthaean questions as follows: after (*a*) a warning against being misled by false prophets or great calamities into thinking that this is the end (verses 4-8; cf. Mark 13:5-8; Luke 21:8-11) and (*b*) a prediction of persecution and promise of help (verses 9-14; cf. Mark 13:9-13; Luke 21:12-19), we have (*c*) an answer to the first question, relating to the destruction of Jerusalem and the scattering of its inhabitants (verses 15-28; cf. Mark 13:14-23; Luke 21:20-24), and (*d*) an answer to the second question, describing the coming of Christ (verses 29-31; cf. Mark 13:24-27; Luke 21:25-28). Then (*e*) there is an exhortation to watchfulness in the situation leading up to the fall of Jerusalem (verses 32-35; cf. Mark 13:28-31; Luke 21:29-33), followed by (*f*) an exhortation to watchfulness for the coming of Christ (verses 36-44; cf. Mark 13:32-37; Luke 21:34-36). "*These* things"—i.e., the fall of the temple and city—will take place within "this generation" (verse 34; cf. Mark 13:30; Luke 21:32); but "of *that* day and hour" (the coming of the Son of Man and end of the age) only the Father knows (verse 36; cf. Mark 13:32). In addition to the parallel accounts in Mark and Luke, it would be helpful to study alongside Matt. 24 the narrative of the opening of the first six seals in Rev. 6, which largely span the same period.

Matt. 24:8; Mark 13:8. *Would you regard the period described by Christ as "the beginning of sorrows" (Matt. 24:8) as commencing when the last martyr of verse 9 joins his fellow-martyrs who have gone before him, bearing in mind the* *connexion between Matt. 24:6-8 and the first four seals of Revelation, and also having due regard to the fifth seal?*

No; I take the description "the beginning of sorrows" (N.E.B., "the birth-pangs of the new age") to refer to the verses immediately preceding. The persecution of verse 9 begins indeed as early as the period covered by verses 6-8 (as is made plain by Luke 21:12, "But before all these things they shall lay hands on you . . ."), but is intensified in the period that follows. I agree about the correlation of verses 6-8 with the first four seals of Rev. 6; but it is not until the fifth seal that we are introduced to the souls of the martyrs, and it is made clear that their number is not yet complete.

Matt. 24:14; Mark 13:10. *Is there any justification for saying that the "gospel of the kingdom" (Matt. 24:14) applies only to the Jews or to the "Jewish remnant," in view of Acts 20:24, 25 where Paul's words suggest that "to testify the gospel of the grace of God" is the same as "preaching the kingdom" (cf. Acts. 28:31, "preaching the kingdom of God")?*

I see no reason for restricting the good news of the kingdom of God to Jewish hearers, although it was, of course, proclaimed to Jews before it was extended to Gentiles as well. On Acts 28:31 ("preaching the kingdom of God and teaching the things concerning the Lord Jesus Christ"), T. D. Bernard says: "Evidently on purpose are the two expressions combined in this final summary, in order to show that the preaching of the kingdom and the preaching of Christ are one: that the original proclamation has not ceased, but that in Christ Jesus the thing proclaimed is no longer a vague and future hope, but a distinct and present fact . . . All is founded upon the old Jewish expectation of a kingdom of God; but it is now explained how that expectation is fulfilled in the person of Jesus; and the account of its

realization consists in the unfolding of the truth concerning him, 'the things concerning Jesus.' The manifestation of Christ being finished, the kingdom is already begun. Those who receive *him* enter into *it*" (*The Progress of Doctrine*, Lecture 5). With Matt. 24:14 and Mark 13:10, on the proclamation of the gospel to all the nations (Gentiles), I should take quite closely Rom. 11:25, where Paul speaks of the incoming of the full number of the Gentiles.

Matt. 24:15; Mark 13:14; Luke 21:20. *With reference to the "abomination of desolation" mentioned in Matt. 24:15 and Mark 13:14, together with the parallel passage in Luke 21:20, which uses different language, Professor William J. McKnight says: "To begin with, no one of the three records makes any reference whatsoever to the temple as the place where the 'abomination' is to be set up. The 'holy place' of Matthew's account is the holy locality, the holy vicinity, the holy environment. It is not the 'holy place' or the 'holy of holies' of the temple; there was a specific word for that. Nor is it the 'outer court' and precincts of the temple; there was a specific word for that. He uses a larger word, which refers to the outlying topography of Jerusalem itself, a word which the Christians of Judaea at the time would be unable to misunderstand"* (The Great Tribulation, p. 42). *Could you comment on this?*

Let me say first of all that I do not believe that the surrounding of Jerusalem with armies (Luke 21:20) is simply synonymous with the standing of the abomination of desolation in the holy place. Matthew is the only Evangelist who speaks of the "holy place" here; Mark refers more vaguely to "the abomination of desolation standing where he ought not" (note the R.V. and N.E.B., which bring out the fact that a *person* is indicated). Matthew's "holy place" does not denote

58

any particular part of the temple precincts or structure; it is a general term denoting the temple area, not "the outlying topography of Jerusalem itself." Paul uses a more explicit term when he refers to what is apparently the same situation in 2 Thess. 2:4, "he takes his seat in the *sanctuary* of God, proclaiming himself to be God." The *sanctuary* (Gk. *naos*) is the central temple-building itself, as distinct from the accessory structures and courts.

Matt. 24:15-28; Mark 13:14-23; Luke 21:20-24. *I find some difficulty in co-ordinating the three accounts of our Lord's eschatological discourse (Matt. 24; Mark 13; Luke 21). In particular, the events of Matt. 24: 15-28 and Mark 13: 14-23 are related by Luke to the Roman siege of Jerusalem and subsequent dispersion of the Jews, followed by the "times of the Gentiles" (Luke 21:20-24); but the events which in Luke follow the expiry of the times of the Gentiles are said in Matt. 24:29 to come "immediately" after the "tribulation" which (according to Luke) must be equated with the events of A.D. 70. Can you throw any light on this?*

The threefold account of the eschatological discourse certainly raises many problems. But on the points you particularly mention, while I agree that the events of Matt. 24:15-28 and Mark 13:14-23 are related by Luke to the Roman siege of Jerusalem and subsequent dispersion of its inhabitants until "the times of the Gentiles" come to an end, I do not think that the events of Luke 21:25-28 necessarily follow the expiry of "the times of the Gentiles"; they may quite well take place within that period.

Mark 13:18 (Matt. 24:20). *Do you regard the prayer in Mark 13:18 as being in principle out of harmony with the general teaching of the New Testament?*

No; I should regard it as an instance of our Lord's characteristic concern for those who were particularly vulnerable in times of distress. In the previous verse He indicates that the hasty flight from Jerusalem when the abomination of desolation is set up will be specially hard for expectant mothers and those with young children. If, in addition to those hardships which would inevitably attend the flight at any time of the year, it took place in winter, their plight would be still worse. Hence His words: "Pray that it may not happen in winter." The questioner explains his difficulty; elsewhere our Lord gives advice (as in Luke 21:36) calculated to keep His followers alert, lest they be taken unawares and seduced into disloyalty to Him, whereas "the principle of this prayer makes the concern of those to whom the prayer applies to be what God has to do, and not what they have to do, or rather, what they should be." But if we see who the people are whom our Lord is concerned about in Mark 13:18, the difficulty will surely disappear; He is expressing much the same concern as He expressed in His words to the weeping women of Jerusalem on the Dolorous Way in Luke 23:28-31.

Luke 21:24. *What is meant by "the times of the Gentiles" in Luke 21:24? When do they begin and end?*

The times (*kairoi*) of the Gentiles are the appointed epochs of Gentile domination of Jerusalem. This domination is something more than the Roman sovereignty which was in force when these words were spoken. Under this phase of Roman sovereignty Judaea and Jerusalem retained a measure of home rule, especially where religious freedom was concerned: Jerusalem had the status of a holy city and might not be profaned by the introduction of idolatrous objects within its walls, even if these were the images on the military standards of the occupying forces; the Romans sanctioned the execution of a Gentile, even if he were a Roman citizen, who behaved insultingly in the temple precincts or trespassed into one of its inner courts, and so forth. By contrast, the times of the Gentiles denote the period during which Jerusalem will be trampled down by the Gentiles, a more violent and ruthless domination, like that foretold in Rev. 11:2. Such a period began with the successful Roman suppression of the first Jewish revolt in A.D. 70, and this would, as I read the passage, be the commencement of the times of the Gentiles of which our Lord spoke. It is much more difficult to say when they came, or will come, to an end.

Matt. 24:29; Mark 13:25; Luke 21:25f. *How do you interpret the statements about the "stars of heaven" in Matt. 24:29 and Rev. 12:4?*

The language in both places is derived from Old Testament prophecy. In the former passage the collapse of established authority is probably meant. But in Rev. 12:4 I have little doubt that the stars which the dragon sweeps from the sky in his earthward fall are his "angels," as they are called in verse 7. Rev. 6:13 presents a closer parallel to Matt. 24:29 than does Rev. 12:4. See p. 138.

Matt. 24:31. *Is the trumpet of Matt. 24:31 the same as that of 1 Cor. 15:52? Does 1 Cor. 15:52 exclude the possibility of there being a "split" resurrection of just and unjust, since this trumpet is "the last"?*

The trumpets of Matt. 24:31 and 1 Cor. 15:52 are probably one and the same, finding a precedent in the trumpet of Isa. 27:13. But I hardly think that this question bears directly on what you call a "split" resurrection. In 1 Cor. 15:51-57 the resurrection of believers only is in view ("those who belong to Christ" as verse 23 puts it; those who are to "inherit the kingdom of God," as verse 50 puts it). I am not aware that there is any reference to a trumpet in those passages which speak unmistakably of the resurrection of the unjust.

Matt. 24:34; Mark 13:30; Luke 21:32. *Do you approve of the translation "race" for "generation" in Matt. 24:34?*

No; our Lord was plainly making a very emphatic declaration, but it would lose all its emphasis if we took it to mean that this race—whether the human race or the Jewish race—would still be on earth to witness the accomplishment of His predictions. The meaning is "this generation," as in Matt. 11:16; 12:41, 42, 45; 23:36. The emphasis is probably moral as well as chronological, echoing the O.T. references to the disobedient generation of the wilderness wanderings (cf. Num. 14:27, 35; Deut. 1:35; Psa. 95:10, with the application of the last-mentioned passage in Heb. 3:10).

Matt. 24:37-39; Luke 17:26, 27. *Does Matt. 24: 37-39 merely mean that things were continuing normally among the people of Noah's day, or were they doing wrong in eating, drinking, marrying, etc.?*

The point is that they were going about their everyday business. We know that the generation that perished in the Flood was outstanding for wickedness, but that is not what our Lord stresses here. Similarly, we know that the men of Sodom in Lot's day "were wicked and sinners against the LORD exceedingly" (Gen. 13:13), but when our Lord compares the days of the Son of Man to the days of Lot, He makes no mention of their wickedness, but simply says that "they ate, they drank, they bought, they sold, they planted, they builded" (Luke 17:28). In both instances the judgment fell on people in the midst of the ordinary affairs of life, and "after the same manner", He said, "shall it be in the day that the Son of man is revealed."

Matt. 24:40, 41; Luke 17:34-36. *The popular view regarding Matt. 24:40f. and Luke 17:34-36, "one shall be taken and the other left," is that the one taken is the good one and the one left the* *wicked one. But is this so in the light of the word "as it was in the days of Noah . . ." (Matt. 24:37; Luke 17:26)? In the days of Noah it was the wicked whom the flood "took . . . away" (Matt. 24:39); only Noah and his family were left. So at the coming of the Son of man it is not the wicked that is taken and the good left?*

I am not sure which is "the popular view." The view which you favour is the Darbyite view; so J. N. Darby puts it: "the taking would be as the taking in the days of Noah in judgment, the left as Noah's family in mercy" (*Collected Writings*, XXIV, p. 341). But the argument is not completely watertight, for the verb "took . . . away" in Matt. 24:39 (Gk. *airō*) is not the same as that used in verses 40 and 41 (Gk. *paralambanō*). The latter verb means "to take with oneself" for better or worse: for better, as when Joseph is bidden to "take" the young child and his mother and escape to Egypt (Matt. 2:13) or when the Lord says to His disciples, "I will . . . receive you to myself" (John 14:3); for worse, as when the devil "takes" Jesus into the holy city and again up a high mountain (Matt. 4:5, 8), or when Jesus' executioners "took" Him from Pilate to the place of crucifixion (John 19:16). Thus in Matt. 24 and Luke 17 the "one" that is taken might be taken for blessing or for judgment, so far as the force of the verb in itself is concerned. If we could say definitely who or what the taker is, it would help; but that is not stated. My own view is that it does not matter much, and that to debate the character of the taking and the leaving may obscure the point which the Lord is making, which is that when the crisis breaks, the ensuing division will penetrate every human stratum and split apart the closest human relationships.

Matt. 25:1. *Who are the virgins of Matt. 25?*

Ten girls in a story who were to take part in a bridal procession; five of them, however, were too late to take part in it and join in the other festivities because they forgot to procure oil for their lamps in time. The point of the parable is: "Don't you be like them (whoever you are); be prepared, for you never know when the moment of crisis will be upon you." The virgins do not "stand for" any body of people in particular; the story is a parable, not an allegory.

Matt. 25:31ff. *I find Matt. 25:31ff. perplexing. When does this session of formal judgment take place? Are the sheep here additional to the believers who are already glorified with the Lord (Col. 3:4, etc.)?*

Yes, there are perplexities associated with these verses, but the answers to your two questions are not really in doubt. The judgment takes place at the Son of Man's coming in glory with His angels (cf. Matt. 24:30; Acts 17:31; 2 Thess. 1:7). Those who are placed as "sheep" on the right hand of the Son of Man are certainly not the elect who have already been manifested with Him in glory, but those whose treatment of His "brethren" is accepted by Him as done to Himself, and requited accordingly.

Matt. 25:46. *In the* Daily Telegraph *of January 24, 1959, a correspondent commented on the meaning of the words* kolasis *("punishment") and* aiōnios *("eternal") in Matt. 25:46, and translated the verse thus: "And these will depart into correction for a period of time, but the just into a period of life." Is this rendering justified?*

The correspondent was incisively and effectively answered by Michael Green in the *Daily Telegraph* of January 29, where it was pointed out that the renderings of the two operative words in the proposed translation of Matt. 24:46 found no support in Arndt and Gingrich's *Greek-English Lexicon of the New Testament*, the latest and most authoritative work of its kind. While *kolasis* did have the sense of remedial chastisement in classical Greek, that sense was largely superseded by the idea of retribution in Hellenistic times: and as for *aiōnios*, when it is used (as here) in an eschatological sense, it means "pertaining to the coming age." Thus "eternal life" is not "a period of life" but the life of the age to come, which (incidentally) endures for ever. I am reminded of a caustic remark by the late Dean Inge, to the effect that arguments like those of the first correspondent mentioned, "based on the supposed meaning of the word *aiōnios*, only prove that the disputant is a poor Greek scholar" (*Things New and Old*, p. 103).

Matt. 26:6; Mark 14:3. *When we read of "Simon the leper" in Mark 14:3 and Matt. 26:6, are we to understand that he was still a leper? If so why was he in a house with others? Or had he been cleansed from his leprosy? If so, why is this not stated?*

He was most probably a cured leper, but you know how a name will stick to a person long after the cause for it has disappeared. We know nothing more about him, much as we should like to: was he, for example, the father of Mary, Martha and Lazarus? The same applies to many people who appear and disappear in the Gospel narratives. There is, to be sure, C. C. Torrey's theory that he was a jar-merchant and not a leper, but it is quite devoid of proof.

Luke 22:20 (Matt. 26:28f.; Mark 14:24f.). *According to some versions, Luke 22:20 should be omitted, because it is not in the oldest manuscripts. If this is so, would it not be a curious omission on Luke's part?*

The situation is, as stated in R.V. margin, that some ancient authorities omit the words, "which is given for you: this do in remembrance of me" from the end of verse 19, together with the whole of verse 20. The result is that we have then a shorter account of the words of institution, in which the cup (verses 17 and 18) precedes the loaf (verse 19a). Certainly the words spoken about the cup in verse 18 are parallel to those spoken about the cup in Mark 14:25 (cf. Matt. 26:29); therefore, if the shorter account in Luke be original, Luke is not really guilty of a "curious omission", since he has already dealt with the cup. Readers of the High Leigh Conference report, *A New Testament Church in 1955*, may remember Harold St. John's reference on p. 90 to "the reverse order, as mentioned in 1 Cor. 10 and in Luke 22, that is, the cup first, and then the bread." The implication is that he accepted the shorter Lukan account as the original text. The longer account, which includes verses 19b and 20, has affinities with the Pauline account in 1 Cor. 11:24f. A decision on the textual evidence in Luke 22 is not easy to make; the witnesses for the shorter account belong mostly to the "Western" text-type, and this text-type is so prone to expanded readings that on the few occasions on which it exhibits a shorter reading its testimony must receive very serious consideration. But the weight of the evidence is probably on the side of the longer reading; in that case we are confronted by another problem which must be solved by other methods than those of unaided textual criticism. You will find a useful discussion of the question in Norval Geldenhuys's *Commentary on the Gospel of Luke*, pp. 554f., 558f.

Luke 22:20. *In Luke 22:20, "This cup is the new covenant in my blood, even that which is poured out for you" (R.V.), does "that which is poured out for you" refer to "this cup" or to my blood?*

Grammatically it refers to "this cup", as is made even clearer in R.S.V. (where the "longer text", of which these words form part, is printed as a footnote variant): "This cup which is poured out for you is the new covenant in my blood." Symbolically the pouring out of the cup expresses the shedding of our Lord's life-blood, as appears from His words in Matt. 26:28 and Mark 14:24, "This is my covenant-blood which is poured out for many."

Matt. 26:29; Mark 14:25; Luke 22:18. *How are we to understand Matt. 26:29, where our Lord says: "I will not drink henceforth of this fruit of the vine, until that day when I drink it new with you in my Father's kingdom"?*

With this verse and its parallel in Mark 14:25 we should take Luke 22:15-18, where our Lord not only uses these words of the cup but says with regard to the passover meal (v. 16), "I will not eat it, until it be fulfilled in the kingdom of God." The age to come was, it seems, sometimes viewed as a banquet, which would be the consummation of the passover. Our Lord takes up and confirms this expectation, but links it with His coming in glory. The kingdom here, then, is the kingdom to be manifested in the future, which will be consummated by His *parousia* and the resurrection of the righteous. These words of Christ constitute the authority underlying Paul's statement in 1 Cor. 11:26, "For as often as ye eat this bread, and drink the cup, ye proclaim the Lord's death *till he come.*" The feast of remembrance, in other words, not only points back to the death of Christ but points on to His appearing.

Matt. 26:50. *What is the point of our Lord's question to Judas in Matt. 26:50, "Friend, wherefore art thou come"?*

It was probably not a question; the pronoun used is not interrogative, but relative. The meaning is best given in R.V.: "Friend, *do* that for which thou art come." The construction is compressed in Greek, as though one might say in English, "Comrade, to your task!"

The Revisers have therefore for intelligibility supplied the imperative "do." (The turn of phrase may also have been designed to remind Judas of his table fellowship with Jesus an hour or two before).

Matt. 26:52; Luke 22:36. *In view of our Lord's words to Peter in Matt. 26:52 "all who take the sword will perish by the sword"), what are we to make of His instructions to the disciples in Luke 22:36 ("let him who has no sword sell his mantle and buy one")?*

It may help us to determine our Lord's meaning in Luke 22:36 if we observe (i) that the disciples misunderstood Him, and (ii) that He had in mind the fulfilment of Isa. 53:12, "And he was reckoned with transgressors." (It is to be noted in passing that, in the best textual tradition, this is the only place in the Gospels where this clause from Isa. 53:12 is quoted; Mark 15:28 is placed between square brackets by Darby, and omitted by R.V., R.S.V. and N.E.B.) Our Lord speaks here with a certain sad irony: since the Son of Man is about to be numbered with transgressors (more particularly, with bandits like the two who were crucified with Him), why should His followers not dress accordingly and wear swords as well as other articles which they had formerly been forbidden to take with them? Taking Him up literally, the disciples revealed that they had two swords with them. But He, realizing that they had not understood Him, dismissed the matter: "Enough!" He said, "that will do." He certainly did not wish them to use the swords for defending Him (as the sequel makes plain), and two swords would have been inadequate for their own self-defence.

Matt. 27:9. *Can you explain the ascription to Jeremiah in Matt. 27:9 of the quotation which appears to come from Zech. 11:13?*

The most probable explanation, to my mind, is that in the source from which the Evangelist drew the quotation, Zech. 11:13 was combined with a quotation or quotations from Jeremiah (whether Jer. 18:2, 3, along with 32:6-15, or Jer. 19:1-13, or some other passage), and that the earlier of the two prophets alone was mentioned by name. You have something similar in Mark 1:2, 3 (R.V., etc.), where the words "As it is written in Isaiah the prophet," introduce two quotations, the former of which is from Malachi and only the latter from Isaiah. Some have emphasized that the prophecy quoted in Matt. 27:9 is there said to have been *spoken*, not *written*, by Jeremiah; but "that which was spoken" is Matthew's regular wording in introducing his "formula-quotations," without any distinction between speaking and writing (see, e.g., Matt. 2:17; 4:14; 8:17; 12:17). I discuss the relevance of the Zechariah quotation at greater length in *This is That* (Paternoster Press, 1968), pp. 108ff.

Matt. 27:11; Mark 15:2; Luke 23:3. *What is the force of our Lord's answer "Thou sayest" to Pilate's question in Matt. 27:11; Mark 15:2; Luke 23:3? Does it mean, as I have heard suggested, "What you say is correct"?*

Our Lord's answer is a qualified affirmative; it means, "What you say is true in a sense, but not necessarily in the sense you intend." His words are amplified in John 18:33-37 so as to bring out their true meaning: "I am a king indeed, but not a king as you understand the word." We may compare His earlier reply to Caiaphas's question, "Art thou the Christ?" which Matthew gives in the form, "Thou hast said" (Matt. 26:64) and Luke in the form, "Ye say that I am" (Luke 22:70). This puts at least some of the responsibility for the form of words used on the questioner. Mark gives His reply in the form "I am," which would be positive enough, but the words which follow add the necessary qualification, "I am indeed the Christ (the Messiah), but the Christ in the sense of the Son of Man, not in the military and political sense which you normally understand by the term."

Luke 23:7-12. *Why is Luke the only evangelist who records our Lord's trial before Herod?*

Luke appears to have had a special interest in members of the Herod family, and special information about them. This could be due to his association with Manaen, foster-brother of this particular Herod (Herod Antipas, tetrarch of Galilee from 4 B.C. to A.D. 39), who was a prominent teacher in the church at Antioch (Acts 13:1). According to good second-century tradition, Luke himself belonged to Antioch. He not only narrates our Lord's "trial" before Herod in Luke 23:7-12, but refers to it also in Acts 4:27, in reporting a prayer of the apostles.

Matt. 27:36. *In the statement in the Passion narrative, "and sitting down they watched him there" (Matt. 27:36), who are "they"?*

The soldiers on duty at the cross. The full stop in the A.V. at the end of verse 35 should be a weaker punctuation-mark, as in R.V., R.S.V. and N.E.B.; the last-named renders the whole sentence rightly: "After fastening him to the cross they divided his clothes among them by casting lots, and then sat down there to keep watch."

Luke 23:35 (Matt. 27:45; Mark 15:33). *Is the eclipse of the sun referred to in Luke 23:45, N.E.B. ("the sun was in eclipse") any help in calculating the day or year of the crucifixion?*

I do not think so, and am interested to see that the word "eclipse" disappears from the 1970 edition of N.E.B. Although

Luke uses the actual verb from which the English word "eclipse" is derived (Gk. *ekleipō*), he can hardly mean an eclipse in the technical sense, as it was the time of the Passover full moon, and an eclipse of the sun cannot take place at full moon. The non-technical sense of the word here is indicated in R.V. ("the sun's light failing") and R.S.V. and the revised N.E.B. ("the sun's light failed"); compare Charles Wesley's line: "Lo! our Sun's eclipse is o'er." In a discussion of this Greek verb in the *Journal of Theological Studies* for 1965 (pp. 331ff.) Sir Godfrey Driver rightly states that "nothing compels the supposition that either here or elsewhere it necessarily connotes an eclipse, and this interpretation can be safely abandoned as scientifically impossible."

Matt. 27:46f.; Mark 15:34f. *When our Lord cried "Eloi, Eloi" on the cross (Mark 15:34; cf. Matt. 27:46), why did some bystanders misunderstand Him and think He was calling for Elijah?*

The effects of crucifixion would prevent clear articulation, and that could be a sufficient explanation of the misunderstanding. Moreover, in the *Palestine Exploration Quarterly* for January-April, 1951, Professor Alfred Guillaume pointed out, on the strength of a spelling variant in some of the Dead Sea Scrolls, that in some parts of Palestine at that time the suffix meaning "my" was pronounced —*iya*. If our Lord pronounced "My God" as *Eliya*, some of His hearers might easily think that He was calling for Elijah.

Matt. 28:19. *What is the exact meaning of the preposition translated "in" (A.V.), "into" (R.V.) in Matt. 28:19? Is it legitimate in any way to infer from it that only at baptism does the Christian become a member of the body of Christ?*

No; in Matt. 28:19 the whole phrase "into the name" must be taken into account. The phrase was perhaps derived from commercial usage (as when we still speak of paying a certain sum "into the name" of so-and-so). The same phrase, "into the name," occurs in a baptismal context in Acts 8:16 and 19:5, where certain believers are "baptized into the name of the Lord Jesus," in the sense of confessing that they are His, acknowledging His Lordship. Those who were baptized "into the name of the Lord Jesus" already acknowledged the one true God; the rank and file of the Gentiles, who are envisaged in the commission of Matt. 28:19, had to learn to "serve the living and true God" (1 Thess. 1:9) as well as to confess Christ as Lord, which they could not do save in the Holy Spirit (1 Cor. 12:3); hence for them baptism into the Triune Name is prescribed. The body of Christ— a Pauline concept—is not in view in Matt. 28:19. Where it *may* be in view in a baptismal context is in a passage like Gal. 3:27, which speaks of believers as being "baptized into Christ"; but by a natural transference of terms baptism can be spoken of as effecting that which it symbolizes.

Luke 24:25. *Does the Greek of Luke 24:25 require the translation, "O foolish men" (R.V.)? Could it simply mean "O fools" (A.V.) and thus denote a man and a woman?*

There is no separate word in Greek corresponding to "men." I suppose the R.V. says, "O foolish men" because the A.V. "O fools" makes our Lord appear to be speaking rather bluntly. Of course "men" may mean "human beings" and not necessarily "males." Perhaps we might render the words: "You foolish people." So far as the Greek is concerned, the two travellers could have been either two men, or a man (Cleopas) and a woman.

THE GOSPEL OF JOHN

John 1:1. *What bearing, if any, has more recent light on the use or omission of the article in New Testament Greek on John 1:1 with reference to the rendering and interpretation of that verse current among Jehovah's Witnesses ("the Word was a god")?*

In the light of the most recent study of the article in New Testament Greek, the J.W. rendering is seen to be "a frightful mistranslation. It overlooks entirely an established rule of Greek grammar which necessitates the rendering, '... and the Word was God.' Some years ago Dr. Ernest Cadman Colwell of the University of Chicago pointed out in a study of the Greek definite article that, 'A definite predicate nominative has the article when it follows the verb; it does not have the article when it precedes the verb.... The opening verse of John's Gospel contains one of the many passages where this rule suggests the translation of a predicate as a definite noun. The absence of the article (before *theos*) does *not* make the predicate indefinite or qualitative when it precedes the verb; it is indefinite in this position only when the context demands it. The context makes no such demand in the Gospel of John, for this statement cannot be regarded as strange in the prologue of the gospel which reaches its climax in the confession of Thomas" (B. M. Metzger, *The Jehovah's Witnesses and Jesus Christ*, 1953, p. 75). See also C. F. D. Moule, *An Idiom of New Testament Greek*, 1953, p. 115f.; N. Turner, *Moulton's Grammar of New Testament Greek*, Vol. III (Syntax), 1963, p. 183. The New English Bible aptly paraphrases the clause: "what God was, the Word was." This is the keynote of the Fourth Gospel: "the deeds and words of Jesus are the deeds and words of God; if this be not true the book is blasphemous" (C. K. Barrett).

John 1:9. *In what sense is Christ "the Light, which lighteth every man that cometh into the world" (John 1:9)?*

I believe that the words "that cometh into the world" refer to Christ and not to "every man." That is to say, the Eternal Word, coming into the world, provides the illumination for all. No spiritual light has ever been received by any one which did not proceed from the Divine Word, even in the days before His incarnation. But John is thinking specially of that fulness of light which flooded the world after the Word became flesh and tabernacled among us. Like most of the themes touched on in the Prologue to this Gospel, this theme of light is taken up and developed in greater detail later in the Gospel; there we learn that there are some who refuse the true light, preferring to remain in darkness. The light will illuminate them if they accept it; by their rejection of it they are self-condemned (John 3:19-21; 8:12; 9:4f., 39-41; 12:35f.).

John 1:13. *Could the opening words of John 1:13 be translated "who was born", thus referring to Christ? If so, what is the force of the expression "not of blood"?*

Our Greek authorities for the verse are unanimous in reading the plural ("who were born..."). The singular ("who was born...") is found in some Old Latin texts and is supported in part by one Old Syriac manuscript. If this reading were established, it would, of course, constitute independent testimony to our Lord's virgin birth. But it cannot be accepted in face of the complete lack of any Greek evidence for it. Yet the Evangelist may have chosen his words carefully so as to suggest an analogy between the spiritual birth of believers and the birth of Christ. Since spiritual birth, however, is the subject of the passage, the expression "not of blood" will emphasize that the divine birthright of the children of God has nothing to do with racial or family ties.

John 1:21. *Was John the Baptist right when he denied that he was Elijah (John 1:21)? How does his denial tally with our Lord's statement in Matt. 11:14?*

John had received no revelation on the subject; Gabriel's statement to Zachariah (Luke 1:17) that John would go before the face of the Lord "in the spirit and power of Elijah" fell short of saying that John would actually be Elijah. Even our Lord's words in Matt. 11:14 did not mean that John was Elijah reincarnated; they meant that John (if those who heard were willing to receive it) was the one who fulfilled the prophecy about Elijah in Malachi 4:5f. In any case, John was wise to leave it to others to make such claims on his behalf; for himself, he was content to be the "voice" of Isa. 40:3.

John 1:32-35. *The Synoptic Gospels represent our Lord's temptation as following immediately after His baptism, whereas John, while not mentioning the temptation, describes events which took place the day after the baptism and the day after that (John 1:35, 43). Can you explain the seeming discrepancy?*

In John 1:32-34, John the Baptist describes what happened at the baptism of Jesus, which took place possibly several weeks before. The "next day" of verse 35 is the day after John's testimony of verses 32-34, and not the day after the baptism itself.

John 3:5. *Would it be true to say of John 3:5 that our Lord referred to a need for cleansing ("water") and to the spiritual character of that cleansing ("the Spirit")? Would this explain the expression, "born of water and the Spirit"?*

Yes, but we should bear in mind the high probability that the prophecy of Ezek. 36:25-27, with its reference to clean water and a new spirit, underlies our Lord's choice of words here. Even where the external application of literal water was practised, as in Essene baptism, John's baptism and proselyte baptism, its significance lay in the fact that it symbolized that inward cleansing which only the Spirit could effect. In our Lord's day, perhaps the most striking way in which the principle of Ezek. 36:25 was translated into practice was the baptism of proselytes. A Gentile who entered the commonwealth of Israel by this rite (in addition to the rite of circumcision, if he was a man) was looked upon as having experienced a new birth. So John the Baptist told his hearers that, to be accepted by God and escape the coming wrath, they must take the outside place, as if they were Gentiles, and accept baptism as the outward and visible sign of their repentance. In John 3 even an upright teacher of Israel is told that he, too, must not rely upon his natural birthright as a member of the chosen nation, but start by taking the outside place and enter the kingdom of God by a spiritual rebirth.

Was the baptism of proselytes practised so early as our Lord's ministry?

"It is disputed how far we can accept this [Jewish proselyte baptism] as older than Christian baptism, but the evidence, though less full than might have been desired, points to the probability that it is older" (H. H. Rowley). I think we may take it as fairly certain that the practice was known in our Lord's time, and indeed that it forms part of the background to the baptism of John. Certain aspects of the practice were debated between the contemporary schools of Shammai and Hillel. The Scriptural justification for proselyte baptism was sought in Ezek. 36:25. Our Lord's words to Nicodemus in John 3:5 probably echo the same passage, and emphasize its spiritual significance: a new birth is necessary for true born Jews as well as for Gentiles before they can enter the kingdom of God.

John 3:8. *In John 3:8 should we read "the wind bloweth" with R.V. text, or "the Spirit breatheth" with R.V. margin?*

Both are good translations of the Greek; here both ideas are probably included. The wind blowing is a symbol of the Spirit breathing. If we used one word instead of three to express "Spirit," "wind" and "breath" (like Gk. *pneuma* and Heb. *ruach*), our thought would move back and fore more easily between the material figure and the spiritual reality. In Ezek. 37, which probably underlies this passage, one and the same Hebrew word is translated "wind" and "breath" in verses 9 and 10 and "spirit" in verse 14.

John 3:13. *In John 3:13 are the words "which is in heaven" (assuming them to be part of the original text) to be understood as spoken by our Lord or as an added comment by the Evangelist?*

I should not care to make a definite pronouncement. But there seems to be no difficulty in the way of taking them as part of what our Lord said if we follow the New English Bible in translating the verse: "No one ever went up into heaven except the one who came down from heaven, the Son of Man whose home is in heaven." The N.E.B. by its use of quotation marks indicates that the clause is part of what Jesus said to Nicodemus.

John 5:26. *What do the words "hath life in himself" mean in John 5:26?*

All living beings apart from God receive life from Him; they have no life in themselves (cf. Acts 17:28). But the life of God is underived and unoriginated; He alone has life in Himself. And within the unity of the Godhead it is the Father who is the Source from which the Son eternally draws. "The Son has not life

only as given, but life *in himself* as being a spring of life" (Westcott).

John 5:30. *Our Lord is reported as saying: "I can of mine own self do nothing" (John 5:30; cf. 5:19; 7:16; 8:28). How could this be if He was able to exercise Godhead authority?*

Because He exercised that very authority in obedience to the Father's will. It belongs to the authority of God (*a*) to have life in Himself, (*b*) to bestow life, (*c*) to execute final judgment. According to John 5:26, the Father has granted the Son to have life in Himself too; according to John 5:19-21, 25, the Son gives life to whom He will because He sees the Father raising the dead and giving them life; according to John 5:22, 27, the Father has conferred on the Son the authority to execute judgment. The Son's exercise of divine authority is thus entirely dependent on the Father's gift, but it is none the less really divine authority.

John 6:70. *Apparently the only Scripture where the indefinite article is used before "devil" is John 6:70. What significance has this when considering the personality and character of Judas?*

In addition to its special meaning "devil", the Greek word *diabolos* has the ordinary sense of "slanderer", "calumniator" or (taking over the meaning of Heb. *satan*) "adversary". In this sense the word appears elsewhere in the New Testament (in the plural) without the definite article (1 Tim. 3:11; 2 Tim. 3:3; Tit. 2:13). Our Lord was not identifying Judas with the personal devil, any more than He so identified Peter in Mark 8:33; but He discerned in Judas's character the qualities of an adversary which later (John 13:2, 27) gave Satan an opportunity for using Judas as his instrument. There are one or two other places in the New Testament where *diabolos* appears in the singular without the definite article, in reference to the devil (e.g. Acts 13:10; Rev. 20:2).

John 7:37ff. *In John 7:37f. is it from Christ or from the believer that the "rivers of living water" flow? What passage is referred to in the words, "as the scripture hath said"? Does the original indicate quotation marks?*

There is no means of indicating quotation marks in the original, and indeed it is unlikely that punctuation signs of any kind were used. The punctuation marks in any translation, as well as the quotation marks where they are provided, depend on the translator's interpretation of the text. There are good reasons for recasting the traditional punctuation of our Lord's invitation in John 7:37f. so as to read it thus:

> He that is athirst, let him come to me;
> And let him drink who believes in me.

This punctuation yields a poetical couplet which fulfils the laws of Hebraic parallelism manifest in so many of our Lord's utterances. Thus far His words repeat the essence of what He had already told the Samaritan woman in John 4:14 about the superior qualities of the living water which He could give. But now He goes on to show that the implanted "well of water springing up unto eternal life" not only refreshes the believer's own soul but flows out to refresh the lives of others. "As the Scripture has said, 'From within him shall flow rivers of living water'." But where exactly does the Scripture speak like this? The reference is probably to such a passage as Zech. 14:8, which foretells how on the day of the Lord "living waters shall go out from Jerusalem"; Ezekiel, giving further details about these waters, adds that "everything will live where the river goes" (Ezek. 47:1ff.). The New Testament interpretation of these and similar prophecies (e.g. Isa. 33:21; Joel 3:18) lies plain for all to read in John's description of "the river of the water of life, bright as crystal, flowing from the throne of God and of the Lamb" for the refreshment of that holy city which consists of the people of God, and for the further blessing of "the nations" at large (Rev. 22:1ff.). It is from the dwelling-place of God in lives that are consecrated to Him that these living waters proceed; and lest there should be any doubt about the meaning of the "rivers of living water" of which our Lord speaks in John 7:38, the Evangelist adds the true interpretation: "this he said about the Spirit."

A. Edersheim (Jesus the Messiah, p. 317) indicates that at the Feast of Tabernacles the ceremony of the water-pouring took place on the last day of the feast, i.e., on one day only each year. I have heard an alternative view, that the ceremony took place on each day of the feast, except the last day, "the great day of the feast," when Jesus stood and cried, "If any man thirst, let him come unto me, and drink" (John 7:37). Which of the two views is the correct one?

Our principal source of information is the tractate *Sukkah* in the Babylonian Talmud, from which we gather that the ceremony of the water-pouring was enacted on the first seven days of the feast, but not on the eighth day (although a prayer for rain was offered on that day). If our Lord's proclamation was made on the day when there was no water-pouring, His point would be that, while no material water was poured on that morning yet spiritual and life-giving water was available to all who would come to Him. His announcement might be regarded as a repetition of that in Isa. 55:1-3; whereas there it is the God of Israel through His prophet who says "come to me" (verse 3), here it is the Son who says so in person.

John 8:6. *What accusation did the scribes and Pharisees hope to lodge against our Lord when they asked Him to make a pronouncement about the woman taken in adultery (John 8:6)?*

If He said that she should not be stoned, they could accuse Him of an offence against Jewish religious law, contradicting the law of Moses. If He said that she should be stoned, they could accuse Him of usurping a right which the Roman government of Judea had reserved to itself—the right of inflicting capital punishment. (We may compare the attempted dilemma over the tribute money). A Roman judge wrote down his sentence before pronouncing it; it was suggested by T. W. Manson that our Lord, discerning His questioners' intention, imitated a Roman judge (whose function He was being incited to usurp) by writing *His* sentence down (with His finger on the ground) before pronouncing it: "He that is without sin among you, let him first cast a stone at her" (verse 7).

John 8:55. *In my (1929) edition of Weymouth's New Testament the last part of John 8:55 reads: "But I do not know Him, and I obey His teaching." I can find no other version with this negative here. Surely it is a very serious error?*

It is a mere misprint, which was corrected in later impressions. The context itself (including the earlier part of the same verse) would make it quite plain that the "not" was intrusive. It is an example of the converse error to that which earned the title of the "Wicked Bible" for an edition of the A.V. in 1631—the accidental omission of "not" from the Seventh Commandment.

John 8:56. *When our Lord said, "Your father Abraham rejoiced to see my day, and he saw it, and was glad" (John 8:56), to what occasion in the life of Abraham did He refer?*

To the occasion described in Gen. 22, it may be, and perhaps to Abraham's words, "God will provide himself the lamb for a burnt offering" (Gen. 22:8). A further possibility, however, in connexion with the same incident is pointed to by Heb. 11:19; if Abraham received Isaac back from the dead "in a parable", the meaning seems to be that Isaac's return from the brink of death was a foreshadowing of the resurrection of Christ, and in so far as Abraham had any appreciation of this, that also would have meant for him a glad seeing of the day of Christ.

John 10:16. *In John 10:16 what is meant by the "fold" and the "one flock", and who are the other sheep?*

In this context the "fold" is the Jewish religious order from which the Shepherd calls His own sheep by name and leads them out; these sheep of His are Jewish believers. The "other sheep" are believers from the Gentiles, who had never belonged to the Jewish fold; they, together with the previous sheep, make up the one flock (the sum total of believers in Christ), following the one Shepherd.

John 10:22. *What was the feast of the dedication mentioned in John 10:22?*

It was the annual commemoration of the purification of the Jerusalem temple by Judas Maccabaeus in 164 B.C., after its three years' pollution by Antiochus Epiphanes, who had turned it into the shrine of a pagan divinity. The festival is still kept by Jews on the 25th day of Kislev (corresponding roughly to our December); its Hebrew name is *Hanukkah* ("dedication").

John 13:8. *In John 13:8 the Revised Standard Version has "no part in me" whereas the older versions have "no part with me." Is there any justification for the change?*

None at all; it is a mistranslation, due (I fear) to carelessness. There is a difference between having no part *in* Christ and having no part *with* Him. That the R.S.V. should have made this mistake is the more surprising in that some members of

70

the committee, such as Moffatt and Goodspeed, who have produced individual translations of their own, have translated the phrase correctly. The N.E.B. rendering, "you are not in fellowship with me," expresses the sense very well.

John 13:31ff. *Why, in Moffatt's translation, do chapters 15 and 16 of John precede chapters 13:31-14:31?*

There is no textual evidence for such a transposition. It is based on such considerations as that John 16:5 ("none of you asks me, Where are you going?") reads rather surprisingly after 13:36 ("Lord, where are you going?") and that 14:31 ("Rise, let us go hence") would come more naturally at the end of our Lord's discourse. But these are not decisive arguments.

John 14:3. *If the word translated "mansions" in John 14:3 really means "resting-places", does not this suggest some sort of basis for the doctrine of purgatory?*

I do not think our Lord means that there are many resting-places or caravanserais *on the way to* the Father's house (although the word in itself could have this meaning, and this interpretation has been favoured by many expositors, including the late William Temple). He says that the many resting-places are *in* the Father's house; that is to say, as B. F. Westcott puts it: "There is room enough for all there: though you may find no shelter among men (16:1, 2), you shall find it amply with my Father."

John 14:13f. *In the light of John 14:13, 14, should we today pray for things to the Lord Jesus Christ, or only to God the Father?*

Christian prayer is normally addressed to the Father through the Son. But in these verses the Son Himself speaks as the answerer of prayer, and there is some ground for reading verse 14, as in R.V.,

"If ye shall ask me anything in my name...". It seems plain from the context of 2 Cor. 12:8 that Paul's prayer for deliverance from the thorn in his flesh was addressed to the Lord Jesus. We may be sure that the prayer of faith is equally heard no matter which Person of the Godhead is verbally invoked.

John 14:31. *Do you think John 14:31 implies a break or journey between chapters 14 and 15, so that the ministry of chapters 15 and 16 was not given in the upper room?*

There are several problems raised by the sequence of thought and event in these chapters. But, if we take them in the order in which they have come down to us, it seems quite probable (though there can be no certainty) that our Lord's words, "Rise, let us go hence," were the signal to leave the upper room. Whether the traditional site of the upper room is the right one or not, the company would have to pass by or through the temple precincts to cross the brook Kidron (John 18:1), and it has been suggested (but not very convincingly) that the great golden vine over the entrance to the holy house may have formed a background for the parable of the True Vine at the beginning of chapter 15.

John 15:4, 6. *What is meant by the expressions "unless you abide" and "if a man does not abide" in John 15:4, 6? Is it possible not to abide in Christ?*

Passages like these are not difficult in themselves; the difficulty arises when we try to make them and other Scriptures square with our theology, instead of using them as the basis for our theology. At the very time when our Lord was speaking there was a glaring example of one who failed to abide in Him—Judas Iscariot, who had just left them. Judas was chosen as his eleven colleagues were (Luke 6:13; John 6:70); their association with the Lord brought them no privileges which

71

were not equally open to him. The plain passages of Scripture which teach the final perseverance of the saints should not be misused as an excuse for soft-pedalling the equally plain passages which speak of the danger of apostasy.

John 17:24. *It is sometimes said that the phrase "the foundation of the world" found in John 17:24 and elsewhere means literally "the overthrow of the world," referring to the "catastrophic" interpretation of Gen. 1:2. Is this right?*

Erich Sauer rightly says in *The Dawn of World Redemption*, p. 20: "Thoroughly false is the translation 'downfall' sometimes offered of the Greek word *katabolē*, used here and in ten other places. The word in question never has this meaning in the Greek language. The proper meaning is 'the laying down of the foundations, founding, establishing'... The sense of the word has nothing to do with the happenings in Gen. 1:2."

John 18:5. *Do you think that "I am he" in John 18:5 is a reference to Ex. 3:14, or is this merely a piece of fancy?*

I think that the words used and the impression they made on the hearers are intended to suggest to the reader that Jesus is deliberately echoing the language of divine self-designation in the Old Testament—perhaps such a passage as Isa. 41:4 ("I am he") even more than Ex. 3:14. We may compare such other passages in this Gospel as 8:24, 28, where Gk. *egō eimi* has a much fuller sense than the unemphatic "it is I." It has been argued, especially by Ethelbert Stauffer (*Jesus and His Story*, 1960, p. 102f., 150), that the Markan form of Jesus' reply to the high priest, *egō eimi*, "I am" (Mark 14:62), similarly constituted a divine claim and was inevitably construed as blasphemy. This is possible, but one cannot be completely sure, for if He had simply wished to say "Yes" to the high priest's question, He might well have said *egō eimi*.

John 19:5. *In John 19:5 the word "Pilate" is italicized. May it therefore be held that it was Jesus who said, "Behold, the man," drawing the chief priests' attention to Himself as the fulfiller of Zech. 6:12 ("Behold the man whose name is the Branch")?*

It is true that the word "Pilate" has been supplied by the translators. But the opening words of verse 5 are little more than parenthetic, showing that Pilate's words in verse 4 ("Behold, I bring him out to you . . .") were accompanied by the appropriate action; the second part of verse 5 then tells us what Pilate went on to say. It is quite possible, however, that John regards Pilate's words "Behold, the man" as an unconscious echo of Zech. 6:12 (which the chief priests might have been expected to recognize, although the Hebrew of Zech. 6:12 has "a man," not "the man"), just as he may see in Pilate's later words "Behold, your King" (verse 14) an echo of Zech. 9:9. (See pp. 177f.)

John 19:34. *Was the act of piercing the Saviour's side (John 19:34) necessary to our salvation, or was it simply necessary to the fulfilment of the Scripture: "They shall look on him whom they pierced" (Zech. 12:10)?*

Since our Lord had already said, "It is finished" and surrendered His life to God (v. 30) when this act of piercing took place, this act can scarcely be thought of as part of His saving work. But John lays special emphasis on the truth of this report (v. 35) not only because it paved the way for the fulfilment of Zech. 12:10, but also because it provided incontrovertible evidence that our Lord had really died. In his Gospel and Epistles John writes with one eye on people who denied the true humanity of Christ, and held that neither His incarnation nor His death could be real. Hence he insists that this proof of Christ's humanity and death was attested by an eyewitness.

John 20:22. *Do you consider that John 20:22 teaches that there was a giving of the Holy Spirit on the occasion when our Lord breathed on His disciples and said: "Receive ye the Holy Spirit"?*

Yes; this event, technically known as the "insufflation", implies a real impartation of the Spirit to the disciples in special relation to the commission of verse 23. It is a matter of interest (and significance, too) that the verb used here is the same as that used in the Septuagint version of Gen. 2:7, when God "breathed" the breath of life into Adam's nostrils.

John 20:23. *Our Lord said to His disciples: "If you forgive the sins of any, they are forgiven; if you retain the sins of any, they are retained" (John 20:23). What authority is conferred in these words, and how is that authority exercised in practice?*

The authority is declaratory in character: it is the authority "to declare and pronounce to his people, being penitent, the absolution and remission of their sins", and the authority to warn the impenitent in the contrary sense. I can think of three ways in which it is exercised. One is in the preaching of the gospel. As the servant of Christ delivers the message with which he is entrusted, he assures those who believe the message of the forgiveness of their sins, and those who reject it of the retention of theirs. Another is in pastoral ministry. When Christians confess their sins, or when they become a prey to doubt and depression, the minister of Christ has the joyful privilege of reassuring them that their sins are forgiven for Christ's sake. And yet another way is in the exercise of church discipline. Those who have erred from the path and, having repented, are restored need to have the absolution and remission of their sins confirmed to them in Christ's name; those who remain obdurate must have the solemnity of their attitude brought home to them, in the spirit of Christ's affirmation that whatever His delegates bind or loose on earth will be ratified in heaven (Matt. 16:19; 18:18; cf. 1 Cor. 5:4f.). See pp. 49f.

John 21:15ff. *The use of the words for "love" in John 21:15-17 is generally explained by saying that* phileō *denotes natural affection and* agapaō *a higher love. Trench, however, seems to present a different interpretation, explaining* phileō *as a personal, unreasoning love, and* agapaō *as the love of a more reasoning attachment. Would you comment on this?*

If any commentator on the basis of either of these differentiations in the Johannine use of the two verbs for love can show satisfactorily what is the difference between the two in John 3:35 and 5:20, I shall be prepared to consider whether there is a difference between the two in John 21:15-17. For both John 3:35 and 5:20 affirm that "the Father loves the Son"; but the verb in the former place is *agapaō* and in the latter place *phileō*. Is the Father's love for the Son in the one place natural affection and in the other a higher love? Or is it in the one place a personal·unreasoning love and in the other a more reasoning attachment? I think not. Again, in the references to the disciple "whom Jesus loved", *agapaō* is used in John 13:23; 19:26; 21:7, 20; but *phileō* in John 20:2; where similarly no distinction can be pressed between the two verbs. In fact, the two verbs appear to have been used interchangeably in Hellenistic Greek. In the Septuagint of Gen. 37:3 *agapaō* is used in the statement that "Israel loved Joseph more than all his children"; but in the following verse, where we are told that "his brethren saw that his father loved him more than all his brethren", the verb is *phileō*. Yet one and the same verb is used in both places in the Hebrew text. Accordingly I am not convinced by those interpretations which see much significance in the change of verb in John 21:15-17.

John 21:18f. *Is it fair and reasonable to assume that, until he was an old man, Peter refrained from telling his friends about the Lord's prediction recorded in John 21:18, 19?*

I see no reason for making this assumption. Besides, the prediction appears to have been made in the hearing of other disciples, so that it was no secret, right from the first.

THE ACTS OF THE APOSTLES

Acts 1:15-26. *Were the eleven apostles over-hasty in co-opting Matthias as a twelfth, to take Judas's place (Acts 1:15-26)? Should they have waited God's time, until Paul was ready to fill the vacancy? Is there any significance in the fact that nothing more is heard in the New Testament about Matthias?*

As regards the last point, nothing more is heard of most of the Twelve by name (so far as the New Testament is concerned), so the absence of any further specific reference to Matthias is neither exceptional nor surprising. For the rest, William Kelly is abundantly justified in his denial that there is any "just ground . . . to question the step of choosing a twelfth apostle, which seems to be thoroughly in keeping with the waiting posture of the disciples. Besides, Acts 2:14; 6:2, would to most minds imply the contrary, and show that Luke does afterwards speak of the Twelve. To suppose that Paul was the intended twelfth is rather to lower his truly peculiar position and extraordinary call" (*Exposition of Acts*, 3rd edition, p. 16). Paul himself would have regarded as preposterous a suggestion which betrays a failure to appreciate the distinctiveness of his apostleship.

Acts 2:16. *Can Acts 2:16 be fairly paraphrased in the following words? "But this (which I now quote to you) is that which has been spoken by the prophet Joel (and if such is to happen in the last days why be surprised at what you now see in our day?)." In other words, does "this" mean the quotation from the past of a yet future event, rather than being a reference to what was happening just then?*

I cannot think that Peter would have expressed himself as he did if that had been his meaning. To his hearers the meaning of his words would certainly have been that they were witnessing the fulfilment of Joel's prophecy. Indeed, "this is that" might be written not only over this passage but over the whole of the New Testament: this is the fulfilment of what in the Old Testament was promised. The last days in this sense have been inaugurated by the passion and exaltation of Christ, as they will be consummated by His coming in glory.

Acts 2:20. *In Joel 2:31, as quoted in Acts 2:20, what is the relevance of the turning of the moon into blood?*

If we take along with these words the preceding statement, "The sun shall be turned into darkness," we may begin to appreciate a relevance in this part of Peter's quotation beyond what is commonly realized. It was little more than seven weeks since the people of Jerusalem had actually seen the sun turned into darkness, during the early afternoon of the day of our Lord's crucifixion. And whatever was the cause of this obscuring of the sunlight (it could not have been an eclipse, since it was full moon), it would very likely have caused the Paschal full moon to rise blood-red in the sky later on that same afternoon. Many of Peter's hearers would remember these phenomena well, and now they learned that they were the predestined harbingers of that day on which the Lord was pouring forth His Spirit and promising salvation to all who called upon His name.

Acts 2:38. *Does Acts 2:38 teach that baptism is necessary in order to be saved?*

No; neither Acts 2:38 nor any other scripture teaches this. Such an idea is contrary to the tenor of the whole New Testament. It is faith-union with Christ that saves. Baptism is the outward and visible sign of repentance and faith. In the apostolic age the outward sign was for the most part so immediately associated with the inward and spiritual grace that both could be spoken of as component parts of one total experience, or by a form of metonymy what was strictly true of the one could be predicated of the other. But we have probably all known people whose Christianity was not in doubt although they had never been baptized, and people whose Christianity was conspicuous by its absence although they had been most canonically baptized.

Do you think it unwise to dogmatize upon the meaning of Acts 2:38, "Repent ye, and be baptized. . . ."?

I think it unwise to dogmatize about the meaning of any Scripture. Where the meaning of Scripture is self-evident, we need not dogmatize; and where it is not self-evident, we should not dogmatize. All that the interpreter of Scripture is called upon to say is: "This is how I understand it, and these are my reasons for understanding it so." Indeed, you will commonly find in ordinary life that it is the more doubtful statements that are most dogmatically affirmed. People will not make dogmatic assertions about whether Sir Winston Churchill was born in 1874 or not, because that is a point which can be readily verified by reference to public records. But they will make very dogmatic assertions about the rightness or wrongness of his policy at some juncture of his political career, because questions like these cannot be verified as matters of fact, but must remain matters of opinion and personal judgment. So, with regard to the interpretation of Acts 2:38, I can give my judgment (which is that remission of sins and the reception of the Spirit are here the sequel to baptism, viewed as the visible token of repentance); but if I say to others, "Unless you accept my interpretation you are wrong," I am simply being foolish.

Acts 2:42. *In Acts 2:42, R.V., the word "and" is omitted before "in the breaking of bread." Does this mean that they continued together in three things rather than in four, and that the fellowship consisted in breaking bread, or in the prayers, or in both?*

The construction suggests that the breaking of bread and the prayers are mentioned as two expressions of the fellowship. But these two acts did not exhaust the fellowship, of course; a further expression of it is mentioned below in verses 44 and 45.

Acts 2:44. *In* The Christian Ecclesia, *p. 45, F. J. A. Hort renders Acts 2:44 thus: "'All that believed together', says St. Luke (this is his peculiar but pregnant description of membership), 'all that believed together had all things common . . .'". Please comment.*

I gather from Hort's remark in parentheses that he understands the phrase rendered "together" (Gk. *epi to auto*) to be a pregnant expression for membership or fellowship in the church. In that case his rendering is literally accurate; the best texts omit "were" and "and" (as found in our common version, "all that believed *were* together *and* had all things common"). Cf. N.E.B.: "all whose faith had drawn them together held everything in common." The phrase rendered "together" seems to have acquired a semi-technical sense of being "in church fellowship" (almost synonymous with Gk. *en ekklēsia*) in the New Testament and early Christian literature.

Acts 4:11. *In Peter's application of Psa. 118:22 to the Sanhedrin, "He is the stone which was set at nought by you the builders, which was made the head of the corner" (Acts 4:11; cf. Mark 12:10f.; 1 Peter 2:7), in what sense were they described as "builders"?*

As early as Psa. 118:22, the words about the rejected stone appear to have been proverbial. There is no emphasis on the Sanhedrin being builders of anything in particular; in so far as the language of the proverbial saying is concerned, they fulfilled the part of the builders simply by rejecting the chief corner stone. One might, of course, think of them as the men who tried to build the edifice of Judaism while leaving out the one "stone" which could bond the whole fabric together, but there is no explicit reference in the context to any such activity of theirs. (In one of the Qumran community documents the members of a rival community, probably the Pharisees, are described as "the builders of the wall," but this is a reference to the unstable wall of Ezek. 13:10 and has nothing to do, in my judgment, with the present passage.)

Acts 6:5, *etc. Is Philip the "deacon" and evangelist of Acts 6:5; 8:5ff.; 21:8, the same as Philip the apostle of John 1:43; Acts 1:13, etc.?*

No, I don't think so. In Acts 6 there seems to be a clear distinction between the twelve apostles and the seven almoners (who may more accurately be described thus than as deacons, having regard to the special form of service for which they were appointed). There is some evidence that certain second-century writers confused the two, and in our own day J. A. Robertson has argued for their identity in his imaginative work *The Hidden Romance of the New Testament*, 1920, pp. 71f. But his argument cannot be sustained.

Acts 7:58. *How was the death of Stephen achieved so easily, without (it appears) any question of procuring the permission of the Roman power, in striking contrast to the death of Christ?*

One concession was allowed by the Roman administration to the Jewish authorities in respect of capital jurisdiction (which otherwise the Romans reserved strictly to themselves); that was where the

sanctity of the temple was threatened or violated. The attempt to fasten a charge of this kind on our Lord was unsuccessful (Mark 14:55-59), but it succeeded against Stephen (Acts 6:13f.). A similar attempt was made (unsuccessfully) against Paul several years later (Acts 21:28; 24:6). (A further suggested explanation is that Stephen's trial took place in the interregnum following Pilate's recall from office at the end of A.D. 36. This date is probably two or three years too late: besides, there was no real interregnum, for an acting prefect was immediately appointed in Pilate's place).

Acts 8:5. *In Acts 8:5, A.V. and R.V. render "the city of Samaria"; R.S.V. and N.E.B. "a city of (in) Samaria." I understand that the manuscripts and other authorities for the text disagree on the presence or absence of the definite article, but since its presence is supported by the Codices Sinaiticus, Vaticanus and Alexandrinus, why do R.S.V. and N.E.B. prefer the indefinite article?*

I suspect that their preference for the rendering "a city" is due not so much to the respective weight of the authorities for the text as to the judgment that it is unlikely that the city to which Philip went was "the city of Samaria" in the sense of the city called Samaria—the Graeco-Roman city (refounded by Herod and renamed by him Sebaste) which stood on the site of Omri's old capital. It would be strange to find Luke designating by the archaic name "Samaria" the city known in his time as Sebaste, but his expression might mean "the (capital) city of (the region) Samaria"; so R. B. Rackham takes it in his commentary on Acts. If we prefer the reading "a city of Samaria"; supported by the Western and Byzantine texts, the city may be Gitta, which, according to Justin Martyr (himself a native of Samaria), was the birthplace of Simon Magus.

Acts 8:16. *In Acts 8:16 the Authorized Version and the Revised Version of 1881 use the pronoun "he" in reference to the Holy Spirit; A.S.V., R.S.V. and Moffatt use "it." Why is this?*

R.S.V. probably took "it" over from A.S.V. without reconsideration. The American Revisers evidently acted deliberately in the matter, for as early as 1881, in the list of their preferred readings and renderings which appeared as an appendix to the British Revised New Testament, Acts 8:16 is annotated: "For 'he was fallen' read 'it was fallen'." Probably the American Revisers believed that the personal Holy Spirit came upon the Samaritan converts, as upon all believers, when first they put their faith in Christ, and that the reference in Acts 8:16 is not to the personal Spirit but to a special endowment with one or more of the gifts of the Spirit. Moffatt may have held the same view. N.E.B. has the personal interpretation: "For until then the Spirit had not come upon any of them."

Acts 8:26; 12:7. *In Acts 8:26 and 12:7 was the angelic visitation actual or visionary?*

It was not visionary if by that word you mean "unreal"; but there are visions of various kinds. When Peter "did not know that what was done by the angel was real, but thought he was seeing a vision" (Acts 12:9), that is as much as to say that he thought he was dreaming; on the other hand, when Cornelius "saw clearly in a vision an angel of God coming in" (Acts 10:3), the visitation, though "visionary", took place when he was wide awake. What is seen in a vision is visible only to the person or persons to whom the vision is given; thus, when Paul saw the risen Christ on the Damascus road, his companions saw no man. I suppose that, in our materialistic age, we are inclined to think that what is seen in a vision is not so real as what is seen with the outward eye under normal conditions, whereas in fact, according to the Bible, it may be more real. What Elisha's servant saw when his eyes were opened by God was a much more adequate view of reality than he could take in with his ordinary eyesight (2 Kings 6:17).

Acts 8:32. *In the quotation from Isa. 53:7 in Acts 8:32, why is it the sheep that is mentioned first as led to the slaughter, followed by the lamb dumb before the shearer, whereas in the Old Testament the suffering Servant is presented "as a lamb that is led to the slaughter, and as a sheep that before her shearers is dumb"? The Old Testament order seems more natural; it is unusual for a lamb (under a year old) to be shorn. Why are the words reversed in Acts?*

The Ethiopian was in all probability reading a copy of the Greek (Septuagint) version of the prophet Isaiah, and in that version the sheep is mentioned first, as in the quotation in Acts. The writer of Acts does not imply that this is the preferable order, but simply records that this was the form in which the Ethiopian read the words. The wording of our Old Testament text accurately represents the Hebrew original, and conforms to what you rightly point out as the more natural order.

Acts 8:37. *Why is Acts 8:37 absent from Darby's New Translation and from the R.V. and most recent versions? Has the omission of this verse any bearing on the principle of believer's baptism?*

The verse is omitted by most recent versions of the New Testament because it is not found in our best ancient authorities for the text—Greek, Latin, Syriac, Coptic and Ethiopic. It first appears in the so-called Western text, probably goes back to the first half of the second century, and certainly reflects early Christian baptismal practice. The principle of believer's baptism is in no way affected by the omission; it is clear even without verse 37 that the Ethiopian was baptized because he believed.

Acts 11:26. *Is there any foundation for the view that "called" in Acts 11:26 means "divinely called"?*

No. The verb *chrēmatizō*, used here in the *active*, means literally "to transact business under the name of..." It must be distinguished from another verb *chrēmatizō*, which, when used in the *passive*, means "to be divinely warned" (as in Matt. 2:12, 22; Acts 10:22). The distinction in meaning between these two verbs of identical form is clarified in Moulton and Howard's *Grammar of N.T. Greek*, Vol. II, p. 265, where the former is linked with *chrēmata*, "business", and the latter with *chraomai*, "to give an oracular response." What is meant in Acts 11:26 is that Antioch was the first place where the disciples of Jesus came to be publicly known as "Christians."

Acts 11:30. *When the church of Antioch sent its gift to Jerusalem (Acts 11:30), since they would most naturally send it to those "serving tables", may we take it that the seven men of Ch. 6 became the basic nucleus for the elderhood in the church (elders being specifically mentioned in Acts 11:30)?*

The survivors of the seven almoners of Acts 6 appear to have left Jerusalem in the persecution that followed Stephen's death. The Hellenistic members of the church, from whose ranks the seven appear to have come, were probably the main target of that persecution. The elders, whom we first meet in Ch. 11, were a body of independent formation, closely associated with James the brother of the Lord.

Acts 12:15. *Was Peter's "angel" in Acts 12:15 his guardian angel, or the psychical counterpart of his physical body, or something else?*

The reference appears to be to his guardian angel (cf. Matt. 18:10), who was evidently regarded as able in a case of emergency to assume the bodily likeness of his human *protégé*.

Acts 13:22. *In what sense can the apparently composite quotation at the end of Acts 13:22 be regarded as a quotation from the Old Testament?*

The words in which God is here said to have borne witness to David ("I have found in David the son of Jesse a man after my heart, who will do all my will") are not explicitly called a quotation, but are plainly based on Psa. 89:20 ("I have found David, my servant . . .") and 1 Sam. 13:14 ("the LORD has sought out a man after his own heart"), while the last clause echoes the language of God about Cyrus in Isa. 44:28 ("He . . . shall fulfil all my purpose"). Technically, the words which we are considering represent a conflation of separate Old Testament passages: such conflations are not uncommon in Acts where they are appropriate to the context (a careful study of Stephen's use of the Old Testament in Acts 7 would be rewarding in this connexion). Actually, the language here ascribed by Paul to God reproduces faithfully, in the form of direct speech, God's mind with regard to David. Samuel's words of 1 Sam. 13:14 are in the third person, but they presuppose a revelation by God to Samuel in the form: "I have sought out a man after my own heart."

Acts 14:23. *What is the correct value of the word translated "ordained" in Acts 14:23? Is it to be equated with "chosen" in 2 Cor. 8:19, where the choice appears to have been that of a number, expressed in some way comparable to a show of hands?*

While the verb *cheirotoneō*, used in Acts 14:23, originally indicated appointment or election by a show of hands (literally by stretching out the hand), it had lost this specific force by New Testament times and had come to mean simply "appoint", no matter by what procedure the appointment was made. In Acts 14:23, therefore, we are simply told that Paul and Barnabas appointed elders in the recently founded churches of South Galatia, but the verb itself tells us nothing about the method of appointment. It is, however, significant that a sufficient interval was left between the founding of the churches and the appointment of elders for the men with the appropriate gifts to approve themselves. The verb in 2 Cor. 8:19 is the same verb *cheirotoneō*, although it is translated "chosen" in A.V.; R.V., R.S.V. and N.E.B. have the more accurate rendering "appointed." How a number of churches appointed this brother to join Paul as their representative in the administration of the collection for Jerusalem we are not told; but it would have required a different procedure from that followed by Paul and Barnabas in Acts 14:23. The verb has a wide enough range to cover a variety of procedures.

Acts 15:14. *Is the Scofield Reference Bible right when it says that Acts 15:14 is "dispensationally . . . the most important passage in the N.T. It gives the divine purpose for this age, and for the beginning of the next"?*

If this passage is important dispensationally, it is remarkable that it should come in the course of a speech by James—"austere, legal, ceremonial", as he is called elsewhere in the *Scofield Bible* (p. 1306). I think that the note to which you refer reads too much into James's words. In Acts 15:14 James is referring back to what Peter has just told the Council of Jerusalem: "Symeon hath rehearsed how first God did visit the Gentiles, to take out of them a people for his name." And if we look back to verses 7 to 11 to see what Symeon (Peter) said, we find that he was reminding his audience of his fruitful visit to the household of Cornelius in Caesarea: "Brethren, ye know how that a good while ago God made choice among you, that by my mouth the Gentiles should hear the word of the gospel, and believe" (verse 7). The word "first" in James's statement in verse 14 points back to the Cornelius incident; it was by the conversion of Cornelius and his household that God began to take from among the Gentiles—as well as from among the Jews—a people for His name. No doubt there are "dispensational" implications in James's words; they indicate quite plainly the advent of the newer dispensation in which the people of God are no longer restricted by racial or national boundaries. But this is surely not the most important statement of this "dispensational" principle in the New Testament. For that we should look rather to Matt. 28:19, 20, or (more fully) to Eph. 2:13-22. James then goes on to find in the submission of Gentile believers to Christ, the Son of David, a fulfilment of the prophecy of Amos that the time would come when David's fallen tent would be erected again and Gentiles would be called by the name of Israel's God (i.e. be brought into allegiance to Him).

Acts 15:29. *Please indicate if the regulations of Acts 15:29 should be taken literally, and if not, when they were rescinded.*

The regulations in question are those enjoined in the letter sent to the Gentile church of Antioch and her daughter churches after the Council of Jerusalem. The main question before the Council was the terms on which Gentiles might be recognized as heirs of salvation and admitted to membership in the church. Some Jewish Christians wished to impose certain conditions over and above faith in Christ, but the Council agreed that faith in Christ must be acknowledged as sufficient, since God Himself had so manifestly shown that this was the sole condition which He required. But when this point of principle was settled, a further question remained for discussion—ways and means of making fellowship (especially table-fellowship) between Jewish and Gentile believers easier in practice. Two main issues were involved—one had to do with relations between the sexes (in which Gentiles were deplorably lax by Jewish standards), and the other

THE ACTS OF THE APOSTLES

had to do with certain kinds of food. The former issue is covered by the prohibition of fornication. It may be that here the word has a technical sense of unions which, while admissible by Gentile custom, were banned by the Old Testament law; but whether the word has this special sense or its more ordinary sense, no question arises in this connexion, because this prohibition is repeatedly enforced throughout the New Testament. The food-laws may be viewed rather differently. It was difficult enough for the ordinary Jew in those days, even after he came to faith in Christ, to reconcile himself to sitting at a table with a Gentile, even if that Gentile was now his fellow-believer. It would be more difficult still if the Gentile ate food which was abhorrent to the Jew's tradition and instinct, and expected his Jewish guest to share it with him. It would be an elementary act of Christian courtesy if Gentile believers abstained from food which offended their Jewish brethren. The reference to "things sacrificed to idols" was applicable to converts from pagan idolatry; this subject is dealt with more fully elsewhere in the New Testament. The prohibition of blood and the flesh of strangled animals applied more particularly to that transitional period in which Jewish and Gentile Christians were learning to live together, although in fact the ban on eating meat with blood survived for long in the Gentile churches. (Indeed, when Alfred the Great promulgated his law-code for the English nation at the end of the ninth century, he prefaced it with the Ten Commandments, extracts from Exodus 21-23, and the apostolic letter of Acts 15:23-29). It is plain from 1 Corinthians that, in the matter of food sacrificed to idols, Paul took an independent line, making the criterion of practice not the antecedents of the food but the spiritual wellbeing of men and women. And 1 Tim. 4:4, 5, may be regarded as rescinding those food-laws which were of temporary application.

Acts 16:34. *Is there any warrant for stating that a more correct translation of Acts 16:34 would be that the jailor in Philippi "rejoiced with all his house that he had believed in God", implying that his faith was the foundation for the baptism of his household, supposed to include infants?*

What the narrative says is that "he rejoiced with all his house having believed in God." Both the verbs "rejoiced" and "having believed" are in the singular, referring to the jailor, but the adverbial phrase "with all his house" (one word in Greek) which comes between them suggests that his household shared his faith and shared his joy, whether it included infants or not.

Acts 17:4. *How can Acts 17:4 be reconciled with 1 Thess. 1:9? The former passage implies that the early Thessalonian church was composed largely of former "devout Greeks" and the latter that its members were formerly worshippers of idols. Does Acts 17:4 mean that the "devout Greeks" were devout worshippers of idols rather than "God-fearers"?*

The "devout Greeks" of Acts 17:4 were certainly God-fearers, i.e. Gentiles who attended the synagogue and were attached to the worship of the God of Israel without going so far as to become full proselytes to Judaism. In Thessalonica, as in many other places where Paul made the synagogue his first base of operations, such God-fearing Gentiles formed the nucleus of his converts. But in Acts 17:4 reference is made only to those who believed as a result of Paul's preaching in the synagogue on three successive sabbaths. Although Luke has nothing to say about Paul's activity in Thessalonica after the third sabbath and before his expulsion from the city, analogy might suggest that he found another base of operations in Thessalonica, serving the same purpose as the house of Titius Justus at Corinth (Acts 18:7) and the school of Tyrannus at Ephesus (Acts 19:9). What analogy suggests is confirmed by the testimony of 1 Thess. 1:9, from which we infer that, by the time Paul left Thessalonica, the majority of the members of the young church there were converts from paganism.

Acts 18:5. *In Acts 18:5 is the verb passive or reflexive in the phrase, "constrained by the word" (R.V.) "pressed in the spirit" (A.V.), "occupied with preaching" (R.S.V.)?*

The verb, so far as its form goes, may be in either the middle or the passive voice; on the whole, I should recognize it as middle, with a reflexive force, as in N.E.B.: "Paul devoted himself entirely to preaching."

Acts 18:18. *Was it Paul or Aquila who had the vow in Acts 18:18? What kind of vow was it?*

As Paul is the subject of the sentence as a whole, it is most probable that it was he who had the vow. The vow appears to have been a temporary Nazirite vow such as any Jew might voluntarily undertake for some special purpose. He let his hair grow for the duration of the vow, and had it shorn, or shaved, at the end of the period (cf. Num. 6:1-21, and the incident of the four men who had a similar vow in Acts 21:23-26).

Acts 18:24. *Was Apollos "eloquent" (Acts 18:24, A.V., A.S.V., R.S.V., N.E.B.) or "learned" (R.V.)?*

In fact he appears to have been both. The Greek word *logios*, so variously rendered (and not found elsewhere in the New Testament) may bear either meaning: in most versions, whichever rendering is preferred in the text, the other is mentioned as an alternative in the margin. Luke, we may be sure, intended either the one sense or the other, and there is just a slight balance of probability in favour of "eloquent."

Acts 20:6ff. *Was there a local church at Troas when Paul and his companions broke bread there, according to Acts 20:7ff.?*

Almost certainly there was, for Paul had spent some time there in evangelistic activity after his departure from Ephesus (2 Cor. 2:12f.), even if it was interrupted by his anxiety to hear Titus's report of the state of the Corinthian church. In any case, there were sufficient Christians in Troas on that particular first day of the week to constitute a very respectable *ad hoc* local church. But had all the people who came together to break bread been Paul's fellow-travellers, it would not have been necessary for them to sit up all night while he talked to them. The believers in Troas surely wanted to make the best use of their time while Paul was there, and hear as much from him as they could.

Acts 20:7. *Is "the first day of the week" in Acts 20:7 to be reckoned according to the Jewish calendar, so that we should think of the disciples as coming together after sunset "on the Saturday night" (so N.E.B.), in which case "the morrow" (v. 7) would simply mean "after break of day" (cf. v. 11)?*

It is not certain. If we take "the morrow" in its strict sense, then "break of day" fell on the second day of the week, Monday, and Luke is following the Greek and Roman reckoning, according to which a new day began at midnight. It may be, as your question suggests, that "the morrow" is used loosely and refers to the part of Sunday that followed dawn. But, in that case, have you considered that you may have discovered an apostolic precedent for Sunday travelling?

Acts 20:8. *Did the torches of Acts 20:8 give off fumes which induced drowsiness, or was it simply hot air and fatigue that overcame Eutychus?*

No doubt Luke's mention of the torches at this point is deliberate, indicating that they were partly responsible for Eutychus's sleepiness. But apart from that he had probably put in a hard day's work, and it was getting on for midnight.

Acts 20:9f. *Was Eutychus really dead or not?*

The point apparently is that Luke says that Eutychus "was taken up dead" (Acts 20:10), whereas in the following verse Paul says: "Do not be alarmed, for his life is in him." In this respect the incident is parallel to that of Jairus's daughter, for the messenger said to Jairus, "Your daughter is dead" (Luke 8:49), whereas our Lord said: "She is not dead but sleeping" (verse 52).[1] I have expressed my mind on the question of Eutychus elsewhere (*The Book of the Acts*, p. 408), as follows: "No wonder then that he was 'taken up dead', as Luke says, 'implying apparently that, as a physician, he had satisfied himself on the point' (Ramsay, *St. Paul the Traveller*, p. 290f.). The treatment which Paul gave the youth—similar to that given in similar circumstances by Elijah and Elisha in the O.T. (1 Kings 17:21; 2 Kings 4:34f.)—suggests artificial respiration. But Paul's words, as he bade the people stop making a fuss, 'for his life is in him' (verse 10), should not be pressed to mean that he was not actually dead for a brief space of time in the strict sense of the word. Luke probably intends us to understand that his life returned to him when Paul embraced him. But it may have been a few hours before Eutychus recovered consciousness." But one should not dogmatize, still less condemn out of hand the alternative interpretation, which is accepted by N.E.B., as earlier by the "Twentieth Century" version and those of Weymouth, Goodspeed and Phillips.

Acts 20:11. *It has been said that Acts 20:11 refers to Paul's partaking of a private meal, as all the verbs in this verse are singular. Is this the right interpretation?*

The presence of the definite article in the phrase "had broken the bread" (R.V.) points back to the phrase "to break bread" in verse 7. The natural inference is that Paul's act in verse 11 represents the fulfilment of the purpose expressed in verse 7. I suggest that in verse 11 the words "had broken the bread" refer to the Lord's Supper, while the following words "and eaten" refer to a fellowship meal. The verbs in this verse are all participles except the last one, "departed"; as Paul is the subject of the whole sentence they must all be grammatically singular, but that by no means excludes our understanding that Paul broke the bread and ate in fellowship with all the Christians who were present.

Acts 20:35. *Is there any significance in the word "himself" in Acts 20:35, so rendered by J. N. Darby ("he himself said") but omitted by A.V.? Does the original construction lay stress on "himself"?*

Yes: the pronoun is emphatic and is rightly rendered "he himself" (R.V. and N.E.B. render it similarly). Paul here certainly refers to an utterance of our Lord during His earthly ministry, not to something spoken by Him after His ascension through His Spirit in the apostles. But the emphatic pronoun is no doubt used to underline the authority of the utterance; it is as though the apostle said: "We have it on the highest possible authority—the authority of the Lord Jesus Himself—that it is more blessed to give than to receive."

Acts 22:16. *What would Paul understand Ananias to mean by the words: "wash away your sins" (Acts 22:16)?*

---

[1] See p. 45.

The imperatives are in the middle voice, and the force of this might best be conveyed by such a rendering as "Get yourself baptized, and get your sins washed away." But Paul, being an intelligent man, would know that the external application of water to his body could not of itself wash away his sins; he would understand that his baptism in water was the outward and visible sign of his inward and spiritual purification from sin by the grace of God, a purification which he appropriated by faith. The meaning is not essentially different from that of Acts 2:38, "Repent, and be baptized every one of you in the name of Jesus Christ for the forgiveness of your sins." In Acts 2:38 the verb is in the passive voice. An example of the middle voice comparable to that of Acts 22:16 is found in 1 Cor. 6:11, where "you were washed" is literally "you got yourselves washed." The reference is probably to the outward washing in baptism as the symbol of the inward washing by the Spirit.

Acts 23:5. *How is it that Paul, who in Acts 9:1f. had an interview with the high priest, says in Acts 23:5 that he did not know who the high priest was?*

The high priest in Acts 9 was Caiaphas; the high priest in Acts 23 (over 20 years later) was Ananias the son of Nedebaeus, and six other men had occupied the office between these two. In A.D. 57 Paul might well fail to recognize the high priest by sight. In any case, it is possible that what Paul meant in Acts 23:5 was something like this: "I did not think that a man who could behave like that could possibly be the high priest."

THE PAULINE EPISTLES

Romans 2:5-7. *Romans 2:5-7 seems to teach that God will render eternal life to those who, by patient continuance in well doing, seek for glory and honour and immortality. How does this line up with the principle of salvation by faith alone, apart from works?*

Since it is in the same epistle that Paul spells out in detail the principle of salvation by faith alone, apart from works, we may be sure that the true interpretation of Rom. 2:5-7 will not contradict that principle. In these verses Paul is not teaching salvation by works, but emphasizing God's impartiality as between Jew and Gentile. We find a similar statement in Acts 10:34, 35, where Peter realizes that "God shows no partiality, but in every nation [i.e. among Gentiles as well as Jews] any one who fears him, and does what is right is acceptable to him." In the Acts passage God showed his acceptance of Cornelius, to whom Peter spoke these words, by sending Peter to him with the gospel so that he and his household might be saved (Acts 11:14). In the Epistle to the Romans Paul repeats, with regard to the Jews, that "the man who practises the righteousness which is based on the law shall live by it" (Rom. 10:5). But the whole argument of the Epistle establishes the point that the Jews have not attained the righteousness which is based on the law (Rom. 9:31) and that the Gentiles, in spite of having the requirements of the law "written on their hearts" are convinced by conscience of failure to keep it (Rom. 2:15). Neither Jews nor Gentiles by nature continue patiently in well-doing; both alike are morally bankrupt before God, and if they are to be justified, it can only be by His grace (Rom. 3:19-30).

Rom. 2:14. *Would you comment on B. W. Newton's translation (and more especially his punctuation) of Rom. 2:14, "For when the Gentiles, which have not the law by nature, do the things of the law...."?*

Bengel and a few others also favoured this punctuation. But it is an unnatural way to construe the Greek order of the words, and does not suit the apostle's argument here, which is that "nature" in some degree supplies to the Gentiles what "law" supplies to the Jews.

Rom. 3:30. *I have noticed that two different editions of the R.S.V. give two different renderings of the last words of Rom. 3:30, one giving "because of their faith" and the other 'through their faith." Why the change, and which is preferable?*

"Because of their faith" is the rendering of the 1946 and 1952 editions of the R.S.V. "Through their faith" is one of eighty-five changes made in the 1962 edition—nearly all of them, like this one, changes for the better. "Through", not "because of", is the proper rendering of the preposition *dia* when followed by the genitive case, as here; the change in the 1962 edition is probably due to the fact that someone spotted the inaccuracy of the rendering in the earlier editions. The N.E.B. also renders "through their faith."

Rom. 5:12. *In Rom. 5:12 death is said to have entered the world in consequence of sin. How can this be reconciled with the evidence that death was in the world long before man appeared?*

The death that is in view in Rom. 5:12 is human death; "death spread to all men [the Greek text says quite explicitly 'all human beings'] because all men sinned." Paul is not concerned here with the death of other forms of life; the fact that such death was present in the world before the appearance of man, therefore, does not affect his argument. Some decades before Paul wrote, a wise Jew of Alexandria summed up the teaching of Scripture on this subject as he saw it in these words: "God created man for immortality, and made him in the image of his own eternity; but through the devil's envy death entered the world, and those who belong to his party experience it" (Wisdom 2:23, 24).

Rom. 5:18. *Does Rom. 5:18 teach that all are automatically freed from the guilt of "original sin"? Is justification in this sense a Scriptural doctrine?*

Justification in any "automatic" sense can scarcely be Sciptural, for justification in Scripture is always linked with faith. The context, I suggest, shows that "all men" in the first half of the verse are all who are in Adam, while "all men" in the second half are all who are in Christ. Exactly the same distinction appears between the two instances of "the many" in the following verse. But in the judgment men will be judged, with perfect equity, "according to their works" and not for belongirg to a fallen race.

Rom. 6:3, 4. *Does Rom. 6:3, 4, refer to baptism in water?*

Yes; not, of course, to the external immersion in water by itself, but to the external sign coupled with the inward reality which is the believers' union by faith with Christ in His death and resurrection-life. We tend too easily to forget that in New Testament times faith and baptism were regularly not two distinct experiences but closely interwoven parts of one experience at the outset of the Christian life.

Rom. 7:14-25. *Do you regard the speaker in Rom. 7:14-25 as regenerate, or is Paul describing his experience as a Pharisee before his conversion?*

I think the speaker is regenerate.

In the preceding verses (7-13) Paul is recounting an early pre-Christian experience, but with verse 14 the tense changes from the past to the present, and Paul is describing an experience which he knew as a Christian. We can well understand that a man of his imperious zeal found it no easy matter to reproduce the "meekness and gentleness of Christ", to win the victory over a hasty tongue, a premature judgment, a resentment at any encroachment on his sphere of apostolic service. The man who speaks in these verses is the man who made it his daily business to discipline himself lest he should be disqualified in the contest of holiness. The passage is summarized in the closing sentence (verse 25b), where "I myself" is emphatic: it is "I by myself" who experience this defeat and frustration in the spiritual conflict, but "I", as a believer in Christ, am not left to "myself", for (as Paul goes on to say) the law of the Spirit of life in Christ points the way to liberation and victory.

Rom. 8:2. *Do you think Weymouth's translation of Rom. 8:2 ("for the Spirit's law—telling of life in Christ Jesus—has set me free . . .") a good one?*

Not so good as that in the later editions of Weymouth: "for the Spirit's law—life in Christ Jesus—has set me free . . ." The point is that Paul is not here simply describing the Spirit as "the Spirit of life"; he is saying that the new principle which energizes believers is "the law of the Spirit" as opposed to the "law of sin" which he served with his flesh (Rom. 7:25) and also "the law . . . of life in Christ Jesus" as opposed to the law which he "found to be unto death" (Rom. 7:10). A simple and literal rendering of Rom. 8:2 would be: "for the Spirit's law of life in Christ Jesus has liberated me from the law of sin and death."

Rom. 8:13a. *What is the death spoken of in Rom. 8:13a: "if you live according to the* *flesh, you will die" (cf. Gal. 6:8, "He who sows to his own flesh will from the flesh reap corruption")?*

It must, I think, be spiritual death, not bodily death, just as the life spoken of in the second part of the verse ("but if by the Spirit you put to death the deeds of the body you will live") must be spiritual and not bodily life. In both Rom. 8:13 and Gal. 6:8 a self-centred life is sterile in relation to God, producing no fruit for eternal life.

Rom. 8:37. *What is the meaning of the phrase "more than conquerors" in Rom. 8:37?*

Paul coins a compound verb *hypernikomen* ("we are super-conquerors") instead of the simple *nikomen* ("we are conquerors") to emphasize the superlative quality of the believer's victory in Christ.

Rom. 9:13. *Does Rom. 9:13 mean literally that God hated Esau?*

A study of the verb "hate" in the Old and New Testament will show that "hate" may be used in the sense of a lesser love, and a study of Malachi 1:2f., from which the quotation in Rom. 9:13 comes, will show that the reference there is not to the individuals Jacob and Esau but to the nations descended from them, Israel and Edom. What is really meant by the terms love and hate here is that Jacob, not Esau, was selected to be the channel for the fulfilment of God's purpose; Israel, not Edom, was the chosen nation. But consider further that in the Bible the election of some is regularly made with a view to the blessing of others through them, and think over the significance of the fact that the "remnant of Edom" in Amos 9:12 becomes in Acts 15:17 (*via* the Septuagint) the "residue of men" who are to seek the Lord, together with "all the Gentiles who are called by my name, says the Lord."

Rom. 9:22b. *In Rom. 9:22b A.V., R.V., R.S.V., N.E.B., and other versions convey*

the idea of God's patient tolerance of "vessels which were objects of retribution due for destruction." *Can you say why Dr. Hugh J. Schonfield in* The Authentic New Testament *translates this part of the verse as "produced with immense pains crude articles prepared for destruction." Why "produced"? Is a point of theology involved?*

I cannot think why Dr. Schonfield translates *ēnenken* (aorist of *pherō*) by "produced"; that is not the meaning of the word. There is another reading of the passage in the "western" text of Romans which runs "What if God, willing to shew his wrath, and to make his power known with much long-suffering towards vessels of wrath fitted unto destruction...."; but this supports his translation as little as does the better attested eastern text. If one of my students served up this translation of the passage in an examination answer I should put a mark of dissent in the margin of his script; but I should not look for some theological motivation any more than I do in *The Authentic New Testament*. The point of theology that is involved in the passage is God's patience with rebellious characters such as Pharaoh, who nevertheless reveal their reprobate nature by their failure to make a repentant response to His patience (cf. Rom. 2:4).

Rom. 11:25-27. *Paul saw a future generation of Jews turning to Christ, their partial and temporary blindness being fully removed. He found confirmation of this in the Old Testament (see the quotation of Isa. 59:20, 21, in Rom. 11:25-27). But does the Old Testament really teach this? Should we have gathered it from the Old Testament, or do we accept it simply because Paul says so?*

It may be, as you say, that if we had only Isa. 59:20, 21 to guide us, we should indeed expect the blessing of "those in Jacob who turn from transgression" but not necessarily of "all Israel." But in

Rom. 11:25-27 Paul is not quoting from Isa. 59 only. He has in mind a number of Old Testament passages, which have enough in common to indicate that they deal with the same theme, although each of them by itself deals only with a partial aspect of that theme. When all of them are taken together, however, the conclusion to which Paul is led by them is irresistible. In addition to Isa. 59, he has in mind the "new covenant" oracle of Jer. 31:31-34, and the Greek version of Isa. 27:9 ("and this is his [Jacob's] blessing, when I take away his sin"), while the phrase "but out of Zion" (in place of "to Zion" of the Hebrew text of Isa. 59:20 or "for Zion's sake" of the Greek version) is apparently based on Psa. 14:7 (repeated in Psa. 53:6). A restoration of "all Israel" is the natural implication of these passages, taken together.

Rom. 12:1. *Does the word "bodies" in Rom. 12:1 refer only to our physical life and powers, or can it be understood in the sense of our whole being, in the light of the newness of life imparted by the indwelling Spirit of God?*

The point that Paul is making is that our bodies, which once were the instrument of indwelling sin, must now be consecrated to God, as an instrument for his service. The idea of our whole being is clearly present when we take verse 2 closely with verse 1: the dedication of the body and the renewal of the mind will together effect that transformation which is involved in the approval and performance of God's holy will.

Rom. 14:1. *A translation of Rom. 14:1 reads: "Although in his faith a man shows weakness, I bid you welcome him to your society without desiring to contest his opinions." Is this correct?*

I think the words quoted are a fair paraphrase of the verse and bring out the sense. A man whose weakness of faith is of the kind described in the following verses of the chapter will not be helped by argument and debate, but rather by being welcomed into a Christian fellowship where, under the Spirit's influence, he can grow into a greater appreciation of the liberty with which Christ has made him free.

Rom. 14:5. *In Rom. 14:5 the observance of special days is evidently the mark of a weak brother. But should we not esteem the Lord's Day above the other days of the week?*

We may esteem the Lord's Day because of the special opportunities of worship, fellowship and witness which it affords. We may voluntarily devote it in a special way to God as part of our "reasonable service", thus acknowledging that all our time is His, just as the special devotion of part of our income to God is an acknowledgment that all our income is His. But this is a very different matter from observing the Lord's Day (or any other day) in a spirit of legal bondage, and criticizing those who do not observe it as we do. It is this spirit that characterizes the weak brother.

Rom. 14:8. *In Rom. 14:8, what does it mean to "die to the Lord"?*

In the previous verse the apostle says: "none of us lives to himself, and none of us dies to himself"—that is to say, in life and death alike our ways are in the Lord's hands, to be directed by His will and for His glory. Having stated the principle negatively in verse 7, he reinforces it by stating it positively in verse 8. The Christian's life is at the Lord's disposal; so is the Christian's death; in living and in dying he belongs to the Lord.

Rom. 14:15. *Do Rom. 14:15 ("destroy") and 1 Cor. 8:11 ("perish") teach that a saved soul can be lost?*

No: the apostle means that a weaker brother's peace of heart may be lost and his Christian growth and testimony ruined if he does something which he has seen another Christian doing, although his own conscience condemns it. The kind of behaviour envisaged is quite permissible in itself, but the "stronger brother" is advised to restrict his personal liberty in such a matter if his example is going to cause such spiritual harm to a "weaker brother."

Rom. 15:16. *The mention, in R.S.V. and N.E.B., of "priestly service" in Rom. 15:16 has been made the ground of a charge of Romanizing or sacerdotal tendencies in these versions. Is this charge justified?*

No; it is the result of ignorance or of something worse. The fact is that "priestly service" is precisely the sense conveyed by the verb *hierourgeo*, which Paul uses here. W. E. Vine, who would not be suspected of sacerdotal tendencies, makes this explicitly clear in his *Expository Dictionary of N.T. Words* iii, p. 74: the word, he says, "is used by Paul metaphorically of his ministry of the Gospel . . .; the offering connected with his priestly ministry is 'the offering up of the Gentiles', i.e. the presentation by Gentile converts of themselves to God."

Rom. 16:26, *etc. Are the "prophets" of Rom. 16:26 and Eph. 2:20 Old Testament or New Testament prophets?*

I take the "prophetic writings" of Rom. 16:26 to be those of the Old Testament; here, as in Rom. 1:2 and 3:21, the apostle insists that the gospel which he proclaims, with its message of justification by faith, is no new-fangled doctrine, but one taught in the Old Testament. The closing doxology of Romans (16:25-27) largely recapitulates the prefatory verses of Ch. 1. The gospel is called a "mystery" in 16:25 because, while it is anticipated in the Old Testament, its full manifestation had to wait for the redemptive work of Christ. There is no reason to suppose that

any prophetic scriptures other than those of the Old Testament were in existence when Paul wrote to the Romans. In Eph. 2:20, on the other hand, I take "the foundation of the apostles and prophets" to refer to the foundational part played in the primitive Church by Christian apostles and prophets; the persons intended are the same as those mentioned in Eph. 3:5 where we are told that the "mystery of Christ"—the inclusion of believing Gentiles with believing Israelites as fellow-members of the body of Christ— "was not made known to the sons of men in other generations as it has now been revealed to his holy apostles and prophets by the Spirit." That Gentiles as well as Israelites would be blessed in Christ was foretold in Old Testament times, as is evident from Rom. 15:8-12; that their blessing would involve full incorporation into Christ was not revealed until after Christ came, when it was made known to Christian apostles and prophets (preeminently to Paul), and through them to the Church at large. A further reference to Christian apostles and prophets occurs in Eph. 4:11.

1 Corinthians 1:12. *Why does Paul in 1 Cor. 1:12 appear to criticize those people who said "I am of Christ"? Is not every Christian entitled to say "I am of Christ"?*

Of course he is. But Paul was criticizing those who said "I am of Christ" in a sense which implied that many of their fellow-Christians were not "of Christ", or at least not so completely "of Christ" as they themselves were. This appears from his indignant question "Is Christ divided?" (1 Cor. 1:13), and also from the wording of 2 Cor. 10:7, "If any man trusteth in himself that he is Christ's, let him consider this again with himself, that, even as he is Christ's, so also are we."

1 Cor. 2:8. *Are "the rulers of this world" in 1 Cor. 2:8 angelic or human rulers?*

Primarily, I believe, they are the principalities and powers of Col. 2:15 who were disarmed and vanquished by our Lord when they assailed Him on the cross. I should not exclude the human rulers—Pilate, Caiaphas, and others—entirely from 1 Cor. 2:8 (compare Acts 3:17); but in so far as they are included, they are the agents of higher and more malign powers than themselves. (We may compare the "world rulers" of Eph. 6:12.)

1 Cor. 2:14. *Is "unregenerate" a proper translation of Gk. psychikos in 1 Cor. 2:14, or does it partake of the nature of commentary?*

This word (rendered "natural" in A.V. and R.V.) is a very difficult word to translate. The translator has first to decide what Paul meant by it, and then choose an English expression which best expresses Paul's meaning. To invent an English adjective "soulish" does not really help, because we shall have to determine what "soulish" means in this context. "Psychic", the English adjective derived from the Greek word, has a peculiar meaning which is out of the question here. The same word is translated "sensual" in Jas. 3:15 (A.V., R.V.), but in modern English "sensual" has a meaning which is not implied by Gk. *psychikos*. Perhaps the French *homme moyen sensuel* comes nearer it; the man in question is one who judges things by the evidence of his senses. Whether he is unregenerate or not is not stated; but if the adjective is to be rendered in English by a negative form, "unspiritual" (R.S.V., N.E.B.) has better warrant from the context than "unregenerate." It would be precarious to imply that regenerate Christians never form judgments on the evidence of their senses and never adopt worldly standards instead of spiritual ones.

1 Cor. 2:16. *When Paul says in 1 Cor. 2:16 "But we have the mind of Christ" does he mean Christians in general, or (more restrictedly) himself and his fellow-apostles or his immediate associates? Does "we" have the same force here as in verses 7, 10, 12 and 13?*

In verse 16 he probably means "we who are spiritual." In the whole paragraph, verses 6-16, "we" means at times "we apostles" or "we who preach and teach the truth" (especially where he says "we speak"), but it tends to expand its scope to embrace all those who are spiritual (e.g. in verse 12).

1 Cor. 4:3. *In 1 Cor. 4:3 Paul says, "I do not even judge myself"; in 1 Cor. 11:31 he says, "if we judged ourselves truly, we should not be judged." Is there a difference between the two kinds of judging?*

Yes; two different words are used. In the latter place R.V. renders, "if we discerned ourselves." There the apostle is emphasizing the necessity of self-examination and self-discipline in the presence of God, so that His judgment may not fall on us for sins tolerated in our lives. In the former passage he is affirming his independence of those who presumed to pass judgment on his apostolic authority and ministry. They have no jurisdiction in this matter, he says; even I myself am not competent to assess the quality of my apostolic service and pronounce a verdict on it; only One can do that, and I shall submit myself to His decision: "It is the Lord who judges me."

1 Cor. 5:5. *What is meant by "delivering to Satan" in 1 Cor. 5:5 and 1 Tim. 1:20?*

We have fuller details in 1 Cor. 5:5 than in the other passage. The incestuous man whose continued presence in the Corinthian church was such a scandal had not only to be excommunicated, but by the apostle's direction the solemn words had to be pronounced by the church when it met to deal with him: "We deliver So-and-So to Satan for the destruction of the flesh, that his spirit may be saved in the day of the Lord Jesus." If a righteous man like Job was "delivered to Satan for the destruction of the flesh", in order that it might be proved that he feared God for God's own sake and not for any material benefits that his piety brought him, how much more might not a sinful man be delivered to Satan, in order that physical affliction might bring him to repentance and turn out for the good of his soul? In either case Satan could take action against the man's body only by God's permission. The ultimate purpose in 1 Tim. 1:20 is also beneficial—that the two false teachers might be brought to a sounder way of thinking and learn not to blaspheme. This was an extreme exercise of the apostolic authority of binding and loosing; we should not dare to do anything of the kind. Yet there is evidence which suggests that God Himself sometimes disciplines offenders against the unity or purity of the church in this kind of way, in response to His people's prayer to Him to deal with a situation which is beyond their scope; and thus we are taught the salutary lesson that "if anyone destroys God's temple, God will destroy him" (1 Cor. 3:17).

1 Cor. 6:4. *Who are the people in 1 Cor. 6:4 who are "least esteemed in the church" (A.V.) or "of no account in the church" (R.V.)?*

They are probably people who have no status in the church at all—the unbelievers before whom the Corinthian Christians were going to law with one another. We should in that case translate either by an indignant question, as R.V. does ("do ye set them to judge who are of no account in the church?"), or by an equally indignant exclamation, as in Moffatt's rendering: "And yet, when you have mundane issues to settle, you refer them to the judgment of men who from the point of view of the church are of no account!" The R.S.V. and N.E.B. renderings concur with this interpretation. The

only feasible alternative is to take the words as a command: "lay them before those church members who are least esteemed"; they may not be qualified for the more serious responsibilities of church government, but they are quite competent to deal with trivial disputes like these. If this sounds ironical, the irony may have been intentional, in view of Paul's statement (verse 5) that he says this to make them feel ashamed of themselves.

1 Cor. 7:7. *When Paul says in 1 Cor. 7:7 that he wishes that all men were as he himself is, does this necessarily mean that he had never been married? Would it not have been necessary for him to be married in order to be a member of the Sanhedrin?*

Quite apart from the question of his membership of the Sanhedrin, it was the regular practice for an orthodox Jew brought up as Paul was to be married at quite an early age (at 18, said the second-century Rabbi Judah ben Tema). Paul's language in 1 Cor. 7 does not require us to suppose that he had never married. There are two other possibilities: (i) that he was a widower, (ii) that his wife left him at his conversion; in either case (i.e. after the death or departure of his wife) he remained celibate. The language of 1 Cor. 7 would be satisfied by any one of these three conditions; in the absence of more positive evidence we cannot say which corresponds to the actual situation.

1 Cor. 7:15. *When Paul says in 1 Cor. 7:15 that "the brother or the sister is not under bondage in such cases" (i.e. where the unconverted wife or husband refuses to go on living with the converted partner), does this imply that the deserted party is free to remarry?*

That seems to be the implication; the marriage bond entered into before conversion is no longer binding if the unconverted partner terminates it on the conversion of the other. It is, of course, an undesirable situation; the converted partner will naturally do everything possible to bring about a reconciliation of the other, in the hope, that, if the other is reconciled, he or she may be won for the same Lord as the converted partner has learned to follow. But if the unconverted partner's refusal to go on with the marriage relationship is final and unalterable, "in such cases the Christian husband or wife is under no compulsion" (N.E.B.). Such is the natural interpretation of the passage. But could one ever be sure that the unconverted partner's refusal to go on with the marriage relationship is final and unalterable? One could, it is evident, where the unconverted partner takes the initiative in divorce and remarriage. It would be difficult to find fault with the converted partner for remarrying in these circumstances.

1 Cor. 7:16. *In 1 Cor. 7:16 is the salvation of the unbelieving marriage-partner held out as "a probability" or an "improbability"?*

The language in itself is ambiguous. Paul has said, "If the unbelieving departeth, let him depart." The believing partner might reply, "Yes, but if I refuse to let him (her) depart, I may win him (her) for the Lord." Paul answers, "But how do you know?" This interpretation is perhaps implied by R.S.V. But the more optimistic interpretation is possible and in the context (I think) preferable. This takes Paul to mean: "If the unbelieving partner is content to remain, let him (her) remain. After all, you (the believing partner) may be his (her) salvation." In the light of Old Testament usage, "how knowest thou whether" may be a way of saying "perhaps"; compare 2 Sam. 12:22; Est. 4:14; Joel 2:14; Jonah 3:9. This interpretation is preferred by N.E.B. and in the context of Paul's apostolic concern I find it the more probable. A mixed marriage of the kind he has in mind is fraught with missionary potentiality.

1 Cor. 7:21. *In 1 Cor. 7:21 what is the force of "use it rather" (R.V.)? I see that it is taken in two contrary senses.*

Again, the wording in itself is ambiguous. R.S.V. text renders, "if you can gain your freedom, avail yourselves of the opportunity", but the footnote alternative is "make use of your present condition instead." Similarly, N.E.B. text has, "if a chance of liberty should come, take it", but the footnote alternative is "even if a chance of liberty should come, choose rather to make good use of your servitude." I prefer the text of both versions to the footnote, partly because it is supported by the tense (aorist) of the imperative "use" (Gk. *chrēsai*), which implies not the continuing of an established attitude but the response to a new turn of events, and partly because this interpretation is more in line with the principle of verse 23, "become not bondservants of men."

1 Cor. 7:25ff. *In 1 Cor. 7:25-38 R.S.V. translates* parthenos *or its plural by "unmarried" (verse 25), "girl" (verses 28, 34), "betrothed" (verses 36, 37, 38). Is not this variation confusing?*

Yes. A further source of confusion is the fact that "unmarried" is used elsewhere in the chapter to render (properly) another Greek word, *agamos*. It is most probable that in the discussion on virgins in verses 25-38 the same category is in view throughout; R.S.V. probably gives the right interpretation on the three occasions when it uses "betrothed" (although this is not a literal rendering), and it might have been well to indicate that this is what is meant in verses 25, 28 and 34 as well.

1 Cor. 7:36ff. *In the course of revising a translation of 1 Corinthians we are faced with the problem of the word "virgin" in 7:36-38. We could, of course, simply render "virgin", as in A.V., but this is too vague. The question then lies between the interpretations "virgin daughter" (as in R.V.), "betrothed" (as in R.S.V.), and* *"married virgin" (i.e. a married woman who, by agreement with her husband, remains a virgin after marriage, living with him in a state of* mariage blanc). *Can you supply any help here?*

We are at a disadvantage here compared with the Corinthians. They knew what the apostle was speaking about, for it was they who had asked the question which he begins to answer at v. 25 ("Now concerning virgins . . ."). But we are in the position of people listening to one end of a telephone conversation; we have to infer what is being said at the other end in order to reconstruct the situation for ourselves. I do not think that a condition of "married virginity" is in view: "let them marry" (v. 36) would hardly be the language used for bringing this situation to an end. The question is, then, whether Paul, in speaking of a man's behaviour to his "virgin", is thinking of a father's duty towards his unmarried daughter, or of a young man's duty towards his fiancée. If the former, the question is: "should he give her to someone in marriage or keep her under his own roof"? If the latter, the question is, "Should he marry her, or should they remain 'partners in celibacy' (N.E.B.)—i.e. in a state of permanent and chaste betrothal?" (This latter situation seems unnatural to us, but it would not necessarily have seemed so to first-century Gentile Christians.) The decision between the two alternatives is complicated by the fact that the verb rendered "marry" in v. 36 is the ordinary word for marrying, which would suggest the latter interpretation; but the verb rendered "giveth . . . in marriage" twice in v. 38 (R.V.) is normally used of a father's giving his daughter in marriage, but is also occasionally used of a bridegroom's marrying a bride, and is so rendered in R.S.V. On the whole, I agree with R.S.V. in taking the reference to be to a man's duty toward his fiancée, because the general tenor of vv. 25-38 seems to point in this direction; the language of the passage is hardly that

which would naturally be used of a father and his unmarried daughter. You are right in being dissatisfied with the bare rendering "virgin"; a translator must make an effort to understand and reproduce the author's meaning.

1 Cor. 10:4. *In 1 Cor. 10:4 is Paul following the rabbinical tradition that the rock which supplied the Israelites with water followed them about during their wilderness wanderings, so that it was available both at the beginning of their wanderings (Ex. 17:6) and towards the end (Num. 20:7)?*

No; in the rabbinical legend it was a literal rock that followed them; in 1 Cor. 10:4 it is a "spiritual rock"—Christ Himself, as Paul expressly says. That is to say, Christ accompanied His people in the wilderness. (The pronoun "them" is not expressed after "followed" in the Greek text of 1 Cor. 10:4 but it is implied.) There is a significant parallel to Paul's statement in Jude 5, where the true text probably affirms that *"Jesus,* having saved a people out of the land of Egypt, afterward destroyed those who did not believe."

1 Cor. 10:16. *At the Lord's Table we frequently hear the expression "the cup of blessing" (1 Cor. 10:16), but where the words of our Lord Himself are quoted it is "the new covenant in my blood" or "my blood of the (new) covenant." Why the difference, and what is the new covenant?*

Paul calls it the "cup of blessing" because over it a blessing or thanksgiving is said (i.e. God is blessed or thanked for providing it). In Jewish usage the cup of blessing, at the end of a meal, is so called because it accompanies the grace after meat. The communion cup was instituted by our Lord "after supper" (1 Cor. 11:25). When Paul says that in blessing God for the "cup of blessing" we are participating in the blood of Christ, he has in mind our

Lord's words of institution which make it clear that the cup symbolizes His blood. In 1 Cor. 11:25 we have our Lord's words; in 1 Cor. 10:16 we have the apostle's words, but the apostle's words are based on our Lord's words and set forth the same teaching. As for the new covenant, this is the new covenant foretold in Jer. 31:31ff., and fulfilled in the sacrifice of Christ (as is shown by Heb. 9:13ff.; 10:15ff.)—the covenant in which God erases His people's sins from the record and implants a new nature within them so that they do His will from the heart.

1 Cor. 11. *It has been held by some expositors that the eleventh chapter of 1 Corinthians is divided into two sections, the first of which ends at verse 16. Is there anything, in your judgment, to confirm this?*

It is a view held not only by some expositors but by most translators, too, for a paragraph division, roughly bisecting the chapter, appears at this point in R.V., A.R.V., R.S.V., Darby, Weymouth, Twentieth Century, Moffatt, Goodspeed, Knox and several others. Verse 1 is closely attached to the preceding chapter; verses 2 to 16 constitute a paragraph dealing with the relative status of men and women in creation and their deportment in the church; verses 17 to 34 form a separate section dealing with proper and improper behaviour at the Lord's Supper. There is a plain transition from one topic to another (even if a related one) at verse 17.

1 Cor. 11:4. *In orthodox Jewish synagogues today men cover their heads for prayer or Scripture reading. Does 1 Cor. 11:4 indicate that this was not the practice in New Testament times?*

It was quite evidently not the practice in the synagogues which Paul frequented; he regards it as a matter of course that

men should pray bare-headed. What is now the established practice among orthodox Jews is certainly very ancient, but plainly it was not in force—or not universally in force—in the decades preceding A.D. 70. There is no evidence of any specific regulation for either men or women with regard to headgear in synagogue in the New Testament period. Among the Greeks it was always regarded as proper for men to worship bare-headed.

In certain lands the veiling of women is a custom which is part of their bondage to a false religion. Therefore on conversion and baptism many of them put aside the veil. In the light of Paul's reference to the veiling of women in 1 Cor. 11:5ff. is this putting aside of the veil contrary to Scripture?

No: if the veil is a symbol of bondage, it ought to be put away. As with so many other external matters, the important thing is not the veil itself, but what it signifies. In the situation with which Paul was concerned, the significance of the veil was quite in keeping with biblical teaching about the status of women; accordingly it was to be retained. But in the kind of situation to which you refer, its significance is contrary to biblical teaching, and therefore it is best to discontinue its use.

1 Cor. 11:6. *In 1 Cor. 11:6 what is the difference between the terms "shorn" and "shaven"?*

To be "shorn" (Gk. *keirō*) means to have the hair cropped close; to be "shaven" (Gk. *xyraō*) means to have it shaved off with a razor. You may find an example of each of the two in Acts, in connexion with a temporary Nazirite vow; in Acts 18:18 Paul had his head "shorn" (i.e. cropped close), while in Acts 21:24 the four members of the Jerusalem church were to have their heads "shaved." This suggests that there was little to choose between the two operations.

1 Cor. 11:10. *In what sense was a woman's veil a sign of authority (1 Cor. 11:10)?*

It was a sign of her personal authority in Christ: not of her submission to her husband's authority, as some commentators have held, nor even of her social dignity and freedom from molestation. In the synagogue service a woman could play no significant part; her presence would not even suffice to make up the quorum of ten (all ten must be males). In Christ she stood on an equality with man; she might pray or prophesy in meetings of the church, and her veil was a sign of this new authority; its ordinary social significance was thus transcended. The angels are envisaged as present at meetings of the church, receiving from the demeanour of the worshippers insight into the character of the new order which God has instituted "in Christ." (See p. 247.)

1 Cor. 11:15. *From 1 Cor. 11:15 it may be inferred that if a woman has long hair, that is her covering, and that therefore she may consider her head covered when praying or, for that matter, covered at any time. Does the language not imply that with long hair, no other covering is required, and that it is with short hair that one is necessary?*

If 1 Cor. 11:15 stood alone, one might easily draw your inference from Paul's statement that a woman's hair "is given her for a covering." But it is not so easy to deduce this meaning from it when we take it along with the earlier part of the chapter. The covering of verse 15 is the one that nature provides; that referred to in the earlier verses is a veil (two different Greek words are used). So the argument seems to be: since nature itself indicates that a woman's head should be covered by providing her with long hair, let her imitate nature and veil her head; if she refuses to wear a veil, let her carry her refusal to its logical conclusion and remove nature's covering as well, by cropping her hair short.

1 Cor. 11:24. *Please comment on the following note in the Tyndale New Testament Commentaries on our Lord's words, "This is my body" (1 Cor. 11:24): "On the other hand, they should not be minimized into giving us a 'Zwinglian' view, that the service is nothing more than an occasion when we think of Christ. There is a very real gift of the Saviour in the sacrament, none the less real for being essentially spiritual."*

By the "Zwinglian" view of the Lord's Supper is meant the view which regards our observance of it as an act of remembrance and nothing more. Now, it is true, as Charles Hodge says in his exposition of the words "in remembrance of me," that "this is the specific, definite object of the Supper, to which all other ends must be subordinate, because this alone is stated in the words of institution." You quote these words in your question, but it is useful to see what Hodge regarded as included in this stated object: "It is of course involved in this, that we profess faith in him as the sacrifice for our sins; that we receive him as such; that we acknowledge the obligation which rests upon us as those who have been redeemed by his blood; and that we recognize ourselves as constituent members of his church and all believers as our brethren. We are thus, as taught in the preceding chapter, brought into a real communion with Christ and with all his people by the believing participation of this ordinance." So Hodge gives a very comprehensive content to the word "remembrance", and rightly so. For "remembrance" or "memorial" in the biblical sense goes far beyond the mental act of remembering. The defect of the "Zwinglian" view (whether it is rightly attributed to Zwingli or not need not concern us here) is that while it properly stresses the character of the Lord's Supper as a memorial, it does less than justice to our Lord's words "This is my body" and "This is my blood", and to the apostle's words that the cup is "a participation in the blood of Christ" and the bread "a participation in the body of Christ" (1 Cor. 10:16, R.S.V.). The "Zwinglian" view cannot account for the fact that those who partake of the one loaf are by that token "one body" (1 Cor. 10:17). It is a matter of common Christian experience that Christ in His Supper communicates Himself to the believer in a special way—not in any external or material sense but spiritually, and to faith. And it is because we participate by faith in Him that we constitute one body in Him and are members one of another. This is probably why the expositor you mention judges the "Zwinglian" view insufficient.

1 Cor. 11:29. *I was surprised recently, in listening to an exposition of 1 Cor. 11:29, to hear the words "not discerning the body" explained as referring to the church. Surely, in view of the context, this is not so, is it?*

Both in 1 Cor. 11:17-34 and in 1 Cor. 10:14-22 it appears that Paul understands the bread which we break as referring not only to our Lord's personal body in which He was crucified and rose again, but also to "the church which is His body." In Ch. 10 this is plain from his words: "The bread which we break, is it not a participation in the body of Christ? Because there is one bread, we, who are many, are one body, for we all partake of the one bread" (verses 16, 17). As for Ch. 11, the point is this. When the Corinthian Christians came together, their behaviour made it impossible for them to take the Lord's Supper in any proper sense. They took it in the course of a fellowship meal, and that was all right. But what was not all right was that the meal was not really a fellowship one, although that was its original intention, because instead of sharing out the food and drink which they brought, the wealthier members ate and drank it themselves, while the poorer members, who had little or nothing to bring, had to go hungry. This was an outrageous denial of Christian fellowship; in other words, it was a failure to "discern the body" which made a mockery of the Holy Communion when the time came to break the memorial bread.

1 Cor. 11:30. *In 1 Cor. 11:30 J. B. Phillips (in Letters to Young Churches) interprets Gk. koimaomai as "spiritual sleep." Is this a permissible translation?*

Permissible but improbable, I should say. Dr. Phillips renders the verse: "It is this careless participation which is the reason for the many feeble and sickly Christians in your Church, and the explanation of the fact that many of you are spiritually asleep." But the context requires something different from a reference to a spiritually unhealthy condition resulting from the Corinthian Christians' unworthy participation in the Lord's Supper. "As there is nothing in the context to intimate that these terms are used figuratively of moral infirmities and spiritual declension, they should be taken in their literal sense. Paul knew that the prevailing sickness and frequent deaths among the Christians of Corinth were a judgment from God on account of the irreverent manner in which they had celebrated the Lord's supper" (C. Hodge). As for the word *koimaomai*, it occurs 18 times in the N.T. In four instances literal sleep is meant; in all the others (leaving 1 Cor. 11:30 out of consideration for the moment) it denotes death. Since literal sleep is out of the question here, it looks as if death is intended.

1 Cor. 12:8ff. *Are the nine gifts of the Spirit set forth in 1 Cor. 12:8-20 available for believers today, or were they withdrawn in apostolic times?*

I should say that they are available today where the Spirit, who distributes His gifts according to His sovereign good pleasure, sees that the situation calls for them. It is true that, according to 1 Cor. 13:8-10, prophecies, tongues and knowledge are to be done away, but only "when the perfect comes." The perfect has not come yet. Some of the gifts enumerated are exceptional in character, and the course of Christian history suggests that they are manifested more particularly at the beginning of some new advance of the kingdom of Christ. They were manifested supremely in the apostolic age, and they have tended to reappear subsequently where similar conditions to those of the apostolic age have reproduced themselves. The literature of the period immediately following the apostolic age makes it plain that they did not come to a full stop with the close of the apostolic age.

1 Cor. 12:10. *Does the gift of prophecy (1 Cor. 12:10) refer to prediction or only to exposition?*

I do not think we can tie it down to one form of utterance. It might take the form of prediction, as it did with Agabus (Acts 11:28; 21:10, 11); it might take other forms. If we think of New Testament prophecy as the declaration of the mind of God in the power of the Spirit, we shall not go far wrong.

1 Cor. 12:13. *In 1 Cor. 12:13 who is the actual baptizer? When did the baptizing take place?*

"In one Spirit were we all baptized into one body . . ."—by whom? By Christ, surely, in fulfilment of John the Baptist's words, "he shall baptize you in the Holy Spirit . . ." (Matt. 3:11; Luke 3:16, A.R.V.). Compare also Acts 1:5 ("you shall be baptized in the Holy Spirit not many days hence") with 2:33 ("having received from the Father the promise of the Holy Spirit, he [Jesus] has poured out this which you see and hear"). The baptism took place, presumably, at the time when the people addressed yielded their allegiance to Christ. It is striking that

Paul wrote these words to a community of Christians whom he had already described as "carnal" (1 Cor. 3:3); nevertheless, taking writer and readers together, he says "we all" were baptized in one Spirit.

1 Cor. 12:31; 14:1. *How are we to understand the term "covet" or "desire earnestly" with regard to spiritual gifts in 1 Cor. 12:31; 14:1, seeing that these are* charismata, *given by the Spirit according to His will, every member being "set" in the body as it has pleased God (cf. 1 Cor. 12:8, 11, 18)?*

The Corinthian church was greatly interested in the more spectacular but less edifying spiritual gifts. Paul counsels them to "desire earnestly the greater gifts" (1 Cor. 12:31)—those which minister to the upbuilding of the believing community. Every church might well cherish an earnest desire for these gifts, and pray God to bestow them. God's good pleasure in granting such gifts is not niggardly; we may be confident that the more we ask, the more we shall receive. But these injunctions seem to be directed to the church rather than to the individual member. On the other hand, when Paul is talking of love, he bids his readers not merely desire it earnestly but actively pursue it (1 Cor. 14:1). And while God in His gracious wisdom allocates His spiritual gifts variously to one and another, the pursuit of love is something that is enjoined upon all.

1 Cor. 13:8. *What is the "knowledge" which is to be "done away" according to 1 Cor. 13:8?*

It is certainly not the knowledge of God, for that knowledge, far from diminishing, will be realized in its fullness "when the perfect comes"; it is then, says Paul, that I shall "know even as also I have been known" (1 Cor. 13:12). The "knowledge" of 1 Cor. 13:8 is that *gnōsis* on which so many Corinthian Christians prided themselves—the esoteric "knowledge" of 1 Cor. 13:2 which enables its possessor to penetrate mysteries, and which, according to 1 Cor. 8:1, "puffs up" or inflates instead of building up. From its association with prophecies and tongues it appears to have been charismatic in origin and character, and thus different from one's personal acquaintance with God or the knowledge which comes through study and experience.

1 Cor. 14. *Is the fourteenth chapter of 1 Corinthians relevant to the present day?*

You will recall that, towards the end of that chapter, the apostle claims that what he writes is "the commandment of the Lord" (v. 37). It is unlikely, therefore, that his directions have lost their relevance. But it is plain what prompts such a question as yours: the greater part of the chapter is devoted to speaking with tongues and prophesying, which are not a practical issue in most churches today. The chapter, therefore, should not be treated as a "directory of public worship", laying down detailed regulations on procedure. But the way in which Paul deals with the activities of speaking with tongues and prophesying is worthy of attention; it reveals certain abiding principles of church procedure, two at least of which are given summary expression: "Let all things be done for edification" (v. 26) and "Let all things be done decently and in order" (v. 40).

1 Cor. 14:2ff. *Is there a difference between the tongues of 1 Cor. 14 and those of Acts 2?*

There is, I think a difference in detail, although both passages are concerned with Spirit-controlled glossolalia (if I may use the technical jargon). The difference is that the tongues of 1 Cor. 14 were "strange tongues" to the hearers (as the quotation of Isa. 28:11f. in 1 Cor. 14:21 implies), and so could not be understood unless they were interpreted;

the tongues of Acts 2 were foreign to the speakers, but immediately recognized by the hearers as the languages "wherein we were born" (verse 8).

1 Cor. 14:16. *What is the "room of the unlearned" in 1 Cor. 14:16? Does it refer to those outside the circle of fellowship, or does "unlearned" connote unregenerate?*

The Revisers' margin probably gives the idea most clearly; it suggests that here the "unlearned" (Gk. *idiōtēs*, as in Acts 4:13) refers to "him that is without gifts." In verse 16 the picture is that of a member of the church giving thanks to God in a tongue not understood by others. How can an "unlearned" brother—one who has neither the gift of tongues nor the gift of interpretation—say "Amen" intelligently to such thanksgiving, especially when there is no one present able to provide an interpretation in the common tongue? In verse 23 the reference is more probably to an outsider, not a church member, who on coming into a place where all were speaking in this unintelligible way (perhaps all speaking at once) would naturally conclude that he had strayed into a gathering of madmen. But if he came into a place where all were exercising the gift of prophecy—uttering in the common tongue words inspired by the Spirit of God—he would recognize and be convicted by the living and powerful word of God.

1 Cor. 14:18. *In view of Paul's claim in 1 Cor. 14:18, "I speak in tongues more than you all", how is it that we have no other reference to his using this gift?*

Presumably because this gift played no part in his *public* ministry (for the reason stated in 1 Cor. 14:19); when he says "one who speaks in a tongue speaks . . . to God" (1 Cor. 14:2) and "he who speaks in a tongue edifies himself" (1 Cor. 14:3), he probably reflects his personal experience. That is to say, his speaking with tongues belonged to the sphere of his private devotions. We should not have known of his possessing this gift even in 1 Cor. 14:18 were it not that his possessing it in an exceptional degree gives him an undeniable right to put it in its proper place in relation to other spiritual gifts. Had he said, "I don't possess this gift myself, and I don't think there is much to it", the enthusiasts would have had an easy answer. As it is, his claim to an unequalled endowment with the gift in a passage whose "entire drift . . . is such as to pour a douche of icecold water over the whole practice" has been well described as "a master-touch which leaves the enthusiasts completely outclassed and outmanoeuvred on their own ground" (H. Chadwick). So today, an attempt to place the gift of tongues in its true perspective would perhaps come best from someone who, like Paul, possesses it but does not attach undue importance to it.

1 Cor. 14:22. *The Revised Version of 1 Cor. 14:22 says that "prophesying is for a sign, not to the unbelieving, but to them that believe." Is the insertion of the words "is for a sign" justified? In other words, is prophesying to the believer the counterpart of tongues to the unbeliever?*

Something certainly has to be supplied after "prophesying" to fill out the sense. But it is questionable whether the words supplied in R.V. give the best sense, although they do preserve the balance of the sentence. In the light of Isa. 28:11f., which Paul has quoted in the preceding verse, the unbelievers intended are people who have ignored the message of God, when it was spoken by normal means, and now require to have it taught to them in a way which cannot be ignored (in the original Isaianic context, through the foreign-speaking Assyrian invaders). If prophesying is a sign to believers, it is not a sign in this sense, so that we cannot say that it is, for the believer, the counter-

part of tongues for the unbeliever. It is probably better to follow the A.V., "but prophesying *serveth* . . . for them which believe", or R.S.V., "while prophecy is not for unbelievers but for believers."

1 Cor. 14:26. *Does the context of 1 Cor. 14:26 suggest that the psalm-singing mentioned in that verse was a solo effort? The other activities mentioned were certainly of this character.*

Yes; I think that the brother who had "a psalm" came prepared to sing it to the others. I believe that in some places the practice has not yet died out, though the others usually join in if they know it.

1 Cor. 14:34. *Would the injunction of 1 Cor. 14:34 ("Let the women keep silence in the churches") apply to all meetings of the church where men are present? Would it apply, for example to a sister giving a report of her missionary service at a welcome home social gathering, or giving a "recitation"?*

To try to relate the injunction to occasions like these, which are not contemplated in the New Testament, involves an overlooking of the relevant differences between the Eastern Mediterranean of the first century and the western world of the twentieth. We do not have to go outside this epistle to discover that the injunction to silence is not absolute; the mention of women's praying and prophesying in 1 Cor. 11:5 speaks for itself, for it appears to envisage these activities at regular meetings of the church where men are present.

1 Cor. 14:36. *What is the meaning of 1 Cor. 14:36, "What! Did the word of God originate with you, or are you the only ones it has reached?"*

The questions are ironical; the Corinthian church was behaving as though it were the vehicle or recipient of a special revelation, which had not been granted to other churches; and Paul asks if this is really so. Something similar is implied in his remark earlier in the same letter: "we recognize no other practice, nor do the churches of God" (1 Cor. 11:16). In more respects than one the church of Corinth was out of step with the other churches, especially those founded by Paul, but it seemed to be taking the line that it was all the others that were out of step.

1 Cor. 15:52. *A preacher has pointed out that the Greek word translated "moment" in 1 Cor. 15:52 is* atomos, *from which our word "atom" comes, and argues that this means that the resurrection body will come into being through a change in the atomic structure of our present body. Is this so?*

This is a change from the claim, pressed in some circles from 1945 onwards, that the phrase "in a moment" really means "in the atomic age." But it is equally baseless. The Greek word *atomos* means "incapable of being cut", and Paul uses it here to indicate a division of time so brief that it cannot be subdivided farther, a "split second", if you like, or (to retain the perfectly correct rendering of our common versions) a "moment." This phrase says nothing whatsoever about the constitution of the resurrection body.

1 Cor. 16:22. *What is the meaning of "Maranatha" in 1 Cor. 16:22?*

It is an Aramaic phrase which found its way into the liturgy of the Church from its earliest days. If we divide it as *Maranatha*, it might mean "Our Lord has come." If we divide it as *Marana-tha* (and this is the more probable division), it means "Our Lord, come!" (*Maran* and *Marana* are alternative forms for "our Lord.") The invocation appears from its occurrence in the *Didache* (early post-apostolic age) to have been used especially at the Lord's Supper (in which our Lord's passion and His last advent are symbolically

brought together), and as for its perpetuation in the church of today, we have only to think of the frequency with which "O come, O come, Immanuel" is sung during Advent. It is in essence the same prayer as the "Come, Lord Jesus" of Rev. 22:20.

2 Cor. 2:5-8, *etc. Do you consider that the brother at Corinth who was disciplined according to 2 Cor. 2:5-8 was the incestuous man of 1 Cor. 5:1? And do we gather from 2 Cor. 12:21 that those who had sinned in the same way as the man of 1 Cor. 5, but not so flagrantly, were left undisciplined?*

It appears to me more probable that the man of 2 Cor. 2:5ff. was someone who had led the opposition to Paul, and done him some personal injury, than that he was the offender of 1 Cor. 5. It is plain from 1 Cor. 6:13-20 that Paul had reason to fear that other members of the Corinthian church were guilty of sexual irregularities, but the case of incest was so flagrant an outrage on public morality, even in a city with the reputation of Corinth, that it had to be dealt with promptly, before Paul was able to come to Corinth and take action in person. Between the writing of the two Corinthian epistles, Paul seems to have paid a visit to Corinth during which his apostolic authority was flouted by those opposed to him in the church. There was a disinclination to accept his direction that those guilty of "uncleanness and fornication and lasciviousness" should be disciplined; hence the language which he uses in 2 Cor. 12:21, written some time after this second visit to Corinth.

2 Cor. 3:1. *In the light of 2 Cor. 3:1, are we justified in maintaining the practice of exchanging letters of commendation, or do the words of this verse have specific reference to Paul alone, and does the phrase "as do some" bear any significance in this regard?*

100

In 2 Cor. 3:1 we are not dealing simply with letters attesting that the bearers are church members in good standing. Paul has in mind certain teachers who made their way to the Corinthian church, armed with letters attesting their authority and ability. "You don't expect *me* to come to you with a letter like that", he asks his own converts, "certifying that I am a recognized apostle, or at least an acceptable evangelist?" It is unlikely that he had specially in mind the letter which the Christians of Ephesus sent to Corinth asking the Christians of that city to give a welcome to Apollos (Acts 18:27); but that was a real letter of commendation. We may compare Paul's commendation of Phoebe (Rom. 16:1f.) and John's of Demetrius (3 John 12). My fellow-elders and myself would think it a grave dereliction of our duty if we allowed a member of our church to leave our neighbourhood for another without in some way commending him or her to the fellowship and hospitality of Christians there.

2 Cor. 5:8. *Paul's words in 2 Cor. 5:8 ("absent from the body . . . present with the Lord") are often quoted to mean that we go straight from life through death into the Lord's presence. But what of 1 Thess. 4:13-17, where it appears that not until the Lord has come and the dead in Christ are raised "shall we ever be with the Lord"? There are other scriptures that come to mind, some of which stress immediacy (e.g. Luke 23:43), while others imply a time of waiting (compare Matt. 27:52, 53). Can you make some comment on this?*

Before the death and rising of Christ those believers who looked for resurrection at the last day knew no other hope than this after death. In so far as they thought of an intermediate state between death and resurrection they thought of it as a time of waiting. Martha's hope for her dead brother was that he would "rise again in the resurrection at the last day"

(John 11:24). Our Lord, to whom she voiced this hope, did not contradict her; after all, He had taught this Himself (cf. John 6:39, 40, 44, 54). But He now taught her something more: that He Himself was the resurrection and the life, and that death had no power over those who were united to Him by faith. Throughout the New Testament, as the passages which you mention illustrate, this two-fold truth is emphasized. On the one hand, the hope of final resurrection is maintained undimmed. Resurrection means "the redemption of the body" (Rom. 8:23); it consummates Christ's redeeming work for all believers. What Paul taught "by the word of the Lord" in 1 Thess. 4:13-17 concerned the lot of the faithful departed at the advent of Christ; that passage says nothing about their lot at death, but this is the subject of 2 Cor. 5:1-8. In the latter passage Paul expresses the assurance that to depart this present life even before the day of advent and resurrection means to "be at home with the Lord"—something "very far better" (Phil. 1:23). Those who are "in Christ" and risen with Him in this life will not be separated from Him when they leave this mortal body; and all that is requisite for communicating with their new environment and enjoying the Lord's presence will be supplied: it has been prepared for them already.

2 Cor. 5:10. *How can a believer "receive good or evil, according to what he has done in the body" (2 Cor. 5:10) if God has blotted out his sins, cast them behind His back, into the depths of the sea, promised to remember them no more, and assured him that for those who are in Christ Jesus there is now no condemnation?*

Whether we are able or not to reconcile these two sets of passages to our own satisfaction, we must recognize that both kinds of statement are equally scriptural, and to emphasize one at the expense of the other is to do violence to the balance of truth. Of the fulness of the salvation which is ours by God's grace there is no doubt. Of the certainty of God's law of sowing and reaping, in the believer as in the unbeliever, in the life to come as in this life, there is equally no doubt. To take a simple case: when a man who has undermined his constitution by drunkenness is converted to Christianity, the new birth which he undergoes does not restore his body to a state of perfect health; the law of sowing and reaping continues to operate in this regard. Of if (which God forbid) a regenerate Christian falls into this or any comparable sin, the fact that he is a Christian does not mean that the law of sowing and reaping is suspended in his case. On the contrary, "the Lord will judge his people" (Heb. 10:30). We may think of those Corinthian Christians who were "weak and sickly" while others slept the sleep of death, because of their misbehaviour (1 Cor. 11:30); they were receiving "the things done in the body", but their eternal salvation was not placed in jeopardy thereby. Indeed, it might rather be safeguarded thereby, if we recall the judgment passed on another erring member of the same church, who was to be delivered "to Satan for the destruction of the flesh, that the spirit may be saved in the day of the Lord Jesus" (1 Cor. 5:5).

2 Cor. 5:14. *What could be advanced against the contention that Paul's statement in 2 Cor. 5:14, "therefore all died", has the effect that in Christ our substitute all are deemed to have suffered the penalty for sin and by His act the sin of mankind has been expiated? In that case no one can with justice be punished for sin; since this would involve a reduction of the efficacy of Christ's substitutionary death. Does not the comment on Rom. 5:15 in the Tyndale Commentary— "'the many' in each case being the great mass of mankind"—point to the same conclusion?*

The Tyndale commentary on Rom. 5:15 goes on to illustrate the point by quoting Calvin's conclusion "that the grace procured by Christ belongs to a greater number than the condemnation contracted by the first man." It will help us to grasp what is involved in the words "all died" in 2 Cor. 5:14 if we consider what is said in verse 15 about these same people. To live *to* Christ is the corollary of dying *with* Christ. There are other passages where Paul speaks about our involvement in the death and resurrection of Christ, and these passages, together with the present one, are mutually illuminating. Let the "all" of 2 Cor. 5:14 be construed as widely as possible—"in Christ", as Paul says lower down, "God was reconciling *the world* to himself"— but we still have to reckon with the possibility, mentioned in the same context, of "receiving the grace of God in vain" (2 Cor. 6:1). For all the provision for human need that the gospel makes, there are still those who choose to contract out of the salvation which it offers and thus forgo its benefits.

2 Cor. 5:20. *To whom is the apostle Paul speaking when he says, "We beseech you on behalf of Christ, Be reconciled to God" (2 Cor. 5:20)? Is this an appeal to the carnally minded Christians at Corinth?*

It is rather a summary of the appeal which he and his fellow-missionaries uttered as ambassadors of Christ. The pronoun "you" after "we pray" is no part of the original text; it is an insertion, italicized as such in the A.V. and R.V. Those whom God entreats by the apostles and whom the apostles beseech on Christ's behalf to be reconciled to God are the people to whom the gospel is proclaimed. The fact that some members of the church of Corinth were carnally minded does not alter the fact that they had heard and accepted the message of reconciliation.

102

2 Cor. 6:17. *In 2 Cor. 6:17 ("Come out from them, and be separate from them"), who are referred to by the word "them"— unbelievers or believers belonging to other associations?*

The unbelievers of verse 14, of course. The whole passage urges Christians not to compromise their faith and witness by making common cause with the idolatries and immoralities of paganism. The use of these words to justify ecclesiastical separation between Christians betokens a grotesque failure to read them in their context.

2 Cor. 9:15. *What is God's "unspeakable gift" of 2 Cor. 9:15?*

The gift of His Son, I have no doubt. Some commentators have thought that the grace of liberality bestowed upon the Christians referred to in Chapters 8 and 9, but the language is adequate only to that gift in which all God's other gifts are summed up and crowned.

Galatians 2:3. *Does Gal. 2:3 mean that Titus was circumcised, although no compulsion was brought to bear upon him?*

I do not think so. The apostle's language is somewhat ambiguous to us, because we do not know as much of the background as he and his Galatian correspondents did. But verses 4 and 5 are probably parenthetical. What Paul says is that when he and Barnabas went up to Jerusalem and took the Gentile Titus with them, the issue of compulsory circumcision was not even raised, although if the Jerusalem leaders had attached importance to this ceremony they would certainly have raised it with regard to Titus. Titus was plainly a test case. But in fact the Jerusalem leaders did not raise the question at all, nor did they exercise any authority over Paul or confer any commission upon him beyond what he already possessed. The mention of circumcision in verse 3, however,

reminds him of a later occasion when it *was* brought up, and so he says parenthetically in verses 4 and 5: "When the matter *was* raised at a later date, it was through some interlopers that it was raised, and for your sakes we made absolutely no concessions whatsoever to them" (I paraphrase and abridge his language).

Gal. 2:10. *When Paul says he was "forward" in remembering the poor (Gal. 2:10) does he mean that he took the lead in doing this?*

No; he means that he was eager to do this very thing; he had in fact, already shown his eagerness in the matter by helping to bring a gift from Antioch for the relief of the Jerusalem Christians in a time of famine (Acts 11:29f.; 12:25). And he continued to show the same zeal when he later organized a collection of money among his Gentile converts for the relief of the poverty of the Jerusalem church. "The poor" in Gal. 2:10, are, of course, those of the Jerusalem church.

Gal. 2:18. *What line of conduct on the part of a Christian preacher can justifiably be described as "building again the things which he destroyed"?*

If we have regard to the context of this expression in Scripture (Gal. 2:18), then we may say that a man who goes back to preaching salvation by law-keeping after preaching the gospel of grace deserves to have his conduct so described. The words could also be used of one who, like Paul, devotes his energy to building up the church after endeavouring to demolish it by persecution (Gal. 1:23).

Gal. 6:5. *What is meant by Gal. 6:5 ("for every man shall bear his own burden") in the light of verse 2 ("Bear one another's burdens")?*

According to Hogg and Vine's commentary on Galatians, verse 5 "is a reminder that each man must, at the Judgment-seat of Christ, answer for himself how he has discharged the obligations of discipleship." Verse 2, on the other hand, "indicates an opportunity for present service to Christ, in sharing the burdens of His people."

Gal. 6:12. *Why does Paul single out circumcision in Galatians for such strong denunciation? Did it acquire a meaning down through the years that it did not have when it was first instituted?*

No; circumcision in itself was a matter of indifference in Paul's eyes (Gal. 5:6; 6:15; cf. 1 Cor. 7:19). But the trouble-makers in the churches of Galatia were pressing the necessity of circumcision upon the believers there, and Paul saw clearly that this was the beginning of a system of legalism which undermined the gospel of grace.

Ephesians 2:1, 5. *In Eph. 2:1, 5 (where A.V. has "dead in trespasses and sins"; "dead in sins") is it being dead in sins or dead to sins (as in Rom. 6:2) that is meant?*

It is death in (or "by reason of") sins that is meant; in grammatical jargon, the dative is instrumental. In Eph. 2:1, 5, Paul is describing his Gentile readers' existing condition at the time when they were "quickened"; the death from which they were raised to new life with Christ was the death which was theirs through sin. The meaning is brought out with perfect accuracy in R.S.V.: "And you he made alive, when you were dead through the trespasses and sins in which you once walked"; the construction is the same as in Rom. 5:10, "while we were enemies, we were reconciled . . .". As in Rom. 5:10 our being enemies was the existing state from which we were reconciled to God, so in Eph. 2:1 our being dead through our sins was the existing state from which we were made alive with Christ.

Eph. 2:5. *Could the expression "with Christ" in Eph. 2:5 be alternatively rendered "through Christ" (the dative case being used in an instrumental sense)?*

I don't think we can take the dative as instrumental here, because it is so obviously governed by the prefix *syn-* in the verb *synezōopoiēsen* ("made us alive together") that "with Christ" is the only natural rendering. There is a further point worth considering in this passage, however; in Eph. 2:1-7 the death from which we were raised with Christ is our own death through our trespasses and sins; whereas in Rom. 6:2-11 it is our death with Christ, our death not *in* sin but *to* sin, from which we were raised with Him.

Eph. 2:8. *What is the gift of God in Eph. 2:8?*

The words "and this is not your own doing, it is the gift of God" are parenthetical; without them, the statement runs straight on: "For by grace you have been saved through faith; not of works, lest any man should boast." What is the point then of the parenthesis immediately following "faith"? Is it faith that is the gift of God? The fact that the Greek word for faith (*pistis*) is feminine, while the pronoun "that" is neuter here, is no barrier to regarding faith as the gift of God; the phrase "and that" is really adverbial. We may compare Phil. 1:28, "a clear omen . . . of your salvation, and that from God," where "that" is similarly neuter, while both "omen" (*endeixis*) and "salvation" (*sōtēria*) are feminine. Jerome, Chrysostom and Theodoret in antiquity, Westcott and Moule in more recent times take "and that . . ." in Eph. 2:8 as referring to "faith." But I am disposed to agree with Calvin and others who take the reference as being not merely to faith but to the subject-matter of the whole preceding clause; the gift of God is His salvation—salvation by grace through faith. It is true, of course, that we should never have exercised faith in Christ on our own initiative; it is the Holy Spirit who persuades and enables us to accept Him as He is offered to us in the gospel; but Paul is saying rather more than this in the present passage.

Eph. 2:21. *In Eph. 2:21 which rendering has the best authority—"the whole building", as in A.V. and N.E.B. (R.S.V. "the whole structure"), or "every building", as in R.V. margin (R.V. text, "each several building")?*

The evidence for and against the omission of the article is rather evenly balanced, although on the whole the case appears to be stronger for its omission. But there is some New Testament authority for the meaning "all", even when the article is absent, so that the rendering "all the building" would be possible whichever reading be preferred. The R.V. rendering suggests that Paul views the various segments of the edifice ultimately combining to produce the finished whole, but this is hardly consistent with the context of this epistle. The point is rather that he is speaking "not of the building as completed, i.e. 'the edifice', but of the building as still 'growing' towards completion. The whole edifice could not be said to 'grow': but such an expression is legitimate enough if used of the work in process" (J. A. Robinson). The whole building operation, that is to say, has the perfecting of a holy shrine for God as its goal.

Eph. 3:5. *In Eph. 3:5 could the phrase "to his holy apostles and prophets" be rendered "by means of his holy apostles and prophets"? In other words, could the dative case be understood as having instrumental force? If this were so, then the prophets could be Old Testament prophets, by means of whom God was now revealing things that they themselves had not understood?*

It is true that the dative case frequently has instrumental force, denoting the

instrument by which something is done. But when the thing in question is done through the instrumentality of a person or persons, the regular construction used is the preposition *dia* ("through") followed by the genitive case. A writer would be specially careful to use this construction to express the instrument or agent with a verb like "reveal", since the dative in association with such a verb as this almost inevitably denotes the party to whom the revelation is made. I should take the apostles and prophets here, as in Eph. 2:20 and 4:11, to be the New Testament apostles and prophets—this without prejudice to the question of the character and duration of the New Testament gift of prophecy.

Eph. 3:15. *What is meant by Eph. 3:15, "from whom the whole family (or 'every family') in heaven and earth is named"?*

The word translated "family" literally means "fatherhood" (see R.V. margin); and I understand the sense to be that all fatherhood is derived from the original, archetypal Fatherhood of God; the closer any fatherhood, natural or spiritual, approaches in character to God's perfect Fatherhood, the more truly does it manifest fatherhood as God intended it to be.

Eph. 3:19. *In Eph. 3:19, according to A.V., R.V., and R.S.V., "to know the love of Christ" is something additional to the things mentioned in verses 16, 17 and 18; in some recent versions (including the N.E.B.) the "breadth and length and height and depth" refer to the love of Christ. Is this correct?*

"To comprehend . . . what is the breadth and length and height and depth" is closely associated with knowing the love of Christ, but there is a distinction between them. I should say that it is the divine purpose ("the plan of the mystery") of verse 9 that is to be comprehended in its breadth, length, height and depth, in all its dimensions as it relates to the universe ("all things" of 1:10). But this divine purpose is so bound up with the knowledge-surpassing love of Christ that the comprehension of the former is impossible apart from the knowledge of the latter.

Eph. 4:5. *Is the "one baptism" of Eph. 4:5 baptism in water?*

So far as I can judge, yes. I suggest that baptism in the New Testament is always baptism in water unless the context shows it to be something else; that is to say, the word is always to be understood literally unless the context indicates a figurative meaning. Moreover, the sevenfold credal summary of Eph. 4:4-6 is divided into three rhythmically equivalent sections $(3 + 3 + 1)$, each of which is dominated by one of the Persons of the Godhead ("one Spirit . . . one Lord . . . one God and Father"). If the "one baptism" were baptism in the Spirit to the exclusion of baptism in water, it would naturally have come in the section introduced by "one Spirit" whereas it comes in the section introduced by "one Lord", alongside "one faith." This is appropriate to baptism in water, which involves a confession of faith in our one Lord.

Eph. 4:8. *What is meant by the statement in Eph. 4:8 that Christ, at His ascension, "led captivity captive"?*

The words are quoted from Psalm 68:18; a similar use of the expression is made in Judges 5:12. In these Old Testament passages the reference is to the train of conquered captives which the victor leads in his triumphal procession. A clue to the meaning of the phrase in Eph. 4:8 may be found in Col. 2:15 where Christ on the cross is viewed as vanquishing the hostile principalities and powers and making a public show of them. They, I suggest, form the "captivity" which in Eph. 4:8 He is said to have "led captive."

Eph. 4:11. *With regard to the "gifts" of Eph. 4:11 it has been said that "the apostles and prophets have long since passed away; they were divinely inspired men and there is not the slightest proof that such men exist today." Is this correct? If so, why is Paul the only apostle known to us who was thus "given"? Where do Barnabas, Andronicus and Junias, etc., come in?*

The apostles and prophets of Ephesians are the foundation on which the new temple is built (Eph. 2:20); this implies that they were given with special regard to the requirements of the New Testament church at its inception. One of the most important qualifications for an apostle was that he should be a witness to the resurrection of Christ (cf. Acts 1:22; 1 Cor. 9:1), and Paul was evidently the last to be so qualified (1 Cor. 15:8). Barnabas, Andronicus and Junias were all "in Christ" before he himself was (Acts 4:36; Rom. 16:7) and were presumably witnesses to the resurrection. When the term "apostle" is used of Christians of a later generation (as it is, e.g., in the *Didache*), it has the more general sense of "messenger" or "missionary." Similarly the church has (happily) never lacked men who declared the mind of God in the power of the Spirit (we can think of some today who exercise such a "prophetic" ministry in this sense), but the prophet in the special New Testament sense appears to have exercised a ministry specially appropriate for the "foundation" phase of the church's life.

Eph. 4:27. *What is the meaning of Eph. 4:27?*

The words "neither give place to the devil" (R.S.V., "give no opportunity to the devil") warn us that by giving way to unrestrained anger we are giving the devil a base of operations in our souls which he will not be slow to exploit. We should afford him no such opportunity. As a practical means of preventing him

106

from establishing a bridgehead of this kind in our lives, Paul (quoting Psalm 4:4) urges us to fix an early termination to our anger, and so be angry (if need be) without letting our anger degenerate into sin.

Eph. 5:9. *Which is the better reading in Eph. 5:9—"the fruit of the Spirit" (A.V.) or "the fruit of the light" (R.V.)?*

"The fruit of the light" appears to be better attested; besides, it fits the context better, forming a contrast with "the unfruitful works of darkness" mentioned in the next verse. "The fruit of the Spirit", which is the reading of the Western texts, has probably been influenced by the wording of Gal. 5:22.

Eph. 5:15. *Who first illustrated the phrase "walk circumspectly" in Eph. 5:15 by reference to a cat walking upon a wall topped with pieces of broken glass? Is it true that Paul uses the word from which "acrobatics" is derived?*

I have no idea who first used the illustration you mention, but one could wish that a moratorium of indefinite duration were placed on its further use. The adverb which A.V. translates "circumspectly" (Gk. *akribōs*) is attached in the most reliable texts not to "walk" but to "see" or "look" (cf. R.V., "Look therefore carefully how ye walk"; N.E.B., "Be most careful then how you conduct yourselves"). It has nothing to do with the word "acrobatics", which is derived from Gk. *akrobateō*, "walk on tiptoe" (*akros*, "tip", "extremity"; *bateō*, "walk"); it is the adverb associated with the adjective *akribēs*, "careful", "accurate."

Eph. 5:18. *If the Holy Spirit already indwells us, why does Paul enjoin us in Eph. 5:18 to "be filled with the Spirit"?*

Being filled with the Spirit implies more than being indwelt by Him. In some believers' lives He has little more than a foothold, because He is almost crowded out by a variety of concerns. Paul is eager that his converts should be under the undisputed control of the Spirit.

Eph. 5:19. *As the word "making melody" in Eph. 5:19 means properly "singing with musical accompaniment", even if it later came to denote singing with or without such accompaniment, do you think that Paul would have used such a word if he had been opposed to such accompaniment?*

The verb (Gk. *psallō*) means primarily to pluck the strings of an instrument, and its meaning develops as you have indicated. The noun for "psalm" (*psalmos*) in the same verse is derived from it. But I think that both words as used here by Paul are irrelevant to the question of instrumental accompaniment, one way or the other. The melody with which he is principally concerned is the melody of the heart, which accompanies the vocal singing. I take it that he refers to the primitive Christian practice of edifying one another in their church meetings by singing to one another, in solos or antiphonally. The words sung might be Old Testament psalms or early Christian hymns, or songs directly prompted by the Spirit. Whether one of the congregation accompanied himself or others on a lute or psaltery would not affect the essential purpose of this form of worship.

Eph. 5:24. *In Eph. 5:24, "as the church is subject", is the construction passive or reflexive?*

Reflexive, I should say. So far as the form itself goes, it might be either middle voice or passive, but in view of the context (the submission of wives to husbands being one particular instance of the submission of believers to one another, inculcated in verse 21) and of similar occurrences of the same construction elsewhere in ethical injunctions, the middle (reflexive) construction is probably to be understood: "to be subject (or submissive)", not "to be subjected."

Eph. 5:26. *The N.E.B. renders Eph. 5:26 ". . . cleansing it by water and word." Is this a correct rendering and, if so, what does it signify?*

It is a correct, though not a verbatim, rendering. I see that in my *Expanded Paraphrase of the Epistles of Paul* I have amplified the same phrase as follows: "cleansing her by the washing of water accompanied by the spoken word." This gives the same sense as the N.E.B. rendering, although it uses more words to express it. As for the significance, I can scarcely do better than quote from an article by Mr. Andrew Borland, Editor of *The Believer's Magazine*, which appeared in that periodical in September, 1954: "If 'having cleansed it with the washing of water with the word' is intended to signify what happened at baptism, then the idea is consistent with the association of purification with the symbolism of baptism. Each individual member of the Church had become dedicated to God at the time of his symbolic purification from sin; and what happened to each separate individual is said to have happened to the entire New Society." To which I would add that the accompanying "word" (Gk. *rhēma*) is probably not here Holy Scripture but the word of confession or invocation spoken by the convert, as in Ananias's words to Paul: "Rise and be baptized, and wash away your sins, *calling on his name*" (Acts 22:16).

Colossians 1:15. *A published statement that "Jehovah's first creation was His Son" is supported by a reference to Col. 1:15 ("the firstborn of all creation") and Rev. 3:14 ("the beginning of the creation of God"). What is the force of these scriptures?*

The term "beginning" in Rev. 3:14 marks Jesus out as the Divine Wisdom by whom God created the universe; it harks back to Prov. 8:22 ("the beginning of his work") and also, perhaps, to the "beginning" of Gen. 1:1. In Col. 1:15 Christ is called "the firstborn of all creation" for two reasons: (i) that He existed before all creation, as the firstborn exists before the rest of the family (in this sense the phrase anticipates "He is before all things" in verse 17); (ii) that all creation is His possession by inheritance as the Father's firstborn. The phrase, that is to say, connotes both primacy in time and supremacy in authority. The one in whom all things were created is not Himself a part of all created things; if that were so, we should have read that in Him all *other* things were created. Indeed, the *New World Translation* interpolates the word "other" at this point; the interpolation is necessary to make the passage mean what the sponsors of the translation believe, but it alters the original sense.

Col. 2:11f. *Does Col. 2:11f. suggest that New Testament baptism is the counterpart of Old Testament circumcision and so is the seal and sign of faith?*

Yes. It is, as Paul says in this very place, not the literal circumcision "made with hands", but the spiritual circumcision ("the circumcision of Christ"), that baptism expresses outwardly. That is to say, baptism is the external and visible sign of that inward cleansing which accompanies the believer's participation in Christ's death, burial and resurrection, "through faith in the working of God."

Col. 2:16. *A certain writer contends that in Col. 2:16 "the sabbath days" (A.V.) should be "weeks", and that the reference is to the meats and drinks associated with them in Old Testament times. What do you think?*

The proper rendering is quite certainly "a sabbath day" (R.V.; similarly R.S.V. and N.E.B.). The Greek word, whether it is used in the singular (*sabbaton*) or in the plural (*sabbata*), can be translated "week" in the New Testament only in certain phrases where the presence of a numeral makes that sense evident, such as "the

108

first day of the week" (i.e. the first day after the sabbath) or "twice in the week" (i.e. twice between one sabbath and the next.) In Col. 2:16 it is as plain as may well be that Paul is warning his readers against those who were trying to impose the observance of the Jewish sabbath on them.

Col. 3:3. *How is our life "hid with Christ in God" (Col. 3:3)?*

Here is J. B. Lightfoot's answer: "The Apostle's argument is this: 'When you sank under the baptismal water, you disappeared for ever to the world. You rose again, it is true, but you rose only to God. The world henceforth knows nothing of your life, and (as a consequence) your new life must know nothing of the world'." Since Christians live "in Christ", and Christ indeed is their true life, it is inevitable that their life should be securely preserved where He is.

Philippians 1:21. *When Paul says in Phil. 1:21, "For to me to live is Christ, and to die is gain", does he say so in special view of his being in bonds at the time, or is it a permanent principle for Christians (with particular reference to "to die is gain")?*

Perhaps Paul was especially conscious of the fact that death would be gain in view of his situation at the time. But anyone who can truthfully say "for me to live is Christ" can also say "to die is gain" because death leads to a fuller experience of the presence of Christ than is possible in this mortal life ("with Christ, which is far better"); yet he knows, as did Paul, that he is immortal till his work is done.

Phil. 2:6. *Can a good case be made out for understanding Gk. harpagmos in the sense of "retaining" in Phil. 2:6?*

I hardly think so. The basic idea of the word is seizing what one does not possess rather than holding on to what one

possesses already. Christ did not consider equality with God as a means of furthering His own interests (if we take the word in an active sense) or as something to be grasped at, as Adam did (if we take it in a passive sense). I prefer the active sense, but am aware that this is a minority view.

Phil. 2:6, 7. *Does Paul mean in Phil. 2:6, 7, that our Lord emptied Himself of equality with God to become a servant?*

No; what Paul means is that our Lord, far from exploiting His equality with God for His own advantage, spent Himself to the uttermost for the advantage of others. The phrase "emptied himself" (A.V., "made himself of no reputation") probably represents an independent Greek translation of the Hebrew words underlying "poured out his soul" in Isa. 53:12; indeed, if one wished to translate Paul's "emptied himself ... even unto death" into Hebrew, one could hardly find better words than the Hebrew original of "poured out his soul unto death" in that Old Testament verse.

Phil. 3:11. *Since the word for "resurrection" used by Paul in Phil. 3:11 appears here only in the New Testament, does it bear a different meaning from "resurrection" in the ordinary sense?*

Probably it does. This is indicated not so much by the fact that the word (*exanastasis*, literally "out-resurrection") is different from the usual word (*anastasis*), but much more by the context. Paul had no doubt that he would one day be raised from the dead, should he pass through death before the Advent; this is plain from such passages as 1 Cor. 6:14 and 2 Cor. 4:14. In the present passage he declares his desire to be conformed to Christ's death in his daily life that thus he may attain the resurrection from the dead. Both of these experiences are to be understood in the same sense as the language of 2 Cor. 4:10, 11. Paul endured many sufferings by reason of his apostolic service, and they might well have got him down, had he not learned to accept them as a sharing in the sufferings of Christ, so that the power of that risen life which was the sequel to Christ's sufferings might be his present experience too.

Phil. 4:3. *As there is no mention in any of Paul's epistles of the Lord Jesus as "the Lamb", or of "the Lamb's Book of life", what is the difference, if any between "the book of life" (Phil. 4:3) and "the Lamb's book of life" (Rev. 13:8)?*

It is not only Paul's epistles that do not give our Lord the designation "the Lamb"; no New Testament writings do so but those of John. Twice in the non-Johannine writings He is *compared* to a lamb: in Acts 8:32 (where Isa. 53:7 is quoted) and in 1 Pet. 1:19 (where He is the antitype of the Passover Lamb). But, by whatever title He may be called, the book of life is His, since He is the Lord of life and holds the keys of death and hades. It is only in Rev. 13:8 that the book is called "the Lamb's book of life"; in the parallel passage in Rev. 17:8 it is simply "the book of life", in which the names of the elect were inscribed "from the foundation of the world" (this suggests that the phrase "from the foundation of the world" in Rev. 13:8 goes with "written" and not with "slain"). In Rev. 3:5; 20:12, 15; 21:27, the same book is referred to as "the book of life" without any express mention of the Lamb; and it is the same book that Paul refers to in Phil. 4:3. The idea occurs elsewhere in the New Testament, without the actual word "book" appearing; cf. Luke 10:20 and Acts 13:48 (where "ordained" probably has the sense "enrolled" or "inscribed").

1 Thessalonians 4:16, *etc. Is the resurrection mentioned by Paul in 1 Thess. 4:16 and 1 Cor. 15:32 the "first" resurrection, including the patriarchs and prophets of ancient history, described by our Lord as "the resurrection of the just" (Luke 14:14) or does it comprise but a small part of the people of God, restricted possibly to those since the early church period?*

It is, in Paul's language, the resurrection of "those who belong to Christ" and will take place "at his coming" (1 Cor. 15:23). I see no reason for excluding from "those who belong to Christ" the patriarchs and prophets who lived and died in faith before He came but greeted His day from afar; they would certainly have been included by our Lord when He spoke of "the resurrection of the just."

1 Thess. 5:10. *What do waking and sleeping in 1 Thess. 5:10 mean ("that whether we wake or sleep, we should live together with him")?*

"Christ died for us, that whether alive or dead, we should live together with Him." So William Kelly paraphrases the verse—rightly, as I judge. The apostle is reiterating the truth taught at the end of Ch. 4. Kelly dismisses as trifling the view held by some that literal waking and sleeping are in view, and goes on: "But even this is not the lowest depth, for there have not been wanting men who wish the apostle to teach that the words bear the same ethical force in ver. 10 as in 6, 7; the necessary inference from which would be that, whether we be spiritually watchful or slothful, we shall alike enjoy the portion of everlasting blessedness together with Christ. Does not this sound uncommonly like moral indifferentism?"

1 Thess. 5:14, *etc. In 1 Thess. 5:14, where A.V. has "unruly" and R.V. "disorderly", R.S.V. renders "idle" (similarly in 2 Thess. 3:6, 7, 11). Is "idle" a new meaning for the word, and is the reference to manual work?*

"Idle" is a possible, but not invariable, meaning for the word that Paul uses (whether in its adjectival form *ataktos*, its

110

adverbial form *ataktōs*, or its verbal form *atakteō*). It is, however, the meaning implied by the context in 2 Thess. 3, and by analogy it is probably the meaning implied in 1 Thess. 5. The situation appears to have been that in the church of Thessalonica some members had been so carried away with excitement by the idea that the Second Advent was imminent that they saw no further need for carrying on their daily work. This meant that, since they were not earning their own livelihood, they became a burden on others. Paul condemns such conduct as a breach of good discipline—which is the basic sense of the word that he uses. No doubt in most, if not all, of the cases it was manual work that was involved, as it was with Paul himself, when he earned his own bread by tent-making; but the principle would be equally applicable to any form of daily work. It is part of Christian order that those who are able to do so should earn an honest living.

1 Thess. 5:19. *Please explain how a Christian can quench the Spirit and grieve the Spirit.*

The quenching of the Spirit (1 Thess. 5:19) would consist primarily in stopping the mouths of those who spoke by the spirit of prophecy. Hogg and Vine in their exposition give the paraphrase: "Do not prevent or obstruct the manifestations of the Holy Spirit's power in others." But it need not be restricted to manifestations of the Spirit in others; if I receive a message from God for others and refuse to utter it, that is also a quenching of the Spirit; Jer. 20:19 describes something of this sort. The grieving of the Spirit (Eph. 4:30) is to be understood in the light of the injunctions that immediately precede and follow. The practices (in thought, word and deed) which the surrounding verses tell us to put away are practices whose indulgence "grieves" the Spirit both in the life of the believer concerned and in the lives of others.

2 Thess. 2:6, 7. *Who first suggested that the restraining power of 2 Thess. 6, 7 was the Holy Spirit?*

So far as I know, it appears to have been Severian, bishop of Gabala in North Syria (*c.* A.D. 400), contemporary and opponent of Chrysostom.

2 Thess. 2:6, 7. *Further to the preceding question, do you suppose that the statement in the Scofield Bible on 2 Thess. 2:6, 7, that the restrainer "can be no other than the Holy Spirit in the church", was derived from Severian?*

No indeed; it is much more likely to go back to the cautiously expressed opinion of J. N. Darby that the restrainer is "the presence of the church on earth with the Holy Ghost dwelling in it" (*Collected Writings* XXII, p. 90). "The Fathers", Darby continues, "may have been right that the external hindrance then was the Roman empire. I can suppose Paul may even have spoken of this as the then hindrance; but by leaning on tradition they [the transmitters of patristic exegesis] went all wrong. The Holy Ghost for all ages taught only the general truth" (pp. 90, 91).

2 Thess. 2:6. *In 2 Thess. 2:6 R.S.V. takes "now" with the participle "restraining" ("you know what is restraining him now"). Is this right, in view of the fact that in Greek "now" does not come between the article and participle to* katechon, *but before the article?*

No; I don't think it is right. William Kelly's discussion of this point in his commentary on 1 and 2 Thessalonians is, I find, convincing. The adverb "now", he says, "is simply resumptive with *kai* ['and'], a particle of transition and not temporal, which is the less necessary as we have subsequently *ho katechōn arti* ['he who now restrains']", where *arti*, unambiguously meaning "now" in the temporal sense, comes after the article plus participle. He stigmatizes the construction adopted by R.S.V. as "a solecism"; this, perhaps, is going a bit too far, for while it would undoubtedly be a solecism if we were dealing with classical Greek, it is hardly so in Hellenistic Greek. Translate: "And now (i.e. 'and as it is') you know what restrains him, in order that he may be revealed in his proper season:"

2 Thess. 2:7. *In 2 Thess. 2:7 (where R.V. renders, "only there is one that restraineth now, until he be taken out of the way"), I understand that the right rendering of the Greek is ". . . until he comes out of the midst", referring to the emergence of Antichrist. Would you please comment on this, and also on the restrainer's identity?*

The suggestion that the clause "until he be taken out of the way" should be translated "until he comes out of the midst" is due to an imperfect acquaintance with Greek idiom. The words taken one by one may seem to yield this latter sense, but in fact the regular usage of the construction in Greek applies, as Alford says, to "any person or thing which is taken out of the way, whether by death or other removal." And this is the sense given in most translations of the passage. The identity of the restraining power, however, is another question. The widest variety of suggestions has been made, ranging from the Holy Spirit at one extreme to the devil at the other. One view, which has become fashionable of late, is that Paul's own ministry was the restraining force; that he meant that the man of lawlessness would not be manifested until his own apostolic course was completed. My own view is that Paul was referring to the forces of law and order which acted as a restraint on the forces of lawlessness for the time being; when the forces of law and order were removed, then the forces of lawlessness would break forth in the regime of the man of lawlessness. C. F. Hogg and W. E. Vine in their commentary on Thessalonians

favour the view that the apostle alluded to Gentile dominion, the course of which had been outlined by Daniel. In Paul's day Gentile dominion was wielded by the Roman Empire, which he acknowledged as "the servant of God, to execute his wrath on the wrongdoer" (Rom. 13:4). Paul himself had cause more than once to appreciate the protection which Roman law afforded him against those who opposed his missionary work. And if something of this sort is in his mind, it may explain his unusually reticent and allusive style in 2 Thess. 2:6f. If he meant the Holy Spirit, or his own apostolic ministry, he could have said so expressly. But it would have put the Thessalonian Christians in a very delicate situation if a letter addressed to them, containing an apparent reference to the prospective removal of the imperial sovereignty, fell into the hands of the police. It was only a few weeks since Paul was obliged to leave Thessalonica in a hurry because his accusers charged him with proclaiming "another emperor, one Jesus" (Acts 17:7); and more explicit wording at this point in his letter might have seemed to confirm the most sinister implications of that charge. On that occasion, Paul's friends in Thessalonica had given security for him, and he certainly did not wish to embarrass them again.

In the preceding answer, you indicate that the phrase in 2 Thess. 2:7 which some have rendered literally "come to pass out of the midst" is a Greek idiom for "be taken out of the way", as our common versions have it. Are there other instances of this idiom in the New Testament?

Two other examples come to mind. One is in 1 Cor. 5:2, "that he that had done this deed might be taken away from among you" (Gk. *ek mesou hymōn*, lit. "out of the midst of you"). The other is in Col. 2:14, "he hath taken it out of the way" (Gk. *ek tou mesou*, lit. "out of the midst"). In neither of these passages is the verb identical with that used in 2 Thess. 2:7, but examples are not lacking in Greek literature where *ek mesou* is used with that verb (*ginomai*, "become"), and always in the sense which our common versions give to 2 Thess. 2:7. There is a detailed and conclusive discussion of the idiom in William Kelly's exposition of Thessalonians at this place; after adducing a large number of classical examples he finds that "the ordinary version is unquestionably correct." If in fact the clause referred to the open emergence of Antichrist, or the manifestation of the mystery of iniquity, we should expect *eis to meson*, "into the midst" and not *ek mesou*.

2 Thess. 2:11. *What is "the lie" of 2 Thess. 2:11?*

"The lie" is the direct denial of "the truth" of verses 10 and 12; from the context of Rom. 1:25, where men are said to have "exchanged the truth of God for the lie," it appears that the essence of "the lie" is the ascription to a creature of the honour and worship that belong to God alone. So in 2 Thess. 2:4 the man of sin claims divine homage; those therefore who prefer "the lie" (that this creature is God) to "the truth" (that the Lord is God) give him the homage that he claims.

1 Timothy 1:18. *What would you suggest are "the prophetic utterances which pointed to" Timothy (1 Tim. 1:18)?*

They were probably utterances by Christian prophets in the church of Lystra and elsewhere at the beginning of Timothy's ministry which made it plain that he was divinely called to that ministry. The recollection of these prophecies would be an encouragement to him in the course of his ministry when other circumstances tended to discourage him. (See the answer on 1 Tim. 4:14, p. 116.)

1 Tim. 1:20. *Wherein lay the blasphemy of Hymenaeus and Alexander (1 Tim. 1:20)?*

We are not told explicitly in this passage wherein their blasphemy lay. They were two prominent men in a group of people who had made shipwreck of their faith through spurning the voice of conscience. That suggests that they were antinomians, teaching that believers should continue in sin that grace might abound (cf. Rom. 6:1). Such teaching was not only blasphemous in itself, but it gave occasion to others to blaspheme too. If it is the same Hymenaeus who appears in 2 Tim. 2:17, his antinomianism was accompanied by false teaching regarding the resurrection of believers: this, he taught, had already taken place. If the Alexander of 1 Tim. 1:20 is identical with the Alexander of 2 Tim. 4:14, then we learn further that he did the apostle a great deal of personal harm and opposed his teaching, but no details are given on these matters.

1 Tim. 2:1-5. *Calvin in his* Institutes *taught that 1 Tim. 2:1-5 does not mean that God wills the salvation of all men but that we should pray for the particular category of men mentioned because they are least likely to be saved—that is, He would have a sample from them. (Cf. 1 Cor. 1:26, 27.) Is not this a case of wresting the Scriptures?*

If we express our disagreement with someone's interpretation of a biblical passage, that is one thing; but if we describe that interpretation as a "wresting" of Scripture, we may be passing a moral judgment and exposing ourselves to the risk of being measured by the standard we use to measure others (Matt. 7:2). Calvin had in mind two basic principles of biblical interpretation: (i) each Scripture should be interpreted in the light of all Scripture; (ii) each Scripture should be interpreted in the light of its own context. With regard to the former, Calvin was not the first or the last expositor to find a difficulty in reconciling the statement that God desires the salvation of all with statements which suggest that He has elected some and not others. It is common form to say that "all" sometimes means "all without exception" and sometimes "all without distinction"; this is true, but if this differentiation is to be applied to the biblical occurrences of "all", it must be applied in the light of the context and not in accordance with the dogmatic framework within which the expositor works. Calvin does pay attention to the context; the apostle plainly makes the fact that God "desires all men to be saved" the reason for his injunction that "all men" should be prayed for. If it is true in general that our prayers should be in accordance with God's will, this kind of prayer is pre-eminently in accordance with it. When, later, Calvin wrote his commentary on the Pastoral Epistles, he said on this passage: "What is more reasonable than that all our prayers should be in conformity with this decree of God [viz. His desire for the salvation of all]? ... God has at heart the salvation of all, because He invites all to the acknowledgement of His truth. This belongs to that kind of argument in which the cause is proved from the effect; for, if 'the gospel is the power of God for salvation to every one who believes' (Rom. 1:16), it is certain that all those to whom the gospel is addressed are invited to the hope of eternal life." The difficulty which he found in giving full value to the natural meaning of words such as those of 1 Tim. 2:4 arose from his failure to see that, according to the general tenor of the Scriptures, the election of some does not necessarily involve the damnation of all the rest. As for the point about kings etc., Calvin felt that in his day, as in Paul's, those in high places were mostly opposed to the spread of the gospel; yet, he takes Paul's meaning to be, that is no reason for not praying for them, because even among them there may be some who will "come to the knowledge of the truth." I do not think that is Paul's reason for making special mention of kings and rulers; it is rather that they stand specially in need of

the prayers of the people of God because of the responsibilities of their office, and because of the momentous issues that hang upon their decisions and actions. Even so, Calvin's interpretation of the passage represents an honest endeavour to expound it in the light of its context and in relation to the rest of Scripture.

1 Tim. 2:8. *What justification has Moffatt for the rendering "at any meeting of the church" in 1 Tim. 2:8 for "in every place" (R.V.)?*

Moffatt's phrase is not a literal translation (as R.V. is) but I believe it is a true interpretation. The word "place", in Hebrew and Greek alike, was sometimes given a special significance among Jews as a place of meeting for divine service; in the present passage there may be an echo of Mal. 1:11, where "in every place" probably refers to the Jewish synagogues in Gentile lands. Some have suggested that "in every place" in 1 Cor. 1:2 similarly means "in every place where Christians meet."

1 Tim. 2:9. *Is there any help from the Greek text as to whether 1 Tim. 2:9 refers to the manner in which women should pray publicly?*

In 1 Tim. 2:9 the Greek is no more conclusive on the point you mention than our English versions; the question is mainly how much force we are to give to the Greek word *hōsautōs*, translated "in like manner." If we treat it as a mere connective particle (R.S.V. "also"; N.E.B. "again"), then the verse refers only to women's dress and deportment, and not to the manner in which they should pray publicly; if we give it its full force (as in A.V. and R.V.), then the latter may well be the point of the verse. That is to say, when men pray, the hands they lift up should be holy hands; when women pray, their attire and demeanour should be chaste. That this is not an unnatural way to understand the Greek construction is suggested by the fact that Chrysostom, whose native language was Greek, understood it thus: women should not approach God to pray, he says, dressed or adorned as if they were going to a wedding (*Homily on Timothy*, 8).

1 Tim. 3:1. *Is there any textual foundation for the A.V. expression in 1 Tim. 3:1, "the office of a bishop"?*

There is no question of text here; it is simply a matter of how best to translate the Greek word *episkopē*. A bishop or overseer is an *episkopos* in Greek, and *episkopē* is the work that an *episkopos* does; hence it is rendered "the office of (a) bishop" in the main English versions from Tyndale to the R.S.V., where "office" has the now rather archaic sense of "duty" or "business", as in the hymn

> Ye servants of the Lord,
> Each in his office wait.

If to our ears the rendering has too official a flavour, a number of alternative renderings are available: "to aspire to leadership" (N.E.B.), "if any one aspires to exercise oversight" (Darby), "whoever aspires to the office of superintendent" (Goodspeed). Newberry's margin translates *episkopē* by "overseership." Which ever rendering we choose, the meaning remains the same; spiritual leadership in any Christian company is a noble service, and whoever aspires to it aspires to an honourable work.

1 Tim. 3:2. *Does 1 Tim. 3:2 mean that an overseer or elder should not marry more than once?*

There is, to be sure, very respectable authority for this interpretation of 1 Tim. 3:2 and Titus 1:6. More probably, however, these passages have in view persons who have been divorced and then remarried (the same applies to 1 Tim. 5:9). Legalized polygamy was so rare in the Jewish and Graeco-Roman world of the first century A.D. that we can scarcely

think that the apostle is primarily forbidding a man to be an elder if he has more than one wife at a time. But in those parts of the mission field today where polygamy is practised, these Scriptures are commonly (and perhaps properly) applied in this sense.

1 Tim. 3:8-13. *The "deacons" of 1 Tim. 3:8-13 are often referred to as those who attend to the "material" as distinct from the "spiritual" affairs of the church. Would the use of Gk. diakonos in such Scriptures as 1 Tim. 4:6, Col. 1:23, 25, Eph. 6:21 suggest that in 1 Tim. 3:8ff. Paul may have had in mind believers doing any form of service in the church?*

I see no warrant for restricting the services of the "deacon" in 1 Tim. 3:8ff. to "material" services. As you point out, the Greek word *diakonos* in the New Testament (together with cognate words) is used to cover a variety of service. It seems likely, therefore, that the deacons of 1 Tim. 3 were men or women who undertook various forms of ministry in the church, without having the special responsibility of pastoral oversight.

1 Tim. 3:15. *In 1 Tim. 3:15 ("which is the church of the living God, the pillar and ground of the truth"), have the words "which is" a causal significance, so as to be equivalent to "because it is"?*

If they have such a causal significance, it is not necessarily implied by the construction, but could be implied by the general sense. And I think that such an implication may well be present. It is important to behave oneself aright in the house of God because of what it is. "Lest it should be thought lightly of, Paul appends a testification of the nobility of the true *ekklēsia*, built on the one foundation" (E. K. Simpson).

1 Tim. 3:16. *Should the definite article be omitted in the statement "God was* *manifest in the flesh" (1 Tim. 3:16)? The expression "the flesh" reminds me of the use made of these words in the early verses of Rom. 8 to denote our old nature, and this would be most inapplicable to our Lord.*

You are quite right in supposing that the definite article is absent from the original text of 1 Tim. 3:16, although the leading English versions insert it. But whether the insertion of the article be required or not by English idiom (I do not think it is), the word "flesh" here denotes our Lord's real humanity (cf. John 1:14) and has nothing to do with the specialized Pauline use of the term to denote the unregenerate self. It is the context, and not the presence or absence of the article, that decides the meaning of the term.

In the writings of two very able expositors (S. P. Tregelles and B. W. Newton) it is suggested that the words "received up into glory" (1 Tim. 3:16, A.V.) should be rendered "in glory He was received up", the reference being to the state, not the place. Is there any substantial support for this rendering?

Yes, this rendering is supported by R.V., R.S.V., Darby, Kingsley Williams ("Plain English"), S. H. Hooke ("Basic English"), among others. The A.V. is supported by Weymouth, Moffatt, Goodspeed and Knox. The rendering "in glory" is preferable; it refers to the manner of our Lord's ascension rather than to the place to which He ascended. When in Acts 1:9 we are told that "a cloud received him out of their sight", we could probably think of the cloud of the divine presence which declares while concealing the glorious Shekhinah (cf. Ex. 40:34; Mark 9:7).

1 Tim. 4:12. *How old was Timothy when Paul wrote to him: "Let no man despise thy youth" (1 Tim. 4:12)?*

The word rendered "youth" might be used of any age up to forty. If Timothy

was sixteen years old when Paul took him as his companion on his second missionary journey (Acts 16:1), he was about thirty-one at this time; if he was twenty on the earlier occasion, he was now about thirty-five—in either case, still a young man in the eyes of a man of sixty or over.

1 Tim. 4:14. *How was Timothy's gift given to him "by prophecy, with the laying on the hands of the presbytery" (1 Tim. 4:14)?*

We may infer from this that the utterance of a prophet or prophets in the church at Lystra marked Timothy out before all the members of the church as one whom God had equipped for the special work that lay before him, as has been suggested in the answer to a question on 1 Tim. 1:18 (p. 113). The elders of the church evidently recognized Timothy's gift when it received this divine attestation, and they manifested their fellowship with him in the exercise of his gift by laying their hands upon him. It appears from 2 Tim. 1:6 that Paul joined them in his act of recognition and laid *his* hands on Timothy too.

1 Tim. 5:3-16. *Is the direction about the enrolment of widows in 1 Tim. 5:3-16 intended to be followed literally in the churches for all time?*

Since the direction appears only here, all that we are entitled to say is that it was intended to be followed literally in the church of Ephesus under Timothy's supervision. This is a good example of the distinction between permanent principles in the New Testament writings and various local and temporary applications of these principles. The permanent principle here, intended to be followed in the churches for all time, is that the church has a responsibility to care for those of its members who are in need or destitute. How this responsibility should be discharged is something that can vary with circumstances. In the world of the New Testament, as in many parts of our world today, widows were particularly destitute. Christian widows therefore became a charge on the charity of the church. They might have no relatives to help them, or their relatives might be unbelievers and unwilling to help them. If they had believing relatives, on the other hand, it was the Christian duty of the latter to help them. The widows of 60 years old and upward who were to be enrolled were perhaps not only to be recipients of the church's charity; if they were still sufficiently able-bodied, they could, in return for their maintenance, be the agents of the church's charity and hospitality to others. (There is objective second-century evidence that this was so.) This may be implied in the requirement that they should have had some experience in showing hospitality, washing the feet of the saints, and so forth. Where social circumstances are sufficiently similar to those of the New Testament world, some arrangement of this sort might well be made; where they are different (as in the western world today), the basic principles will be put into practice in more appropriate ways.

1 Tim. 5:17. *In 1 Tim. 5:17 does the word "especially" in the phrase "especially those who labour in preaching and teaching" mean that the other elders do not teach or that they do not stand in such need of "double honour (honorarium)" as those who teach?*

All elders should be "apt to teach" (1 Tim. 3:2)—ready to give instruction in the Christian way by precept and example —but some have teaching as their special gift. If, as the context suggests, material recompense for the time and energy devoted to the spiritual service is indicated by the word "honour", it may be that in the situation with which Paul and Timothy were concerned the preparation and exercise of a teaching ministry occupied much of the time which an elder might otherwise have given to gainful employment; it would therefore be fitting for those who benefited spiritually from his ministry to help to support him materially, as Gal. 6:6 also directs. This situation is still common, and the apostolic injunction remains valid.

2 Tim. 2:6. *Is J. N. Darby right in his translation of 2 Tim. 2:6: "The husbandman must labour before partaking of the fruits"?*

As Darby says himself, "the structure of the phrase is somewhat obscure", and the translation he offers is a possible one; but almost certainly the commoner rendering is to be preferred: "It is the hardworking farmer who ought to have the first share of the crops" (R.S.V.).

2 Tim. 2:17f. *Were Hymenaeus and Philetus proponents of "realized eschatology" (2 Tim. 2:17, 18)?*

Of an "over-realized eschatology", rather. But we cannot be quite sure what form was taken by their teaching "that the resurrection is past already." Half a century later Polycarp mentions the false teaching (of gnostic stamp) "that there is neither resurrection nor judgment" and describes anyone who maintains it as "the first-born of Satan" (Polycarp to the Philippians 3:5). This may be a later development of the teaching of Hymenaeus and Philetus. Their teaching could have arisen from a distortion of Paul's own teaching that the believer has died and risen with Christ. With Paul's teaching we may compare that in John 5:25, according to which the hour "now is" when the dead, hearing the voice of the Son of God, shall live. Teaching like this is the true Biblical "realized eschatology", but not so exhaustively realized that it removes the expectation of resurrection and judgment to come.

2 Tim. 2:19-21. *How do you regard Darby's translation of 2 Tim. 2: 19-21, which seems to underline the "exclusive"*

117

principle that separation from evil is "God's principle of unity"?

The rendering of this verse in Darby's translation is: "if therefore one shall have purified himself from these in separating himself from them, he shall be a vessel to honour ...". The phrase "in separating himself from them" is a gloss on the text, indicating that Darby interpreted it to mean that in order to be "a vessel to honour" a man must withdraw from those who are "vessels to dishonour." So indeed, he says in his footnote: "here he has to purge himself from among them (the vessels)." I regard it as much more probable that a Christian is called upon to cleanse himself from the defilements mentioned elsewhere in this chapter (just as cups, etc., have to be rinsed clean from impurities) than that he is called upon to separate from his fellow-Christians. My gloss on the text has no more authority than J. N. Darby's, but, for what it is worth, here it is: "In a large house there are many vessels—not only gold and silver ones, but vessels of wood and earthenware as well. Some of them are for honourable service, and some for service to which no honour attaches. So whoever purifies himself from these polluting things will be a vessel for honourable use, set apart for the use of the Master Himself, and available for any good service." The words "if a man purifies himself from these" have much the same force as "Let everyone who names the name of the Lord depart from iniquity" in verse 19. The real trouble behind so many questions about these verses is their misuse to support a theory of ecclesiastical discipline which, as originally propounded, would call upon Christians to "cleanse themselves" by separating from all fellow-Christians who do not accept their discipline.

2 Tim. 3:16. *The New English Bible rendering of 2 Timothy 3:16 ("Every inspired scripture has its use ...") shows "scripture" with a small initial while* the same word in Rom. 4:3 has a capital initial. Is it possible that the translators in the former case were thinking of the basic sense of Gk. graphē as "writing"?

This may well be so; on the other hand, the simple reason could be that the translator of Romans used a capital and the translator of 2 Timothy a small "s", and no care was taken to impose uniformity. But it is probable that in 2 Tim. 3:16 the N.E.B., like the R.V., uses "scripture" in the general sense of "writing." "Every writing has its use for teaching the truth and refuting error"—that is, of course, not true. But "every *inspired* writing"—or, as the N.E.B. has it, "every inspired scripture", or, as the R.V. has it, "every scripture inspired of God"—certainly has this use. In Rom. 4:3, on the other hand, the word plainly has its special sense of divinely inspired writing, without any explicit mention of its inspiration; hence N.E.B. rightly renders: "what does Scripture say?"

2 Tim. 4:10. *In the reference to Demas in 2 Tim. 4:10 could the verbal form translated "having loved" be legitimately rendered "having been loving", with the implication that his departure from Paul was the outward manifestation of a hidden process that had been on continuous operation over a long period?*

It may be true that such a process had been going on within Demas for some time, but this cannot be inferred from the tense of the verb; the form used is the aorist participle (*agapēsas*), and the aorist would be the most inappropriate tense to use of a continuous process. It is more likely to refer to the event which inaugurates such a process (that is what grammarians calls the "ingressive" aorist); if so, we might translate: "having conceived a love for the present age." What form his love for the present age took is impossible to discover: extremes of interpretation at one end and the other are John Bunyan's portrayal of Demas operating a silver mine and the view ascribed to James Butler Stoney that Demas left the apostle in order to go on a missionary journey of his own, his love for the present "world" (A.V.) being presumably love for the souls of its heathen millions!

2 Tim. 4:11. *Is Paul's call for Mark's ministry (2 Tim. 4:11) a tacit admission that he was wrong in his dispute with Barnabas (Acts 15:39), or may we see in it the issue of his forgiving spirit?*

Certainly, if there was anything in Mark's departure from Perga (Acts 13:13) that required Paul's forgiveness, Paul had forgiven him. Whether Paul, on mature reflection, concluded that he had been at fault in his dispute with Barnabas is not clear. It has, indeed, been suggested that when he wrote of heavenly love as not being "provoked" (1 Cor. 13:5) he had in mind his sharp "contention" with Barnabas over Mark, for the verb (*paroxynō*) in the one place corresponds to the noun (*paroxysmos*) in the other. But it would probably have been unwise for Mark to join a second missionary expedition in which Paul was one of the leaders. Barnabas no doubt discerned in his cousin promising qualities which could be developed better under his personal care than they would if Paul were present too. It certainly did Mark good to spend more time in the company of such a "son of encouragement" as Barnabas was, and in due course his latent capacities became manifest and were appreciated by Paul himself.

HEBREWS AND THE "GENERAL" EPISTLES

Epistle to the Hebrews. *How did the Epistle to the Hebrews receive its title, and is there sufficient authority for us to refer to it as such?*

The problem of the original addressees of this book is almost as great as the problem of its authorship, and in some ways is more important. The oldest extant manuscripts, lists of New Testament writings, and references to the book in the Fathers, unanimously entitle it "To (the) Hebrews." There is, as Westcott says, "no evidence that it ever bore any other address. Though there is no reason to suppose that the title is original, it expresses at least the belief of those by whom the Epistle was placed among the apostolic Scriptures, and describes truly the character of those for whom it was written, so far as their character can be determined from its general scope, as men who by birth and life were devoted to the institutions of Israel." But, granted that the recipients were probably Christians of Jewish descent, it is as Christians that the author writes to them; and we must not infer from the traditional title that the epistle's exhortations to "hold fast our confession" and its warning against "falling away from the living God" are in some sense "not for us." As regards naming the epistle, how else could we intelligibly refer to it than by its ancient and universally accepted title?

Heb. 1:4. *In Heb. 1:4 how has our Lord "by inheritance obtained a more excellent name" than the angels? How can He who is the Son inherit that which He already has?*

We must not press the word "inheritance" here to imply that He obtained at some point in time something that He did not already possess. The "more excellent name" of verse 4 is the name of "Son" (as verse 5 makes clear), and it is evident from verse 2 that this name was His in the beginning (for "Son" is the antecedent of the adjective clause "by whom also he made the worlds"). Although the verb *klēronomeō* primarily means "inherit," it can be used in the wider sense of "obtaining" or "acquiring"; hence R.S.V. renders the second clause in verse 4: "as the name he has obtained is more excellent than theirs"—but even so there is no implication that there ever was a time when it was not His. He holds the name of "Son", as He has inherited all things (verse 2), by the Father's appointment.

Heb. 1:5. *When the words "I will be to him a Father, and he shall be to me a Son" are applied to our Lord in Heb. 1:5, do they refer to Him in manhood or in deity? And how is their present application related to their apparent application to Solomon in 2 Sam. 7:14, from which the Hebrews quotation seems to be taken?*

While the mutual relationship of the Father and the Son is an eternal one within the unity of the Godhead, the words you quote from Heb. 1:5 refer properly to Jesus as the Messiah. The same is true of the words quoted from Psa. 2:7 in the first part of the same verse ("Thou art my Son; this day have I begotten thee"). The anointed king of Israel was in a special sense acknowledged by God as His son, and this acknowledgement is uniquely appropriate to the final and greatest Prince of the house of David. In its original context, of course, the first half of 2 Sam. 7:14 (quoted here) refers to Solomon as much as the second half of the verse. But it is in the Messiah, not in Solomon, that the holy and sure promises made by God to David and his house find their perfect fulfilment (cf. Isa. 55:3, quoted in Acts 13:34), and thus some of the language used in these promises passes beyond Solomon and other immediate successors of David to find its ultimate satisfaction in Christ.

Heb. 1:7. *In what sense does God make "His angels spirits (or rather 'winds', as in R.V.), and His ministers a flame of fire" (Heb. 1:7)?*

This is a quotation from the Septuagint of Psa. 104:4, where the Hebrew text means: "who makest the winds thy messengers, fire and flame thy ministers" (cf. R.S.V.). That is to say, wind and fire are servants of God, hasting to carry out His errands. But the force of the Septuagint and New Testament construction suggests rather that the angels of God fulfil His commands with the speed and power of wind and fire. Another possibility is that our author thinks of God as turning angelic beings into wind and fire, so that their evanescence is contrasted with the Son's eternal dominion (cf. verse 8).

Heb. 2:9. *At the end of Heb. 2:9 should we read "for every man" (with A.V., R.V., etc.), or "for every thing" (with J. N. Darby)?*

The grammatical point is that the Greek form used (the genitive of the word meaning "all" or "every") may be either masculine or neuter. While it is true, as we learn from Rom. 8:19ff., that even the inanimate creation is to benefit by the redemptive work of Christ, the present passage in Hebrews is concerned with His work for mankind. I therefore prefer Darby's footnote alternative "every one", which is also the R.S.V. rendering (cf. also N.E.B. "for us all").

Heb. 4:15. *What is the point of the words "yet without sin" in Heb. 4:15?*

These words indicate that our Lord was exposed to all the testings and temptations that come His people's way, without ever being mastered by them and sinning against God.

Heb. 6:2. *What is the "laying on of hands" in Heb. 6:2?*

It is most probably the laying on of hands which in some other New Testament contexts is associated with the impartation of the Spirit (cf. Acts 8:17; 19:6).

Heb. 6:4. *Are the "partakers of the Holy Ghost" in Heb. 6:4 true believers?*

One might easily think so. But have you ever known people who experienced what appeared to be a perfectly genuine conversion, took part energetically in gospel witness, were baptized, took communion, entered wholeheartedly into the fellowship of a Christian church—and then suddenly, deliberately, inexplicably and (so far as one can judge) irrevocably gave the whole thing up? Such people are by no means unknown. They often become the worst opponents of the gospel, actively trying to dissuade others from accepting it; they are far more difficult to win than raw pagans, and it really does seem "impossible to renew them again unto repentance." Were they real? No, if continuance be the test of reality (and it is). But no one could have told this at the time. When the seed sown among rocks and thorns began to spring up, no doubt it looked promising enough; it was the passage of time that showed the difference. Yet that seed enjoyed the sunshine and the rain as much as the seed that fell on good ground. And these people whom we have in mind shared in a sense all the privileges enjoyed by the children of God with whom they were associated. (Simon Magus might be cited as a New Testament example of such a person.) The Lord knows those who are His; but the warnings of this epistle are recorded in order that we may put all our confidence in Him and none in self. It is evident, too, from verse 9 that the writer did not really believe that his readers were apostates, such as are described in verse 4 to 8.

Heb. 7:3. *Do we gather from Heb. 7:3 that Melchizedek was of heavenly origin?*

The words "without father, without mother, without genealogy, having neither beginning or days nor end of life" refer to the fact that in the narrative of Gen. 14:18-20 Melchizedek, priest-king of Salem (Jerusalem?), is introduced suddenly and disappears as suddenly, nothing being said about his ancestry or his progeny, his birth or his death. The silences of Scripture, in our author's view, are as much the product of divine inspiration as its statements, and these very silences concerning one who was in himself an ordinary man (though a great one) make him a fitting picture of our Lord in His royal and perpetual priesthood. It is by these providential silences, and not because of a "heavenly origin", that Melchizedek in the biblical record has been "made like unto the Son of God."

Heb. 7:22. *What is the meaning of the word "surety" in Heb. 7:22? Does it have the same meaning as "mediator"? And is the suretiship exercised Godward or manward or both?*

A surety is something more than a mediator. The old covenant was dispensed through a mediator, namely Moses (cf. Gal. 3:19), but no one was qualified to be a surety or guarantor that its terms would be carried out on the manward side. The people themselves gave an undertaking (Ex. 24:3, 7), but they were unable to make it good. But the new covenant has a perfect guarantor; that is one of the reasons why it is called a "better covenant." As the representative and high priest of His people He is an acceptable surety on their behalf in the sight of God; and to His people He is the surety that all God's covenant-promises are sealed to them in Him.

Heb. 7:27. *What is meant by "daily" in Heb. 7:27? Do we not gather elsewhere that the high priest brought a sin-offering for himself and then for the people only on the great day of atonement?*

The annual sin-offering is the only regular one prescribed in the law, so far as the high priest's service is concerned. But there were other occasions when a similar atonement had to be made (cf. Lev. 4:3), and such an occasional sin-offering may have been in our author's mind when he used the expression "daily." While there is no explicit command for a daily sin-offering to be presented by the high priest, yet inadvertent sinning, of the kind provided for in Lev. 4:3, could well have been a daily hazard. The high priest occupied a special position; an inadvertent sin on his part affected the people whom he represented; it was wise therefore to take precautions against the very possibility of his having committed an inadvertent sin. That the high priest in the first century A.D. offered sacrifices daily is indicated also by Philo, the Jewish theologian of Alexandria. But in the special ceremonies of the day of atonement these daily or occasional sin-offerings were summed up and "raised, so to speak, to a higher power" (A. B. Davidson).

Heb. 9:1-5. *Why is the golden altar of incense omitted from the list of sacred furniture in Heb. 9:1-5?*

If it *is* omitted, I cannot think why. Some commentators have suggested that the incense-altar was a later addition to the original text of Exodus, but even if this could be established, it was certainly included in the text of Exodus known to the author of Hebrews. But perhaps it is not omitted from Heb. 9:1-5. The "golden censer" of verse 4 (A.V.) may be in reality the golden incense altar (cf. R.V. margin, R.S.V., N.E.B.). The Greek word *thymiatērion*, while normally rendered "censer," may denote any instrument for the burning of incense, and could well mean the

122

incense altar here. In that case a further question arises, why it is associated with the holy of holies instead of the holy place. This association is not unique: in 1 Kings 6:22 the incense altar is called "the whole altar that belonged to the inner sanctuary" (R.S.V.), the reason being possibly that on the day of atonement the blood of the sin-offering had to be sprinkled on the horns of the incense altar as well as on the mercy-seat (Ex. 30:10; Lev. 16:15), and also because the holy of holies was never entered without incense (Lev. 16:12).

Heb. 9:4. *Were the pot of manna and the rod ever placed actually in the ark, as Heb. 9:4 states?*

The Old Testament does not say so explicitly. The pot of manna was laid up "before the LORD . . . before the testimony" (engraved on the tables of stone) being placed in the ark according to Ex. 25:16, 21. Aaron's rod was similarly placed "before the testimony" (Num. 17:10). These expressions might suggest to us that the pot and the rod were put in front of the ark, outside it. G. H. Lang, in his exposition of Hebrews, apparently takes "wherein" to mean "in the tabernacle which is called the Holy of holies" (cf. Heb. 9:3) rather than "in the ark"; but this puts a strain on the natural construction of the passage. It is certain that by the time when the ark was placed in Solomon's temple it contained nothing but the tables of the law (1 Kings 8:9); Delitzsch thinks that "the very terms of this statement may almost seem to imply that other things had been here formerly." Since the Old Testament tells us nothing about the pot of manna outside Ex. 16:33f., and nothing about Aaron's rod after Num. 20:8-11, it is open to anyone to surmise that, even if they were not placed inside the ark at first, they were put there subsequently, and lost perhaps when the ark was captured by the Philistines. But that would simply be calling upon imagination to take the place of evidence.

Heb. 9:16f. *Are there good grounds for the view that the Testator in Heb. 9:16, 17, is the victim by whose blood the new covenant is ratified rather than simply the One whose last will and testament it is?*

I do not think so, although the view that the covenant victim is referred to has the strong support of B. F. Westcott. The difficulty is that to find the covenant victim there involves an unnatural straining of the language. The fact is that the Greek word variously rendered "covenant" and "testament" (*diathēkē*) has a range of meaning wide enough to include both these ideas. It denotes a settlement or disposition of any kind, including one which takes effect only on the death of the one who made it (i.e., a last will and testament). It is not true to say of *any* kind of covenant that "where a covenant is, there must of necessity be the death of him that made it." But our author, who has just spoken of Christ as "the mediator of a new covenant" or settlement, goes on to say (if one may paraphrase his argument): "Now there is one kind of settlement which depends for its validity on the death of him who made it (namely a testament), and that kind of settlement is particularly relevant here, for the new 'settlement' could not have come into effect apart from the death of Him who made it, its Mediator and Surety." The idea of a testament may have suggested itself the more readily to his mind in view of the "eternal inheritance" mentioned at the end of v. 15. Westcott argued that the one who "made" the covenant could be regarded as the covenant victim since the covenant-maker is identified representatively with the covenant victim, so that "in the death of the victim his death is presented symbolically." But it is not always true that the covenant-maker is thus identified with the covenant victim.

The covenant with Abraham in Gen. 15:1-18, and the covenant with Israel in Ex. 24:3-8, were made by God, but it is suggested that God was identified representatively with the covenant-victims on those occasions. "The death of him that made it" must mean "the death of the testator," as A.V. and N.E.B. simply and rightly put it.

Heb. 9:23. *What are the heavenly things of Heb. 9:23 and how came they to need cleansing?*

The cleansing of the sanctuary amounted to making it fit for use in the worship of God, as is indicated (so far as the earthly sanctuary is concerned) by Num. 7:1 and Lev. 16:16, 33. The "heavenly things" which required to be cleansed by means of better sacrifices than their earthly copies denote the whole heavenly order of worship in which we are called to participate. What, after all, *is* God's holy temple? Heb. 3:6 indicates that it is the community of His redeemed people—they are God's habitation in the Spirit, according to Eph. 2:22; His "spiritual house", according to 1 Pet. 2:5. But in order to become His habitation, his house, His heavenly temple, they required to be cleansed by a sacrifice infinitely superior to any that the material sanctuary knew.

Heb. 10:12. *In Heb. 10:12, do the words "for ever" go with what precedes or with what follows?*

A.V. and R.V. both attach "for ever" to the words which precede, rendering ". . . had offered one sacrifice for sins for ever," and putting a comma after "for ever," not before it (similarly R.S.V. and N.E.B.). But the position of the adverbial phrase in the Greek of this verse is as ambiguous as it is in English, and there is no conclusive argument against putting the punctuation mark before instead of after it. It might be argued that thus the abiding character of Christ's high priesthood is emphasized

(cf. "a priest for ever" in Heb. 7:3, where the same Greek phrase, *eis to diēnekes*, is used). But I agree with B. F. Westcott in his commentary: "The sacrifice was efficacious for ever, through all time, being appropriated by each believer. The connexion of *for ever* with the following *sat down* is contrary to the usage of the Epistle; it obscures the idea of the perpetual efficacy of Christ's one sacrifice; it weakens the contrast with *standeth*; and it imports a foreign idea into the image of the assumption (*sat down*) of royal dignity by Christ." (I have replaced the Greek words in this quotation by the English equivalents.)

Heb. 10:22. *Does the wording of Heb. 10:22, "and almost all things are by the law purged with blood", mean that some things were not purged with blood? If so, what were they?*

There is a slight difference of emphasis in the rendering of the R.V.: "And according to the law, I may almost say, all things are cleansed with blood . . .". The principle of ceremonial cleansing by means of blood was general but not universal. In rare cases, atonement was made by incense or by gold (Num. 16:46; 31:50; see 1 Pet. 1:18). There were several other exceptions, like that of Lev. 5:11-13, where an Israelite, in deep poverty, brings the priest an ephah (about half a bushel) of fine flour, of which a handful is burned upon the altar. The priest makes atonement and the offerer is forgiven, for his flour is accepted as a sin-offering, without either oil, incense or blood.

Heb. 10:26ff. *To whom do the words of Heb. 10:26ff. (beginning "For if we sin wilfully . . .") apply? Is it possible for a believer to sin wilfully?*

It would be good if the answer "No" could be given to the last part of the question, but experience suggests otherwise. The people whom the writer warns against the dreadful possibility envisaged in these verses are those whom he couples along with himself as committed and recognized Christians. He is not thinking of their being overtaken by a sudden temptation and succumbing to it, but of deliberate apostasy from Christ, embraced as a settled policy. If a man renounces the work of Christ as the ground of his salvation, where else will he find a "sacrifice for sins"? The language of the writer is not obscure; the difficulty arises when we try to accommodate his teaching within the framework of our accepted system of doctrine. But when that difficulty arises, we should modify our framework rather than try to persuade ourselves that the biblical text does not quite mean what it appears to mean and, above all, we should beware of thinking that the words cannot refer to us. Some very unlikely people have apostatized before now. On the other hand, the writer is far from wishing to shake his readers' confidence and security in Christ; instead, he encourages them with the assurance of his belief that he and they alike, far from falling back and being involved in destruction, will persevere in faith and save their souls (verse 39).

Heb. 10:29. *What is meant by "the blood of the covenant, wherewith he was sanctified" (Heb. 10:29)?*

Just as the people of Israel were sanctified in the sense of being set apart for God by the covenant blood shed at the foot of Sinai (Ex. 24:8; Heb. 9:18-20), so by the sacrifice of Christ, by His "blood of the new covenant," the new people of God, among whom the man in question was publicly reckoned before his apostasy, have been set apart for Him.

Heb. 11:3. *What exactly is to be understood from Heb. 11:3?*

The visible, material universe came into being by pure creation—out of nothing. It was not fashioned from pre-existent material, as most pagan cosmogonies

taught. It is by faith, says the writer, that we understand this; he means, no doubt, that it has been revealed in Scripture, and could not have been discovered by study or research. Here, as in Heb. 1:2, "world" represents Gk. *aiōnes*, and denotes the whole space-time continuum. The "word of God" by which the worlds were framed is His command (Gk. *rhēma*); cf. Psa. 33:6, 9.

Heb. 11:35. *What is meant by "a better resurrection" at the end of Heb. 11:35? Does it imply that there are degrees in the resurrection of believers?*

The meaning will become quite plain if one looks at the beginning of the verse in the R.V.: "Women received their dead by a resurrection." This is a reference to such incidents as the raising from death of the Sidonian widow's son by Elijah (1 Kings 17:22) and of the Shunammite's son by Elisha (2 Kings 4:34f.). But the martyrs referred to in the later part of the verse endured torture in expectation of a *better* resurrection than that; those boys were raised from the dead to resume bodily life and in due course to die again; the martyrs looked for a resurrection to the immortal life of the age to come.

Heb. 12:14. *Is the holiness in Heb. 12:14 holiness in status or in practice? If the former, why are we told to follow after it? If the latter, does this not imply salvation by character?*

It is certainly practical holiness or sanctification that is meant. But the words "without which no man shall see the Lord" do not teach salvation by character any more than does our Lord's beatitude: "Blessed are the pure in heart: for they shall see God" (Matt. 5:8). Sanctification in this sense is as much the work of God as justification is; merit is excluded from the one as from the other. And while salvation, in the sense of pardon and cleansing from the guilt of sin, is the gift of God's grace, the highest blessing of all is the vision of God, that beatific vision which the greatest saints have coveted as the most utterly desirable thing in time or eternity.

Heb. 12:24. *When Heb. 12:24 speaks of Christians as having come to the "sprinkled blood that speaks more graciously than the blood of Abel", are we to infer that the blood shed on the cross is now literally and actually present in heaven?*

No; this very epistle is careful to make it clear that whereas the high priest in Old Testament times entered into the holy of holies on the day of atonement "*with* blood not his own" (Heb. 9:25), our Lord entered into the heavenly sanctuary once for all not "with" but "*through* his own blood" (Heb. 9:12)— that is to say, by virtue of the perfect sacrifice which He offered when He yielded up His life on the cross. We come "to the blood of sprinkling" in the sense that, when we put our trust in Him, His sacrificial death avails to cleanse our conscience from sin.

James 1:1. *If ten tribes were not distinguishable in New Testament times, who are the twelve tribes of Jas. 1:1?*

The ten tribes (other than Judah and Benjamin) were not completely indistinguishable in New Testament times; for example, Anna the prophetess belonged to the tribe of Asher (Luke 2:36). But the expression "the twelve tribes" could be used comprehensively even if the possibility of distinguishing between them no longer existed; thus Paul speaks to Agrippa of "our twelve tribes, earnestly serving God night and day" (Acts 26:7). As thus used by Paul, the phrase is practically synonymous with "all the house of Israel" (Acts 2:36). As used by James, the phrase refers to the sum-total of believing Israel; he assumes that his readers hold "the faith of our Lord Jesus Christ" (Jas. 2:1).

Jas. 1:2. *What are the "divers temptations" mentioned in James 1:2?*

They are the "various trials" (R.S.V.) that test our faith, for when we receive them in the proper spirit, our faith and patience are strengthened by them, as verse 3 shows. They are, of course, different from the "temptations" of verses 13 and 14, where James is thinking of those temptations to evil which arise from our inner propensities.

Jas. 3:6. *How can the tongue set on fire the whole wheel of nature (Jas. 3:6)?*

By the mischief it does. The "whole wheel of nature" is a figure for the whole course of human life. Just as excessive friction in the axle of a wheel can make the axle red-hot, so that fire spreads outwards along the spokes and sets the whole wheel alight, so the mischief engendered by an irresponsible tongue can enflame human relationships and cause irreparable destruction to the whole round of life.

Jas. 5:14. *Can the anointing of James 5:14 still be practised today, with beneficial results?*

That it is still practised today with beneficial results I believe to be true. I have no eyewitness knowledge of any such incident, but I have met Christians who have been so anointed and have recovered. Naturally it is the successful instances that tend to be remembered and recorded. In *The Origins of the Brethren*, p. 78f., Dr. H. H. Rowdon refers to a letter written by Anthony Norris Groves from Bagdad on October 15, 1831, in which he tells how Francis William Newman, who had joined him there, fell dangerously ill but was anointed by his companions and recovered. (Dr. Rowdon points out that according to other evidence the recovery was gradual.) But during that year Groves had lost his wife and then his baby daughter through the plague; whether anointing was used in their case, as prayer was certainly offered for them, I do not know. If someone had sufficient leisure to investigate examples of this anointing over a wide area of place and time, and to compare the incidence of successful and unsuccessful applications, his research would make interesting reading.

Is the sickness mentioned in Jas. 5:14 any sickness? Does the promise hold good for any sickness? Or is the sickness definitely linked with some known sin committed by the individual concerned (as verse 16 suggests)?

Verse 15 does not indicate that in all cases envisaged in verse 14 some specific sin is linked with the sickness; the language is provisional: "*if* he has committed sins . . .". Then the thought of the forgiveness of sins leads James on in verse 16 to deal more generally with confession of sins and praying for one another within the church, with a view to healing; and here perhaps sickness resulting from sin (cf. 1 Cor. 11:30) is more specifically in view. There are obvious problems raised for elders who are invited to act in accordance with verse 14, but where the request for this action is made in simple sincerity, I know of no elders who would refuse, although they might sometimes hope that the sick person's faith was stronger and more efficacious than their own. In the case of an obviously terminal illness the wording of the prayer would no doubt be modified so as to be appropriate to the circumstances, but even there the praying and anointing in response to the patient's desire would bring some positive benefit.

1 Peter 2:12. *What is the "day of visitation" in 1 Pet. 2:12? When will presumably unconverted Gentiles "glorify God"?*

The general thought is similar to that in Matt. 5:16, "that they may see your good works, and give glory to your Father who is in heaven." But here the idea of a "day of visitation" is added. This phrase is normally associated with judgment (cf. Isa. 10:3), but not invariably so; Jerusalem's "time of visitation" (Luke 19:44) would have been for her blessing had she recognized and grasped it. If God were to visit in mercy the persecutors of those to whom Peter was writing, the believers' example would serve as a powerful instrument in His hands for disposing the persecutors to repent and accept His salvation; in that case the former persecutors, as a result of the believers' good works, as they watched them, might well give glory to God. If, on the other hand, they refused to repent, they would be constrained to acknowledge their error on their judgment-day and thus bear witness to the righteousness of the persecuted believers' conduct; such confession and testimony would redound to God's glory.

1 Pet. 3:18ff. *What is the meaning of 1 Pet. 3:18-22?*

Perhaps it would be helpful to expound these verses by means of an expanded paraphrase. "When Christ suffered once for all for sins, suffering as the Righteous One on behalf of us who were unrighteous, His death marked the end of His physical life; it was by the Spirit that He was raised to life again and in the Spirit that His resurrection life is maintained. [Compare Paul's language in Rom. 1:4; 8:11; 1 Cor. 15:45; 2 Cor. 3:17.] It was in the power of the Spirit, too, that He went and made proclamation to the imprisoned spirits—those spiritual beings that disobeyed God's ordinance in the days of Noah (Gen. 6:1-4) and are accordingly 'kept in everlasting bonds under darkness unto the judgment of the great day' (Jude 8; cf. 2 Pet. 2:4). [The substance of His proclamation to them is not stated, but the analogy of Col. 2:15 suggests that His victory on the cross sealed their doom finally.] It was in those days of

Noah, while the ark was being constructed, that God in His patient grace gave men a prolonged opportunity to repent, but they refused to repent, and only a handful of persons, eight in all, were brought safely through the flood by means of the ark. Their salvation then, when they were upborne by the water, has its antitype in your salvation now set forth in figure by the water of baptism. The baptismal water is not like an ordinary bath, which removes external impurities from the body; it symbolizes an inward and spiritual cleansing, it is the response which a purified conscience makes to God (cf. Heb. 10:22). It is not the water of baptism in itself that effects this inward cleansing, but the saving event which baptism signifies—the resurrection of Jesus Christ, in which His people share by faith. And Jesus not only rose from the dead; He has entered heaven itself and occupies the place of supremacy at God's right hand, supreme over the highest of created beings. This is the seal of His triumph, and in that triumph His people share by faith."

With reference to the foregoing answer, on 1 Peter 3:18ff., may there not be the further point that baptism now saved these readers from their former life, associations, etc., just as the Flood put a barrier between those who escaped it and the corruption of their former environment, and just (similarly) as the Red Sea and the cloud put a barrier between the redeemed Israelites and Egypt (1 Cor. 10:1f.)?

Yes, indeed. As you go on to say, such an understanding of the passage rounds off Peter's comments on salvation elsewhere in the epistle—in 1:5, 9, 10; 2:2. And it adds weight to the suggestion (which I am disposed to accept) that this epistle, especially from 1:3 to 4:11, is addressed more particularly to recent converts—"newborn babes" (2:2)—so as to bring out the meaning of their baptism.

1 Pet. 3:18ff. *Is there any particular difficulty about the "spirits in prison" if, as the Tyndale Commentary on 1 Peter says (p. 142f.), "the word* pneumata, *spirits, alone and without qualification, is not thus used anywhere in the Bible to describe departed human spirits"?*

I think the statement you quote from the Tyndale Commentary is right. Wherever the spirits of departed human beings are clearly intended, qualifying words are added to show this, e.g. "the spirits of just men made perfect" in Heb. 12:23. This creates a presupposition that it is not the spirits of departed human beings that are intended in 1 Pet. 3:19. Of course 1 Pet. 3:19 might constitute an exception to the general rule if this were demanded by the context, but I see nothing in the context to demand this.

1 Pet. 3:19. *Is there ground for accepting Moffatt's reading of 1 Peter 3:19: "it was in the Spirit that Enoch also went and preached to the imprisoned spirits"? Is it possible to say anything about the nature or purpose of the message?*

Moffatt's introduction of Enoch into this verse (you will find it also in E. J. Goodspeed's *American Translation*) is based on a conjecture first published by William Bowyer in 1772 and later popularized by J. Rendel Harris and others. Rendel Harris used to say that there was nothing more certain in life than a good conjectural emendation, but a conjectural emendation is really good only if it imposes itself immediately and universally as self-evidently right, and this cannot be said of the intrusion of Enoch into 1 Peter 3:19. The suggestion is that "Enoch" fell out of the text at an early date because of its similarity to the group of words immediately preceding, *en hō kai* ("by which also"); and it is argued that Enoch would then be represented as doing what he is said to have done in the apocalyptic Enoch literature of the first or second century B.C.—proclaiming doom to the fallen angels—but this is a flimsy argument. What our text says is that it was Christ who by the Spirit went and made proclamation to them.

1 Pet. 4:1-3. *What is the meaning of the first three verses of 1 Pet. 4?*

Peter, I suggest, is saying much the same thing as Paul says in Rom. 6, but in different language. "Since therefore Christ suffered in the flesh" will then mean "Since Christ has died"; "arm yourselves with the same thought" will be Peter's equivalent to Paul's "consider yourselves dead to sin" (Rom. 6:11), and the parenthetic "for whoever has suffered in the flesh has ceased from sin" may be understood in the sense of our having "died to sin" (Rom. 6:2). Or we may compare Rom. 6:7: "he who has died is justified from sin"—that is, he is quit of sin. Death pays all debts; the man who has died with Christ (or, in Peter's language, has armed himself with the same mind as Christ showed by suffering in the flesh) has his slate wiped clean, and can start his new life in Christ freed from the entail of the past.

1 Pet. 4:6. *Who are "the dead" to whom the gospel is said to have been preached in 1 Pet. 4:6?*

Not, I think, people who were dead when the gospel was preached to them, but people who were dead at the time when the epistle was written. They heard the gospel, they believed, but subsequently they died. It might be asked, then, what good the gospel did them, since they died just as unbelievers die. Peter answers that the believing dead are not deprived of the benefits of the gospel. While "according to men" (i.e. from the human point of view) they were "judged in the flesh" (i.e. suffered bodily death, the penalty of sin), yet "according to God" (i.e. from God's point of view) the spiritual life which they received when they believed the gospel does not end

with bodily death, but endures for ever. There may also be a reference (as in Rom. 8:11) to the resurrection hope, which the indwelling Spirit of God guarantees in advance to the believer.

In the light of Jer. 18:7-10; 26:3, 13 etc. ("if that nation concerning which I have spoken, turn from their evil, I will repent of the evil that I thought to do unto them . . .") should we not beware of being too dogmatic and literal in our interpretation of prophecy? The sparing of Nineveh is an example. Are not the pronouncements of judgment intended to be warnings to lead men to repentance?

Yes; the passages to which you refer are of great importance for our understanding of Old Testament prophecy. It would probably not be going too far to say that every prediction of judgment in the Bible must be understood as subject to the condition "unless there is repentance" —whether that condition be expressed or only implied. The case of Nineveh which you adduce is an apt illustration: "Yet forty days, and Nineveh shall be overthrown" was a conditional, not an absolute pronouncement, the condition being "unless it repents." The men of Nineveh did not know whether this condition was implied or not, but took appropriate action in case it was implied (Jonah 3:9). Jonah knew well enough that the condition was implied, and that was what annoyed him; he would have preferred the message of judgment to be unconditional (Jonah 4:2). No prophecy could have been more explicit; the time-limit for its fulfilment was exactly stated, and yet it was not fulfilled because Nineveh repented. The fact is, judgment is God's "strange work" (Isa. 28:21), to which He girds Himself reluctantly, as to an uncongenial responsibility, only when it is clear to Him that the situation is otherwise irremediable. But when He sees a glimmer of repentance, He sets His work of grace afoot with joyful haste; this is His proper work, in which His heart delights. Stern disciples like Jonah may disapprove of their Lord's readiness to forgive and forget; those who have a truer sense of His mind will rejoice to know Him as "a gracious God, and full of compassion, slow to anger, and plenteous in mercy" (Jonah 4:2), for otherwise they themselves could never have hoped for His forgiveness. A later rabbi, who had caught the true spirit of the God of Israel, represents Him as saying: "Give me a loophole of repentance as tiny as the eye of a needle, and I will drive a chariot and horses through it." This principle ought to be carefully considered. When, for example, we meet an Old Testament prophecy of judgment, which has never been fulfilled, we should not necessarily conclude that it must therefore be fulfilled in the future. Perhaps there was, in God's sight, no need for its fulfilment, since the implied "unless" was satisfied. There is nothing mechanically inevitable about the ways of God, as though His decrees were the dictates of blind fate. But where he pledges himself by His own name to act in grace, where He assures His people of the triumph of His cause and theirs, where He stands engaged to bring the weakest believer safely through to final salvation, there "we can confidently say, The Lord is my helper, I will not be afraid; what can man do to me?" (Heb. 13:6).

2 Pet. 1:19. *How do you interpret the rise of the day-star in 2 Peter 1:19? Is not the rendering "whereunto ye do well that ye take heed in your hearts, as unto a lamp shining in a dark place, until the day dawn, and the day-star arise" unnatural?*

Yes, it is an impermissible wresting of the word-order to take the phrase "in your hearts" out of its proper setting and construe it with "take heed." The meaning of the passage should be gathered from the context. At a time when the apparent postponement of the Lord's coming with power was causing some Christians to wonder whether the blessed hope would ever come to pass, the readers of this letter are assured that the apostolic preaching about His coming was no invented fable, but something unshakably true. Two proofs of this are adduced: (i) the transfiguration, which was a foreview of the consummated kingdom of God, witnessed by the apostles, and (ii) the prophetic writings, a surer basis for faith even than the transfiguration. To the promise contained in these writings they must pay careful heed, until the time when it begins to be fulfilled. The signs which herald the approach of the Lord's glorious appearing will then be welcomed in their hearts like the first dawning of a new day, like the morning star rising in the sky as the harbinger of sunrise. The heart is the seat of understanding, and the words teach a lesson similar to that of Mark 13:29, "when you see these things taking place, you know that he is near, at the very gates."

2 Pet. 1:20. *What is meant by the words, "no prophecy of Scripture is of private interpretation" (2 Peter 1:20)?*

The meaning seems to be that no prophecy should be interpreted on its own, in isolation from its context or from the general tenor of prophetic Scripture. This is because the Holy Spirit is the primary author of all prophecy (verse 21), which accordingly bears one consentient witness, in accordance with which every individual prophecy must be understood. A corollary of this is that no prophecy should be interpreted in accordance with the reader's private ideas or preferences, because it was not from private ideas or preferences that the prophecy arose.

2 Pet. 2:1ff. *Are the persons spoken of in 2 Peter 2 the same as those mentioned in 2 Timothy 3:1-8? Would they be* believers who have degenerated into this condition? Timothy is told to "turn away" from such in the same way as he is told to "withdraw" himself from the contentious characters of 1 Timothy 6:3-5.

The false teachers excoriated in 2 Peter 2 may not be the same individuals as those described in 2 Timothy 3:1-8, but they are the same sort of people, those who are further characterized in 2 Timothy 3:13 as "evil men and impostors" who "will go on from bad to worse, deceivers and deceived." As for the question whether they are believers who have degenerated into this condition, the antinomian heretics of 2 Peter 2 at any rate are viewed as false professors, who received a considerable measure of enlightenment, but in the end showed their real unregenerate nature (verse 22); and the implication of 2 Timothy 3 also is that the withstanders of the truth described there are people who never had anything more than an outward veneer of true godliness. Whatever may be said about the contentious characters of 1 Timothy 6:3-5, it is worth observing that the words, "from such withdraw thyself", found at the end of verse 5 in A.V., are lacking in R.V., R.S.V., etc., because they are insufficiently attested.

2 Pet. 3:10ff. *How does 2 Peter 3:10ff., with its description of the dissolution of heaven and earth on the day of the Lord, to be followed by the inauguration of the eternal state, tie up with resurrection as the hope of the church? It seems strange to find an epistle written to Christians pointing them on to this final consummation as the event which they ought to be "looking for and earnestly desiring" (R.V.).*

It would be a self-centred hope that was fixed on our own advantage. The hope of the church cannot be other than the hope of the church's Lord. So Sir Edward Denny puts it in well-chosen words:

Thy sympathies and hopes are ours,
    Dear Lord! we wait to see
Creation all, below, above,
    Redeemed and blessed by Thee.

Our Lord's hope does not stop short of the consummation variously described in 1 Cor. 15:24-28 and Eph. 1:9f.; and so neither can ours. Our personal "hope of salvation" at the coming of Christ (1 Thess. 5:8f.; cf. Tit. 2:13) is but part of this wider hope which is equally ours in Him.

2 Pet. 3:15. *Which of Paul's writings is referred to in 2 Peter 3:15?*

The reference to Paul is prompted by the admonition "count the forbearance of our Lord as salvation," which might be reminiscent of Rom. 2:4, "God's kindness is meant to lead you to repentance." The exhortation to "be zealous to be found by him (the Lord) without spot or blemish, and at peace" (2 Peter 3:14) has a parallel in 1 Cor. 15:58 (as you point out) or 1 Thess. 5:23. But unlike Paul, Peter looks on to the ultimate dissolution of the present creation and its replacement by a new one, without taking into his purview the preceding stages as Paul does (say) in 1 Cor. 15:23-28. The end may well be viewed as a complex of events rather than as one instantaneous event, but it is possible so to concentrate on the individual events that make it up as to forget that in itself it is the one decisive act of God in Christ.

1 John 2:1. *What is the difference between our Lord's advocacy in 1 John 2:1 and His high priesthood in the Epistle to the Hebrews?*

His advocacy is one of the many forms of His high-priestly ministry on our behalf. Like all the other forms of this ministry, His advocacy is based on the atonement He made for His people's sins (cf. Heb. 2:17). To this Charles Wesley has given immortal expression in the stanza beginning, "Five bleeding wounds He bears...", in the hymn "Arise, my soul, arise." John mentions His advocacy in the situation that arises "if any one does sin" (R.S.V.). Other aspects of His high priesthood mentioned in the Epistle to the Hebrews (apart from His ensuring His people's never-failing acceptance before God) are His strengthening them to meet and resist temptation (Heb. 2:17f.), His sympathizing with their weakness and providing the necessary mercy and grace to help them in time of need (Heb. 4:15f.), and His intercession on their behalf (Heb. 7:25). Some idea of what is involved in this intercession may be gained from a consideration of Luke 22:31f. and John 17:6ff. His intercession is not to be envisaged as though He were "*standing* ever before the Father with outstretched arms, like the figures in the mosaics of the catacombs, and with strong crying and tears pleading our cause in the presence of a reluctant God; but as a *throned* Priest-King, asking what He will from a Father who always hears and grants His request. Our Lord's life in heaven is His prayer" (H. B. Swete).

1 John 2:2. *In what sense is Christ a propitiation "not for our sins only, but also for the whole world" (1 John 2:2)?*

In the sense that the atoning sacrifice which has availed to wipe out our sins is sufficient to do the same for all. Jesus is not only the personal Saviour of each believer; He is "the general Saviour of mankind." According to the Gospel of John, He is "the true light that enlightens every man" (John 1:9) or, in the forerunner's words, "the Lamb of God, who takes away the sin of the world" (John 1:29). We must therefore not rest content with the assurance of our own salvation but spread the joyful message worldwide.

1 John 2:9-11. *Is the "brother" in 1 John 2:9-11 more particularly a fellow- Christian, rather than one's relative by natural birth?*

Since John concentrates throughout this epistle on the heavenly family, into which believers have been introduced as children of God, it is probable that he is thinking more especially of a brother in Christ. But the principle would not be restricted to brethren in that sense; it is, in fact, unlimited in its scope. The incident of Cain and Abel, who were natural brothers, is adduced in Ch. 3:12 as a warning against hatred; and it is certain that any Christian who cherishes feelings of enmity and hatred in his heart against a brother-man has failed to learn the first lesson in the school of Christ.

1 John 2:15. *Is the "world" (kosmos) in 1 John 2:15 ("Love not the world") different from the "world" (kosmos) in John 3:16 ("God so loved the world")? If so, by what criterion do we distinguish in sense between two occurrences of the same word?*

We can make the distinction only by having regard to the context. In John 3:16 it is primarily the people in the world (mankind) who are in view; this is made plain by the words "whosoever believeth ..." which cannot refer to inanimate nature or to a world-system, but to human beings. In 1 John 2:15 it is the "godless world" (N.E.B.), i.e. the world-system organized in rebellion against God, that is in view—the current climate of opinion, as we might say. This is made plain by John's summing up of "all that is in the world" in the following verse; the lust of the flesh and the lust of the eyes and the pride of life denote the things on which children of God are not to set their affection. Not only is "world" (*kosmos*) different in sense in the two places; "love" (*agapaō*) is also different in sense: in John 3:16 it is a self-sacrificing love; in 1 John 2:15 it is an acquisitive love. It is not the Greek word in itself that makes the difference (it can have as wide a range of meaning as its English counterpart); it is the context in which is it used.

1 John 3:8. *How can a child of God be of the devil (1 John 3:8)?*

He cannot; that is the point John is making. The characteristic of a child of the devil is that he sins; the characteristic of a child of God is that he doesn't sin. This does not exclude the possibility that the child of God may commit an occasional sin; John has already pointed out that divine provision is made for this contingency in the propitiation and advocacy of our Lord (1 John 2:1, 2). But no one whose course of life is characterized by sin can claim to be a child of God.

1 John 3:9. *What is the meaning of "his seed" in 1 John 3:9?*

"His seed" is almost certainly "God's seed", but the clause "his seed abides in him" may be taken in two ways, according to our understanding of the phrase "in him." It may mean (i) that "God's nature" (so R.S.V.) abides in the believer or (ii) that God's offspring—i.e. God's children—abide in Him, that is in God, and cannot sin because they are the offspring of the unsinning God. One way or the other, the new birth involves a radical change in human nature; for those who have not undergone it, John implies, sin is natural, while for those who have undergone it, sin is unnatural—so unnatural that its practice constitutes a strong refutation of any claim to possess the divine life.

1 John 4:20. *With reference to 1 John 4:20 ("he who does not love his brother whom he has seen, cannot love God whom he has not seen"), I have a difficulty. It is not easy to love some of our brethren and sisters because of the inconsistencies which we cannot help seeing in them; it seems so much easier to love God, knowing how much He has done for us.*

Perhaps it may help if we remember that the love for one another which the New Testament enjoins is not a matter of feeling, but a steadfast seeking of one another's good. Where God is the object of our love, we cannot, of course, promote His welfare by any act of ours, but we can obey Him, and obedience indeed is laid down as a test of our love to Him. "For this is the love of God, that we keep His commandments" (1 John 5:3); and one of His principal commandments is "that he who loves God should love his brother also" (1 John 4:21). You rightly refer in a postscript to our Lord's commandment "that you love one another as I have loved you" (John 15:12), and add that this implies a self-sacrificial love. It certainly does, and it is God's love for us, with all our inconsistencies (not to use a stronger word), that enables us to love our brothers and sisters, with all *their* inconsistencies. This is not something which comes naturally to us; to love the unloveable is a mark of that divine love which has been shed abroad in the hearts of believers through the Holy Spirit, and its presence is a proof of the presence of the Spirit Himself. Just as, in the Old Testament, love for one's neighbour is the counterpart of love for God, so, in the New Testament, love for the people of Christ is the proof of our love for Christ Himself.

1 John 5:6, 8. *Is the water mentioned in 1 John 5:6, 8, the water of John 19:34?*

Considering the importance attached in the context to the "blood and water" of John 19:34; I should not care to say that there is no reference to it in 1 John 5:6, 8. The Evangelist appears to regard the effusion of blood and water from our Lord's side as a combined testimony to the reality of His humanity and the genuineness of His death. But the primary reference of the water in 1 John 5:6, 8, as I see it, is rather to His baptism. John knows of false teachers who held "the Christ" to be a spiritual being that descended on Jesus of Nazareth at His baptism but left Him before His death.

From their point of view, the Christ came by water but not by blood. Hence John emphasizes that He came "not with the water only, but with the water and with the blood"; He was proclaimed as the Son of God as truly in His death as He was in His baptism. The water and the blood bear witness as they are media for the supreme witness-bearing of the Spirit, who not only by His descent at Jordan (cf. John 1:32-34) but by the sacrifice of the cross (cf. Heb. 9:14) testifies to the truth of our Lord's person.

1 John 5:7. *Why is 1 John 5:7, as it appears in A.V., missing from so many later versions?*

The verse that appears in the A.V. as 1 John 5:7 is not in the original Greek text, nor in any Greek manuscript earlier than the fifteenth century, nor in Jerome's Latin text, nor in the R.V., nor in the R.S.V., nor in the Jerusalem Bible, nor in the N.E.B., nor in many other authorities too numerous to mention. J. N. Darby does not have it in his *New Translation* (1871), and refers to it in a footnote as "having, as is well known, no real manuscript authority, and inserted by some here without adequate warrant." The doctrine of the Trinity is, of course, well enough established in the New Testament apart from this passage (cf. Matt. 28:19; 1 Cor. 12:4-6; 2 Cor. 13:14; Eph. 4:4-6). The interpolation first appears in a Latin treatise by a Spanish Christian named Priscillian who died in A.D. 385. Erasmus felt obliged to include it (reluctantly) in his third edition of the Greek New Testament (1522) because of an incautious promise he had made, and so it found its way into successive early printed editions of the Greek Testament and thence into the A.V.

1 John 5:16. *What is the "sin unto death" in 1 John 5:16?*

I suggest that it is, quite literally, a sin which has death as its consequence.

Compare 1 Cor. 11:30, and possibly 1 Cor. 5:5. But the only way in which it may be known that a sin is "unto death" is if death actually ensues. What John is doing, in that case, is to make it plain that he does not advocate praying for the dead. Another possibility is that John has apostasy in view, as though these who "went out from us" (2:19) have put themselves beyond the reach of prayer; but this I doubt.

3 John 4. *What is meant by "walking in the truth" (3 John 4)?*

Living a Christian life. "The truth" is Christianity in its fullness; when one who professes allegiance to Christianity lives a life in conformity with his profession, then he does not merely pay lip-service to the truth but "walks in the truth." In effect, walking in the truth is the same thing as walking in the light (1 John 1:7).

3 John 9f. *If you were Gaius, would you continue to recognize Diotrephes as an elder after receiving the third epistle of John?*

I don't know: perhaps I should not have recognized him as an elder even before receiving John's epistle. If I judge his description correctly, he was probably a self-appointed dictator of the type that is not unknown even today when there is not a sufficiently firm church administration to keep such people in their proper place.

Jude 11. *What is "the way of Cain" in Jude 11?*

It is the way which is devoid both of faith (cf. Heb. 11:4) and of brotherly love (cf. 1 John 3:11f.). In the early days of Christianity there was one heretical (Gnostic) group which actually venerated Cain and his successors as champions of right, and claimed to be akin to him "and to the men of Sodom and Esau *and Korah*" (as Epiphanius informs us).

Jude 22f. *Are two or three classes described in Jude 22 and 23?*

The A.V. and N.E.B. give two classes; the R.V. and R.S.V. distinguish three. The difficulty is due mainly to the uncertainty of the Greek text and in part to the question whether *diakrinomai* should be rendered "make a difference" (A.V.), "be in doubt" (R.V.; cf. R.S.V., N.E.B.), or "dispute" (Darby, Mayor). I think that most probably two classes are envisaged; those who are responsible for maintaining due order in the churches must use different methods towards those who persist in inculcating subversive and immoral doctrine and those who have been misled by false teachers.

THE BOOK OF THE REVELATION

Revelation 1:3; 22:10. *Since the Book of Revelation is called a "prophecy" (Rev. 1:3), should we not regard everything in it as belonging to the future—at least, to what was future when John received the visions?*

This would be a valid inference only if "prophecy" meant "prediction" and nothing more. But God's revelation through His servants the prophets (among whom John is counted in Rev. 22:9) might refer to past, present or future. And John himself was commanded to write down what he saw, both "what is and what is to take place hereafter" (Rev. 1:19), in words which imply that part of his visions had reference to a situation already in existence.

Rev. 1:4, *etc. What is meant by the "seven spirits" of Rev. 1:4; 3:1; 4:5; 5:6?*

Most probably this is a symbolic representation of the one Holy Spirit in the sevenfold fulness of His grace and power. The way in which the "seven spirits" are mentioned in Rev. 1:4f. between "him who is and who was and who is to come" and "Jesus Christ the faithful witness," as though enjoying equality of status with the Father and the Son, confirms this. They are not identical with "the seven angels who stand before God" in Rev. 8:2. When in 3:1 and 5:6 Jesus is said to have "the seven spirits of God," this denotes the fact that He possesses the Spirit in unlimited measure (cf. John 3:34). The language in 4:5 is reminiscent of Zech. 4:2-10. At an early state in the history of the interpretation of Revelation, the expression "the seven spirits" were correlated with the seven designations of the Spirit of the Lord in Isa. 11:2, according to the Septuagint, where the Messiah has resting upon Him "the spirit of wisdom and understanding,

the spirit of counsel and might, the spirit of knowledge and godliness, the spirit of the fear of God." We may compare the lines in the ancient hymn *Veni Creator*:

> Thou the anointing Spirit art
> Who dost thy sevenfold gifts impart.

Rev. 2-3. *Do you believe that we have a panorama of church history in the Letters to the Seven Churches in Rev. 2 and 3?*

Nothing that I know of church history suggests to me that the seven letters correspond to seven successive stages in the course of church history, in such a way that the letter to Ephesus is specially applicable to the church of apostolic days, and the letter to Laodicea to the church of the period immediately preceding the Second Advent. I have seen this view expounded, but have never found it convincing. While the letters were applicable first and foremost to the seven churches to which they are addressed, they have a permanent message for other churches, for the seven churches of Asia between them cover most of the conditions in which churches have found themselves throughout the Christian era. An excellent exposition of the abiding spiritual message of the seven letters is given by E. M. Blaiklock in *The Seven Churches* (Marshall, Morgan & Scott, 1951). "While institutions grow old and enthusiasm decays", he writes, "as happened at Ephesus, while good men face bitter trials, as they did at Smyrna, while rulers sit in the place of God, as they sat at Pergamum, while subtle error saps the strength of men, as it did at Thyatira, while specious appearance takes the place of truth, as it did once in Sardis, while high courage faces opportunity's open door, as Philadelphia saw, and while worthlessness walks with head in air, as it did in Laodicea, the two chapters have a word to say to men." It is all right to say (as some say today) that we are living in Laodicean days, if we mean that we ourselves are Laodiceans, because then we may pay heed to the injunction of Rev. 3:18. It is dangerous to say it if we mean that others are Laodiceans while we are not; such a spirit of complacency is the essence of Laodiceanism and is very difficult to cure.

Rev. 2:7, *etc. Who is the "overcomer" mentioned repeatedly at the end of the Letters to the Seven Churches in Rev. 2 and 3?*

The Christian who maintains his confession to the end without faltering in face of direct persecution or the more subtle temptation to compromise at certain points.

Rev. 2:4. *Did the church of Ephesus regain its "first love" (Rev. 2:4)?*

Yes, if the testimony of Ignatius (about A.D. 110) may be trusted. According to him, the church of Ephesus showed him great kindness when he was on his way from Antioch to Rome to be exposed to the wild beasts in the arena: "You are imitators of God," he wrote to the church in reference to this kindness, "and, having kindled your congenial task by the blood of God, you brought it to perfect fulfilment." Ignatius's words give us reason to think that the Ephesian church paid heed to the Lord's exhortation: "Remember then from what you have fallen, repent and do the works you did at first" (Rev. 2:5).

Rev. 2:6, *etc. Who were the Nicolaitans, and what was their doctrine?*

The form of the word "Nicolaitans" suggests that they were the followers of one Nicolas, but the idea that this Nicolas was the proselyte of Antioch mentioned in Acts 6:5 cannot be traced earlier than *c.* A.D. 180. The works and teaching of the Nicolaitans are to be inferred quite plainly from the Letter to Pergamum in Rev. 2:12-17; they were evidently a party who believed in making the Christian path in a pagan world a little smoother by urging some measure of compromise with idolatry—so much compromise, at least, as would satisfy imperial and social requirements. The self-styled prophetess of Thyatira apparently taught something very similar, although no express mention of Nicolaitans occurs in the Letter to Thyatira. But John (or, rather, the risen Christ speaking through John) stigmatizes such compromise as "the teaching of Balaam" (cf. Num. 31:16).

Rev. 4:4, *etc. Who are the twenty-four elders and four living creatures of Rev. 4:4, etc.?*

They are probably a senior order of angels, rendering priestly service to God in heaven, including the presentation of the prayers of the saints (5:8). The number twenty-four may correspond intentionally to the twenty-four priestly courses of 1 Chron. 24. The four living creatures represent rather the powers of creation serving the Creator; their antecedents may be found in the living creatures (cherubim) of Ezekiel's visions (Ezek. 1:5ff.; 10:1ff.).

Rev. 5:9. *What value should be attached to S. P. Tregelles's insistence that "us" ("thou...hast redeemed us") should be retained in Rev. 5:9 (The Hope of Christ's Second Coming, p. 77)?*

Tregelles was influenced by the fact that "us" appears in this verse in the Codex Sinaiticus. He was strongly supported by B. W. Newton (*Thoughts on the Apocalyse*, Appendix B). But they both accepted the reading "them" and "they" in verse 10 for "us" and "we" of the Received Text, which logically demands the omission of "us" in verse 9 with several ancient authorities, the R.V., and most recent editors. J. N. Darby (who points out that Codex Sinaiticus "is very incorrect in the Apocalypse") and W. Kelly are among those who reject "us" in verse 9—a point of considerable importance, as its retention would have lent more support to their interpretation of the passage.

Rev. 6:6. *What is the significance of the oil and the wine in the words "see thou hurt not the oil and the wine" in Rev. 6:6?*

The message associated with the opening of the third seal implies the scarcity and rationing which are the natural sequel of the warfare announced at the opening of the second seal. Wheat and barley (the staple forms of solid food) are to be sold at about ten or twelve times their normal price, and olive oil and wine (the staple forms of liquid food in "Bible lands") must be used very sparingly.

Rev. 6:8. *Why is the rider on the pale horse in Rev. 6:8 given dominion over only one fourth of the earth? Also, are the four horsemen part of the present scene, or are they yet to appear?*

If death and Hades are given dominion over a fourth of the earth, the implication is that a quarter of mankind are wiped out by the four scourges here mentioned— sword, famine, pestilence and wild beasts. In a more general sense, of course, death has dominion over all men "in Adam" (Rom. 5: 12-14; 1 Cor. 15:22); but that is not the sense intended here. Had Death and Hades been given dominion over all mankind in the sense of Rev. 6:8, then all mankind would have died in the period introduced by the breaking of the fourth seal, and human history on earth would have come to a full stop. The trumpets later in the book are attended by a larger degree of destruction than the seals, and the plagues emptied from the seven bowls of chapter 16 are more destructive than the trumpet judgments.

Expositors differ on the question whether the four horsemen belong to the part of Revelation which deals with "things that are" or to the part which deals with "things that are to be hereafter." My own tentative view would be that since Christ is seen in Ch. 5 as taking the sealed scroll immediately on His return to heavenly glory, fresh from the place of sacrifice, the events accompanying the breaking of the seals are those of A.D. 30-70. I suggest that the cry under the sixth seal, "Fall on us and hide us" (Rev. 6:16), is identical with the cry foretold by our Lord in Luke 23:30, and is associated with the same crisis. Several Bible students have marked the rather close correspondence between the first six seals of Rev. 6 and our Lord's Olivet forecast of the immediate future to be fulfilled within a generation (see p. 57) (Matt. 24; Mark 13; Luke 21).

Rev. 6:13. *What would be your opinion of the phenomenon in the sixth seal (Rev. 6:13), where the stars are seen to fall from heaven "as the fig tree sheds its winter fruit when shaken by a gale"?*

I believe the reference in Rev. 6:12, 13 is identical with that in Matt. 24:29, and that here, as there, the collapse of established authority is meant or, as William Kelly put it, "an overwhelming revolution which overthrows existing institutions and governmental order" (*Lectures on the Revelation*, p. 148). The language echoes that of such Old Testament passages as Isa. 34:4 and Joel 2:31; 3:15, where a similar visitation of divine judgment is portrayed. See pp. 59f.

Rev. 6:17ff. *One well-known exposition of the Book of Revelation says that the great tribulation does not begin until after the seventh seal; another says it is perfectly clear that it is completely finished before the sixth seal. Which is right?*

Much confusion of thought on this subject is caused by failure to distinguish carefully between the great tribulation endured by the people of God at the hands of a godless world-power and the great tribulation endured by that world-power and its followers at the hands of God unless they repent. The former is the result of the devil's wrath against the godly; the latter manifests the wrath of God against their oppressors. It may be "perfectly clear" that the former is finished before the sixth seal; but when the sixth seal is broken the "kings of the earth" and their followers realize with terror that *their* great tribulation is about to fall on them. So both commentators could be right, but the great tribulation which the one has in view is not the same as that intended by the other.

Rev. 7:5-8. *In Revelation 7:5-8, why is Dan omitted and replaced by Manasseh, which one would expect to be included in Joseph?*

The traditional answer to this question is that Dan is omitted because Antichrist was expected to come from that tribe (an expectation based by Irenaeus on the Septuagint version of Jer. 8:16). Another suggestion is that Dan once stood where Manasseh now stands, the confusion being due to an obscurity in the manuscript; but this suggestion is purely conjectural, unsupported by any textual evidence. So no certain answer can be given. We may compare the omission of Simeon from the blessing of Moses (Deut. 33)—although that omission probably has quite a different explanation.

Rev. 9:1, *etc. Please comment on the revival of the rendering "bottomless pit" in Rev. 9:1, etc., in the Revised Standard Version.*

I think this return to the A.V. rendering of Gk. *abyssos* in place of "abyss," as in R.V. and A.R.V., is a retrograde proceeding. The N.E.B. prefers "abyss." The

rendering "bottomless pit" depends on a false etymology, and is rather absurd when one thinks about it. In Luke 8:31 and Rom. 10:7 the R.S.V. renders the same word by "abyss," which makes it the more surprising that this rendering was not used for the occurrences of the word in the Apocalypse.

Rev. 10:7. *What is the "mystery of God" referred to in Rev. 10:7?*

It is the eternal purpose of God, formerly kept secret but now to be revealed and consummated. The mystery (foretold through the prophets) is to be fully unfolded when the seventh angel sounds his trumpet, and a consideration of what happened when this angel did sound (Rev. 11:15ff.) will indicate the chief features of the mystery.

Rev. 11:15. *What are the kingdoms of Rev. 11:15?*

Perhaps there is only one kingdom in this verse. The R.V. rendering is, "The kingdom of the world is become *the kingdom* of our Lord, and of his Christ"— the italicization of the second occurrence of "the kingdom" indicating that it has no equivalent in the Greek. The meaning may then be that "the sovereignty of the world has passed to our Lord and his Christ" (N.E.B.). Otherwise, taking the R.V. wording as it stands, the meaning is that Gentile world dominion has been replaced by the eternal kingdom of our Lord and His Messiah. This is in line with the visions of Daniel 2 and 7, and their interpretation; "the kingdom of the world" may sum up the four Gentile world-empires or may refer to the last of the four, and the kingdom which replaces "the kingdom of the world" is the "everlasting dominion, which shall not pass away" foretold in Dan. 7:14 (cf. Dan. 2:44).

Rev. 12:1-6. *If the woman in Rev. 12 is Israel (a mystical woman), should not* the *"man child" also be interpreted mystically? If she is Israel, when did Israel receive the wings of a great eagle to be carried to a place of refuge in the wilderness? If the "man child" is Christ, surely the woman should be the Virgin Mary, and when was she carried to the wilderness on the wings of an eagle?*

I think we may dismiss the identification of the woman with the Virgin Mary. It goes back at least to the middle of the fifth century, when it was suggested by a writer called Quodvultdeus, who interpreted the woman as Mary, but Mary viewed as a type of the Church. The identification of Mary with the woman crowned with twelve stars has no doubt played its part in the exaltation of our Lord's Mother as the queen of heaven, but it is hardly in keeping with her historical portrayal in the New Testament. However, in view of the widely attested tendency in Biblical literature to oscillate between corporate and individual personality, there would be nothing surprising in the presentation of the Messiah as coming to birth from the travail of the messianic community, i.e. the people of God in Old and New Testament times together. The "man child" is destined "to rule all the nations with a rod of iron"—language traditionally associated with the Davidic Messiah and going back ultimately to Psa. 2:9. But in Rev. 2:26f., at the end of the letter to Thyatira, the same language is used of the faithful overcomer. This accords with the association of the saints in the royal and judicial dignity of the Son of Man which is found both in the Old Testament (Dan. 7:22, 27; cf. Psa. 149:5-9) and in the New (e.g., Luke 12:32; 22:29f.; 1 Cor. 6:2f.). Thus it is at least to be borne in mind as an open possibility that the "man child" of Rev. 12 should be understood corporately of the Messiah together with His followers. But I find it most satisfactory to understand much of Rev. 12 as being a flashback to events

preceding the time at which John received his visions, serving as an introduction to a new section of his prophecy. The woman I should think of as the messianic community or "Israel of God," especially as manifested locally in the Palestinian church, the mother-church *par excellence*; and I should identify the incidents of verses 6 and 14-16 with the fortunes of that church during the war of A.D. 66-70. The "remnant of her seed" will be Christians in other parts of the world, the targets of attack in 13:7.

Rev. 13:1, *etc. Are the ten horns of Rev. 13:1; 17:3 to be identified with the ten horns of Dan. 7:7?*

I do not think so. In Dan. 7 the ten horns grow out of the head of the last of four beasts; in Rev. 13 and 17 they grow out of the head of a beast who combines features from all four of Daniel's beasts, and who may thus be envisaged as more ferocious than any single one of Daniel's beasts. I take the ten horns of Dan. 7 to signify a succession of rulers who followed Alexander the Great, the little horn of verse 8 being Antiochus Epiphanes, on whom John's imperial Antichrist is in some degree modelled. See p. 141 below.

Rev. 13:18. *Have you any views on the number of the beast in Rev. 13:18?*

I have no desire to add to the number of interpretations, which must considerably exceed six hundred and sixty-six. One of the wisest remarks on the subject was made by Provost George Salmon of Trinity College, Dublin, who laid down "three rules by the help of which I believe an ingenious man could find the required sum in any given name. First, if the proper name by itself will not yield it, add a title; secondly, if the sum cannot be found in Greek, try Hebrew, or even Latin; thirdly, do not be too particular about the spelling" (*Introduction to the N.T.*, p. 251). For my part, I shall rest content (or nearly content) with "Nero Caesar" until someone shows me a more convincing solution. The question whether any instance was known of "Nero Caesar" being spelt in such a way as to yield an exact numerical total of 666 was answered affirmatively in the 1950s when the required spelling was found on an Aramaic document of Nero's reign from the Wadi Murabba'at, west of the Dead Sea.

Rev. 16:12. *Who are the kings of the east in Rev. 16:12?*

Any territory east of the Euphrates would satisfy the wording. John and his original readers would naturally think in the first instance of the Parthians and their allies.

Rev. 17:3ff. *In Rev. 17 what is signified by (a) the woman, (b) the beast, (c) the seven heads, (d) the ten horns?*

The woman is the city of Rome; the beast is the Roman Empire, from which the city drew her sustenance; the seven heads are given a twofold significance, being (i) the seven hills of Rome (verse 9) and (ii) seven successive emperors (verse 10); the ten horns are ten subordinate rulers who were to attack and destroy the city.

Rev. 17:10. *Who are the "seven kings" of Rev. 17:10?*

I have elsewhere suggested that they are the Roman Emperors Augustus, Tiberius, Gaius, Claudius and Nero (the "five" who "have fallen"), Vespasian (the one who "is" at the time of the vision) and Titus (the seventh who "has not yet come" and "must remain only a little while"). This calculation omits Galba, Otho and Vitellius, whose brief reigns intervened successively between Nero (54-68) and Vespasian (69-79); if one or more of these three should be included in the reckoning, then the identification of the first five must be modified.

Rev. 19:7f., *etc. Who constitutes the bride of Christ in Rev. 19?*

The elect of all ages, I should say. This seems evident from Chapter 21, where John, invited to see "the bride, the wife of the Lamb" (v. 9) is shown the same body of people under another figure, that of "the holy city Jerusalem" (v. 10). This city of God has the names of the twelve tribes of Israel inscribed on her gates and the names of the twelve apostles inscribed on her foundation-stones; this I take to mean that the city, or the bride, comprises the people of God in Old and New Testament times alike.

Rev. 20:3ff. *Do you identify the Messianic reign with the millennium of Revelation 20?*

Not completely; as I see it, the millennium of Rev. 20 is included as a later phase of the Messianic reign but is not co-extensive with it. Our Lord's Messianic reign began with His exaltation ("Sit at my right hand ...") and goes on until God has put all His enemies beneath His feet (1 Cor. 15:25). The millennium begins at a later point, when the faithful martyrs and confessors of Rev. 20:4 are raised from the dead to share His dominion.

Rev. 20:4. *In Rev. 20:4 we read of "souls of those who had been beheaded for their testimony to Jesus" and who had refused the mark of the beast. Were they from John's perspective a past or a future company?*

For John they were both. They included the souls of Rev. 6:9, but by contrast with the situation denoted by the breaking of the fifth seal the full tale of martyrs was now complete.

In Rev. 20:4 it is said that the "souls" mentioned in the foregoing question "lived" (A.V.) or, according to the New American Standard Bible, "came to

141

life." *I take it that the translators of the latter version regarded the Greek verb as an ingressive aorist. Since the word is used in this way in Rev. 2:8 and Rom. 14:9, as well as in the following verse of our present chapter, where each time resurrection is in view, do we not have strong reason to believe that this is what is implied in Rev. 20:4?*

Yes. The R.S.V. and N.E.B. also render "came to life" (N.E.B. "came to life again"), with this implication. Those souls that John saw when the fifth seal was broken had not ceased to exist, but they were disembodied; the white robes given to them in 6:11 are scarcely their resurrection bodies, which they are to receive when all their fellow-martyrs have joined them. For the completed company of glorified martyrs we may consider Rev. 7:9-17; 14:1-5 (those "redeemed from mankind as first fruits for God and the Lamb"); 15:2 ("those who had conquered the beast and its image"—by the means specified in 12:11).

Rev. 20:10. *The middle clause of Rev. 20:10 is variously translated in our versions: e.g. "where the beast and the false prophet are" (A.V.), "where are also the beast and the false prophet" (R.V.), "where the Wild Beast and the false Prophet were" (Weymouth). The Companion Bible gives the A.V. text but has a note in the margin: "are. No verb. Read 'were', or 'were cast'." Can you give some help on this point?*

The verb "are" in A.V. is italicized, because no verb is expressed in the Greek; it is left to be supplied from the context. The literal translation of the clause is "where also the beast and the false prophet"; this is intolerable in English, which demands that the verb be expressed.

It is not certain whether the better verb to supply would be the verb "to be" either in the present tense (A.V., R.V.) or in the past (R.S.V., Weymouth), or the same verb as in the preceding principal clause: "the devil that deceived them was cast into the lake of fire and brimstone, where also the beast and the false prophet were cast" (compare also N.E.B.). On the whole, the latter rendering would be my preference. The adverbial relative *hopou*, used here, can mean "whither" as well as "where" in the New Testament (cf. Rev. 14:4).

Rev. 21:14. *According to Rev. 21:14 the foundations of the walls of the New Jerusalem bear "twelve names of the twelve apostles of the Lamb." But, if we include Matthias (Acts 1:26) and Paul (Rom. 1:1; 2 Cor. 12:12, etc.), there were thirteen apostles. Who are the twelve of Rev. 21:14?*

They are, I do not doubt, the twelve who accompanied our Lord in the days of His flesh, with Matthias replacing Judas Iscariot. The apostleship of Paul was of a different order to theirs (see p. 75 above).

Rev. 22:17. *Is the twofold "Come" of Rev. 22:17 addressed to the Lord or to the thirsty person mentioned later in the verse?*

To the Lord, I think. If the Spirit is the Spirit of prophecy (cf. Rev. 19:10), then "the Spirit and the Bride" will be practically equivalent to "the prophets and the saints" (H. B. Swete). It looks as if each church member who listened to the Apocalypse being read aloud was expected at this point to break in with his personal "Come!" (in Aramaic *Marana-tha*), in response to the assurance of verse 12: "Behold, I come quickly."

PART II

Answers on Various Subjects

Ancient Literature and Archaeology

Josephus on Jesus and James

Have the references in the "Jewish Antiquities" of Josephus to Jesus (xviii. 63f.) and to his brother James (xx. 200) any evidential value?

They might have some slight evidential value if we did not have the much more positive and substantial testimony of the New Testament documents. There is no reason to doubt the authenticity of Josephus's account of the death of James. It was known to Origen about A.D. 230. The way in which James is introduced there as "the brother of Jesus, the so-called Christ", would suggest that Josephus has made some earlier reference to this Jesus. Such a reference has come down to us in the passage from Book XVIII to which you allude, and while this passage appears have received some embellishments from Christian copyists (for it was Christians and not Jews who preserved the writings of Josephus), in its main elements it is certainly genuine. As Josephus composed it, it may have run something like this: "About this time there arose a source of further troubles in one Jesus, a wise man and a wonder-worker, a teacher of those who gladly welcome strange things. He led away many Jews, and many Gentiles also. This man was the so-called Christ. When Pilate, acting on information received from the principal men among us, condemned him to be crucified, those who had first attached themselves to him did not abandon their allegiance, and the tribe of Christians, which is called after him, is not extinct even today." The tone is detached and mildly hostile.

Population of Jerusalem

What would the population of Jerusalem and of Palestine have been in New Testament times?

Professor Joachim Jeremias, in his work *Jerusalem in the Time of Jesus*, pp. 78, 83, reckons that the normal population of the city was around 25,000-30,000, but that an influx of some 125,000 pilgrims at Passovertide raised it temporarily to around 150,000. In the same work, p. 205, he gives reasons for thinking that the population of all Palestine in those days was between 500,000 and 600,000.

The Holy Sepulchre

What light have recent discoveries thrown on the question whether the Church of the Holy Sepulchre was within the north wall of Jerusalem at the time of our Lord's death, or outside it?

In 1963 archaeological excavations in the Old City, directed by Dr. Kathleen Kenyon, revealed a quarry of this period, south of the Church of the Holy Sepulchre, which must have been outside the second north wall of Jerusalem. If this quarry was outside the wall, then the site of the Church was *a fortiori* outside it. Her account may be read in the *Palestine Exploration Quarterly* for January-June 1964. This does nothing, of course, to prove that our Lord was crucified and buried on the site of the Church; but if the excavations had shown that the wall ran *north* of the Church, that would have been proof that the site was not authentic. The question remains open; if ever it is settled, it will be settled on objective archaeological grounds and not on grounds of ancient tradition or modern sentiment.

The Holy Sepulchre and the Third North Wall

Further to the foregoing question, if the quarry south of the Church of the Holy Sepulchre must have lain outside the Second North Wall, would not the same reasoning suggest that it must have lain outside the Third North Wall (Agrippa's Wall)—which is impossible?

This problem has been recognized by Dr. Kathleen Kenyon, who says that it "needs further consideration of all the available evidence"; at present she is not prepared to say that it is impossible that the quarry area should have lain outside the Third North Wall. The quarry was one belonging to the period of the kings of Judah, which was sealed off in the 7th century B.C. The site then remained unbuilt upon until the early 2nd century A.D., when it was filled in with material including pottery of the 1st and early 2nd century A.D. Had it lain within the Second North Wall it would certainly have been filled in and built upon long before. Agrippa's Wall, the Third North Wall, built between A.D. 41 and 44, ran very largely along the line of the present north wall, and enclosed not only the new suburb of Bezetha on the north-east, but an undeveloped area on the north-west. But for the destruction of the city in A.D. 70 this undeveloped area would no doubt have been built over in a matter of decades. Agrippa's Wall was left incomplete; had Agrippa ("Herod the king" of Acts 12) been able to complete it, Josephus assures us twice over that the city could never have been taken by the Romans. The filling in and building over of the quarry area is probably to be assigned to Hadrian. The lines of Hadrian's city (A.D. 135) are followed essentially by the present walls. (Its south wall ran well to the north of the former south wall, and actually as Dr. Kenyon's excavations have shown, to the north of the *north* wall of the Jebusite city, which David captured.)

Jerusalem in Abraham's Day

If the north wall of Jebusite Jerusalem, recently discovered by Miss Kenyon, was built about 1,800 B.C., was the city there in Abraham's time? How would

this affect the belief that Abraham's offering of Gen. 22 was on the site where Solomon's temple was later built (and the present Dome of the Rock), since the site would presumably have been inside the city?

It may well be that the recently discovered north wall was there in Abraham's day. But the temple area, as it later became (the present Haram esh-Sherif), would have been outside the wall, since the north wall of Jebusite Jerusalem ran *south* of the temple area. Jebusite Jerusalem was apparently confined to the hill Ophel, the "stronghold of Zion" where David took up his residence after he captured it (2 Sam. 5:6-9). This area is not enclosed by the present walls. It is evident from Gen. 22 that the place where Abraham offered his sacrifice was not in a built-up area; the "ram caught in a thicket by its horns" and other details in the narrative suggest that it was out in the open and this would not contradict the tradition that the place was the site of the later temple. But the validity of the tradition is questionable; it is not certain that "the land of Moriah" of Gen. 22:2 is to be identified with "Mount Moriah" of 2 Chron. 3:1.

Jerusalem and the Israelite Conquest

If, as is implied by Josh. 15:63 and Judg. 1:21, together with 2 Sam. 5: 6-10, Jerusalem was not taken by the Israelites until its capture by David, how can we account for the statement in Judg. 1:8 that it was captured by "the children of Judah" at an early stage in the Israelite settlement in the land?

One explanation was suggested by the late Pearce Hubbard in a lecture on "The Topography of Ancient Jerusalem" delivered at the Centenary Annual General Meeting of the Palestine Exploration Fund in June, 1965, and published in the *Palestine Exploration Quarterly* for July-December, 1966. This is that the Jerusalem of Judg. 1:8 (and of Josh. 10:1, 5, 23;

12:10) was a settlement on the south-western hill, distinct from the well-fortified Jebusite settlement on the south-eastern hill, which remained in Canaanite hands until David's day. Further archaeological research would be necessary to determine whether this architectural judgment can be sustained or not.

Jewish Control of Jerusalem

It has been pointed out that on June 7 1967, Jews gained control of the site of Ancient Jerusalem for the first time since the Roman crushing of the Bar-kokhba revolt in A.D. 135. On how many occasions did Jews have absolute control of the city after the Babylonian destruction of 587 B.C.?

If by "absolute control" you mean "not subject to any degree of non-Jewish overlordship", then the answer to your question is: on three occasions. (i) In May, 142 B.C., as a result of the military and diplomatic efforts of Judas Macca-baeus and his brothers over a period of 25 years, "the yoke of the Gentiles was removed from Israel" (1 Macc. 13:41), and Israel enjoyed independence under the Hasmonaean dynasty of priest-rulers, with their capital at Jerusalem, until the Roman occupation of Jerusalem in the summer of 63 B.C. (ii) From the repudiation of Caesar's overlordship in the summer of A.D. 66 to the Roman conquest of the temple and city in the summer of A.D. 70 Jerusalem was under Jewish control. (iii) From the outbreak of the second Jewish revolt, led by Barkokhba, in A.D. 132 until its reduction by the Romans three years later Jerusalem was again under Jewish control; the Jewish state issued its own coins then, as it had done during the first revolt. One might add the periods during which Herod (37-4 B.C.), his son Archelaus (4 B.C.-A.D. 6) and his grandson Herod Agrippa I (A.D. 41-44) controlled Jerusalem as rulers of the Jews, but while technically they ruled as "friends and allies of the Roman people", actually they were dependent on Rome.

Christianity at Pompeii

Is there any evidence to show that Christianity had reached Pompeii before its destruction in A.D. 79?

There is a little evidence, but it is not unambiguous. One piece of evidence is a charcoal inscription on white plaster in the atrium of House No. 22 on the Vico del Balcone Pensile. The Latin text was scarcely intelligible when it was first uncovered, and it has faded considerably since then. But the word CHRISTIANOS ("Christians" in the accusative plural) seems unmistakable, although it is no longer possible to determine what the inscription said about them. Attempts to reconstruct the original wording have rarely convinced any but their respective authors. Another piece of evidence is the word-square believed to yield the solution *Pater Noster* with Alpha and Omega, discovered in the course of excavations at Pompeii in 1925. If this word-square is indeed a Christian formula (see *The Spreading Flame*, pp. 356f.), then it also attests the presence of Christians there before A.D. 79. Since there were Christians at Puteoli, 25 miles west of Pompeii, nearly twenty years earlier according to Acts 28:13f., it is antecedently probable that there were Christians also at Pompeii.

Christianity at Herculaneum

Further to the foregoing question, is there not some evidence for the presence of Christianity at Herculaneum as well as at Pompeii before A.D. 79? A room in the "Bicentenary House" is supposed to have been a Christian chapel because of a cross-shaped depression on a wall and what may have been an altar or fauld-stool on the floor in front of it.

That is so, but the inference is not completely certain. There is indeed a cross-shaped depression in the stucco wall-panel of an upper room in the house referred to, but the large number of nail marks scattered over the area has been thought by some to indicate that it was something quite ordinary, such as a wall cabinet, that was once nailed in this position and then removed. The identification of the piece of wooden furniture on the floor as possibly an altar or fauldstool is entirely dependent on the identification of the depression in the wall-panel as the mark of a cross which was formerly nailed there. It is a probable, but not absolutely certain, witness to the presence of Christianity in Herculaneum before its destruction. Quite apart from this evidence, it is on general grounds likely that Christianity had in fact reached Herculaneum by that time.

The Dead Sea Scrolls

What is the value, from a Biblical point of view, of the scrolls recently discovered at Qumran, in the Dead Sea region?

Their value is manifold, but they make two contributions of outstanding importance to Biblical study—they give us information about the condition of the Hebrew text of the Old Testament at a date a thousand years earlier than the oldest Hebrew Biblical manuscrips previously known, and they throw much welcome light on the Jewish background and environment of Christian origins. On the former score, they confirm that the Hebrew text of the Old Testament was transmitted with exceptional accuracy during the first nine centuries A.D. Here and there they help to restore the original text; e.g. in Isa. 21:8 they confirm that the true reading is, "Then he who saw cried" (without any reference to "a lion" as in A.V. and R.V.), and Isa. 53:11 they confirm the Septuagint reading: "After the travail of his soul he shall see light." On the latter score, some ludicrous exaggerations have received unwarranted publicity, such as that our Lord Himself may have studied for a time at Khirbet Qumran, the headquarters of the community which owned the scrolls, or that Khirbet Qumran "is perhaps, more than Bethlehem or Nazareth, the cradle of Christianity." Such wild surmises tend to bring the serious study of the subject into disrepute. But the relation of the community (possibly a branch of the Essenes) to Christian beginnings is a question of fascinating importance.

The Founder of Christianity and the organizer of the Qumran community (who preceded Him by more than a century) taught their respective followers a way of life. The two ways of life did not completely coincide, and one might consider what were the factors which enabled the one to survive the catastrophe of A.D. 70 while the other disappeared then, to be rediscovered as a historical antiquity in our own day. We shall understand both better if we give due weight to the resemblances and differences between them.

The resemblances are due not only to the general fact that both movements drew upon the spiritual heritage of Israel's faith, enshrined in the Old Testament writings; they are due more particularly to the fact that both originated in a nonconformist environment within the Jewish nation. In *The Scrolls and Christian Origins* (1961)—one of the best books on this subject—Matthew Black traces the Essene and Qumran movements back to an ancient ascetic strain or wilderness tradition in Israel, represented in earlier days by the Kenites, Nazirites and Rechabites. This train, he believes, continued to flourish in the post-exilic period as a nonconformist tradition in two main groups—a northern and a southern. From the southern group came the men of Qumran; it was against the background of the northern group that, a century and more later, Jesus began to proclaim in Galilee the gospel of the kingdom of God (although the evidence of the Fourth Gospel is that He had earlier and later associations with the southern group as well).

147

At one point after another throughout the New Testament some interaction between Qumran and early Christianity is indicated. It is of the essence of the gospel story that it is not something insulated from the contemporary world but part and parcel of the on-going course of first-century thought and action.

When God does a new thing in the earth, as He did pre-eminently in the Incarnation, the event cannot be exhaustively accounted for in terms of what went before (although what went before constitutes a providential preparation for the event); but when once the event has taken place, it is fed into the stream of history as a real dateable occurrence, playing its part in the historical pattern of cause and effect, or challenge and response.

Even in their most sober and restrained presentation, the discoveries at Qumran, with the light they shed on biblical studies, are exciting enough. They do not constitute, as the publisher's blurb on one American book once put it, "the greatest challenge to Christian dogma since Darwin's theory of evolution"—that is as rare a gem of wishful thinking as I have come across in this connexion! But they do provide us with new and most welcome background and context for the more intelligent study of the New Testament and Christian origins. When any object is viewed against a new background, the object itself takes on a fresh appearance, and against the background supplied by the Qumran discoveries many parts of the New Testament take on a new and vivid significance. Above all, those passages which express the remnant consciousness and eschatological outlook of early Christianity take on a new significance, by comparison and contrast alike, when they are viewed in the light of this contemporary movement which was also characterized by a remnant consciousness and an eschatological outlook.

We should be restrained from premature dogmatism when we consider how incomplete our knowledge of the Qumran community still is. Even when all the documents that have been discovered are published the reflection that they may represent but a fragment of what the library originally contained will continue to impose counsels of caution.

Truth is one and indivisible; and the more truth we receive, the more light is shed on the truth we already know, and the better able we are to appreciate the old and the new together. It was a Christian apostle who said, "We cannot do anything against the truth, but only for the truth" (2 Cor. 13:8). The men of Qumran would gladly have endorsed his words; we, too, may take their lesson to heart.

In the Tyndale Lecture in Biblical Archaeology for 1956, entitled The Teacher of Righteousness in the Qumran Texts, *it is stated that the Teacher of Righteousness probably received that name from Hos. 10:12, where R.V. margin gives "teach you righteousness" as a variant rendering for the text, "rain righteousness upon you." What about Joel 2:23, where E. B. Pusey supports the rendering, "He will give thee the Teacher unto righteousness" (instead of "he giveth you the former rain in just measure"), and interprets it of our Lord?*

Certainly Joel 2:23 may have been in the minds of those who called the leader of the Qumran sect "the Teacher of Righteousness", as well as Hos. 10:12. (Since Hosea is probably the earlier of the two prophets, the Joel passage may echo this.) But in both places I think the figure of rain is primarily what the text means, although the members of the Qumran sect apparently preferred to take the root in the sense of "teach" and applied it to their founder. I do not accept Pusey's exegesis of Joel 2:23.

T. H. Gaster, in his translation of the non-Biblical Dead Sea Scrolls, holds that the title "Teacher of Righteousness" designates an office not a person; and that it denotes a sort of apostolic succession of priests. He states categorically that the Qumran brotherhood "did not believe, as has been supposed, in a martyred messianic 'Teacher of Righteousness', who reappeared posthumously to his disciples and whose Second Coming was awaited." Is this a fair statement of the matter?

For the most part, yes. The title "Teacher of Righteousness" could have been applied to more than one person. But it is used predominantly of one outstanding man, the effective founder and first leader of the brotherhood. It is also used of a figure who was expected to arise "in the latter days"; there is no evidence to show that this future Teacher of Righteousness would be the first Teacher of Righteousness risen from the dead (as some have held). The second categorical statement which you quote from Gaster is right, and deserves the widest publicity. There is no evidence that the Teacher of Righteousness was martyred, still less that he was crucified; when his death is referred to, it is spoken of as his "being gathered in." And there is no evidence that his followers looked upon him as in any sense a Messiah. They did cherish the messianic hope in a very interesting form, but the Teacher of Righteousness was not an object of that hope. Gaster's translation, though free, is generally reliable.

It was reported early in 1958 that the official organ of the Russian Young Communist League, Komsomolskaya Pravda, has affirmed, in the first Russian Communist comment on the discovery of the Dead Sea Scrolls, that they present "conclusive proof" of "the mythical character of Moses and Jesus." Would you comment on this report?

It was said long ago that, if Moses did not exist, it would be necessary to invent him, for the history of Israel is inexplicable without him. So far as available reports go,

the argument in *Komsomolskaya Pravda* concentrated on our Lord more than Moses. The scrolls, it was said, belong to the first and second centuries B.C. (which is largely true), and have enabled scholars to conclude "that the image of the 'Divine Messenger' existed among the Essenes long before the New Testament writes of the birth of the mythical Christ. The principal traits of Jesus were, consequently, developed before the appearance of Christianity." In so far as the image of the Divine Messenger, or the traits of the Messiah, existed among the Essenes before the time of Christ, they were derived from the Old Testament. And the presence of those traits in the Old Testament has been recognized from the earliest days of Christianity; in fact, our Lord's fulfilment of these traits was from the first treated as one of the strongest evidence for His Messiahship. The Communist argument is a complete *non sequitur*. It is strange that people who are so far advanced in some branches of knowledge should lag so far behind in others—in certain phases of history, for example, including the history of Christian beginnings. I suspect that Marxian dogmatism has a distorting effect on the study of history. I do not know if there is a Russian translation of the Qumran texts comparable to Theodor Gaster's English version of *The Scriptures of the Dead Sea Sect*. If there is, an intelligent and unprejudiced Young Communist need only consult it in order to appreciate the fallacy of the statement quoted. If there is not, then plainly here is an opportunity for some Russian Hebraist to fill this gap in his compatriots' knowledge. If these comments are read in Moscow or Leningrad, I hope someone will take the hint.[1]

Is there any likelihood that Russian readers would be allowed to have access to unbiased accounts of the Dead Sea

---

[1] The gap has been filled (1971) by I. D. Amusin.

Scrolls and their significance, as you suggest in your last answer?

The widely publicized comment in *Komsomolskaya Pravda* may have been the first Russian *Communist* comment, but it was not the first Russian comment. In the *Journal of the Moscow Patriarchate*, Vol. 12 (1957), pp. 54-64, there was a careful and objective study "On the Tenth Year of the Discovery on the Shores of the Dead Sea" by Michael, then bishop of Smolensk. Bishop Michael pointed out (i) that the Scrolls revealed the existence in first-century Palestine of a Jewish sect more akin to primitive Christianity than the Pharisees and Sadducees, providing a fertile soil for the gospel seed, but (ii) that, despite this kinship, there were basic differences between the sect of the Scrolls and the early Christian Church.

A more scholarly account of the matter appeared in 1960, from the pen of Professor I. D. Amusin of Leningrad, one of Russia's most distinguished Semitists: *The Manuscripts of the Dead Sea* (published at Moscow by the USSR Academy of Sciences). Chapter V of this work was entitled "The Qumran Manuscripts and Early Christianity." In discussing other views on this last subject, Professor Amusin mentioned "radicals" or agnostics like Edmund Wilson, J. M. Allegro and A. Powell Davies and, at the opposite extreme, the proponents of "clerical" or "orthodox" views like Bishop Michael of Smolensk and "even so highly competent an English Semitist and Biblical scholar as H. H. Rowley." Between these extremes are the "liberals" like W. F. Albright, F. M. Cross, W. H. Brownlee, Millar Burrows and (be it said with all due modesty) the present writer. Liberal as these are, they are insufficiently emancipated from church dogma, with special reference to the divine personality of Jesus Christ. For his part, Professor Amusin relates the Qumran discoveries to the Leninist line on the rise and progress

of early Christianity, in such a way as to suggest that he is insufficiently emancipated from his own brand of dogma. Other Soviet scholars have also in various ways assessed the possible relation (or lack of relation) between the Qumran texts and early Christianity.

Extra-Canonical Literature

1. The Apocrypha:

What is the value of the Apocrypha? Is it profitable to acquire a knowledge of the books contained in it?

The books called the Apocrypha are a collection of Jewish literature—historical, legendary, poetical, didactic and apocalyptic—which appeared in the centuries between the *c.* 300 B.C. and *c.* A.D. 100. They form no part of the Hebrew Bible and do not appear to be quoted as authoritative in the New Testament. Most of them formed part of the Septuagint, the Greek version of the Old Testament current in the early church. They provide valuable information about the history and religious outlook of the Jews in the closing centuries B.C., and thus are useful for the study of the New Testament background. Jerome (*c.* A.D. 400) distinguished them carefully from the books in the Hebrew Bible, saying that although the church "does not receive them within the canonical scriptures", yet she "reads them for the edification of the people, not to confirm the authority of ecclesiastical dogmas." I have discussed them further in *The Books and the Parchments*, Ch. XIII, and in *Tradition Old and New*, Ch. VIII.

2. "The Book of Jubilees":
What is the Book of Jubilees?

The Book of Jubilees is a Jewish work of the second century B.C. which re-tells the Pentateuchal history from the Creation to the Exodus, adding some legendary material, and dividing the period into 50 parts of 49 years each. The aim of the work appears to have been a reformation of the Hebrew calendar, so that the year comprised 364 days and was divided into four equal quarters. It was held in high regard by the Qumran sect.

3. "Secret Mark"

There was a brief report in the press in 1960 about a "secret Gospel of Mark" said to have come to light. Is anything further known about it?

Professor Morton Smith of Columbia University, New York, came upon a reference to it in 1958 when he was studying ancient documents at the Mar Saba monastery south-east of Jerusalem. On the back of a Dutch book, printed in the 17th century, he found a handwritten copy of a Greek letter which on stylistic grounds he would assign to Clement of Alexandria, towards the end of the 2nd century. The chief interest of this letter lies in the fact that it refers to a longer edition of Mark's Gospel (current at Alexandria), which included "secret" sayings of Jesus not found in the canonical Mark. According to the author of the letter, Mark came to Alexandria from Rome, where he had already published his shorter Gospel (which was in essence Peter's witness to Christ). At Alexandria he expanded it and added some "secret" sayings. The Gnostic leader Carpocrates took this expanded Gospel and mixed spurious material with it. The expanded Gospel inserted after Mark 10:34 the story of the raising of a rich young man from the dead; this story has resemblances to the raising of Lazarus in John 11. The narrative then goes on to tell of James and John's request to Jesus (cf. Mark 10:35ff.). At the end of this incident there is a reference to Salome, presumably the mother of James and John (cf. the parallel narrative in Matt. 20:20ff.), who in several Gnostic Gospels plays a larger and more colourful part than she does in the New Testament. We shall have to wait until the full text of this discovery is published before we can pass judgment on it with any confidence. If, however, the expanded Gospel gives more details of the process of initiation into the mystery of the kingdom of God than are given in the canonical Mark, we may have to do with a Gnostic edition of the original Gospel. Early Alexandrian Christianity, which claimed Mark as its founder, had a decidedly Gnostic flavour about it.

4. "The Gospel according to Thomas"

What is the "Gospel according to Thomas"? Can it properly be described as a "Fifth Gospel"?

Towards the end of last century and early in the present century a few papyrus fragments containing sayings ascribed to Jesus were discovered at Oxyrhynchus in Egypt. Each saying was introduced by the words: "Jesus said." Some had been independently preserved in other early Christian writings; most were entirely new. It was evident that they came from a Greek collection of sayings of Jesus, compiled in the 2nd century. About 1945 a Gnostic library, consisting mainly of Coptic documents, was unearthed at Nag Hammadi, west of the Nile, about 60 miles north of Luxor. One of these documents proved to be a Coptic translation of this collection of sayings of Jesus, described in its colophon as "The Gospel according to Thomas." It begins: "These are the secret words which the living Jesus spoke and Didymus Judas Thomas, wrote down. 'Whosoever listens to these words shall never taste death. Let not him who seeks cease until he finds, and when he finds he shall be astonished; astonished he shall attain the kingdom and when he attains it he shall rest...'" In all, this document contains 114 sayings ascribed to Jesus. Some (like the one quoted) are obviously based on sayings recorded in the canonical Gospels; some may be based on authentic recollection; some are improbable; and some reflect heretical tendencies. To this last class, for example, belongs one which has been quoted in the press: "Wretched is the body which is bound to a body. And wretched is the soul bound to these two together." This echoes the disparagement of marriage which was fashionable (especially among Gnostics) in the early Christian centuries— a disparagement which arises from the false idea that the body is intrinsically evil and the soul intrinsically pure. For all the interest of the "Gospel according to Thomas", it is quite without warrant to describe it as a "Fifth Gospel", as though it had any claim to stand alongside the canonical four. A useful English edition is *The Secret Sayings of Jesus*, edited by R. M. Grant and D. N. Freedman (1960).

Petrine Tradition and Archaeology

What was really discovered with any relation to the apostle Peter in the excavations conducted in the early 1940's beneath St. Peter's in Rome?

About A.D. 200 a presbyter of the Roman church, Gaius by name, was engaged in a controversy with a Christian of Asia Minor named Proclus, a member of the Montanist party. When Proclus tried to support his case by appealing to the names of John and other eminent early Christians who were buried in Asia Minor, Gaius retorted that he could point out at Rome the "trophies" (i.e. funeral monuments) of Peter on the Vatican hill and of Paul on the Ostian road. What was discovered beneath the high altar of St. Peter's appears to be the "trophy" or monument which Gaius associated with Peter's name. It is dated by its archaeological context around A.D. 160, a little less than a century after Peter's death. Nero's gardens, where many Christians were martyred in the aftermath of the great fire of Rome in A.D. 64, lay in the immediate vicinity.

Is there any evidence that Peter was ever in Rome, apart from his reference to "Babylon" in 1 Pet. 5:13?

If that reference were the only evidence, the case would be a precarious one. In interpreting the New Testament references to Peter, and in evaluating the evidence for his career after he disappears from the New Testament record, it is best to put unhistorical papal claims out of our minds. There are some sturdy Protestants who suppose that their first duty towards such texts as "Thou art Peter . . ." in Matt. 16:18 or the "Babylon" reference in 1 Pet. 5:13 is to explain them in such a way as to spike the papal guns. But the interpreter's first duty is to understand the texts in the light of their context, and to avoid letting his judgment be deflected by theories or traditions which have nothing to do with the case. There is no historical evidence that Peter was the founder of the Roman church or that he was ever bishop of Rome. Quite apart from the consideration that such a local charge would have been inconsistent with his apostolic commission, there is good contemporary evidence for believing that the institution of the single or monarchical bishop was not established in Rome until well into the second century A.D. But that Peter did visit Rome towards the end of his life, and that he met his death there, can be supported by the same kind of evidence as John's residence in Ephesus, although the evidence is rather stronger for Peter in Rome than it is for John in Ephesus. In both cases there is literary evidence stretching back to the second century; but in Peter's case there is a good deal of archaeological evidence too. I should not base an argument on "Babylon" in 1 Pet. 5:13, but its identification with Rome is accepted by Eusebius (4th century) on the authority of Papias (2nd century); and neither of these writers was at all interested in defending Roman claims. I am disposed to accept the identification myself (together with the A.V. interpretation "the church that is at Babylon") because (*a*) it is known—and that not only from the Book of Revelation —that "Babylon" was current as a sobriquet for Rome among Jews and Christians of that period; (b) there is no independent evidence for a visit by Peter to Babylon on the Euphrates, as there is for his visiting Rome. If it be asked what the apostle to the circumcision was doing so far west, it may be said that there were few cities in the world then where he could find such a concentration of his proper constituency as in Rome.

I saw a reference some time ago to a report that the bones of Peter had been found in Jerusalem. Do you know what lay behind this report?

I fancy that the report was based on the discovery between 1953 and 1955 of a number of ossuaries (earthenware receptacles for disarticulated bones) on the Mount of Olives near the church called "Dominus Flevit", the traditional site of our Lord's weeping over Jerusalem. Many of the names scratched on these ossuaries are names which appear in the New Testament (Judah, Martha, Mary, Salome, Sapphira, etc.), in addition to many others which are not paralleled in the New Testament. One of the ossuaries bears the inscription "Simon Bar-Jonah" or "Simon Bar-Zenah" (the last word is indistinct). On the supposition that the former decipherment is correct, it is as naive to leap to the conclusion that the bones in this ossuary are those of the apostle as it is to leap to the conclusion that another collection of bones found some years earlier under St. Peter's high altar in Rome were his because nearby there was a Greek inscription scratched on a wall saying (perhaps) "Peter is in here." As for the ossuary inscription, "Simon Bar-Jonah" would have been about as common a name in first-century Judaea as (say) John Macdonald is today in the Highlands of Scotland or David Jones in Wales. Over 90 years ago the French archaeologist Clermont-Ganneau found near Bethany another collection of ossuaries with inscriptions including such names as Martha, Mary, Lazarus, Simon —but he did not leap to the conclusion that he had found the bones of the famous family of Bethany (including those of Simon the leper of Mark 14:3). In 1947 the late Professor E. L. Sukenik leaped to the conclusion that the name "Jesus" which he found on two ossuaries referred to our Lord—not, of course, suggesting that His bones were contained in them— but the references were almost certainly to two other bearers of the same name— Jesus the son of Judas and Jesus the son of Aloth.

Antichrist

Why did Luther and other Reformation leaders identify the Papacy with Antichrist?

We shall not understand their doing so unless we realize something of the intensity of their conviction that they were living in the last days—an intensity which it is difficult for Christians in a less eschatologically-minded age to appreciate. But with this conviction they looked around for the Antichrist of the last days, and had no difficulty in finding him in the Papacy, for in their eyes the Papacy was far and away the greatest enemy of the gospel. And it must be agreed that not even the warmest defender of the papal cause could describe the Renaissance Popes as *friends* of the gospel. It was in keeping with this eschatological outlook that many of Luther's friends, and followers thought of *him* as the promised Elijah. Spalatin did so as early as 1522, and when news came of Luther's death in 1546, Melanchthon broke it to his students at Wittenberg with the words: "Alas, gone is the chariot of Israel and the horseman thereof." So also the hymn-writer Nicolaus Hermann could sing:

> Elijah, ere the last great day,
> On earth should we be hearing,
> Proclaiming to this evil world
> That Christ is soon appearing;
> But our beloved man of God

Has sounded late his voice abroad;
The end must now be nearing.

(There were eschatological stirrings in the other camp as well, and there it was not overlooked that Luther's name lent itself rather easily to numerical analysis which yielded a total of 666.)

Apostasy

What is an apostate, from the Christian point of view?

From the Christian point of view, an apostate is one who, having once deliberately professed the Christian faith, later as deliberately repudiates it altogether.

Apostolic Succession

How would you demonstrate from Scripture the erroneousness of the doctrine of apostolic succession?

I should not suggest that the doctrine is erroneous; on the contrary, I should try to demonstrate from Scripture what the true doctrine of apostolic succession is. The true apostolic succession is the steadfast continuing in the apostles' teaching and fellowship. An apostolic church is one in which the apostolic teaching is maintained; where the apostolic teaching is maintained in its purity, the apostolic fellowship will not be far away. Provision is made in the New Testament for the maintenance of a true apostolic succession in this sense; see, for example, 2 Timothy 2:2, where Paul instructs Timothy to impart the teaching which he had received from Paul "to faithful men, who shall be able to teach others also." So the continuity of apostolic teaching would be maintained from generation to generation, the canonical Scriptures providing a permanent standard by which the apostolicity of this transmitted teaching would be tested. It was to safeguard the pure transmission of the apostolic teaching that emphasis was first laid on the importance of the continuous succession of bishops in a church, especially in a church of apostolic foundation.

Baptism

Do you feel able to join in the words, "I acknowledge one baptism for the remission of sins"; and if so, how do you interpret them?

I have no option but to acknowledge one baptism for the remission of sins, for the New Testament knows but one Christian baptism (Eph. 4:5), and Peter on the day of Pentecost described Christian baptism as being "for the remission of . . . sins" (Acts 2:38). I remember, too, how Paul at his conversion was commanded: "Rise and be baptized, and wash away your sins" (Acts 22:16). I do not recognize any dispensational frontier after the descent of the Spirit at Pentecost which would give baptism a different significance in the early apostolic age from that which it came to bear later. I interpret the words in question in the light of the fact that what is true of the reality symbolized is often predicated of the symbol itself: in baptism, part of the spiritual reality which is thus outwardly symbolized is the removal of the believer's sins.

What is the baptism of the Spirit?

The baptism of the Spirit is the act of the exalted Christ in which He imparts His Spirit to those who believe on Him, in fulfilment of such promises as those of Mark 1:8; John 16:7, and thereby incorporates them as members of His body. This baptism of the Spirit took place initially on the day of Pentecost, when Christ "poured out" the promised gift on His people (Acts 2:33) and thus constituted them the fellowship of those baptized with (in) His Spirit (sometimes called the "Spirit-baptized fellowship" for short); into this fellowship believers have been incorporated in a long and numerous succession over the centuries, as they in turn have through faith been baptised into Christ.

In one of his works W. Graham Scroggie interprets Gal. 3:27; Eph. 4:5; Col. 2:12 and Rom. 6:3, 4, in terms of the baptism of the Spirit (as opposed to water-baptism). Might this have some bearing on the interpretation of such passages as Mark 16:16; Acts 2:38 and even 1 Cor. 15:29? Does the Greek text throw any light on this matter?

This question is not one in which reference to the Greek text will give much additional help. When baptism in the Spirit is contrasted in the New Testament with baptism in water, the contrast is not with Christian water-baptism but with John's. Baptism in the Spirit and baptism in water in Christ's name are two elements in "Christian initiation" which the New Testament does not separate. The order in which they are experienced may vary (compare Acts 8:12-17 and Acts 10:44-48), but whichever precedes the other, both form part of one whole, baptism in the Spirit being the inward work of grace and baptism in water being the outward sign. In 1 Cor. 12:13 it is in the one Spirit that believers, without discrimination, have been baptized into the one body of Christ. But this baptism in the Spirit did not supersede baptism in water; baptism in water continued to be the public ordinance by which believers were welcomed into this Spirit-baptized fellowship. Therefore I do not ask myself whether the baptism into Christ mentioned in Gal. 3:27; Eph. 4:5; Col. 2:12 and Rom. 6:2, 3, is water-baptism or Spirit-baptism, as though it must be either the one or the other. That in each of these four passages the original readers of the letters would have immediately understood water-baptism I have no doubt. But it is not the external dipping in water in itself that incorporates or engrafts believers into Christ as members of His body; that is the inward and spiritual work of which the outward washing is the visible token. So the four verses mentioned certainly *imply* baptism in the Spirit, even if they do not explicitly name it. In Acts 2:38 the reception of the Spirit is the sequel to repentance and baptism in the name of Christ. This initial baptism in the Spirit plainly did not exclude water-baptism. As for Mark 16:16, this is probably a compressed form of the fuller wording of Matt. 28:19 (as you know, Mark 16:9-20 is not part of the original Gospel of Mark, but a later summary of resurrection appearances); and whatever was the point of the practice alluded to in 1 Cor. 15:29, it does not seem to have had anything to do with an inward work of the Spirit.

Barth, Karl

I am considerably perplexed by the variety of opinions I hear expressed about the orthodoxy of Karl Barth. According to some evangelical leaders, he was the pioneer in a return to truly biblical theology; according to others, he was a dangerous neo-modernist, all the more dangerous because of his use of orthodox terminology. Where does the truth lie?

It lies much more with the former representation than with the latter. Barth stood squarely within the Reformation tradition. The variety of opinions about his theology is partly due to the dialectic form of his thought and language, which makes it possible to select sets of quotations from his work in such a way as to give two totally different impressions of it. The merit of such a study as G. C. Berkouwer's *The Triumph of Grace in the Theology of Karl Barth* (Paternoster Press, 1956) is that it takes adequate account of the Barthian dialectic and thus does justice to the whole trend of Dr. Barth's thought. Much of Dr. Barth's own work, whether in the German original or in English translation, is written in a style which daunts all but the hardiest specialists in systematic theology. There are, however, a few of his books which can be commended to the more general reader who wants to hear the man speak for himself, such as his *Credo*, his *Dogmatics in Outline*, and (of all his books the one which I appreciate best) *The Knowledge of God and the Service of God*, an exposition of the *Scots Confession* of 1560, delivered as the Gifford Lectures in the University of Aberdeen in 1938. There is no point in continuing to criticize him on the basis of writings which he later considered himself to have outgrown as belonging to his "egg-shell" stage. Two assessments of Barth which can be recommended for further study are C. Brown, *Karl Barth and the Christian Message* (Tyndale Press, 1967), and T. H. L. Parker, *Karl Barth* (Eerdmans, 1970).

Belial

What does Belial mean?

Belial is compounded of two Hebrew words, *beli* and *ya'al*. The meaning of *beli* is "no" or "without"; *ya'al* is usually understood to mean "profit", and so the whole word would mean "no profit" or "worthlessness." "Men of Belial" or "sons of Belial" are, then, "worthless fellows", "good-for-nothings." But *ya'al* may also mean "ascending", and Belial might accordingly mean the place from which there is no ascending, i.e. the realm of the dead. In favour of this view is the fact, for example, that in Psa. 18:4 (where R.S.V. renders it as "perdition") it appears in synonymous parallelism with "death" and "Sheol." In later Judaism and in its one N.T. occurrence (2 Cor. 6:15, Gk. *Beliar*) the word is used personally, practically as a designation of the devil.

Biblical Criticism, Interpretation, Texts, Versions, etc.

What is lower criticism?

Lower criticism, as it used to be called, or textual criticism, as it is commonly called today, is a branch of literary study which endeavours, by carefully comparing and assessing the existing copies of a document which has itself been lost, to determine as accurately as possible what its original wording was. A. E. Housman described it as "the science of discovering error in texts and the art of removing it." It was called lower criticism because it logically precedes higher criticism as the foundation of a building must be laid before the superstructure is erected.

What is higher criticism?

Higher criticism is a branch of literary study which endeavours to establish, on the basis of internal and external evidence, the composition, date and authorship of any work, Biblical or non-Biblical. Sir Robert Anderson spoke of its application to Biblical literature as "a system of study which has thrown new light upon many parts of Holy Scripture, and has brought us new proofs of its authenticity and accuracy, proofs of a kind that preceding generations knew nothing of." He went on to deplore the fact that the name "higher criticism" had been wrongly assumed by what he called "pseudo-criticism"—a system of thought based on disbelief in the supernatural character of the Biblical revelation (*Pseudo-Criticism*, 1904, p. 1ff.). Unfortunately this has not always been borne in mind, and one finds even people who ought to know better referring to higher criticism as something to be denounced and using "higher critic" as a polite swearword. Anyone who investigates the structure and literary relationships of (say) the Book of Job or the Epistle to the Hebrews and tries to discover when or by whom these books were written is practising higher criticism.

Biblical Interpretation

We are taught that the Holy Spirit is the Divine Interpreter of Holy Scripture. But how can we be sure that any particular interpretation is Spirit-given, especially when dealing with passages on whose interpretation spiritual men differ? And how can we answer Roman Catholics who claim that they are not exposed to such uncertainty since they have the infallible interpretation of the Church?

To take the last part of the question first, I may quote from *A Catholic Commentary on Holy Scripture* (1953): "There is of course no 'official' view on any but a minute handful of Biblical texts, and as will be seen from the Commentary there is the amplest room for diversity of interpretation within the bounds of orthodoxy." Evangelicals would agree that the main lines of the Christian interpretation of the Old Testament are laid down in the New Testament. For the rest, the Holy Spirit's interpretative work is not of the kind that would enable us, for example, to decide between variant readings or renderings. His work in this regard is to enable us to see in all the Scriptures the saving revelation of God embodied in Christ, that through our contemplation of Christ, His likeness may be reproduced and reflected in our lives. The central message of the Bible— salvation by God's grace received through faith in Christ—has been vindicated in the believer's experience. An interpretation of Scripture which is consistent with this saving message is more likely to be Spirit-given than one which is not.

The Septuagint

Is the Greek used in the Septuagint similar to that of classical Greek, nearer to classical Greek than to New Testament Greek, or similar to the "Koinē" Greek generally used by the New Testament writers?

The Greek of the Septuagint, like that of the New Testament, is *Koinē* or Hellenistic Greek (i.e. Greek of the kind which became current after the conquests of Alexander the Great). But in many areas of the Septuagint the translators retained the idiom of the original Hebrew to a point where Septuagint Greek becomes something on its own, unlike ordinary Greek, whether Hellenistic or otherwise. It is certainly quite unlike classical Greek.

Since the Septuagint was made before Antiochus Epiphanes destroyed many ancient Hebrew manuscripts, has it more value than many evangelical scholars care to admit, especially in view of the fact that the New Testament writers often quoted from it (especially in Hebrews)?

I do not know that evangelical scholars as such have an assessment of the Septuagint peculiar to themselves. The Septuagint, as reflecting one form of Hebrew text current in the third and second centuries B.C., is a witness of high value. But it was only in Judaea that copies of the Law were seized and destroyed by the officers of Antiochus; when the persecution ceased and religious liberty was regained, it was a simple matter to procure copies from elsewhere, and especially from the flourishing Jewish settlements in Mesopotamia. We now have from the last two or three centuries B.C. copies of Hebrew scripture representing both the ancestor of the later Massoretic text and also the form of text which the Septuagint translators had before them, so that a more precise assessment of their relative worth can be made than was formerly possible. For the most part, the ancestor of the Massoretic text emerges from a critical comparison of the two bodies of evidence with its superiority established. As for the use of the Septuagint by New Testament writers, they probably did as we do—quoted the version in common use among them unless they had special reason to depart from it here or there.

Sometimes, where an Old Testament passage is quoted in the New Testament, it is quoted from the Septuagint in a form considerably different from the Hebrew text. What are we to make of this?

In some places the Septuagint probably represents a Hebrew text varying slightly from that which has come down to us. Thus, when the last clause of Isa. 28:16 is quoted in the New Testament (cf. Rom.

9:33; 10:11; 1 Peter 2:6), it appears with the verb "shall not be put to shame", following the Septuagint (which reflects Hebrew *yēbōsh*), instead of "shall not make haste", which is the reading of the Massoretic Hebrew (*yaḥish*). It is then the province of textual criticism to decide, if possible, what the original Hebrew wording was—whether one or the other of these, or (say) *yaḥil*, implied by other versions (cf. N.E.B. "shall not waver"). But these are not the most important instances of the problem you refer to. There are places where the Septuagint gives an interpretation of a Hebrew expression instead of a literal rendering of it. For example, the Septuagint translator of Psa. 40:6 doubtless read the words "ears hast thou digged for me" in his Hebrew text just as we do. But he knew that the "digging" or hollowing out of ears is part of the process of forming a complete body; therefore, since the part implies the whole, he reproduced the clause by the Greek words, "a body hast thou prepared for me." Where a New Testament writer quotes such an interpretation, he adopts it as being the true interpretation of the original; this is manifestly so when the Septuagint wording of Psa. 40:6 is quoted in Heb. 10:5ff., for the writer there applies it to the body which Christ received at His incarnation and which He offered up once for all (verse 10).

Samaritan Bible

What is the date of the earliest known copies of the Samaritan Pentateuch?

They are usually believed to belong to the eleventh or twelfth century A.D. The Samaritan edition of the Pentateuch (despite the comparatively late date of its oldest surviving copies) probably goes back to the fourth century B.C. At that earlier time it was not exclusively Samaritan; some typically "Samaritan" manuscripts of the Pentateuch have been found in the Qumran caves, alongside those which exhibit the traditional Jewish text,

and others which exhibit the kind of Hebrew text which must have lain before the Septuagint translators. I have given a fuller account of the Samaritan Bible in *The Books and the Parchment*, Chapter 10.

Greek New Testament Text

Which is the most reliable text of the Greek New Testament? What is your opinion of J. J. Griesbach's edition?

At present there are no more reliable editions of the Greek New Testament than (i) the edition published by the British and Foreign Bible Society in 1958, edited by Erwin Nestle and G. D. Kilpatrick; (ii) the latest edition of the "Nestle" text issued by the Stuttgart Bible House and edited by K. Aland (1963); (iii) the edition published by the American Bible Society and several others in 1966, edited by K. Aland, M. Black, B. M. Metzger and A. Wikgren. Griesbach's text (first edition, 1774-7; second edition, 1796-1806) marked an important advance in its day, but it has been antiquated by the abundant discoveries made in the nineteenth and twentieth centuries.

Is there any truth in the statement that the Sinaitic and Vatican manuscripts are two remaining copies of fifty Greek Bibles prepared for Constantine by Eusebius in A.D. 331?

Both the manuscripts you mention were copied in the fourth century, but there is no particular reason for thinking that either of them was one of the fifty which Constantine had prepared for presentation to the churches of his new capital, Constantinople.

How many Greek manuscripts of the New Testament are available today as compared with those available to Westcott and Hort?

If by "available" is meant "conveniently available for use" (e.g. in photographic reproduction) and not simply "known to exist", the answer is that they had available to them for their edition of 1881 no New Testament papyri, 29 uncials (out of some 45 then known to exist), 150 cursives (out of nearly 1,000 then known to exist) and "comparatively few lectionaries" (out of above 400 then catalogued). At a recent count there were known to exist 85 papyri, 268 uncials, 2,792 cursives and 2,193 lectionaries, 5,338 manuscripts in all; and the number is constantly rising.

The bulk of our extant manuscripts of the Greek New Testament exhibit what is called the Byzantine text. The weight of this evidence is said to be favourable to the "Received Text" underlying the King James Version. It is also said that the Sinaitic and Vatican manuscripts represent a small family of documents containing a type of text which the church rejected before the end of the fourth century, so that the Revised Version, which relies mainly on these two manuscripts, is unreliable as compared with the King James Version. Could you comment on these statements?

The "Received Text" is the designation commonly given to the text of the earliest printed editions of the Greek New Testament, although in actual fact it was first so used in the publisher's blurb advertising an edition printed at Leiden in 1633. The earliest printed editions of the Greek New Testament, from which the sixteenth and seventeenth century English versions were translated, were based for the most part on fifteenth century manuscripts—although Erasmus was in such a hurry in preparing his printed Greek text of 1516 that, when the Greek manuscript which he was using for Revelation proved to be mutilated at the end, he translated its last verses from Latin into his own Greek and sent the copy to the printer, and to the end of its days the Received Text has retained two words in Rev. 22:18 which are not found in any Greek manuscript, but were supplied by Erasmus.

The wide circulation and establishment of the Byzantine text from the fourth century onwards is due to the central and dominating position that Byzantium (Constantinople) played in the Eastern Roman Empire after it became Constantine's capital in 334. The form of text which was used in the Constantinopolitan church, from the time of Chrysostom (347-407), was disseminated from there over Greek-speaking Christendom. There is no evidence of its being used earlier, either in manuscripts or in translations made from Greek into other languages or in Biblical quotations by Christian writers. It is a well edited fourth century type of text, drawing upon several types of text which were in circulation earlier. Before the centralizing influence of Constantinople, there were types of Greek text associated with a number of cities and regions—Alexandria, Caesarea, Antioch and the West. The Alexandrian text is represented by the Sinaitic and Vatican codices and by the Coptic versions. At the time when the Revised Version of the New Testament was being prepared, this text represented the nearest attainable approach to the original text, and in adopting it the Revisers gave the English-speaking world the most reliable text of the New Testament that was then accessible. (The quality of their translation is quite another question.) But Westcott and Hort, whose influence in the Revision committee was paramount, exaggerated the archaic status of the Alexandrian text, which they called the "Neutral" text, considering that it represented the apostolic text with practically no deviation. The Alexandrian text is, in fact, a text edited about the beginning of the third century according to the best traditions of Alexandrian philological scholarship; but there were other rival types of text in circulation, in Egypt itself as well as elsewhere. Until fairly recent years it looked as though it might be possible, first to establish the main local types of text current in the early third century, and then to construct by their means an archetype which might reproduce the original text as nearly as made no difference. But the discovery in recent years, in rapid succession, of manuscripts going back to the second century has shown that a different methodology must be adopted. None of the third-century editions can stake an exclusive claim to represent the first-century-text, and the fourth-century Byzantine edition even less so. Whereas the King James Version for the most part represents one text-type (the Byzantine), as also does the Revised Version (the Alexandrian), such later versions as the R.S.V. and N.E.B. represent an eclectic text. As the introduction to the N.E.B. New Testament puts it: "There is not at the present time any critical text which would command the same degree of general acceptance as the Revisers' text did in its day. Nor has the time come, in the judgment of most scholars, to construct such a text, since new material constantly comes to light, and the debate continues. The present translators therefore could do no other than consider variant readings on their merits, and, having weighed the evidence for themselves, select for translation in each passage the reading which to the best of their judgment seemed most likely to represent what the author wrote." In the present state of the question this is certainly the path of wisdom.

Bible Translations and Paraphrases

Can a clear distinction be drawn between a translation and a paraphrase?

No, the frontier between the two cannot be accurately defined. On the one hand, a work such as Robert Young's *Literal Translation of the Bible* is so much a word-for-word rendering that it comes near to being a "crib" rather than a translation; on the other hand. James Montgomery's hymn "Hail to the Lord's Anointed" (or Isaac Watts' "Jesus shall reign where'er

the sun") is self-confessedly a "paraphrase" of Psalm 72 and does not pretend to be a straight translation. The delimiting of the frontier between the two becomes a matter of practical concern in regard to a number of modern versions, whether "modern speech" versions like the New English Bible and J. B. Phillips's *New Testament in Modern English,* or interpretative versions like the *Amplified New Testament* and K. S. Wuest's *Expanded Translation.* Generally speaking, the more interpretative expansion a translator introduces in order to bring out the sense, the more does his version deserve to be called a paraphrase rather than a straight translation; this being so, one might describe the versions of Phillips and Wuest (for example) as paraphrases. But in any biblical translation worthy of the name the translator's judgment must play a part, even if only when he has to decide which punctuation marks to use, and where to place them. For example, a translator who left our Lord's words to the penitent robber in the form, "Verily I say unto thee today shalt thou be with me in paradise", without any mark of punctuation, would be evading his duty; but in carrying out his duty he would be bound to exercise his interpretative judgment.

Please comment on the following statement on the Revisers of the 1881 New Testament:"The Revisers did not know the grammar of the article although Moulton's eighth edition of Winer's Grammar had been published previously."

It is an exaggerated statement. In the year when the first edition of W. F. Moulton's translation of G. B. Winer's *Grammar of New Testament Greek* appeared (1870), Moulton took his place as a member (the youngest member) of the Company of New Testament Revisers. The translation was dedicated to Dr. C. J. Ellicott, Bishop of Gloucester, who was Chairman of the New Testament Company throughout its deliberations: in the preface to his translation of Winer, Moulton said: "if this book succeeds in accomplishing anything for the accurate study of the Greek Testament, it will be through what I have learned from Bishop Ellicott's wise counsels, and from his noble Commentaries on St. Paul's Epistles." And F. J. A. Hort, pre-eminent among the Revisers, in a lecture-course delivered in 1891, described Moulton's Winer as standing "far above every other" work as a *Grammar* to be used alongside the standard commentaries; presumably he had formed this opinion ten to twenty years before. So some of the Revisers were acquainted with the grammar of the Greek article as set forth by Winer and his translator. But on the whole the Revisers tended to approach the Greek New Testament with the standards of classical Greek literature of the fifth and fourth centuries B.C. in the forefront of their minds, and this affected their treatment not only of the Greek article but of other features of Greek grammar also. In addition, they tended to translate literally except where English idiom would be positively violated by a literal rendering, and this means that the incidence of the article in the Revised New Testament sometimes reflects Hellenistic Greek rather than English usage. It is easy but unprofitable for us today to criticize the Revisers; in the ninety years since they completed their work the study of New Testament Greek in general, and of the New Testament use of the article in particular, has been carried forward beyond the stage of knowledge that was available to them.

Why does the British Revised Version spell "spirit" with a small "s" in all references to the Spirit of God in the Old Testament? The Authorized Version, American Standard Version and Revised Standard Version do not agree with this.

I do not remember that I have seen any explanation of the Revisers' policy of not capitalizing "spirit" in the Old Testament when the Spirit of God or the Holy Spirit is referred to. I can only think that a substantial majority of the Old Testament company held that the reference in the relevant Old Testament passages is not to the *personal* Spirit of God. The New Testament Revisers appear to have thought differently. Thus in Luke 1:15 (R.V.), before the birth of Christ, the angel tells Zacharias that his son John the Baptist will be "filled with the Holy Ghost" (margin, "Holy Spirit"); and in Luke 4:18 (R.V.) our Lord reads Isa. 61:1 in the form "The Spirit of the Lord is upon me," whereas the Old Testament revisers rendered the passage: "The spirit of the Lord GOD is upon me."

Can you give an opinion of the translation of the Bible by Ferrar Fenton?

This translation is a notable performance, when one considers that it is the unaided work of a business man whose special training did not lie in the field of biblical languages, but who believed that his commercial experience was a divine preparation for the task of Bible translation. One is not predisposed in favour of his version by his own estimate of its excellence: he characterized his fifth edition as being, he believed, "the most accurate rendering into any European language, ancient or modern, ever made, not only in words, but in editing, spirit and sense." And it must be said that he gets off to an astonishingly bad start by his translation of Gen. 1:1, "By Periods GOD created that which produced the Solar Systems; then that which produced the Earth." But the bulk of the work is much better than that. His rendering of the poetical parts of the Bible goes with a fine rhythmical swing, and his marking of supposed objections in the course of Paul's arguments is helpful. But in view of his limitations (unrecognized by himself) his renderings require to be checked by reference to more trustworthy versions.

Can you tell me something about a New Testament which I have picked up second-hand? It is The Corrected English New Testament: A revision of the "Authorized Version" *by Samuel Lloyd, with a preface by Bishop Handley Moule; its publication coincided with the centenary of the British and Foreign Bible Society in 1904.*

It is a revision of the Authorized Version on the basis of Nestle's Greek text, which the British and Foreign Bible Society adopted for its centenary edition of the Greek New Testament in that same year. Dr. Lloyd revised the A.V. with a lighter touch than the Revisers of 1881 had used.

What is your opinion of the Bible versions by J. Moffatt and R. A. Knox?

The techniques of translation used by these two men were so different that their renderings must be considered separately. Moffatt's version was at one time the most popular of all Bible versions in modern speech, but nowadays it has been overshadowed by more recent works. His New Testament rendering is better than that of the Old Testament, because his Greek was better than his Hebrew, but even in the New Testament his version suffers from being based on a generally discredited edition of the Greek text (Von Soden's). Generally, his rendering is characterized by idiomatic vigour and freedom (although the idiom is at times Scots rather than English); he tends, however, to be over-colloquial. He is too ready to resort to conjectural emendation and in general allows himself excessive liberties with the text, especially in rearranging it. To get a grasp of the general argument of an Old Testament prophetical book or a New Testament epistle one of the best courses is still to read it through in Moffatt's version; but when it comes to more precise and detailed study his version is not adequate.

Knox had a much finer sense of appropriate style than Moffatt had, and from the literary point of view his version is one of the best of all modern English versions. The main defect of his version arises from the fact that, as instructed by the ecclesiastical authorities who commissioned it, he used the Latin Vulgate as his basic text (while referring constantly to the Greek and Hebrew originals). It is a delightfully readable translation, with some of the qualities of a "period piece", but like Moffatt's (although for different reasons) not suitable for detailed verbal study.

Does the new Revised Standard Version undermine the doctrines of our Lord's Deity and Virgin Birth?

These doctrines, and the other basic doctrines of the Christian faith, can be established as conclusively from the R.S.V. as from the older English versions. The nativity narratives of Matthew and Luke, in the new version, state the virginal conception of our Lord quite unambiguously. The formally heretical footnote which mars the American Standard Version of 1901 at John 9:38 has not been reproduced in this revision. In Titus 2:13 and 2 Pet. 1:1 it reads (with the English R.V.) "our great God and Saviour Jesus Christ" and "our God and Saviour Jesus Christ," a rendering which gives Jesus the title "God" more explicitly than does the American Standard Version, which follows the A.V. in these two places. The R.S.V. is not immune from criticism, any more than other versions, but the charge that it undermines or perverts Christian doctrine does not lie. As one of the new revisers has said, "no doctrine of the Christian faith has been affected by the revision, for the simple reason that, out of the thousands of variant readings in the manuscripts, none has turned up thus far that requires a revision of Christian doctrine" (F. C. Grant).

Occasionally the Revised Standard Version of the Old Testament presents in the text a rendering based on the Septuagint or another ancient version, and indicates in a footnote that the Massoretic Hebrew text reads otherwise. In these places are the readings of the versions more accurate than those of the Massoretic text?

Sometimes they are. Considering the length of time over which the Hebrew text was copied and re-copied, the wonder is that the Massoretic text is so accurate. But of its quite remarkable accuracy there can be no doubt; it must be conceded that (by and large) the Jewish scribes who transmitted the Hebrew Old Testament were much more painstaking than the Christian scribes who transmitted the Greek New Testament. (There are circumstances which go far to explain these two different levels of accuracy.) But in a handful of places the Massoretic text is defective, and in some of these the Septuagint (or one of the other ancient versions) has preserved the original text. A simple example is in Gen. 4:8, where two Hebrew words have fallen out of the Massoretic text after the clause "And Cain said to Abel his brother . . ." (they are preserved in the Samaritan, Septuagint and Latin Vulgate editions). But it is striking in how many places where the Septuagint has been judged by the R.S.V. translators to preserve a reading which is defective in the Massoretic text, *Hebrew* evidence for the reading hitherto known only from the Septuagint has come to light in the Biblical manuscripts from Qumran (e.g. the reading "sons of God" for the Massoretic "sons of Israel" in Deut. 32:8).

What is your opinion of George M. Lamsa's translation of the Bible (A. J. Holman, Philadelphia, 1961), which claims to be based on ancient eastern manuscripts?

Mr. Lamsa's translation is based on the Peshitta, the Bible of the Syriac-Speaking churches. But the Peshitta is itself a translation (from the Hebrew, and partly from the Greek, in the Old Testament, and

from the Greek in the New Testament); a translation of the Peshitta is therefore one remove farther from the original than a translation from the Hebrew and Greek texts would be. Syriac, or Eastern Aramaic, which is Mr. Lamsa's native tongue, is distantly akin to the Galilaean Aramaic (a form of Western Aramaic) spoken by our Lord and His apostles, and sometimes, as Mr. Lamsa emphasizes, a form of words in the Peshitta may be quite close to the form actually used by our Lord. But we cannot depend on this, and in fact there are manuscripts of an "Old Syriac" version of the Gospels substantially earlier than the Peshitta, one of which bears traces of Palestinian dialect and might therefore be thought to come nearer to our Lord's Aramaic speech than the Peshitta does.

Brethren History

I have been re-reading Sir Edmund Gosse's Father and Son. *To which group of Brethren did the elder Gosse belong? I find very little mention of well-known Brethren.*

Sir Edmund Gosse points out in the preface that, to avoid offence, he altered the names of several individuals referred to. But even in this book the evidence is clear that Philip Henry Gosse was associated with the Open Brethren. Certainly B. W. Newton's *Thoughts on the Apocalypse* would not have been favoured reading in an Exclusive household in the 1850's, as (according to *Father and Son*) it was in the Gosse household! Again, the "Mr. S" who baptized young Edmund, in the neighbouring town (Torquay) to the Devonshire village (St. Marychurch) where he and his father lived, was Leonard Strong (formerly of Demerara). In the biography of Henrietta Soltau, daughter of Henry William Soltau of Exeter (*A Woman who Laughed*, by M. Cable and F. French, p. 41) we are told how Henrietta and her sisters sometimes had as a companion on their sea-shore excursions "little Edmund Gosse, a child of precocious scientific attainments under whose tuition they learnt to observe the habits of the little creatures which lived in the pools and among the rocks of that fascinating Devonshire coast." Later on in *Father and Son* mention is made of "some enormous Evangelical conference" which father and son attended in London in 1864. The reference is to the Meetings on Prophecy held at Freemason's Hall in that year—meeting which were addressed not only by the elder Gosse but by such other well-known "Open Brethren" as J. L. Harris, William Lincoln, Charles Hargrove, Leonard Strong, H. W. Soltau and the Earl of Cavan. But P. H. Gosse became rather detached from the main movements among Brethren after his removal to Devonshire, where he devoted himself to the pastoral responsibility for a small congregation in St. Marychurch. His prophetic standpoint (which combined the historicist interpretation of Daniel and the Revelation with "partial rapture" views) would not have commended itself to many even of his "open" brethren, while some of his other theological opinions—e.g. those published in *The Mysteries of God* (1884)—were even less acceptable. More information may be gathered from the straightforward biography of him written by his son, although it is not nearly so interesting as *Father and Son*—a book which, for all its interest, had for its author's credit better have remained unwritten. (See also F. R. Coad, *A History of the Brethren Movement*, pp. 182f., 221f.)

Why do you say in your answer to the previous question that Sir Edmund Gosse's book Father and Son *"had for its author's credit better have remained unwritten"?*

For this reason. It is perfectly certain that Sir Edmund Gosse had no intention to expose his father's foibles to public ridicule; no man of decent feeling (as he

was) would wish to do any such thing. But nevertheless that was bound to be the effect of what he wrote; and for one person who knows about the elder Gosse from his own writings or from Sir Edmund's biography of him, there are probably a hundred who know only the picture portrayed in *Father and Son*. If (as we must believe) Sir Edmund did not foresee that this would be the effect of the book, he must be convicted (in this respect at least) of a serious lack of good judgment—not to say good taste—which does him little credit. And there are many who have reacted to the book as did the late Professor C. H. Turner of Oxford: "I remember well", says his biographer, "to what depths of indignation he was moved by Edmund Gosse's *Father and Son*: the one thing he could not understand was what seemed to him *impietas* in the most sacred of all relationships."

Is Samuel Butler, author of The Fair Haven, *the same as the Samuel Butler who was one of the signatories of the "Letter of the Ten"? What do you think of his approach to Christianity? He discards as inaccurate much of the New Testament—e.g. Matthew's account of the resurrection.*

No; the author of *The Fair Haven* had no connexion with Bethesda Chapel, Bristol. (I wonder if someone will write and ask what the "Letter of the Ten" was; it may be that a new generation of readers has grown up which is unacquainted with such ancient landmarks!) The Samuel Butler about whom you enquire is best known as the author of *Erewhon*. In *The Fair Haven* he set about launching an attack on Christianity under the pretence of defending it; he reckoned that people would conclude that a system of thought which could only be maintained by such weak arguments as he deliberately used was indefensible. But he reckoned without the inability of the earnest evangelical public in England to recognize satire when they saw it. Some of the best known evangelical periodicals of the day, not realizing that they were being led up the garden path, gave the author credit for being an honest defender of the faith, although they felt that his arguments could be strengthened here and there, and mildly regretted that on certain points he conceded more than was necessary to the opposition. A man of Samuel Butler's mentality must have savoured the irony of this reaction to the full! He rightly saw that the heart of the defence of Christianity is the truth of Christ's resurrection, and if you read *very* carefully between the lines of his treatment of this subject, you may discover what he really believed about it—namely, that our Lord did not actually die on the cross, but revived in the tomb.

In the last question reference is made to the "Letter of the Ten", described in your answer as an "ancient landmark." What was the "Letter of the Ten"?

The "Letter of the Ten" was a document, drawn up and signed by Henry Craik, George Müller and eight other leaders in Bethesda Chapel, Bristol, and approved by a church meeting on June 29, 1848. After affirming their wholehearted adherence to the Scriptural doctrine of the Person of Christ, the signatories declared their policy regarding the reception of Christians from the sister-church at Plymouth, where a leading teacher was charged (whether rightly or wrongly) with maintaining views subversive of this doctrine. Because the Bethesda policy did not conform with the disciplinary policy of J. N. Darby and his followers in this matter, the "Letter of the Ten" became one of the outstanding documents in the case between Open and Exclusive Brethren. You will find the text of the Letter in F. R. Coad, *A History of the Brethren Movement*, Appendix C.

It is said that among the early Brethren "attempts at unprofitable ministry by unfit persons were graciously repressed by the elders." How was it done, and could it be done today?

It can be done today as effectively as yesterday by elders whose spiritual stature commands the confidence of the believers in general. It is a well attested fact that J. N. Darby asked B. W. Newton to sit where he could conveniently take the oversight of the ministry in the Plymouth meeting, and so restrain what was manifestly unprofitable and unedifying. The author of *Peculiar People*, who writes under the pen-name "Septima" (a daughter of C. Russell Hurditch, and second wife of H. Grattan Guinness), says that her maternal grandfather would break in upon a tedious discourse on a Sunday morning with "Now, dear brother, I think we'll sing a hymn." And it is recorded that at one of the large open conferences in Yeovil W. H. Bennet "sweetly but decidedly" terminated a good man's attempt at unprofitable ministry after ten minutes or thereabouts by rising and saying: "Beloved brother, I think it is the general feeling of the meeting that you have said enough upon this subject."

As one reads about the earlier days of the Brethren movement, time and again cases turn up of quite eminent Brethren teachers being denounced by their fellows for holding and teaching false doctrine. One hears very little of this thing today. Is it because we are more orthodox than our fathers were, or is it because we have not the same concern for sound doctrine?

I am fairly well acquainted with teachers among "Open Brethren" at the present time, and I know of no false doctrine that is held or taught by any of them. But that does not mean that we are more orthodox than our fathers were. We read of men like C. E. Stuart and F. W. Grant being excommunicated by their brethren, allegedly for false doctrine, but actually because in their expounding of true biblical doctrines they advanced interpretations with which their brethren did not agree. The history of the Brethren does reveal, very occasionally, one or another who taught something which was logically, although not intentionally, subversive of the gospel. But most of the mutual excommunications of which we read were due to quite reasonable diversities of interpretation of Scripture truth. It is all too easy to interpret orthodoxy as meaning "what *I* think" and heterodoxy as meaning "what *the other man* thinks." Happily we are encouraged to study the Scriptures for ourselves, and not to toe this or that party-line. The result is that on a number of subjects we do have diversities of interpretation, but we have learned by experience that it is better to get together and confer about them, or if necessary to express courteous criticism of them, than to excommunicate one another. Another factor for which perhaps we should be grateful is that printing is so much more expensive nowadays. A couple of generations ago it was all too cheap and easy to engage in a prolonged pamphlet-warfare which might do untold harm by spreading a local or personal difference far and wide and enlisting partisan support on either side. I have a considerable collection of such polemical pamphlets, and I regard it as a great mercy that we see so little of this sort of thing today.

I have been informed that a number of early Brethren teachers (e.g., Darby, Kelly, Mackintosh) taught that the reception of the Holy Spirit was an event subsequent to conversion. I find what appears to be the same teaching in G. H. Lang, The Churches of God, p. 149. What would be your comment on this?

No doubt your informants had in mind such passages as these: "There must be faith in the work of Christ, as well as in His Person, in order to a person's being sealed. . . . That a person may be born again, and not have received the Holy Ghost, is perfectly certain according to Scripture, for 'whosoever believeth that Jesus is the Christ is born of God', and this the disciples did while Christ was on earth, but could not have the Holy Ghost, which did not come until the day of Pentecost; though they had life, and were clean through the word" (J. N. Darby, *Collected Writings*, XXXI, p. 398f.). Again, with reference to Acts 2:38, "it is evident that the reception of the Holy Ghost as here spoken of, has nothing whatever to do with the bringing men to believe and to repent. It is a subsequent operation; it is an additional separate blessing; it is a privilege founded on faith already working in the heart. So far is it from being true that a man receives the gift of the Holy Ghost the moment he believes, that it may well be doubted whether there ever was such a case since the world began. I do not mean to deny that the gift of the Holy Ghost may be practically on the same occasion, but never in the same moment: at least, I should like any one to produce me one proof from the Word of God, or one instance from practical experience. I have never seen, nor ever heard of such a case, and (what is more) I believe that Scripture precludes the possibility of it" (W. Kelly, *Lectures on the New Testament Doctrine of the Holy Spirit*, p. 172). These quotations will serve to illustrate the point made about early Brethren teachers. (One does not go to C. H. Mackintosh for original contributions to doctrine.) Darby and Kelly distinguished the Holy Spirit's work in regeneration from His coming to take up His permanent abode in believers.

My comment on all this would be that Luke and Paul for the most part refer to different occasions when they speak of people receiving the Holy Spirit. Luke generally refers to that powerful coming of the Spirit which is attended by outward manifestations of an exceptional character. It was so with Cornelius and his household, although in their case the outward manifestations and the inward operation of the Spirit coincided, since it was necessary that Peter should have visible and audible proof immediately of what is essentially an invisible and inaudible visitation (Acts 10:44-46); it was so with the Ephesian disciples of Acts 19:6; and something of the same sort is implied of the converts on the day of Pentecost (Acts 2:38) and the Samaritan converts of Acts 8:17. (How could Simon the sorcerer have *seen* there and then "that through the laying on of the apostles' hands the Holy Spirit was given" if there had not been outward manifestations?) This reception of the Spirit might be experienced before baptism (Acts 10:44), after baptism (Acts 2:38), or after baptism *plus* the laying on of apostolic hands (Acts 8:16; 19:5f.). But when we turn to Paul's writings, it is assumed that all believers have the Holy Spirit indwelling them. Even "carnal" Christians like those in Corinth are told not only that they are corporately "God's temple" with the Spirit of God dwelling within them (1 Cor. 3:16), but also that the body of each one of them "is a temple of the Holy Spirit within you, which you have from God" (1 Cor. 6:19). Again it is taken for granted that all the Christian readers of the Epistle to the Ephesians "were sealed with the Holy Spirit of promise" when they believed (Eph. 1:13). Perhaps, however, the most conclusive passage for Paul's teaching on the subject is Romans 8. In that chapter not only does the Spirit impart life to believers; it is His presence within them that guarantees their resurrection on a coming day (verse 11); in fact, the life which He imparts here and now is the first instalment of their coming resurrection life (verse 23). Those who are directed by Him are the sons of God; it is a sign that He has been received when believers address God as Father (verses 14-16). I should find it impossible in the light of this chapter to suppose that any Christian does not have the Holy Spirit; indeed, this is the natural sense of Paul's own words in verse 9: "Any one who has not the Spirit of Christ, does not belong to him." It makes no difference to the meaning of this verse if we substitute a crib-rendering of it for a real translation (as has been done) and say: "But if any one Spirit of Christ has not, this one is not of Him." What the verse really means is shown with crystal clarity by the New English Bible: "if a man does not possess the Spirit of Christ, he is no Christian." (I heard some years ago of a man who was converted through reading this verse in the New English Bible; he realized that he did not possess the Spirit of Christ, and therefore was no Christian; and accordingly he took the steps necessary for becoming a Christian.) See also p. 214.

Could you give a brief outline of what is meant by "Needed Truth"?

I will try to do so, subject to correction by those who know more about it than I do. *Needed Truth* is the title of a Christian periodical, the official organ of a group of churches of God which draw a rather sharp line of demarcation between themselves and other Christians. It first appeared in 1887 under the editorship of four brethren then in fellowship with independent or "open" churches. The line of teaching which it inculcated had been expressed a few years earlier in a pamphlet entitled *The Church and Churches of God: A Suggestive Outline of Truth*, by a young man of exceptional devotion, Frederick Arthur Banks. Not long after the inauguration of *Needed Truth*, its editors and others who agreed with their teaching withdrew from their former "unwalled" fellowship to form a new one with clearly defined boundaries. While those brethren who hold this teaching readily agree that all believers in Christ are by Him baptized in one Spirit into one body, their distinctive doctrine recognizes a narrower church fellowship than that of membership in the body of Christ. This narrower fellowship comprises the churches of God—the churches of God being a term restricted to the local churches where this teaching is held and practised. The New Testament situation, in which there was but one church in any one city, no matter how many meeting places there may have been in the city, is taken as a permanently valid pattern. In addition to elders in the individual local churches, there are elders over the districts in which these churches are grouped. New Testament precedent for this district supervision is found in the Council of Jerusalem described in Acts 15. While we agree with these brethren that the doctrine of the church is an essential part of the faith once delivered, we consider that an interpretation of this doctrine which has the effect of erecting barriers between believers should send us back to discover where along the line of argument some flaw has occurred which leads to such a conclusion. The brethren with whom I am linked in church fellowship gladly acknowledge that all these churches are true churches of God, but the acknowledgment would not, I think, be reciprocated. If a plain and up-to-date statement by one of their leading teachers is desired, it is provided in a twenty-page pamphlet entitled *Churches of God in Apostolic Teaching*, by Mr. T. M. Hyland, the present editor of *Needed Truth*, obtainable from Needed Truth Publishing Office, Assembly Hall, George Lane, Hayes, Bromley, Kent.

Calendars and Chronology

According to the traditional Jewish Calendar the year of creation was 3761 B.C. Can you explain the 243 years of difference between this reckoning and that which appears in the margins of our ordinary Bibles (4004 B.C.)?

The Jewish chronology to which you refer is propounded in a rabbinical treatise called *Seder Olam* ("The Order of the World"), traditionally ascribed to a writer of the second century A.D. called Jose ben Halafta. It is based on an interpretation of Daniel 9:24-27 which

views the "seventy weeks" or 490 years as running from the destruction of Solomon's temple by the Babylonians to the destruction of Herod's temple by the Romans.

Josephus says in his Jewish War (*vi. 270*) *that the temple of Jerusalem was destroyed by Titus 639 years after its restoration in the time of Haggai. This estimate exceeds the commonly accepted chronology by some fifty years. Is there any explanation of this discrepancy?*

This discrepancy involves a lengthening of the period of the Second Temple, while the discrepancy pointed out in the previous question involves a shortening of the same period; but both are apparently due to varying interpretations of Daniel's prophecy of the seventy weeks. Josephus appears to have followed a Pharisaic interpretation which reckoned the seventy weeks as beginning with the Jews' deliverance from exile in the first year of Cyrus and the last week as beginning with the accession of Alexander Jannaeus, the great enemy of the Pharisees (see his *Antiquities*, xiii. 301). According to the received chronology this interval (538-103 B.C.) was one of 435 years, but the interpretation followed by Josephus expanded it to 483 years.

If Herod the Great was still alive when our Lord was born, why is he said to have died in 4 B.C.? What was the date of our Lord's birth? If an error was made in calculating the year, why has it never been corrected?

The reckoning of the Christian era— usually attributed to Dionysius Exiguus early in the 6th century A.D., though it has been suggested that the system may go back some 300 years earlier—was complicated from the outset by an arithmetical error of some four years. In terms of the dating of events by the era of the foundation of Rome (A.U.C.) it was reckoned that Herod died in A.U.C. 754, and this year was accordingly renamed A.D.1. In fact (and there was ample evidence at the time to show this), Herod died in A.U.C. 750. But by the time the error was discovered, the use of the common era was too firmly established to be revised, and so we have to say that Herod died in 4 B.C. and that our Lord was born not later than that year, and possibly two years earlier (cf. Matt. 2:16). Our Lord may thus have been six years old in the year we conventionally call A.D.1.

Why was the birth of Christ chosen as the epoch rather than his death? Does history record any opposition to so great a change?

To Christians, of course, it seemed a most unexceptionable and appropriate method of reckoning dates; and its general convenience has led to its adoption by non-Christians, who thus bear tacit witness to the centrality of Christ in history. For internal purposes Jews and Muslims follow their own calendars (reckoned respectively from the year of the creation of the world and the year of the Hijra, i.e. Muhammad's flight to Medina, in A.D. 622), but for more general and international use they follow the "common (i.e. the Christian) era." Dionysius chose the supposed year of our Lord's incarnation as his starting-point because that event was, as he put it, "the beginning of our hope." The questioner points out that in the Roman Catholic Church saints are canonized from the date of their death, but the purpose of Dionysius was quite different from the establishment of an anniversary; in fact, the particular day on which his era started was March 25, the festival of the annunciation of our Lord's birth to Mary by Gabriel.

Does the date of the Flood of which Sir Leonard Woolley found traces at Ur correspond with that which S. H. Langdon found at Kish?

Let an expert speak: "Woolley himself equates these traces of a heavy local deluge (at Ur) with that mentioned in the Gilgamesh Epic and in the historical texts and dates them after the first pottery-bearing levels (Al Ubaid) and before the first written records. Similar bands of clay deposits were found by Langdon at Kish, sixty-five miles to the north, in the same year, but these appear to be of an earlier date" (D. J. Wiseman, *Illustrations from Biblical Archaeology*, 1958, p. 15.)

In Gen. 11:26 we read that "Terah lived seventy years, and begat Abram..."; in verse 32 Terah is said to have died in Haran when he was 205 years old (which would make Abram 135 at the time); according to Acts 7:4 it was after his father's death that Abraham left Haran for Canaan, but Gen. 12:4 tells us that he was only 75 at the time. How can this discrepancy of 60 years be accounted for?

The older chronologers accounted for it by supposing that Terah was 70 years old when his first son (Haran?) was born, but that Abram was not born until his father was 130. In that case he is mentioned first among Terah's three sons in Gen. 11:26f. not because of seniority but because he was the most outstanding of them. A still older solution appears in the Samaritan Bible, according to which Terah's age at death was 145. It has been argued (e.g. by P. E. Kahle) that this reading also appeared at one time in some Septuagint texts, and that it was on one of them that Stephen's statement was based. Those, however, who believe that the more difficult reading is normally to be preferred may dismiss this solution as an easy way out.

According to Gal. 3:17, the law was given 430 years after the promise to Abraham. But in Ex. 12:40 the Israelites' sojourning in Egypt is said to have lasted 430 years, and in Gen. 15:13 Abraham is told that his seed will be afflicted 400 years. How are these statements to be reconciled?

The statement of Gal. 3:17 is explicit enough; it gives the period between the promise to Abraham and the giving of the law as 430 years. (Even so, we might note in passing C. F. Hogg and W. E. Vine's remark in their commentary on this verse: "Paul is not concerned here with the exact duration of the interval . . . The number of years cannot have been less than four hundred and thirty in either case. That the period was a considerable one is all the argument requires.") The Samaritan and Septuagint texts of Ex. 12:40 make 430 years cover "the sojourning of the children of Israel, which they sojourned in Egypt *and in the land of Canaan.*" The italicized words are an added gloss; the Hebrew text (represented by our common versions) is original; the Samaritan and Septuagint editors, however, misunderstanding the force of this chronological datum, corrected it to what they reckoned to be the facts of the case. In my judgment the chronological note of Ex. 12:40 originally denoted not duration of time but a point of time, that point being the year of the Exodus, reckoned from an initial fixed date which was not necessarily that of the descent into Egypt, but more probably (as W. F. Albright has suggested) the Era of Tanis. According to Gal. 3:17 the fixed date from which the 430 years were calculated to the Exodus coincided with the promise to Abraham. The 400 years of Gen. 15:13 either represent the same figure in round numbers or else (as rabbinical tradition held) are reckoned from the birth of Isaac. The actual duration of the sojourn in Egypt is indicated in Gen. 15:16, "they shall come back here in the fourth generation"; from various relevant genealogical lists it appears that the Israelites did in fact leave Egypt in the fourth generation after their arrival there. But to those who are tempted to become over-absorbed in such

studies Thomas Fuller's remark may be commended: "Chronology is a surly cur, that hath bit many a man's fingers."

Can the 480th year mentioned in 1 Kings 6:1 be explained if the Exodus took place in the 13th century B.C.?

This figure is commonly regarded as equivalent to "the twelfth generation." This is more probable than the view that the chronological note in 1 Kings 6:1 "may be a late gloss in the text" (*New Bible Commentary Revised*, 1970). The Septuagint version speaks of the 440th year, which could represent another way of counting the generations (reckoning 40 years to a generation).

Canon of Scripture

The books of Esther, Ecclesiastes and the Song of Songs do not appear to have been quoted by our Lord or the apostles, and thus lack the seal of such authority. When were they introduced into the Old Testament, and by whom?

I believe there may be an allusion to the refrain of Ecclesiastes ("Vanity of vanities") in Rom. 8:20. The three books mentioned belong to the third division of the Hebrew Bible, called the Writings, which was substantially complete by our Lord's time, although its limits (with particular reference to these three books) were finally established by Jewish authorities in the period following A.D. 70. Esther is lacking in the earliest *Christian* list of Old Testament books known to us (from about A.D. 170). I have discussed the canonicity of these books in Chapter VIII of *The Books and the Parchments* (1963) and in Chapter VIII of *Tradition Old and New* (1970).

How would you answer those who say that since the Church chose or decided the Canon of the New Testament, therefore in matters of doctrine the Church is an authority above even the Scriptures?

By denying that the Church in any official sense chose or decided the Canon of the New Testament. The first occasion on which an ecclesiastical body made a pronouncement on this subject was the Synod of Hippo in A.D. 393, and that Synod did not confer upon the New Testament books any authority which they did not already possess, but ratified the general consensus of Christian people over the previous two or three centuries. As Bishop Westcott put it, "The extent of the canon was settled by common usage, and thus the testimony of Christians becomes the testimony of the Church." Or, in the words of F. J. Foakes-Jackson, "The Church assuredly did not make the New Testament; the two grew up together." I have dealt with this question at greater length in *The Spreading Flame*, pp. 221-237.

Catechumens

What were "catechumens" in the early church? Do we have their equivalent today? Is Luke 1:4 relevant in this connexion?

Catechumens in the early church were converts who were in course of receiving instruction in the rudiments of the Christian way before being baptized. Early as the catechumenate is, it is later than the apostolic age. It is plain from the New Testament records that no such interval for instruction came between conversion and baptism; the necessary further instruction was given after baptism, not before it. The point about Luke 1:4 is that the Greek verb rendered "thou wast instructed" in R.V. is *katēcheō*, the verb from which "catechumen" is derived. But in Luke 1:4 it is not used in any technical sense; cf. R.V. margin, "thou wast taught by word of mouth"; R.S.V. and N.E.B., "you have been informed." Theophilus was not a "catechumen" in the post-apostolic sense.

Christ

HIS SONSHIP

Is it right to speak of our Lord as the "Eternal Son", seeing that this title is not used in the Scriptures?

The important question is not whether the title is used in Scripture, but whether it expresses a Scriptural idea. The Divine Sonship of our Lord is linked in the New Testament with His incarnation (Luke 1:35), with His baptism (Mark 1:11), with His transfiguration (Mark 9:7), and with His resurrection (Rom. 1:4); but it cannot be held to have had an absolute beginning with any one of these events. A passage like 1 John 4:9 ("God sent his only Son into the world") clearly implies that Christ was the Son of God before the moment of His being sent; Heb. 1:2 equally clearly implies that the One through whom God made the worlds bore the relation of Son to Him then. And, whether we read "the only begotten Son" or "God only begotten" in John 1:18, the One who is there said to have His being in the Father's bosom cannot be other than His Eternal Son.

When did Jesus find out that He was the Son of God?

We know that at His baptism He heard the voice of God addressing Him directly as His Son (Mark 1:11; Luke 3:22). But many years before that, His words to Mary when she found Him in the temple— "I must be about my Father's business", or better, "I must be in my Father's house"—suggest that by the age of twelve He had some consciousness of His Divine Sonship.

Further to the last two answers, would you comment on the quotation of Psa. 2:7 in Acts 13:33; Heb. 1:5 and Luke 3:22 (if you consider that the manuscript support in the last-named passage warrants it)? Does not the context require us to interpret the word "begotten" there of the assumption of a new official

171

dignity rather than in its more usual sense?

Yes. In Heb. 1:5 and 5:5 the context is not defined precisely, and there it is rather the relationship itself that is emphasized than any particular occasion. But in the other two New Testament passages the reference appears to be to our Lord's baptism. This is certain in Luke 3:22; even if we do not follow the Western text there in reading "this day have I begotten thee," it is plain that the words "Thou art my Son" (as in Mark 1:11) echo Psa. 2:7. Our Lord, of course, did not become the Son of God for the first time at His baptism, but at His baptism He was acclaimed by God as His Son and "anointed . . . with the Holy Spirit and with power" (Acts 10:38) to enter upon His messianic ministry. This is probably the point of the quotation in Acts 13:33 too. Note that the A.V. "again" in that verse has no authority; it is in the following verse that the resurrection is introduced (cf. Rom. 1:4). The raising up of verse 33 is our Lord's being publicly raised up by God and presented to Israel at the outset of His ministry as the Servant-Messiah.

His Headship

If Christ is "the head of the body, the church" (Col. 1:18, etc.), is it correct to describe Him also as "Head of the new creation"? Is the new creation identical with the church, or are we dealing with two different senses of headship?

Even if at the present time the new creation is co-terminous with the church (cf. 2 Cor. 5:17; Eph. 2:10), it will one day be much wider in range than the church. The church has been begotten by God in order to be "a kind of firstfruits of His creatures" (Jas. 1:18); when the church is glorified, all creation will be "delivered from the bondage of corruption into the liberty of the glory of the children of God" (Rom. 8:18-22); when God's tabernacle is with men and they are all

"His peoples" (the plural is the preferable reading in Rev. 21:3), the nations will walk by the light which illuminates the church, but they will not be included in the church (Rev. 21:24). Christ is not said in so many words to be Head of the new creation in Scripture, but He may rightly be described thus, as He is both its originator and ruler. Similarly He is described elsewhere as "the head of every man" (1 Cor. 11:3) and "the head of all principality and power" (Col. 2:10). But when He is said to be "head over all things to the church which is his body" (Eph. 1:22f.), a vital union is suggested because here and nowhere else we have the head and body as correlatives. His relation to His church is represented by this figure as being organic in a unique sense. We should, however, note with care the purpose for which the church is envisaged in Scripture as the body of Christ, and not extend the figure to areas to which it is not applied in Scripture.

What do people mean when they speak of our Lord's two natures?

They mean that He is not only altogether God, but also (since His incarnation) altogether Man. The Biblical doctrine on this fundamental subject is summed up as follows in the *Westminster Shorter Catechism*: "The only Redeemer of God's elect is the Lord Jesus Christ, who, being the eternal Son of God, became man, and so was, and continueth to be, God and man in two distinct natures, and one person, for ever."

Is it correct to claim that worship due to God alone was accepted by our Lord? It is urged by some that, in the passages which seem to suggest that He did, the terms rendered "worship" should be understood to mean homage, obeisance, or the like; and the inference is drawn that this disposes of our Lord's implied claim to deity.

The Greek words, like the English word "worship", take their precise sense from the person to whom the worship is paid. When we dignify the mayor of an English borough with the title "worshipful", we are not paying him divine honours; we are simply according him such dignity as becomes his position. The Greek verb most commonly rendered "worship" is *proskyneō*, which is used of paying homage to a king or the like as well as paying worship to God. Thus, in the Septuagint of 1 Chron. 29:20 it appears in the clause "they worshipped the LORD, and the king"—which means, of course, that they paid divine honours to God and royal honours to the king. It is unlikely that in all instances those who are said to have "worshipped" Christ intended to pay Him divine honours. J. N. Darby translates "did him homage" even in such places as Matt. 2:11 and John 9:38, and justifies his procedure in the preface to the second edition of his translation of the New Testament: "And this [a discussion of such forms as 'ye' and 'you'] leads me to the use of the words 'do homage' instead of 'worship,' which I do only for the sake of other people's minds not used to such questions. I have not a doubt of the justness of the change, and just because in *modern* English 'worship' is used for what is rendered to God only; when the English translation [i.e. the A.V.] was made it was not, and the use of it now falsifies the sense in three-quarters of the passages it is used in. It is quite certain that in the vast majority of instances of persons coming to the Lord they had not the least idea of owning Him as God. And it falsifies the sense in a material point to use the word now. That we worship Christ who do know He is God is another matter. In the English Bible it is, or at least was, all right, because worship did not mean what it does now. The man when he is married says, 'With my body I thee worship' . . . It would not have been worth mentioning but for simple souls."

But for us there is no doubt about the kind of worship that is to be paid to our Lord; it is the same kind of worship as is to be paid to the Father, who has ordained that all should "honour the Son, even as they honour the Father" (John 5:23), and has declared that He Himself is glorified when every knee bows in Jesus' name and every tongue confesses that He is Lord—i.e. when Jesus receives such worship as is due to God alone (Phil. 2:10f.). It is on the tenor of such scriptures as these, and not on the meaning of the Greek verb taken by itself, that we can most securely base our conclusions.

In most of the New Testament, and especially in such verses as 1 Cor. 8:6; Eph. 4:6; John 17:3; Jude 4, the name "God" seems to be applied exclusively to the Father. Does this mean that there is a sense in which Christ is not God?

No; the common restriction of the name "God" to the Father throughout the New Testament avoids ambiguity, follows Old Testament usage, and also accords with the fact that, within the eternal unity of the Godhead, the Father is the "Fount of Deity." The Son is begotten by Him, the Spirit proceeds from Him; but the reverse is never suggested, and is, in fact, inconceivable. Again, within the Godhead, the Father is the source of authority; He sends the Son and sends His Spirit, but is never sent by Them. But if we ask the New Testament writers whether Christ is altogether God as well as altogether Man, they leave us in no doubt about the answer; not only do they designate Him by such titles as "our great God and Saviour" (Tit. 2:13, R.V., R.S.V., N.E.B.), but repeatedly, as if it were the most natural thing in the world, they apply to Him Old Testament passages which in their original context refer unambiguously to Jehovah, the God of Israel.

Could Jesus be truly man if He was truly God at the same time?

173

Yes; not only could be, but actually was so. Because God made man in His own image, it was possible for God to manifest Himself perfectly in flesh, i.e. in a real human life (1 Tim. 3:16). So perfectly, indeed, did He thus manifest Himself that Jesus could say: "He who has seen me has seen the Father" (John 14:9)—not, of course, that Jesus *was* the Father but that in His incarnation He became the perfect revelation of the Father. When all this, and more, has been said, it remains a mystery *how* He combined Godhead and manhood in His one person, being "divinest when He most was man"; but since "no one knows the Son except the Father" (Matt. 11:27), it is a mystery which we need not expect to penetrate.

HIS PARENTAGE AND UPBRINGING

How did Mary find out that her son was the Son of God?

By Gabriel's announcement to her: "The Holy Ghost will come upon you, and the power of the Most High will overshadow you; therefore the child to be born will be called holy, the Son of God" (Luke 1:35).

Did Mary have other children than our Lord? Can we be sure of the correctness of the translation of the words "brothers" and "sisters" as used of His blood-relations?

The natural implication of such passages as Matthew 13:55f. and Mark 6:3 is that the brothers and sisters there mentioned were younger children of Mary. Sometimes, where the sense demands it, the words "brothers" and "sisters" do have a wider meaning. But the onus of proving that they have that wider meaning in the passages referred to rests upon those who deny that literal brothers and sisters of our Lord are meant. Those who accept the dogma of Mary's perpetual virginity do not believe that our Lord had literal brothers and sisters; there is no reason why

those who do not accept this dogma should not take the terms in their literal sense.

It has been suggested that our Lord's parentage was not so humble as is commonly believed; that the Greek word which denotes Joseph's trade implies not a humble artificer but a very rare craftsman and therefore a person of standing in the community and certainly not poor. What would you say on this?

Joseph was a *tektōn*—a word which is usually rendered "carpenter" but may have the wider significance of "builder." In either case there is no suggestion that he was a "very rare craftsman"—no more rare than any other carpenter or builder. Certainly he did not belong to the most depressed class of society; there was always work for a carpenter or builder to do. We might, if we wished to classify his rank in present-day terms, describe him as belonging to the lower middle class. But the low standard of living and the heavy burden of taxation would mean that he and his family could not live very far above subsistence level.

Is it true that the Virgin Mary had a sister of the same name? John 19:25 suggests that Mary the wife of Clopas was sister to Mary the mother of Jesus. Or does that verse refer to four women, the second one ("his mother's sister") being nameless?

If we take John 19:25 by itself, it is natural to understand "Mary the wife of Clopas" as being in apposition with "his mother's sister." But if we compare it with Mark 15:40, we are led rather to the conclusion that "his mother's sister" should be identified with Salome, who (as a comparison with Matt. 27:56 indicates) was the mother of James and John, the sons of Zebedee. In that case, John 19:25 mentions four women—the mother of our Lord (who is not mentioned in the parallel accounts in the other Gospels) and three others.

Is it the Virgin Mary who is referred to in Matt. 27:56 as "Mary the mother of James and Joses" (compare Mark 6:3)?

I do not think so: first, because it would have been more natural to refer to the Virgin as "the mother of Jesus" (as in John 2:1; Acts 1:14), since He is the central figure; second, because "Mary the mother of James and Joses" is more naturally identified with "Mary the wife of Clopas" in John 19:25. The James whose mother this Mary was is distinguished in Mark 15:40 as "James the less"—by contrast, I suggest, with James the Lord's brother, whose stature in the Church of Jerusalem in the apostolic age would make him overshadow any other James (especially after the execution of James the son of Zebedee). According to the second-century writer Hegesippus, Clopas was brother to Joseph the carpenter; we have no means of assessing the truth of this statement.

PHYSIQUE

Why is our Lord usually portrayed in pictures and such representations with an attractive face and personality, when God says that He has "no beauty that we should desire him"?

Artists must portray what they see in their mind's eye; we cannot answer for their representations of our Lord. But it is not *God* who says of the Servant that he has "no beauty that we should desire him" (Isa. 53:2); it is people who formerly saw nothing attractive in him, but now lament their previous blindness because their eyes have been opened and they are able to appreciate Him as he really is.

HIS FINANCIAL SUPPORT

The Lord and His disciples toured Palestine north, south, east and west for three and a half years. How was this financed?

Mainly, it appears, by voluntary gifts and free hospitality. Here and there the Gospel narratives provide hints of how

their material needs were met; we have the reference to the well-to-do women who "ministered to them of their substance" in Luke 8:3, and the instructions to the Twelve when they were sent out two by two (Matt. 10:9-11) suggest a pattern of maintenance which probably did not greatly differ from that followed when our Lord and His disciples journeyed together.

HIS LANGUAGES

It is often said that our Lord read from the Greek Septuagint in the synagogue at Nazareth (Luke 4:16-19). If so, He and His hearers were bilingual as they also spoke Aramaic. Is it possible that He studied the Scriptures in Hebrew as well? What are your general observations?

It is most unlikely that the Scriptures were read in the Nazareth synagogue in any language other than Hebrew. Luke naturally reproduces the lesson read by our Lord in a form approximating to that of the Greek Bible because he was a Greek, writing in Greek. No doubt our Lord used Greek when addressing such people as the Syrophoenician woman or Pontius Pilate, but Aramaic would be His habitual speech, and He would certainly read the Scriptures in their original Hebrew text.

If, as you say in the preceding answer, Aramaic was our Lord's habitual speech, does this mean that the Greek in which His words are reproduced in the Gospels is only a translation of what He actually said? But why then should we have a few of His sayings reported in Aramaic (e.g. Talitha cumi) with a translation?

It is generally accepted that Aramaic was the common speech of Palestinian Jews (especially Galilaeans) in our Lord's time, and an examination of the Greek form in which His words are reported strongly suggests that they are (often very literally) translated from that language. It is particularly interesting, for example to see how much of His teaching acquires poetical form when we try to envisage the Aramaic wording underlying the Greek of the Gospels. An analogy to the retention of a few phrases in the original Aramaic might be presented by an English biography of a Frenchman, in which the Frenchman's words would normally be quoted in English, but at times, for vividness, some specially impressive or memorable utterances (such as *C'est magnifique, mais ce n'est pas la guerre*) would be left untranslated (possibly with an English rendering added in a footnote). But it is the Greek text of our Gospels that is our primary source; attempts by philologists to recover the Aramaic wording of the sayings of Jesus reported in our Gospels do not enjoy canonical authority.

His Righteousness

C. H. Mackintosh (Notes on Genesis, 6th ed., p. 64) speaks of sin attaching to the life which our Lord gave up on the cross: "He rose triumphant, in the power of a new life, to which righteousness as distinctly attaches itself, as did sin to that life which He gave up on the cross." Has such a statement Scriptural support?

In saying that sin was attached by imputation to the life which our Lord gave up on the cross, Mackintosh probably intended to summarize the Scriptural teaching on this subject. But his language is open to objection, and it is far better to adhere to the language of Scripture, as in 2 Cor. 5:21; Gal. 3:13; 1 Peter 2:24. Of course, righteousness attached as perfectly to our Lord's life before His crucifixion as to His resurrection life; but Mackintosh did not intend to deny this.

While Reformed theology speaks of the righteousness of Christ as imputed to believers, it has been pointed out that the expression "the righteousness of Christ" does not occur in Scripture. Is
there any difference between the righteousness of Christ and "the righteousness of God" (2 Cor. 5:21; Phil. 3:9)? Is Christ's righteousness something personal to Himself?

If the actual expression "the righteousness of Christ" does not occur, the reality denoted by the expression is fundamental to the New Testament gospel. Something very close to "the righteousness of Christ" appears in Rom. 5:18 ("one man's act of righteousness") and 5:19 ("one man's obedience"). Since Christ's act of righteousness leads to "justification of life", since through His obedience the many "will be made righteousness", it is difficult to press any great distinction between the righteousness of Christ in its justifying efficacy and "the righteousness of God" which we become "in him" (2 Cor. 5:21) or the righteousness "which is through faith in Christ, the righteousness from God that depends on faith" (Phil. 3:9). The righteousness of Christ is something personal to Himself in the sense that He alone exemplified God's perfect standard; but His people enter into the good of it by faith, since He is the One "whom God made . . . our righteousness" (1 Cor. 1:30).

His Teaching

What was our Lord's reason for teaching in parables? The reason given in the Gospels appears to suggest that He was not prepared to reveal His teaching openly, but modern scholars seem almost uniformly to reject this view.

The passage you refer to is Mark 4:11f. and its parallels (Matt. 13:11-17; Luke 8:10). A consideration of these parallel passages, together with the passage in Isa. 6:9f. which they echo, gives us the sense. To those whose eyes were open, whose ears were alert and whose minds were receptive, the parables were luminous, revealing "the mystery of the kingdom of God." To the others, however, they

176

remained riddles; the Aramaic word for "parable" can also mean "riddle", and if we have regard to the Aramaic targum of Isa. 6:10 which appears to be quoted in Mark 4:12, we may render our Lord's words: "To you has been given the mystery of the kingdom of God, but to those outside everything takes the form of riddles, so that (the prophet's words are fulfilled in them): 'They see indeed but do not perceive; they hear indeed but do not understand; else they would turn again and receive forgiveness'." Our Lord's reason for parabolic teaching, then, we may say, was that those whose eyes were opened might appreciate the truth all the more clearly, while He was sadly aware that for those who closed their eyes the outcome would simply be greater blindness.

His Priesthood
Is it right to refer to Christ as "the great high priest" before His ascension?

The title "high priest" is not given to our Lord in the New Testament outside the Epistle to the Hebrews, and in the interests of clear thinking it is best to restrict its use to the sense which it has in that Epistle, where His high priesthood begins with the offering and presentation of His perfect self-sacrifice. This does not mean that He did not act before His passion in a manner which was essentially high-priestly, or at any rate priestly. We may think, for example, of His intercession for Peter (Luke 22:32), and especially of His prayer for His disciples in John 17. That has frequently, since the sixteenth century, been called His high-priestly prayer, and in view of the fact that He offered it from the standpoint of His finished work (John 17:4), we may learn from it something of the nature of His present intercession on His people's behalf (Heb. 7:25; Rom. 8:34).

To the suggestion that our Lord's present intercession can be understood if we think of Him as offering for His people now such prayers as that which He offered for Peter on earth (Luke 22:32), it has been replied that He is not only praying but also doing for His people now what He did for Peter and all His people on earth: "Why only his word, and not his greatest deed?" Would you comment on this?

Yes; the question "Why only his word, and not his greatest deed?" is asked by my colleague Gordon Rupp in an essay on "The Finished Work of Christ in Word and Sacrament" (contributed to *The Finality of Christ*, ed. D. Kirkpatrick, 1966), in the course of which he drops the remark that if he could take only one epistle to a desert island with him, it would be the Epistle to the Hebrews. My comment on his question is that I quite agree, provided that we recognize (as Professor Rupp, of course, does) that our Lord is not bearing His people's sins now, or making purification for them, since He did this once for all so perfectly on the cross that it needs neither continuation nor repetition. But His ministry of intercession in heaven is based on that finished work; in this sense He is still doing for His people what He did for them on earth, making not only His word but (much more) His greatest deed available for their blessing. Professor Rupp quotes appraisingly James Moffatt's comment on Heb. 7:25, "His intercession . . . has red blood in it." But Charles Wesley, as usual, says the *mot juste* in the stanza "Five bleeding wounds He bears . . ."— which is admittedly the language of poetry and not of dogmatic prose. (I wonder why that stanza, the greatest one in the hymn "Arise, my soul, arise," is omitted in *Hymns of Faith?*)

His Death
Do the words of John 19:31, "for that sabbath day was a high day", signify that in that year passover fell on a weekly sabbath, or that the sabbath was

not the weekly one, but a midweek sabbath because of passover? If the former, why does John emphasize it? If the latter, does it not follow that Jesus was crucified midweek?

"That sabbath day was a high day" because it was not only the weekly sabbath but also the day of the passover, by the temple reckoning. John emphasizes it because it was trebly important that the bodies should not remain on the crosses overnight on that occasion: first, because they ought not to remain overnight in any case (Deut. 21:23); secondly, because it would have been an additional desecration to allow them to remain until the sabbath (which began at sundown); thirdly, because that sabbath was no ordinary sabbath, but coincided with the passover. The word *paraskeuē* by itself, as used in John 19:31, simply means "Friday" (i.e. sabbath eve), but that Friday was in addition Passover Eve (John 19:14).

It has been suggested that pious Christian sentiment has lingered excessively over the crowning of Jesus with thorns and His flagellation, whereas in fact the crowning with thorns was intended, like the purple robe and mock sceptre, for purposes of ridicule, not to inflict pain, while the flagellation is mentioned only in a passing phrase. (Cf. A. N. Wilder, Theology and Modern Literature, 1958, p. 109.) Would you comment on this?

It is true, of course, that there is a strain of Christian piety which has dwelt too much on our Lord's bodily sufferings, to a point where the true significance of his atoning sacrifice is in danger of being overlooked. With regard to the historical facts: the crown of thorns was certainly part of the apparatus of ridicule when the soldiers celebrated a mock coronation of our Lord. There is a good study of "The Crown of Thorns in John 19:2-3" by H. St. J. Hart in the *Journal of Theological Studies* for 1952 (p. 66ff.), where it is suggested that the crown of thorns was

intended to imitate the "radiate crown" of a divine ruler. But while the primary purpose of the crown of thorns was ridicule, yet if the author of the study I have mentioned is right in thinking that the thorns were those of *Phoenix dactylifera*, it could well have caused acute pain also. As for the flagellation, there is no doubt about its intention and effect; the Roman scourge was an abominable instrument of torture, under which it was not unknown for men to die. It was not necessary to give it more than a passing mention, because readers of the gospels would know only too well what a Roman scourging was like. See pp. 249f.

Is "cross" the best translation of stauros, the Greek word used in the New Testament for the instrument on which our Lord was executed?

There are two words used in the Greek Testament for this instrument; one is *xylon* (derived perhaps from the Septuagint version of Deut. 21:22, 23, quoted in Gal. 3:13) and the other is *stauros*. The former word, used in this sense five times in the New Testament, is translated "tree" in the older versions, but it can be used of anything made of wood, such as cudgels (Matt. 26:47, etc.) or stocks (Acts 16:24); as used of the cross, it means a wooden gibbet (and so it is rendered in N.E.B.). The word *stauros* means a stake; when used of an instrument of execution it may mean a stake for impalement (as among the Assyrians) or (as in the New Testament) the instrument used for the Roman practice of crucifixion. There are numerous places in Greek literature outside the New Testament where *stauros* means "cross" in this latter sense. But neither Greek *stauros* nor Latin *crux* nor English "cross" says anything definite about the shape of this instrument of execution. There was no standard shape, although the Gospel references to bearing one's cross suggest a cross-beam to be fixed to an upright. In addition to the conventional shape of the cross in Christian art (†), which was convenient for fixing the "title" to the upper projection of the upright plank, the T shape was quite common; there was also the X shape (St. Andrew's cross) and the Y shape; there might be an upright only with no cross-beam, the arms being then stretched up above the head; or a board with the general shape of a door might serve quite well. There can be no objection to the word "cross" as a translation of *stauros*, provided we do not think it denotes one particular shape of gibbet. (See also p. 191.)

What was the "cup" to which our Lord referred in his prayer in Gethsemane? Was it a cup of "poison" that the devil offered Him in order to forestall His death on the cross? Does Heb. 5:7 (A.V. He "was heard in that he feared") mean that it was such a cup that He feared, and was He answered because of that fear?

We shall find a commentary on the reference to the cup in Gethsemane in John 18:11 where our Lord, expressing the resolute embracing of the Father's will which came to expression in the garden, says, "Shall I not drink the cup which the Father has given me?" As for Heb. 5:7, we should note the rendering of R.V. and R.S.V., "he was heard for his godly fear", or of N.E.B., "because of his humble submission his prayer was heard" —that is, because of His obedient acceptance of the Father's will in preference to His own natural desire to be spared the cross. (That such a desire was natural will be clear to anyone who gives a little thought to what crucifixion was like.) Some commentators have seen a contradiction between Heb. 5:7 ("he was heard") and the fact that the cup was not removed from Him, and have either amended the text by inserting "not" before "heard" or suggested that it was from fear of death (rather than from death

itself) that He was delivered or adopted some other interpretative procedure. But, whether or not Heb. 5:7 refers to Gethsemane (and I am sure that this is its main, though not necessarily exclusive, reference), we shall understand it better if we realize that the language of this passage is influenced by the Greek version of Psa. 22. In particular, "he was heard" echoes Psa. 22:24, "when he cried to him, he heard"; our Lord accepted and drained the cup—in other words, He entered into death, but having done so, He was delivered out of it. If ever you come across a pamphlet by the late William Hoste entitled *Christ in Gethsemane* (published many years ago by John Ritchie, Kilmarnock), you will find in it a clear and satisfying answer to your question and others related to it.

HIS RESURRECTION

Is the New Testament doctrine of the resurrection of Christ satisfied by the view that He continued to live on in the lives of His followers?

No. It is true, of course, that a Christian in New Testament times (or in modern times) could say with Paul "Christ lives in me"; but that was the consequence of Christ's resurrection, not the resurrection itself. The only evidence that we have for the resurrection of Christ makes it plain that the body which was taken down from the cross and laid in Joseph's tomb was no longer in that tomb when the third morning came, and (more important still) that Christ appeared alive again to various people who knew Him, not only on Easter Day but intermittently for some six weeks thereafter. Our subjective experience of the power of the risen Christ is the result of the objective fact of His rising from the dead on the third day. It was to the objective fact, not to the subjective experience which follows from it, that Paul referred when he said: "If Christ hath not been raised, then is our preaching vain, your faith also is vain" (1 Cor. 15:14).

179

Were the souls of the righteous dead of Old Testament times held captive by Satan until our Lord Himself set them free at His Resurrection?

Even an uncanonical writer like the author of the Book of Wisdom knew that "the souls of the righteous are in the hand of God, and no torment shall touch them" (Wisdom 3:1). Many Old Testament saints were subject to lifelong bondage through fear of death until Christ came to abolish it (Heb. 2:15; 2 Tim. 1:10), but some had sufficient faith to see that a man who walked with God in this life would not be bereft of His presence and protection in the life to come (cf. Psa. 73:24; 139:8). The idea that the soul of a man like Abraham, who was justified by faith, was held captive by Satan is without Scriptural support and is incredible in itself.

Church

CHURCH—LOCAL

Is it true that in New Testament and early Christian times the local church embraced all the Christians in a city, while it might be divided into several smaller congregations for practical purposes, and that elders were elders of the whole church in the city, not elders of the individual congregations?

As a matter of history this appears to have been the practice. But it is not a matter of principle. If it were, how could it be applied to Christians in country districts, which were evangelized at a later time than urban populations? Some groups of Christians have nonetheless adopted this as a point of principle, with the result that ecclesiastical relations have to be modified every time that a city extends its boundaries. Andrew Miller pointed out the arbitrary nature of a system which required that a congregation in Woolwich be reckoned part of the same local church as that in Islington, eight miles away, but not of the same local church as the congregation in the adjoining borough of Plumstead, because in his day Plumstead lay just outside the administrative area of Greater London.

Does common sense, experience, tradition or plain Scripture teach that a local church and elders have no authority over another local church and elders?

Plain Scripture certainly gives not the slightest foundation for the idea that one local church and its elders have any authority over another local church and its elders. An apostle, whose commission extended far beyond the frontiers of any one local church, could issue directives to several churches by virtue of the authority invested in him by the Lord. But when the church of Colossae was tempted to go astray in matters of doctrine, no suggestion was made that the neighbouring church of Laodicea should take the situation in hand. And when, later, the church of Laodicea in her turn grew lukewarm, no suggestion was made that the church of Philadelphia might intervene in an attempt to raise the temperature. The New Testament does clearly teach the administrative independence of each local church, and her direct responsibility to the Lord; although this does not in any way impair the fellowship which ought to exist between churches. Subsequent tradition has introduced a quite different principle. For example, there is a long-standing tradition in Central and Western Europe that the churches in that area (and not in that area only) should submit to the authority of the historic church of the city of Rome and its administration. This traditional claim is rejected by all heirs of the Reformation, but is it always rejected for the best reasons? The fundamental reason why (as Article XXXVII puts it) "the Bishop of Rome hath no jurisdiction in this Realm of England" is that, according to the New Testament, no bishop, of whatsoever kind, has any jurisdiction in any church but his own. As for common sense and experience, they teach (in my judgment) that an immeasurable amount of ecclesiastical trouble might be avoided if the New Testament precedent were followed in this matter.

If the churches of the New Testament were independent of one another's control and unconnected by any formal federation, what was the nature of the fellowship between them, and what is the nature of the fellowship which should exist between similar churches today?

The New Testament churches all acknowledged the supremacy of Christ. Churches of apostolic foundation generally recognized the authority delegated by Christ to their founder-apostle or apostles. For the rest, the bond between them was one of practical love. Hence Paul's concern to have his Gentile churches contribute to the material aid of the Jerusalem church. As for churches today, the following words of the late J. B. Watson are worthy of careful consideration: "The bond of fellowship between churches is to be that of a common obedience to the same Lord and subjection to His Word, not that of conformity to decisions imposed from without, or that secured by creeds or governmental forms laid down by representative councils. The unity thus exhibited will be that of the Spirit, the effect of which toward the world will be that which only the steady pressure of truth manifest in life can produce."

In a booklet entitled Departing from Iniquity *or* Inconsistency, *by G.R.C., there is a statement that "the doctrine which asserts the independence of local assemblies is iniquitous." How does this statement stand in the light of our Lord's letters to the seven churches in Rev. 2 and 3?*

It is plain that each of these seven churches is treated independently; there is no suggestion of a federation of Asian churches which might check moral or doctrinal deviations on the part of one of its member-churches. Perhaps the author of the statement you quote has failed to grasp what is meant by the "independence of local assemblies." This expression does not imply that there should be no fellowship or mutual concern between local churches; it does not imply that local churches can never co-operate for a common purpose, or that one church can say to another: "I have no need of you." But it does imply that each local church is *administratively* independent; in this sense it is directly responsible to the Lord and not to any other church or group of churches.

What are the essential conditions to be given to a young person allowed to join one of our churches?

The one Scriptural condition for membership in any local church is that which God Himself requires and with which He has declared Himself satisfied—namely, faith in Christ, or new life in Christ. A Scripturally constituted church will gladly welcome anyone who makes a credible profession of faith in Christ. But after the initial reception, a young person (or an older person, for that matter) will have much to learn about the privileges and responsibilities involved in sharing the church's fellowship, worship and witness; and those who care for the church's spiritual wellbeing will see to it that new members are taught these necessary things.

CHURCH LEADERSHIP
Elders and Deacons.

Should elders constitute the ruling body over a local church, to such an extent that they never inquire of other brethren in order to ascertain their views on church matters?

Of course not. The elders are spiritual trustees, responsible both to the church and to the Lord. They cannot discharge their trust without being as fully acquainted as possible with the mind of the church. The more they maintain complete fellowship with the church in all their work of oversight and make it plain that the welfare of the church is their earnest concern, the more will they enjoy the confidence and respect of their brethren and sisters.

Should church elders control the routine financial and temporal business of the church, including repair and maintenance of the building where they meet, etc., or should this work be seen to by deacons, on the basis of Acts 6?

It is certainly preferable that the elders should delegate such duties as you mention to other competent members of the local church, and thus free their own hands for the work of spiritual oversight and teaching to which they have been called. These other brethren may be called deacons if you will (though the work of a deacon in the New Testament has a wider scope). The principle of Acts 6:1-6 is applicable here, even if the actual circumstances do not repeat themselves. It may be, of course, that in a small church a very few members have to do all the work, spiritual and material alike. It may not be superfluous to remark that all such work should be carried out in fellowship with the whole church, and in particular that a full account should be given at regular intervals of the receipt and expenditure of the church's money.

What provision is made in Scripture for ensuring a proper succession of elders in an assembly?

It stands to reason that elders who are concerned with the spiritual well-being of the local church will promote its well-being (among other ways) by taking into their counsels from time to time younger men who manifest the appropriate qualities, so that the supply of responsible

leaders will not dry up, to the impoverishment of the church. They will do this, of course, in fellowship with the church as a whole, which ought to know, approve and acknowledge its spiritual guides. This principle appears clearly in 2 Tim. 2:2, where provision is made for a continuous supply of faithful and capable teachers in the church. So long as the principle is recognized, the procedure for putting it into effect is a matter of minor importance.

It is frequently said that it is the duty of the elders of a church to arrange for adequate and systematic Bible teaching in the church by inviting speakers from outside their own church to conduct series of ministry meetings. If the implication of this is that the elders themselves are not competent to give the believers the teaching that they need, how does this square with the apostolic requirement that an elder should be "apt to teach" (1 Tim. 3:2)?

Certainly every elder should be "apt to teach" in the sense that he should be able to instruct less mature Christians in the basic principles of the Christian faith and in the practical implications of these principles. A man who is unable to do this lacks one of the essential qualifications of an elder. But such teaching need not involve the public ministry of the Scriptures; there are many fine elders who have not the gift of public utterance. It is certainly the duty of the elders to see that provision is made for the spiritual needs of the Christians under their care. For the most part they will make this provision themselves, in dependence on the grace and power of the Holy Spirit; but at other times they may decide that what the church needs in present circumstances is a particular line of ministry for which none of themselves is specially gifted, but which a certain person known to them *can* impart in a most acceptable manner. They will therefore invite him to pay them a visit, in order that the church (including the elders) may profit by the gift that God has given him.

Should an elder retire from the ministry of oversight when the church feels that he is getting past his usefulness?

A man of spiritual discernment (and of course no one who is not a man of spiritual discernment can exercise spiritual oversight) would recognize that he was getting past his usefulness before the church did, and would no doubt take appropriate action. It is, after all, the man who does the work who is the true overseer, not the man who has the title. Ceasing to do the work is itself retirement, for practical purposes. But we must distinguish between different situations. Many a spiritual leader loses his bodily vigour as he grows older, yet his wise judgment, based on long experience, is such that his guidance is eagerly sought and followed by his younger brethren. There is the sadder situation in which advancing years bring mental deterioration with them; when this happens, a man's fellow-elders must deal with him in Christian gentleness and with appreciation of all the help that he has given when he was in full possession of his faculties. Saddest of all is the situation when the deterioration manifests itself in personality and character, when a man who once served the Lord and His people well as a spiritual guide is no longer capable of doing so, but insists on having things all his own way (especially in the absence of fellow-elders who could deal with him graciously and firmly) just because he likes the illusion of power that it gives him. Several of these problems were discussed at the High Leigh Conference of Brethren in 1955, and I take leave to quote two contributions to the discussion. Mr. Harold St. John said: "Surely, a godly man who knows that his ministry, and his powers of expression, are definitely waning, will willingly submit to discipline, and be prepared to retire into the shadows.

But I do not think it would be right to take an elder brother, who may have served a particular church, off the oversight. I would sooner allow him to act as a sort of emeritus professor, giving him still the opportunity of doing what he can, while, at the same time, he will learn to grow old gracefully." And on the question of how to deal with an elder who, because of spiritual deterioration, has become a serious hindrance to a small church, Mr. B. H. Mudditt said: "The brethren must avoid any open rupture. And they must avoid anything in the way of a whispering campaign behind his back. In a case within my own knowledge they laid this before the Lord in prayer. They prayed that God Himself would solve the problem; and in a very simple way, within three months, the whole problem was completely solved, and by the direct intervention of God. And that fact demonstrated to the assembly that God was still on the throne, and was ready to hear and answer the specific prayers of His people. Another result was that all the other elders ever since have 'gone softly'!" I think you will find that these two quotations between them go far towards providing an answer to your question.

Is it correct to say that no local company of Christians has the right to the designation "church" unless and until elders and deacons are in evidence?

No; elders and deacons are necessary for the well-being of a local church, but not for its being. When Paul and Barnabas appointed "elders in every church" of South Galatia (Acts 14:23), the implication of the language is that the churches were there before elders were appointed in them. I know that the maintenance of due order by properly appointed elders is a "mark" of the true church—something by which it may be recognized for what is, but we must not confuse such a "mark" with the essence. "Apart from the eternal high-priesthood of Christ, no ministry is essential to the Church in the sense that the Church could not exist without it. On the other hand, in an imperfect world of sinful and fallible men and women, some ministry is necessary in the sense that the Church cannot be fully effective for its tasks without it" (T. W. Manson, *Ministry and Priesthood*, 1958, p. 72).

What is involved in the spiritual guidance which church elders are expected to supply, apart from their administrative activities?

First and most important, their lives should be examples which their fellow-believers can safely follow. Next, they should be "apt to teach"; that is to say, they should have a thorough judicious and experimental knowledge of the Word of God and of His will therein unfolded, so that they can apply what they know not only to their own lives but to those for whose spiritual and moral welfare they are responsible. And in this connexion it is worth emphasizing that they should be the sort of men to whom their fellow-Christians will readily go with their spiritual and moral problems, knowing that these problems will be treated with sympathetic wisdom *and in complete confidence.*

Should church offices come under review periodically?

It is highly desirable that they should be reviewed, as a matter of accepted procedure, every two or three years. Where this is done, it is easier to avoid the painful situation which sometimes arises when (say) someone who has been Sunday School superintendent for forty or fifty years does not realize that he is no longer fit for this work and cannot be persuaded by tactful suggestions to resign. If, in the ordinary course of events, it were understood that the question of reappointing the existing superintendent or appointing a new one should come up at stated intervals, a fresh appointment would probably have been made long before, and no resentment caused.

Should deaconesses be recognized or appointed by assemblies?

Whether they are called deaconesses or not is a small matter; but that women as well as men might serve as deacons in apostolic churches is plain from 1 Tim. 3:8-13, where the "women" of verse 11 (R.V.) appear to be women who performed service of this kind, rather than deacons' wives (as in A.V.). Phoebe was a "servant" (Gk. *diakonos*) of the church at Cenchreae (Rom. 16:1). In *A Return to Simplicity* (the report of the 1956 High Leigh Conference of Brethren), p. 28, Mr. E. W. Rogers says concisely: "My view is that the Scripture provides for deacons and deaconesses in the local church." I agree.

Would not our churches tend to prosper spiritually if they each maintained a full-time resident brother for pastoral service—especially for visiting work?

What is of first importance is that proper provision should be made for pastoral service. If the elders, from their knowledge of the situation, judge that this provision can best be made by enabling someone who is suitably qualified to give his whole time to this service, good and well. This is done in some places. In others it is found sufficient if two or more share this responsibility between themselves, in which case it may not be necessary for any one to devote his whole time to it. While visiting is important—especially the visiting of those who are unable to attend meetings regularly—pastoral service is not confined to this; the ministry of the Word is also an essential part of pastoral service. It may well happen that one brother who is excellent in visitation is not so well qualified for the regular ministry of the Word, while someone else who can minister the Word acceptably is not so good at visiting. It is a pity when one man is expected to discharge all the pastoral responsibilities, including those for which he is not so well qualified in addition to those which he is properly equipped to do. Where the various responsibilities can be shared among those who are qualified to discharge them, whether on a full-time or on a part-time basis, this is better, though it is not always feasible. Where financial considerations arise, of course, we must give effect to the Scriptural principle that "the labourer is worthy of his hire" (1 Tim. 5:18).

Who should choose the deacons—the church, the existing deacons (if any) or the overseers?

If by deacons is meant persons to carry out such responsibilities as were discharged by the seven of Acts 6:3-6, then that passage suggests that they should be chosen by the church and installed in office by the elders.

Could you say something about the function of trustees in relation to the responsibilities of the elders or oversight of a church? Should the elders ever consult them, or vice versa, especially where questions of doctrine arise?

The usual situation is that the trustees are appointed to make sure that the building owned by the church continues to serve its proper purpose—to see that the terms of the trust are fulfilled. The elders of the church are responsible for the spiritual well-being of the people of God committed to their care, and with this the trustees as such will not interfere. In most situations with which I have had to do there has been a considerable overlapping in personnel between elders and trustees, so that the one body was well acquainted with the proceedings of the other, but it need not always be so. Sometimes the trustees are charged with the administration of some money to be used for the maintenance of the building;

in such a case consultation with those who use the building (possibly represented for this purpose by the deacons) would be desirable. A major problem arises if the doctrines stipulated in the trust are no longer maintained by the church, or doctrines contrary to these are authoritatively taught. Then the trustees have to protect the terms of the trust. If, for example, the trust prescribes the teaching and practice of infant baptism and the church later comes to the conclusion that believers' baptism only should be taught and practised, it might be best for the church to look for another building, for the trustees have their duty to perform, regardless of their personal views on baptism. When a conflict of this character arises, it is not to the question page of *The Harvester* that it will have to be carried. All this suggests that care be taken in listing doctrines to be annexed to a trust-deed. Those charged with drafting such a document will want to safeguard the basic evangelical verities, without being too specific about detailed interpretations and applications on which there may be reasonable differences of opinion, bearing in mind that the beliefs which unite Christians are more important than those which divide them.

CHURCH CONSTITUTION

Where a church constitution has been drawn up, and a division unfortunately develops in its ranks, what action is the party which holds to the constitution justified in taking in order to maintain its control of the building?

If it holds to the New Testament, there is one course of action which it is justified in taking. The example of R. C. Chapman will illustrate it. When, under the influence of his ministry, a Strict Baptist congregation in Barnstaple renounced Strict Baptist principles, "some Christians in Barnstaple," he relates, "who held the strict views which we had by then abandoned, demanded that we should give up the use of the chapel. I carefully examined the Trust Deed, and found that in not one particular, did we set aside its provisions. *Yet* we gave them the chapel, just as I should give my coat to a man who demanded it. You will not be surprised when I tell you that ere long the Lord gave us a much better chapel."

Is decision by majority vote in church matters a desirable procedure?

It may be all right when the question is where to go for the annual church picnic, or the like; but where matters of conscience or principle are concerned, it is best to wait until the sense of the meeting manifests itself with sufficient unanimity. (This does not mean that any individual or group can enjoy the unlimited use of the veto! We remember C. F. Hogg's oft-repeated remark: "Majority rule is bad; minority rule is worse.") Here again the experience of R. C. Chapman is instructive. When he went to Barnstaple to minister to the Strict Baptist congregation mentioned in the preceding answer, it was on condition that he was free to teach all that he found written in the Scriptures. When a visiting brother urged him to set aside the congregation's rule that none but baptized believers might take communion, he relates: "I replied that I could not force the consciences of my brethren and sisters; and I continued my ministry, patiently instructing them from the Word. I well knew at that time that I could have carried the point with a large majority, but I judged it to be more pleasing to God to toil on to bring all to one mind."

When the elders are evenly divided over a question affecting the welfare of the church and matters have reached a complete impasse, is there any action that the church can take to relieve an intolerable situation?

Considering the duty of elders to set a good example to the others, I should have thought that such a situation within their ranks would have provided a rare opportunity for the exercise of Christian forbearance and yieldingness. One might have expected to see the grace of Christ so animating the whole body of elders that each side would insist on letting the other side have its way. Where this is not so, it might be a good thing for the meeting of elders to consist of an odd number of members, so as to avoid an even division. But where a division in the eldership becomes public property in the church, and matters reach an impasse, the elders might as well confess their unfitness to serve in such a capacity and resign *en bloc*. The church might then be given an opportunity of indicating which brethren command its confidence.

Should a church always pay the expenses of a visiting speaker, even when he is known to be quite well off?

Yes, always. Whether he is well off or not has nothing to do with the principle (and in any case, it is a matter on which you might be quite misinformed). And remember that a speaker who drives his own car incurs expense as well as one who travels by bus or train or taxi. If a speaker does not wish to recoup himself, then he can take what you give him and use it for the Lord's work. But many churches do not realize how largely their good name depends on the care which they take to ascertain and cover all the expenses which a speaker may reasonably be expected to incur in accepting an invitation to visit them.

Ought we to give gifts for the purchase of books to preachers who are in "secular" employment?

The giving of gifts, unlike the repaying of expenses, is a matter of grace, not obligation, and cannot be subject to regulations! But a congregation may feel grateful to a preacher for his ministry, and desire to show its appreciation in a tangible form. They may conclude that, since he is sufficiently well-to-do, it would be embarrassing to offer him a monetary gift, but that a book-token would be a graceful and acceptable expression of their thanks. If that is the sort of situation you have in mind, I should warmly commend the spirit thus displayed.

Is there any valid distinction between inviting a speaker to preach on a certain day and inviting him to expound the Scriptures in the course or at the end of a communion service? Does the latter practice involve the rejection of the Holy Spirit's guidance?

No more and no less than the former practice. Whether we meet for the holy communion or for prayer, to hear the Word of God or to take part in collective gospel witness, we should be subject to Christ as Lord and responsive to the Spirit's guidance—as on all the other occasions of life. It is a mistake to think that the Spirit guides in some unique way at the Lord's Table. If we do not seek His guidance in all our week-day activities of work and recreation, we need not expect to enjoy it on Sunday morning.

Was a "free for all" system of ministry practised among the early Brethren such as Müller and Chapman?

No; and it is to be hoped that no such system is practised among the Brethren of today. The practice current among early Brethren was well expressed by G. V. Wigram about 1844 when he was asked if he admitted "a regular ministry." His reply was: "If by a regular ministry you mean a *stated* ministry (that is, that in every assembly those who are gifted of God to speak to edification will be both limited in number and known to the rest), I do admit it; but if by a regular ministry you mean an *exclusive* ministry, I dissent. By an *exclusive* ministry I mean the recognizing certain persons as so *exclusively* holding the place of teachers, as that the use of a real gift by any one else would

be irregular" (*On Ministry in the Word*, quoted by S. P. Tregelles, *Three Letters*, 1849, p. 13). Nor was this a principle admitted in theory only; it was a recognized practice that attempts at unprofitable ministry by unfit persons were restrained by the elders. See p. 165.

Is it against Scriptural principles to book speakers one or two years ahead?

No more than it is to book them one or two *days* ahead. We do not know what a day may bring forth; therefore in short-term as in long-term bookings we should practise the lesson of Jas. 4:15 and say, "If the Lord wills, we shall live and we shall do this or that."

What was the origin of the "conversational Bible reading"?

Such an informal institution probably had no formal origin. That Christians who share a common interest in the Bible should discuss it when they meet, or even arrange to meet for the purpose of discussing it, is a very natural thing. If the use of the Greek verb *dialegesthai* (meaning "to converse") is anything to go by, Paul appears to have conducted conversational Bible readings in the synagogues at Thessalonica (Acts 17:2), Athens (Acts 17:17), Corinth (Acts 18:4) and Ephesus (Acts 18:19-19:8); and when the synagogue doors in the last-named place were shut against him, he continued his conversational Bible readings in the lecture-hall of Tyrannus (Acts 19:9). This may not have been the origin of the Bible readings to which your question refers, but it certainly provides an excellent precedent for them.

Should our church leaders take more interest in, and become more aware of, current thinking in modern theology, or would this be a waste of time?

Teachers of Biblical doctrine would be well advised to have some idea of the religious teaching that is being currently purveyed, whether in specialist circles or (more important still) in popularized form. If they know what those whom they teach, or for whose instruction they are responsible, are being exposed to in this regard, they will understand more clearly how to frame their instruction so as to confirm what is good and refute what is harmful. This is not a waste of time; fresh advances along the path of truth can be made in the course of exposing error, as is shown by the Epistle to the Colossians. This applies not to theology only in the stricter sense; it is at least equally urgent in the field of ethics. Christian leaders will be able to give much more direct help to young people (and at times to older people too) if they know what way of life is being commended to them as desirable through many media of communication— popular literature, television, etc.—in the permissive climate of modern western society.

Would you care to comment on the statement in F. R. Coad's History of the Brethren Movement: *"It is doubtful whether Biblical criticism in itself does anything to weaken the radical views on church order which are distinctive of Brethren" (p. 258)?*

Very gladly: as a professional practitioner of Biblical criticism I would express myself less tentatively than Mr. Coad and say that Biblical criticism strengthens these radical views on church order. By Biblical criticism in this context I understand the historical and philological study of the New Testament documents and of the oral teaching which can be discerned behind them, as distinct from their dogmatic study. The views on church order which I hold, and in the practice of which I find congenial fellowship in the church to which I belong, are held by me as a result of, not in spite of, the critical study of these foundation documents of Christian faith and practice. The striking

affinity between the findings of Henry Craik and B. H. Streeter in this field (mentioned on p. 256f. of Mr. Coad's book) is highly relevant to your question.

Ought not Christians to be discouraged from travelling miles to a place of worship, passing one or two (often small) meetings on the way? I wonder how many smaller churches could be strengthened if we all worshipped with the nearest one.

The problem which you raise is largely the product of our present-day Western way of life, with its swift and easy means of locomotion which are naturally not envisaged in the New Testament. It is normal and natural to belong to a neighbouring church. But there may be many reasons, some of them good reasons, for attending a more remote one. For example, one may pass a strong church in order to help a weaker one. This may operate, for aught I know, as frequently as the reverse tendency, which I should regret as much as you. Or other considerations may enter into the question. Sometimes a remoter place of worship is more conveniently accessible than a somewhat nearer one. Or a family may move house a few miles away, and continue to attend the church to which they belonged before. Parents may attach themselves to a church where they believe their children will find more spiritual help and fellowship. Or I may think that the nearest church is not sufficiently Scriptural: e.g., being a "tight" brother, I may have an easier conscience about going to a more distant meeting than to one which is close at hand but "loose"—or *vice versa.* I know that all these considerations play their part in practice, although some are less valid than others. No rules can be laid down, of course, but where there is a reasonable choice, the decision which church to join should not be taken "unadvisedly or lightly, but reverently, advisedly, discreetly, and in the fear of God." And I might add that "Where can I *give* most?"

should be a more decisive question than "Where can I *get* most?"

Can a company of Christians who exclude from their membership or from attendance at their gatherings people of another colour or race than their own claim to be a Scripturally gathered church?

To ask the question is to answer 'it, is it not? In a free country any group of persons may form themselves into a society for any lawful purpose, religious or otherwise, and can draw up their own rules of membership and admission. If they wish to exclude certain people because the colour of their skin—or, for that matter, the colour of their hair—is unacceptable, let them do so. But any such group is deluding itself if it imagines that it has any right to be regarded as a Christian church. If it could have the opportunity of a five minutes' visit from the apostle Paul, he would deal as faithfully with that company as he dealt with Peter at Antioch. And if it were pleaded that this was not now a question of fellowship between Christians of Jewish and Gentile birth, but between dark-skinned and light-skinned Christians, he would wonder if his hearers had taken leave of their senses if they imagined that pigmentation was in the slightest degree relevant to local church fellowship, and he might point out that among the esteemed prophets and teachers in that very church of Antioch there was one "Simeon that was called Niger" (Acts 13:1)—and it is not difficult to guess why he was called that! No, when we look at such a question in the light of the New Testament the answer is obvious. It may be that the questioner has in view a social environment differing both from that in which Paul lived and that in which these answers to questions are written. Even so, to be conformed to this world in a matter so contrary to the Biblical principles of Christian fellowship is an example of the kind of "worldliness" that is really a menace to the Christian cause.

How should a Christian act when he finds himself in a church ruled by a dictatorial minority, or finds the church hopelessly divided on matters affecting its basic constitution? If he leaves there is no guarantee that he will find perfect peace, with no disturbing element anywhere else.

You have gone far towards answering your own question by the sentence which you have added to it. It may be said that a church ruled by a dictatorial minority is not following apostolic church order, and the same is no doubt true of a company at sixes and sevens over its constitution. Perhaps different advice could be given to different persons in accordance with a variety of circumstances. But I can think of a few instances in which someone, finding himself faced with a situation such as you have described, has left it, and a few years later (owing to the kindly operation of *anno domini* and other factors which the Lord uses to achieve His purpose) the situation changed so radically that, if he had stayed and stuck it out, he would have found himself able to give the church just the help and guidance required in the changed circumstances. So long as the opportunity remains open to discover and follow the guidance of Scripture, the situation is not hopeless.

Confession

Should there be public confession of sins?

The confession should be as public as the sin. A sin committed against God alone need be confessed to God alone; a sin committed against an individual should be confessed to that individual; a sin committed against the church should be confessed to the church; and if a sin is committed before the general public, the confession should have the same publicity as the sin had. And where the sin is of a kind that calls for material or moral restitution, such restitution is a necessary part of the confession.

189

The New Covenant

Why does the new covenant have a Mediator, when everything connected with it depends on God and not on man?

Jesus is the Mediator of the new covenant in a different sense from that in which Moses mediated the old covenant. Moses was God's spokesman to the people of Israel; he stood between God and the people on the occasion when the Sinai covenant was inaugurated and offered the sacrifices by which it was ratified. But our Lord's mediatorship in relation to the new covenant involves His suretiship as well; He is the One in whom God makes His covenant effective with His people; His is the covenant blood which was shed for many (Mark 14:24). It is true that the validity of the new covenant depends entirely on God; but the Mediator of the new covenant (apart from whom it could never have been bestowed upon us) combines Godhead and manhood in one person. (See also p. 122.)

Creation

There was a press report recently that life had been produced synthetically in a laboratory. Has this any bearing on the biblical doctrine of creation?

It is not at all certain, I gather, that this report should be taken at face value. But if and when a living organism is synthesized in a laboratory, it will not affect at all the truth that God is the Creator of all life as of everything else. Such a breakthrough would be due to the discovery and application of the laws which are part of the world that God has created. By whatever means life comes into existence, God is its author. We shall still say:

"To all Thou givest, to both great and small;
In all life Thou livest, the true life of all"

whether that life is synthesized in a laboratory or comes into being in circumstances with which we are thus far more familiar.

In Evolution and Christian Thought Today, edited by R. L. Mixter, p. 48, the statement is made that "it is generally asserted that God created time just as he created matter." Do you agree that time can be said to have been created?

Yes; it is an aspect of the world that God created. When, in Heb. 1:2 and 11:3, we are told that "the worlds" were made through the Son or by the Word of God, the Greek word used (*aiōnes*) implies the universe of space and time. Time, as we know it, is bound up with the cycle of nature and the biological process, and is thus part of the created order. God Himself is not controlled by time but "inhabits" eternity (Isa. 57:15) and the hope which He has set before His people includes liberation from the inexorable course of time and participation in His own eternity. It will stretch the mind of anyone who is concerned about this question of created time to follow Augustine's wrestling with it in the eleventh book of his *Confessions*.

Creeds

Do the Apostles', Nicene and Athanasian Creeds support or deny the sufficiency of Scripture?

These formularies are in the main confessional summaries of the Christian doctrine of God. They presuppose the sufficiency of Scripture in the sense that "they may be proved by most certain warrants of Holy Scripture" (Article VIII). They are in no sense substitutes for Scripture nor do they usurp its authority. Their special emphases are to be accounted for in the light of the situations in which they took shape. It is a curious fact that the titles by which all three are familiarly known are, strictly speaking, misnomers. I have written at greater length about them in *The Spreading Flame*, Chapters XXIV–XXVI, XXXI. A fuller and more authoritative treatment is given in *Early Christian Creeds*, by J. N. D. Kelly (Longmans, 1950).

In the creed which is recited at an Anglican communion service, do the words "by whom all things were made" refer to the Father or to the Son?

The relevant words (from the Nicene Creed) are: ". . . one Lord Jesus Christ, the only-begotten Son of God, begotten of his Father before all worlds, God of God, Light of Light, very God of very God, begotten, not made, being of one substance with the Father, by whom all things were made. . . ." While formally the last clause might refer to the Father, yet actually each phrase or clause in this section of the creed refers to the Son. The Scriptural foundation for the statement, of course, may be found in John 1:3; Col. 1:16, or Heb. 1:2b. The preposition translated "by" is Gk. *dia* ("through"), as used in these three New Testament passages.

What is meant by the statement in the Apostles' Creed that our Lord "descended into hell"?

That He entered the realm or state of the dead and remained there until the third day.

Crucifixion

Does the reported discovery of the bones of a crucified man near Jerusalem throw any light on the New Testament narrative?

The reference is to one of several first-century ossuaries discovered in 1968 on Ammunition Hill, north of Jerusalem. The first official report of the discovery appeared in the *Israel Exploration Journal* in January 1970. The ossuary in question contained bones which were unmistakably those of a crucified man. Crucifixion had been suspected in some earlier instances, but now for the first time the evidence is unambiguous. The man, whose name (according to the inscription on the ossuary) appears to have been John, son of Ezekiel, was in his middle twenties. He had been crucified with three nails—one driven through each wrist or forearm and a third driven through both heels together. This last nail was still *in situ*, as it had turned and could not be readily removed. Both shin-bones had been smashed by a single blow. The discovery illustrates in particular the crucifixion narrative of the Gospel of John: that is the only Gospel to mention the nails (John 20:25) and the breaking of the legs (John 19:31-34).

Demon Possession

Where can I find help on the question of demon-possession, as described in the Gospels?

Among books that are readily accessible today you would find real help in A. Rendle Short, *Modern Discovery and the Bible* (1942), p. 89ff., and *The Bible and Modern Medicine* (1953), p. 109ff., and J. Stafford Wright, *What is Man?* (1955), p. 131ff. Both these authors refer to an important work on the subject written over sixty years ago—J. L. Nevius, *Demon Possession and Allied Themes* (Revell, 1892)—which is not easily procurable now, but will repay careful study if it can be got hold of. Nevius's investigation of the phenomenon (especially in China) left him in no doubt that the demons had an objective reality. Merrill F. Unger's *Biblical Demonology* (Van Kampen Press, Wheaton, Illinois) is another valuable work on the subject, and so is W. M. Alexander's *Demonic Possession in the New Testament* (Edinburgh, 1902). The author of this last book was a remarkably versatile scholar, holding doctorates in medicine, science and divinity; but ecclesiastical politics led him to withdraw the book from circulation a year or two after its publication, and only second-hand copies are obtainable.

Dispensationalism

What is "dispensationalism" and why are

191

many Christians so dead against it as to describe it as "heresy"?

According to Dr. Frank Gaebelein, "dispensationalism is not a theology but rather a method of interpretation helpful in grasping the progress of revelation in the Bible" (foreword to C. C. Ryrie, *Dispensationalism Today*, 1965). It distinguishes a number of successive stages in God's dealings with the world, and uses this distinction as a means of classifying the data of the Bible so as to appreciate the movements towards the consummation of God's increasing purpose. You may find something of the sort in Paul's writings, for example (without the use in this regard of the terms "dispensation" and "dispensationalism"): in Rom. 5:14 the period from Adam (i.e. from the fall) to Moses (i.e. to the lawgiving) is distinguished from the period that followed; in Rom. 5:20 and Gal. 3:19 the age of law, introduced through Moses, is treated as a parenthesis in God's dealings with mankind; to the main stream of His dealings belong the promises to Abraham and his descendants which have been fulfilled in Christ (Rom. 4:13ff.; Gal. 3:6ff.). The objections to which you refer arise when the method of interpretation is treated as if it were integral to the revelation itself (so that a preference for some other method is deplored as erroneous), or when God is envisaged as having different gospels for different times or different groups of people, or when only a restricted group of writings (the captivity epistles, for example) is regarded as having direct relevance for the church of the present day. If, as has been said, a heresy is a truth carried to its logical conclusion, exaggerations like these may lead in a heretical direction. One eccentric dispensationalist, the late S. D. Gordon, went so far as to say that "there is no cross in God's plan of atonement" (*Quiet Talks about Jesus*, p. 116)— the cross being, presumably, a saving after-thought on God's part, when His

earlier and "painless" plan for procuring atonement had been frustrated. Heretical implications may easily be found here, but such a viewpoint would be as thoroughly repudiated by dispensationalists in general as by other evangelical believers.

Doctrine

Does doctrine really matter?

Perhaps this question has been prompted by the tendency of some people to split doctrinal hairs and to behave in general as if the points of interpretation on which Christians disagree are the things that matter most. That tendency ought to be discouraged. On the other hand it is foolish to say, as some do, that it is the life and not the doctrine that matters, for my behaviour is profoundly influenced by the doctrine which I hold. If I believe (as I do) that Jesus Christ is the Son of God and the Saviour of the world, then I must pay the most careful heed to His teaching and example in the ordering of my life. On the other hand, if I believed the doctrine of Karl Marx to be more authoritative than that of the gospel, my way of life would be directed in accordance with that belief. Perhaps it will suffice to say that the central doctrines of Christianity matter infinitely; but our interpretations and refinements of these doctrines do not matter nearly so much as we think. Or, to put it otherwise, the doctrines which unite Christians are of superlative importance; the doctrines which divide them ought to be examined to see whether in fact they are full-orbed Christin doctrines, or only partial appreciations of them.

Who were responsible for drawing up the Westminster Catechisms and Confession of Faith?

They were the main documents drawn up by the Westminster Assembly of Divines, a commission set up by the English Parliament in 1643 to reorganize the liturgy, discipline and government of the Church of England. The Assembly consisted of 121 theologians, supplemented by ten peers and twenty members of the House of Commons; a commission of Scottish divines attended in a consultant capacity. They tended to Presbyterianism or Independency in church policy, Puritanism in practical theology and Calvinism in doctrine. (See also pp. 205f.)

According to a recent report (the accuracy of which has been questioned) signals have been received from outer space which indicate the presence elsewhere in the universe of intelligent beings, perhaps inhabiting another planet (not necessarily one of the planets of our solar system). Is any Biblical doctrine affected by such a report?

Not *adversely* affected. It has always been held by Christians that there are other created intelligences in the universe than ourselves. Whatever be the basis for the report to which you refer, one day well-authenticated evidence for this kind of thing may well be forthcoming. But if we feel uneasy about it, it may simply be that our God (i.e. our idea of God) "is too small." There are far more wonderful things in God's creation than we have dreamed of yet, and as more and more of them come to light, the more abundant reason we shall have for admiring the Creator's power and wisdom.

Are principles more important than persons?

No; persons are more important than principles. If it is our own principles that we have in mind, we should remember that principles vary according to the individual perspective. You know the conjugation which runs: "I have principles; thou hast prejudices; he is an obstinate fool." If it is the principles of Holy Scripture that we have in mind, we should remember that these principles are concerned in the main (if not indeed alto-

gether) with personal relations: God's "I-thou" relations with us, and our relations with one another. The point could be illustrated in this way, which is relevant to the background against which the question is asked. Regular readers of the question-and-answer page in *The Harvester* have probably concluded that I hold rather rigorist principles on the subject of divorce and remarriage because, when I am asked for an exegesis of the New Testament pronouncements on the subject, I find no room for either divorce or remarriage, where Christian husbands and wives are concerned. But here is a living situation: John and Mary, once married, have been divorced, and now John has married Ann, and Mary is married to James. How is this situation to be dealt with in terms of pastoral responsibility? If rigorist principles are pushed to their logical conclusion, they cannot be helped at all. But just as truth pushed to its logical conclusion in the intellectual sphere may become heresy, so truth pushed to its logical conclusion in the practical sphere may become tyranny. Here are four persons, and probably several others who are indirectly affected, who have to be helped. Anyone exercising pastoral responsibility in the matter must consider first and foremost what action is dictated by Christian charity and compassion towards all the persons concerned, knowing that thus the will of God is most likely to be done and the honour of Christ most likely to be upheld. And it will often be discovered that love will find a way through where logic reaches a dead end.

Further to the previous question, while your statement that persons are more important than principles would fit the example which you give in your explanation, would it fit the situation at Antioch described by Paul in Gal. 2:11-16?

I think it would. The serious feature of Peter's "play-acting" (as Paul called his conduct since it did not accord with his real convictions) was the devastating effect it was bound to have on Gentile Christians. They would inevitably feel that they were regarded as second-class church members at best. Let us suppose (if such a thing were conceivable) that a missionary statesman from Europe or America, visiting the Central African mission field, refused (owing to pressure from people at home) to sit at table with African Christians or even take the Lord's Supper along with them. A missionary on the field who felt it necessary to denounce such conduct publicly would not simply be contending for bare principle's sake but would have the interests of the African Christians very much at heart. In such a case the claims of their well-being would outweigh considerations of courtesy to a distinguished visitor. And in the Epistle to the Galatians as a whole, while Paul contends for evangelical principle, it is the injury done to his converts that moves him to white-hot indignation.

Easter

Is Easter a pagan festival and, if so, ought Christians to observe it?

The *name* Easter is of pagan origin, being derived from the name of a Germanic spring-goddess. But it is certainly not of her that we think nowadays at Eastertide. In most European languages the word for Easter is derived from *pascha* ("Passover"), and "Easter" itself is used in the sense of "Passover" in the A.V. of Acts 12:4. A festival is pagan if it is celebrated in a pagan way; it is Christian if it is celebrated in a Christian way. Christians at Eastertide think of Christ their Passover who was crucified for them, and of Christ who rose from the dead as the first fruits of those who sleep (1 Cor. 5:7; 15:20), although Eastertide is not the only season when they think of Him thus. If they desire to observe the yearly anniversary of His resurrection as well as

the weekly "anniversary", then let them observe it, as Paul says, "in honour of the Lord" (Rom. 14:6).

Ecumenism

Would you agree with the statement in Doctrine in the Church of England *(1938), referring to the various denominations, that "just in so far as their very existence as separate organizations constitutes a real division ... it becomes true to affirm that, if any are in schism, all are in schism"?*

If I were compelled to use the term "schism" of any believers in Christ, I should restrict it to those who draw narrower frontiers of fellowship than those which Christ has drawn, and who refuse intercommunion with Christians who do not toe their party-line.

Since the Brethren movement came into being as a means of promoting unity among Christians and removing the sectarian barriers that separated them, how has it come about that in some quarters "separation" rather than "unity" has become the Brethren's watchword?

Biblical separation is another word for holiness. Brethren have in large measure endeavoured to promote holiness of life, in common with many other reforming movements that have arisen in the course of Christian history, but there is a difference between biblical separation and unbiblical separatism, and sometimes the two have been confused. And it was an early confusion of the two that started the unhappy business in the Brethren movement. J. N. Darby wrote a tract entitled *Separation from evil God's principle of unity* which expresses characteristically the essence of the exclusivism which derives from his teaching. So fundamental in his eyes was the position there stated, that "it seems to me", he said, "that one who would deny the abstract principles of that tract is not on Christian ground at all . . .

Is not holiness the principle on which Christian fellowship is based? And the tract is really and simply that" (*Collected Writings*, I, p. 573). But this argument is sufficiently refuted by the example of Anthony Norris Groves. Groves' judgment may be questioned by those who think differently from him, but not his holiness of life; he is, in the words of W. B. Neatby, "one of the Church's great saints." If Darby's tract had simply been an exposition of biblical holiness, Groves would have found it most congenial. As it was, he set against its teaching his own attitude to fellow-Christians whose doctrines, practices and associations left (as he saw it) much to be desired: "I would infinitely rather bear with all their evil than separate from their good." But Darby was too sensible a man to follow his own declaration to its logical conclusion and deny that Groves was on Christian ground at all. The New Testament does occasionally enjoin putting away certain persons and withdrawing from others, but these are presented as regrettable and occasional exceptions; they cannot be elevated to the first principles of Christian fellowship. If an attempt nevertheless is made to treat separation from evil as the basis of unity, the result must be progressive division and subdivision. For, no matter how radically one may separate from evil, there will always be a little evil left to separate from again. No matter how pure the communion to which one belongs, it can always be made a little purer. You may reduce your communion to a membership of two, but you will discover some residual evil in the other person if you keep an eye open for it; and when you have withdrawn from him, you will still not be entirely separate from evil. Before his death Darby himself was plagued by some of his followers who carried his separatist principles further than he did himself; there is a record of a meeting in April, 1881, at which he spoke for more than an hour about the evil of "New Lumpism", "Clean Groundism",

and similar tendencies within the Exclusive fold. And in the extreme exclusivism especially associated with the late James Taylor, Jnr., of Brooklyn, N.Y., we have an awful warning of the lengths to which sane Christians can be driven when separation is made an end in itself. When an obviously absurd conclusion is reached, it is advisable to go back in the chain of deduction and find out where the error crept in; in this case it crept in at the beginning of the process, when "separation from evil God's principle of unity" was accepted as a major premiss. Nothing is here said against the duty which lies on all who name the name of Christ to depart from iniquity; but God's principle of unity is the common life in Christ into which believers are brought by the Holy Spirit.

What is the World Council of Churches?

According to a statement adopted by the first assembly of the World Council of Churches at Amsterdam in 1948, "the World Council of Churches is a fellowship of Churches which accept Jesus Christ as God and Saviour. They find their unity in Him ... The Council desires to serve the churches, which are its constituent members, as an instrument whereby they may bear witness together to their common allegiance to Jesus Christ, and co-operate in matters requiring united action ... the Council disavows any thought of becoming a single unified church structure independent of the churches which have joined in constituting the Council, or a structure dominated by a centralized administrative authority. . . ." The definition in the first sentence was revised at the New Delhi assembly in 1961 (which met under the uncompromising slogan, "Jesus Christ the Light of the World") as follows: "The World Council of Churches is a fellowship of Churches which confess the Lord Jesus Christ as God and Saviour according to the Scriptures, and therefore seek to fulfil together their common calling to the glory of one God, Father, Son and Holy Spirit." The constituent churches include most of the major Protestant bodies (here "Protestant" is used to embrace "Anglican") and most of the Eastern Orthodox Churches, although the latter have qualified their membership with explicit reservations, arising from their understanding of the doctrine of the church.

Ekklesia

Is there any difference between the terms "assembly" and "church"?

In the Biblical sense of the terms, none whatsoever. They are alternative translations of the Greek word *ekklēsia*; another alternative translation is "congregation", which Tyndale used in his version, and to which the New English Bible has returned when the reference is to a local company.

In the Greek word ekklēsia *(translated "church" or "assembly" in N.T.) does the prefix* ek- *convey the idea of being called out from mankind, or only called out in the sense of "summoned"?*

The prefix *ek-*, whatever be its importance for the etymology of the Greek word, has little direct bearing on the Biblical force of *ekklēsia*. As used in the New Testament of the people of God, this word has as its background not its pagan Greek usage but its occasional usage in the Greek of the Septuagint to represent Heb. *qahal*, applied to the nation of Israel when called together as the assembly or congregation of Jehovah. The *ekklēsia* of a Greek city was the citizen-body, summoned to meet in discharge of its political and legislative functions. The "assembly" in the Ephesian theatre (Acts 19:29-41) was composed of the citizen-body of Ephesus; only it was not a "regular assembly" (verse 39) because it had not been legally summoned or called together. Neither in the Biblical nor in the extra-Biblical sense of the word is the idea of being "called out from

mankind" in view. To be sure, the people of God are taken out from the nations (Acts 15:14)—from Gentiles as well as from Jews—but that is not the point of the word *ekklēsia*.

Election

Are "election to salvation" and "election to damnation" correlative terms?

In certain theological systems they are, but it is important to test all theological systems by Scripture, and to remember that, when the teaching of Scripture is systematized, something is usually left out in the process. The term "election" has become so involved in theological controversy that the sense of the Biblical teaching on the subject might be better grasped if we used a non-theological word like "selection" in its place. Christ selected twelve men to be apostles (Luke 6:13); He selected Saul of Tarsus to be a "chosen vessel" (Acts 9:15); but His selection of these men for a special purpose implies no disparagement of others who were not so selected. God selected Israel from among the nations (Acts 13:17)—to the great benefit of the other nations, not to their disadvantage. When the election of the people of God in this age is in question, it is not so much their "election to salvation" as their election to holiness that is emphasized. This is so, for example, in Eph. 1:4 and 1 Pet. 1:1f.; and similarly, in Rom. 8:29, the purpose for which God foreordained those whom He foreknew v/as that they should be "conformed to the image of his Son." In none of these places is there any suggestion of "election to damnation" as a correlative. We should beware of generalizing from such particular references as those in Rom. 9:22 ("vessels of wrath made for destruction") and 1 Pet. 2:8 ("they stumble because they disobey the word, as they were destined to do"). The general analogy of Biblical teaching on this subject indicates that some are chosen or selected by God—not in order that others, apart from them, may be left in perdition, but in order that others, through them, may be blessed. See p. 235.

Is it more Scriptural to say that Christ died for His people (the elect) or that He died for all?

To say that He died for His people is certainly Scriptural ("Christ loved the church and gave himself up for her", according to Eph. 5:25); but it is equally Scriptural to say that He died for all: He "gave himself as a ransom for all, the testimony to which was borne at the proper time" (1 Tim. 2:6). And when Scripture says "all" in a context like this, it means "all." Some readers who are not sure of this statement may find it profitable to consider certain exegetical comments of John Calvin. On Matt. 26:28 and Mark 14:24 ("which is shed for many") he says: "By the word *many* he means not a part of the world only, but the whole human race." As for Luke 22:20 ("which is poured out for you"), this reminds believers to apply to themselves personally what has been provided for all: "let us not only remember in general that the world has been redeemed by the blood of Christ, but let each one consider for himself that his own sins have been expiated thereby." Again, on Rom. 5:18 ("the free gift came unto all men to justification of life") he says: "Paul makes grace common to all men, not because in fact it extends to all, but because it is offered to all." And he shows what he means by saying that it does not extend to all in the words which immediately follow: "Although Christ suffered for the sins of the world, and is offered by the goodness of God without distinction to all men, yet not all receive Him." Similarly in his will, composed at the age of 54, shortly before his death, he wrote: "I testify indeed and acknowledge that, as a suppliant, I pray Him so to accept me as washed and cleansed by the blood of the Supreme Redeemer, shed for the sins

of the human race, that I may stand before His judgment-seat under the form (i.e., vested with the righteousness) of that same Redeemer." I reproduce these quotations not because I think Calvin was infallible but because his words will (very properly) carry more weight than any words of mine.

Have we any means of knowing what the ultimate proportion of elect and non-elect members of the human race will be?

No. Some estimates have indeed been made, but on doubtful authority. For example, Mr. William Fisher, elder in the parish of Mauchline, Ayrshire, in the latter part of the 18th century, is recorded in a well-known Scottish literary composition as having estimated one elect to ten non-elect;[1] but that may have been the speculative effort of a man who, convinced of his own election, preferred to keep the number small and select. More recently, and more seriously, the Rt. Hon. J. Enoch Powell, preaching in Great St. Mary's, Cambridge, interpreted certain words of our Lord as assertions "that his salvation will not be for all, not even for the majority" and insisted that "ignorance, incapacity, perversity, the sheer human propensity to error are sufficient to ensure a high failure rate."[2] They are sufficient, indeed, to ensure a 100 per cent failure rate, but for the grace of God. Once the grace of God begins to operate, however, the situation is transformed. When, in Rom. 5:15, 19, it is said that the free gift of God's grace in Christ has abounded for "the many" and that the obedience of that one man will make "the many" righteous, no valid exegesis can make "the many" mean a minority, for (as Calvin reasonably puts it in his exposition of this passage) "if Adam's fall had the effect of producing the ruin of many, the grace of

---

[1] Robert Burns, *Holy Willie's Prayer*, Stanza 1.
[2] *Sermons from Great St. Mary's*, edited by H. W. Montefiore (1968), p. 96.

God is much more efficacious in benefiting many, since admittedly Christ is much more powerful to save than Adam was to ruin."[1] C. H. Spurgeon, the greatest English Calvinist of the 19th century, is said to have prayed more than once, "Lord, hasten to bring in all Thine elect, and then elect some more."[2] I cannot discover any theological objection to such a prayer, bearing in mind the sovereignty of God's grace. If one thing is more certain than another about the God of the Bible, it is this, that in His zeal to save, He will inaugurate means to bless His creatures beyond our wit to conceive or anticipate.

Eschatology

In church history different doctrines have been emphasized at different times and have later lost their emphasis. Do you think that the emphasis placed upon eschatology during the last century has now lost its importance and that God has perhaps some other truth that needs greater emphasis?

It is undoubtedly true that at certain periods in Christian history the providence of God has so ordered it that aspects of truth have been recovered and emphasized when their recovery and emphasis were most necessary for the health of the church. An outstanding example is the recovery in the first half of the 16th century of the doctrine of justification by faith. But no evangelical Christian would say that this doctrine could ever lose its importance. As for eschatology, the quickening of interest in it at the beginning of the 19th century was perhaps stimulated by such events as the French Revolution and the Napoleonic Wars, and later by the loss of the temporal power of the Papacy in 1870. However that may be, Christianity bereft of its eschatological

content is not Christianity rightly so called. To whatever degree the early 19th century saw a general revival of eschatological interest, it is the 20th century that has witnessed its special revival among Biblical theologians and students of the origins of Christianity, so much so that several schools of thought are nowadays distinguished in eschatological categories, such as "thoroughgoing eschatology", "realized eschatology" and so forth. Since this answer was first published, we have witnessed the emergence of a new school of thought associated with Jürgen Moltmann, author of *The Theology of Hope* (German edition, 1965; English translation, 1967). All this may indicate that, like other aspects of Christian doctrine, this one is revived not only at the time but among the people where such a revival is most necessary. And it could be that another important aspect of truth is being revived right now, or waiting to be revived.

What is the meaning of "realized eschatology"?

"Realized eschatology" is a name given to that phase of New Testament teaching according to which the age of fulfilment has already come. When, for example, our Lord says, "If . . . I cast out demons, then the kingdom of God has come upon you" (Matt. 12:28; Luke 11:20), or "he who does not believe is condemned *already*" (John 3:18), or "The hour is coming, *and now is*, when the dead will hear the voice of the Son of God" (John 5:25), or "*Now* is the judgment of this world" (John 12:32), He is using the language of "realized eschatology"; the last things are already here. But alongside statements like these there are others, including statements made by our Lord Himself, which affirm that the kingdom of God, and the resurrection and judgment, are not only here already but in another sense are yet to come: alongside "realized eschatology" (or, as I prefer to call it,

---

[1] *Calvin's Commentaries: Romans and Thessalonians*, translated by R. Mackenzie (1961), pp. 114f.
[2] A. C. Underwood, *A History of the English Baptists* (1947), p. 204.

"inaugurated eschatology") we find also "future eschatology." The kingdom of God, which was effectively inaugurated by the passion and trimph of Christ, still awaits its consummation.

Should we describe certain beliefs about the Second Advent as heretical?

To deny the Second Advent itself would be heretical, for the Second Advent is an essential element in the apostolic teaching. But there is room for a wide diversity of interpretation when we try to relate the Second Advent to the course of events associated with the end time. There are at least half a dozen quite distinct schools of interpretation found among evangelical Christians in this matter, and none can claim superiority over the others in point of sanctity or scholarship, nor should any of them be called heretical. It is better to study the Scriptures for ourselves and thus be fully persuaded in our own minds than to adhere too rigidly to any one school; but sometimes it is good to have the reservation at the back of our minds that the other man *may* be right. On the certainty of the Second Advent we can be firm; but "concerning the times and the seasons" there is much that will not be known until the momentous event has actually taken place.

Are the parousia, epiphaneia, *and* apokalypsis *of our Lord distinct events in point of time, or are they synchronous?*

His advent, manifestation, and revelation (to turn the Greek terms into English) are not merely synchronous; they are three alternative designations of one and the same event.

Is the statement historically justified that the doctrine of the "secret rapture" was first expressed in the course of an Irvingite meeting?

So S. P. Tregelles thought: "I am not aware", he wrote, "that there was any

definite teaching that there would be a secret rapture of the Church at a secret coming, until this was given forth as an 'utterance' in Mr. Irving's Church, from what was there received as being the voice of the Spirit. But whether anyone ever asserted such a thing or not, it was from that supposed revelation that the modern doctrine and the modern phraseology respecting it arose" (*The Hope of Christ's Second Coming*, 2nd edition, 1886, p. 35). This simply means that Tregelles could not trace it farther back. But Tregelles was not converted until about 1832, when he was 19 years old; he had no first-hand acquaintance with the events in question before that time. The "utterance" referred to appears to have been delivered in January, 1832, in Edward Irving's church in London, by Emily Cardale, and was accepted by the congregation as inspired. But, in his unpublished reminiscences contained in the "Fry MS", B. W. Newton says that on the second Sunday that the Brethren's original chapel in Plymouth was used (some time in 1831) Captain Percy Hall taught the secret rapture in the morning and G. V. Wigram denounced it in the evening. (Wigram later changed his mind on this subject.) It seems highly probable that the idea was introduced into both groups from one of the Albury Conferences (held in 1826 and the following years, and attended by members of both the Darby and the Irving circles). Newton makes some mention of the body of men who launched these conferences— the banker Henry Drummond and others —and adds: "Soon Irving joined, and ruined it all by suggesting the Secret Coming." Of course, from Newton's point of view, anyone who introduced the secret rapture into a discussion would ruin it! We should bear in mind that, when the Albury meetings began, Irving had not yet been identified with the heretical views on the Person of Christ for which he was later condemned, and a prophetic interpretation would not then have been regarded as suspect just because

199

it came from him. In any case, it may have been suggested by others independently. According to William Kelly's pamphlet *The Rapture of the Saints: Who suggested it? or rather, On what Scripture?* (1903), J. N. Darby's own account was that, around 1830, a consideration of 2 Thess. 2:1f. led him to the conclusion that the rapture of the saints would take place before the day of the Lord. He was considerably helped in getting his mind clear on the subject by a suggestion made by a an ex-clergyman of the Church of Ireland named Tweedy. It does not appear, however, what Tweedy's precise suggestion was—whether it bore directly on the interpretation of 2 Thess. 2:1f. or on some related subject. G. H. Lang wondered if his suggestion was that in the Synoptic Gospels the disciples are addressed as Jews and not as Christians ("Inquire of the Former Age", *The Disciple*, January 1954, p. 57). But whatever the origin of the "secret rapture" doctrine may have been, that is irrelevant to its validity or otherwise (unless we believe in imputing "guilt by association"). Its validity must depend on whether or not it is taught in Scripture.

Does the Greek word translated "coming" in 2 Thess. 2:1 convey the same meaning as the word translated "presence" in Phil. 2:12? If so, would this lend weight to the "secret rapture" theory of the Second Advent? If the sense in 2 Thess. 2:1 is limited to "arrival," would it tend to weaken such a theory?

The Greek word is the same in both places; it is the word *parousia*. Its primary sense is "presence," and it is in this sense that it is used in Phil. 2:12, in opposition to "absence" (Gk. *apousia*). But its commonest use in the New Testament, with reference to our Lord's advent, is linked with its contemporary usage to denote an official visit by some distinguished person. When thinking of such a visit, one may concentrate on the moment of arrival, with all the attendant pageantry of welcome and presentation, or one may take into view the stay (or "presence"), whether of long or short duration, which follows the arrival. In *Touching the Coming of the Lord* (1919) the late C. F. Hogg and W. E. Vine suggested that the Lord's *parousia* was the period of His "presence" with His people between the removal of the Church and His glorious manifestation to the world. I am doubtful about this interpretation, but either way I do not see that it really affects the "secret rapture" theory. If that theory is to be established, it must be on the basis of Scriptural evidence and not on the exact meaning which we attach to the word *parousia*.

From such passages as Phil. 4:5; Heb. 10:25, 37; Jas. 5:8 and Rev. 22:20, coupled with Paul's use of "we" in 1 Thess. 4:15, 17, and 1 Cor. 15:51f., are we to understand that the Christians to whom these truths were originally revealed believed that the Lord was actually going to return in their own lifetime (as distinct from the mere possibility of His so returning)? If this is a legitimate interpretation, could it be that the Lord did intend to return at that era, and if so, do the Scriptures give any indication why His coming was delayed?

Of the passages you mention, Phil. 4:5 may be left out of the reckoning, in view of the possibility that "The Lord is near" refers to His permanent nearness to His people rather than to His imminent advent. But this does not change the general picture; you might have quoted Phil. 3:20, "*we* wait for a Saviour." So far as Paul himself is concerned, he sometimes associates himself with those who will be alive on earth at the Lord's return (e.g. 1 Thess. 4:15, 17; 1 Cor. 15:51f.; Phil. 3:20), and sometimes with those who will be raised from the dead at that time (e.g. 1 Cor. 6:14; 2 Cor. 4:14). Clearly Paul did not know in which of the two groups he would find himself; he *hoped* that he would still be alive at the time, so that he might be "clothed upon" with his heavenly habitation without having to pass through a disembodied phase. But as time went on he appears to have reckoned more and more with the possibility, and even the probability, that he would die first (cf. 2 Cor. 5:1-10); indeed, in Phil. 1:21-24 he writes as if this would be preferable to continuance in mortal body, so far as his personal interests were concerned. Plainly Paul had no definite means of knowing whether the Lord would come in his lifetime or not. As for other Christians of the early apostolic age, it is plain, I think, that the Thessalonians believed that the Lord would come very soon, while they were still alive, and that they were bewildered and dismayed when some of their number died before His coming. But this was because Paul had to leave Thessalonica without giving them all the teaching that he had hoped to give. When he heard about their bewilderment and dismay, he wrote to reassure them that the faithful departed would suffer no disadvantage at the Second Advent compared with those who were still alive. There are, indeed, two New Testament passages which might be interpreted in such a way as to link the Advent closely with the conversion of Israel: these are Acts 3:19-21 and Rom. 11:25-27. These two passages display quite different time-perspectives: the former envisages Israel's conversion as an early possibility, while the latter views it as the sequel to the completion of the Gentile world-mission. The former perspective disappeared quite soon, probably before any New Testament book was in being. As for those passages which stress the imminence of the Second Advent, what they stress is a moral imminence rather than a chronological one. The times and seasons which the Father has reserved within His own jurisdiction remain concealed so that each successive Christian generation may live with the healthy realization that it *may*

be the generation to witness the Advent. But if future generations of Christians are to look back on the first twenty centuries A.D. as "the early period of church history", and still look forward, as we do, to the Second Advent, it will be as true for them as it was for those who first read the words of Heb. 10:37 that "yet a little while, and the coming one shall come and shall not tarry."

In the last answer you refer to the possibility that Christians in generations yet to come may look back on the first 2,000 years A.D. as "the early period of church history." Are there Christians who believe that the church will be on earth for thousands of years yet to come? Do they believe that the Lord will come as foretold in 1 Cor. 15 and 1 Thess. 4?

There are Christians who make all kinds of dogmatic statements about the Lord's coming. The answer to both your questions is "Yes"; but it is just as unwarranted to assert that the Lord will not come for thousands of years yet as it is to assert that He will come before the end of the present century. The fact is, we do not know. It would be safer to say that, so far as the teaching of Scripture is concerned, Christians who believe that the Lord will come as foretold in 1 Cor. 15 and 1 Thess. 4 and elsewhere are equally prepared to envisage His coming within this generation or after the lapse of further centuries or millennia. Christians today who confidently expect His advent in their own lifetime may have to be reminded of the possibility that (as B. B. Warfield put it) the church of the 20th century is "still the primitive church"; Christians today who in their thinking postpone His advent to the remote future should be reminded that the present hour may be later than they think. But the date of the Second Advent is the least important aspect of the doctrine; for us, as for first-century believers, it is now the last hour; the coming of the Lord is at hand; our

201

salvation is nearer than when we first believed. Last century, in an age of eschatological excitement, these wise words were spoken: "though time intervene between Christ's first and second coming, it is not recognized (as I may say) in the gospel scheme, but is, as it were, an accident. For so it was, that up to Christ's coming in the flesh, the course of things ran straight towards that end, nearing it by every step, but now under the gospel, that course has (if I may so speak) altered its direction, as regards His second coming, and runs, not towards the end, but along it, and on the brink of it; and is at all times equally near that great event, which, did it run towards it, would at once run into. Christ, then, is ever at our doors" (J. H. Newman, *Parochial and Plain Sermons*, p. 241).

Eternity

Please comment on the statement: "There is no word in either Hebrew or Greek that connotes what we mean by 'eternal', in the sense of 'never-ending.' The Biblical expressions so translated mean 'age-abiding' and are indefinite as regards duration."

When the Biblical writers wished to express the simple idea of endlessness they could do so quite easily by means of the phrase "no end", as in Isa. 9:7, "Of the increase of his government and of peace there shall be no end" (Heb. 'ēn qēṣ), or Luke 1:33, "of his kingdom there shall be no end" (Gk. *ouk estai telos*). The Gk. adjective *aidios*, used in Rom. 1:20 of God's "everlasting power and divinity" and in Jude 6 of "everlasting bonds", also has this sense. As for the words and phrases based on Heb. 'ōlām or Gk. *aiōn*, these in themselves express indefinite duration, but the context or the inherent sense may make the indefiniteness more explicit. Thus, when the kingdom which has no end (according to the passages quoted above) is elsewhere called an "eternal kingdom" or one that "shall

stand for ever" (cf. Dan. 2:44; 2 Peter 1:11; Rev. 11:15), we know that '*ōlām, aiōn, aiōnios* in such places involve the idea of endlessness. Or where God is called "the Everlasting God" (Heb. 'ēl 'ōlām, Gen. 21:33) or the "eternal God" (Gk. *aiōnios theos*, Rom. 16:26), we must understand the words to connote eternity in the fullest sense. As for "eternal life" (Gk. *zōē aiōnios*), that is probably an abridged way of saying "the life of the age to come"—the life of the resurrection-age, which through Christ is possessed and enjoyed already by believers in Him, without their waiting till the resurrection at the last day to receive it. It is primarily a unique quality of life, but since the resurrection-age is endless, endlessness must also be a feature of the life which belongs to it. The believers' eternal life, in fact, is a sharing in their Lord's unending risen life (Rom. 6:4-11) or, as it is elsewhere called, His indissoluble life (Gk. *akatalytos*, Heb. 7:16). It is actual usage, not etymology, that determines the meaning of words and phrases; failure to remember this is often the cause of our being misled with regard to the meaning of Scripture.

How can the incident of death change the unfathomable love of God for His human creation? Would He who exhorted us to forgive until seventy times seven do otherwise Himself?

Who says that the incident of death changes God's unfathomable love? His judgment is regularly said to be passed upon the deeds done in the body—i.e. in this mortal life, which consequently appears to be a period of probation. We may be sure that God will never act inconsistently with His own character, and that all will receive His forgiveness save those who refuse His forgiveness, which He has pledged in Christ to all who truly repent. But we should not blunt the urgency of the New Testament insistence that now is the decisive time for repentance and faith.

If aiōnios (*"eternal"*) *means* "*everlasting*", *how are we to read it in (say) Rom. 16:25 and Jude 7, to give only two examples?*

The adjective *aiōnios* is derived from *aiōn* ("age") which, like its Hebrew equivalent *'clam*, denotes indefinite duration, whether backward in time, forward in time, or in both directions. Thus God is God "from age to age" (Psa. 90:2), i.e. everlastingly in both directions. His existence had no beginning and will have no end. The idea of eternity can be emphasized by the use of the plural "ages" (e.g. "to the ages", Rom. 1:25), or by compound expressions such as "to all the ages" (Jude 25), "to the ages of the ages" (e.g. Gal. 1:5) or even "to all the generations of the age of the ages" (Eph. 3:21). The context alone can decide whether such expressions connote absolute eternity or very long duration. We read of "the everlasting hills" (literally "hills of age", Deut. 33:15; Hab. 3:6), and Mount Zion "abides for ever" (Psa. 125:1); but they had a beginning and will have an end: God was there before them and will continue after them (Psa. 90:2; 102:25-27). The city gates of Jerusalem are apostrophized as "everlasting doors" (R.S.V. "ancient doors", literally "doors of age") in Psa. 24:7, 9; the "ancient high places" of Ezek. 36:2 are literally "high places of age"; the "years of ancient times" (Psa. 77:5) are literally "years of ages." In the New Testament the prophets are said to have prophesized *ap' aiōnos* (literally "from an age" or "from eternity"), which simply means "from of old" (Luke 1:70; Acts 3:21), and the expression "through times eternal" in Rom. 16:25, to which you refer (A.V. "since the world began"; R.S.V. "for long ages"), has much the same meaning. A remoter antiquity is denoted by the phrase "before the ages" in 1 Cor. 2:7. As for Jude 7, it is plain that the fire which consumed Sodom and Gomorrah is not still burning; it may not even have been long-lasting, but its effects certainly were, so that we might interpret the use of *aiōnios* here as an instance of "transferred epithet." In addition to these uses of the words, however, there is a use which is bound up with the New Testament doctrine of the two ages—the present age and the age to come. While the present age is still running its course, the powers of the age to come have already been set in operation by the coming of Christ, and those who are united to Him, while they still live temporally in "this age", belong spiritually to "that age" and enjoy here and now "the life of the age to come"—"eternal life." The adjective "eternal" here denotes primarily the character of this life (it is not the mortal life of the body, but the resurrection life of Christ shared with His people); but because the age to come is unending, the life which belongs to it is unending.

Evangelicalism

What is Neo-evangelicalism? Would you subscribe to it?

It is a term which has significance, I think, only in an American context; it has been devised to indicate not a deviation in doctrine from evangelicalism as commonly understood but certain features of method, approach, co-operation and so forth which have not traditionally characterized evangelicalism in the United States. According to Dr. Harold J. Ockenga, who is said to have coined the term, neo-evangelicalism breaks with modernism (because of its commitment to historic Christianity), with neo-orthodoxy (because of its commitment to Biblical authority) and with the attitudes summed up in the American term "fundamentalism" (because of its commitment to the belief that the gospel "must apply to the social scene, that there must be an application of this to society as much as there is an application of it to the individual man"). Another feature is its inclusivism as opposed to exclusivism, as seen, for example, in the Billy Graham crusades. The periodicals *Christianity Today* and *Eternity* would, I suppose, be cited as organs of neo-evangelicalism. In Britain the term would have little meaning, and not simply, as a writer in *The Banner of Truth* suggested some time ago, because "the distinguishing features of British evangelicalism for most of this century have . . . been those now manifest in this movement in the U.S.A." Would I subscribe to it? To some of its features, perhaps, but not to the label itself. I have no hesitation in answering to the designation "evangelical" (not in any partisan or sectarian sense), because it clearly implies commitment to the Evangel; but I should insist on remaining an *unhyphenated* evangelical.

When, in your last answer, you say that you suppose the periodicals Christianity Today *and* Eternity *would be cited as organs of neo-evangelicalism, do you intend this as a criticism of these periodicals?*

No; I myself am a contributing editor of the former and a consulting editor of the latter. I simply decline to wear the "neo-evangelical" label myself. Nor have I any fault to find with the inclusivism for which neo-evangelicals are criticized, as seen, for example, in the Billy Graham crusades. Since I myself do not like to be excluded by fellow-Christians, a simple application of the Golden Rule teaches me not to exclude other fellow-Christians. What I believe to be the proper attitude is expressed in the doggerel lines of Edwin Markham:

He drew a circle that shut me out—
Heretic, rebel, a thing to flout!
But love and I had the wit to win:
We drew a circle that took him in.

But this attitude is very comfortably accommodated within plain unhyphenated evangelicalism.

In your answer to the last question but one, you say that you have no hesitation in answering to the designation "evangelical" but that you would insist on remaining an unhyphenated evangelical. But you would call yourself a "conservative evangelical," would you not?

No indeed. What other people call me is their own business, but for myself, although I hold many views which are termed "conservative", I hold them because I believe them to be true, not because they are conservative, still less because *I* am conservative. Other views of mine are probably quite radical by most traditional standards, but I hold them too because (rightly or wrongly) I believe them to be true.

Excommunication

Did "cutting off" in the Old Testament always mean capital punishment? If not, was it sometimes excommunication, and what did that amount to?

Either death or excommunication (outlawry or banishment) would be an effective way of cutting someone off "from among his people." In Exod. 31:14 it plainly implies death. In some places (e.g. Gen. 17:14) it may denote excommunication: an excommunicated person would be put outside the scope of the covenant between God and His people, and be regarded as an outlaw. What this would have meant in earlier Old Testament times may be gathered from the descriptions of Cain (Gen. 4:14), Ishmael (Gen. 16:12) and David (1 Sam. 26:19b)—not that these were formally excommunicated in the sense we have in mind. But in, perhaps, the majority of the references to "cutting off", a divine judgment seems to be indicated; this is certainly so in those places where God says, "I will cut him off from among his people" (e.g. Lev. 17:10). See p. 8.

Faith

Is not reason a necessary complement to faith, to prevent its degenerating into fanaticism, credulity, superstition, or mere adherence to tradition? Are not Evangelicals at fault when they neglect secular knowledge and experience?

As for the last part of your question, I should not say that Evangelicals are more prone than others to this form of neglect. To the true Evangelical all truth is God's truth, and when his mind has been illuminated by the divine revelation, he is able to appreciate the whole universe of knowledge and experience better than before. As regards reason, it is a gift of God; in fact, it is part of the image of God in man. It cannot lead sinful man to the knowledge of God as He really is; this knowledge is a matter of revelation, to be accepted by faith. But while faith leads us into regions which reason cannot reach, there is nothing unreasonable about it. It transcends reason; it does not run counter to it. Reason, indeed, is more truly what God intended it to be when it is clarified by faith in God. God encourages His people to use their reason. In the Old Testament He challenges Israel to come and reason with Him (Isa. 1:18); in the New Testament there is ample evidence of the apostles' readiness to reason with their audiences about the credentials of the gospel, and the Epistle to the Romans is one sustained argument by a man whose rational power, impressive by nature and enhanced by training, was enlightened by grace and used by the Spirit of God as a chosen instrument for His purpose. Tertullian's *credo quia absurdum*, "I believe it because it is absurd", may have been effective rhetorical hyperbole, but it is a very unapostolic sentiment.

Fate

Is it true that everything we do, and everything that happens to us, is fixed unchangeably in advance long before our birth?

No. This idea is bound up with pagan notions of fate, and has nothing to do with the Biblical teaching about God's fore-ordaining grace and Fatherly providence. For example, when I start to deal with a question like this, I decide in my own mind how to answer it. I am well aware that many antecedent factors in my life, and very probably in my heritage, influence the way in which I answer it; but the final decision about the answer lies within my free choice. If everything were fixed unchangeably in advance, our personal responsibility for our actions would be dissolved; but nothing is taught more clearly in the Bible that that "each of us shall give account of himself to God." In fact, this needs to be specially stressed today, when so many schools of thought minimize personal accountability, to a point where people plead that their actions are the result of their parentage, or their environment, or just to "something that came over them."

Federal Headship

What is meant by Adam's "federal headship," to which I find reference in the literature of the Darby-Newton debate?

The federal headship of Adam is an important feature in what is known as "federal theology" or "covenant theology"—a system of classifying the theological data of the Bible, propounded by Reformation divines of the late sixteenth and early seventeenth centuries, preeminently by Johannes Cocceius (1603-69). It was unknown to the primary Reformers (e.g. Calvin), but was adopted in the Westminster Confession of Faith (1647). You will find a summary of it in L. Berkhof's *Systematic Theology*, pp. 211-218, 262-301. The adjective "federal" is derived from Latin *foedus*, meaning a "covenant" or "treaty"; "federal headship" is thus another expression for "covenant headship." The question is: "What is Adam's relation to mankind, by virtue of which his sin involved the race in death?" The answer of covenant theology, which may be expressed concisely in the words of the Westminster

Shorter Catechism, is this: "When God had created man, he entered into a covenant of life with him, upon condition of perfect obedience; forbidding him to eat of the tree of knowledge of good and evil, upon the pain of death . . . The covenant being made with Adam, not only for himself, but for his posterity; all mankind, descending from him by ordinary generation, sinned in him, and fell with him, in his first transgression." This "covenant of life," which is by definition a covenant of works, is nowhere expressly mentioned in Scripture; those who appeal to Hosea 6:7 in support of it simply show the precariousness of its foundation. Since, according to the hypothesis, Adam entered into it on behalf of his posterity as well as in his own name, he became thereby the "federal head" of the human race, and the human race was involved in his breach of covenant when he committed his act of disobedience. Those who reject this construction of the matter must suggest a better explanation of mankind's involvement in Adam's fall, as stated in Rom. 5:12-21; I hope my own attempt to expound these verses in the Tyndale Commentary on Romans may be accounted a better explanation. One attractive feature of the doctrine of Adam's covenant of works and his federal headship is that it provides a fitting counterpart to the doctrine of the new covenant of grace and redemption mediated by Christ and Christ's status as head of the new creation. But the covenant which is rendered old by the new covenant of the gospel is plainly said in Scripture to be the covenant made with Israel at Sinai (2 Cor. 3:7-18; Heb. 8:13). While the explanation of Adam's relation to the old creation in terms of covenant headship is not completely satisfactory, we may rightly acclaim Christ, the archetype and representative of the new humanity, as

"Adam, descended from above,
Federal head of all mankind."

(See also pp. 192f.)

Forgiveness

In view of Jer. 31:34, "I will forgive their iniquity, and I will remember their sin no more" (cf. Heb. 8:12; 10:17), is the request of pardon for sin in connexion with salvation an insult to God and His Word and the testimony of the Holy Spirit, and to the perfect work of Christ?

No. The Lord commended the publican's prayer (Luke 18:13), taught his disciples to pray for forgiveness (Matt. 6:12; Luke 11:4), and prayed that His enemies might be forgiven (Luke 23:34). Peter urged Simon the sorcerer to pray for forgiveness (Acts 8:22).

What good is forgiveness to anyone who would not thank you for it, or who prefers to go without forgiveness rather than plead for it?

Even if it does not do him much good, it would do you great harm to withhold your forgiveness from him. If you cherish an unforgiving attitude towards him, you cannot pray for him; if you forgive him in your heart, you can then pray for him, and that may do him good:

"more things are wrought by prayer
Than this world dreams of."

Fundamentalism

What is a Fundamentalist?

The term appears to have been coined about sixty years ago by the then Editor of the *Watchman-Examiner* to denote those who accepted the doctrines expounded in *The Fundamentals*—a set of twelve books containing articles in defence of the Christian faith by a variety of eminent evangelical scholars, and widely distributed through the English-speaking world. But why coin a new and rather unbeautiful word to denote people who hold the historic faith of the Christian Church? Nowadays the term is commonly used to denote one who holds extreme traditional and literalist views, and has well been called "a refined theological swearword." It is better not to use it, either in praise or in blame. As for the articles in the twelve books, most of them were not "fundamentalist" in the more restricted sense of the term which is current today; they were simply dedicated to the defence of the basic Christian doctrines. One of the contributors, Dr. James Orr, in his essay on "Science and Christian Faith" (Vol. IV, Chapter IV), could refer with sympathy to Rudolf Otto's *Naturalism and Religion*, finding there evidence of a not unwelcome "newer evolution . . . which breaks with Darwin on the three points most essential to his theory." But it is most unlikely that a present-day "fundamentalist", as commonly understood, would acknowledge any affinity with Otto.

Gifts, Spiritual

What is the connexion between a man's natural ability and his spiritual gift? Does he receive a spiritual gift after conversion, or is it merely a matter of putting to work those abilities which he received at birth and developed in life?

There is a special sense of the term "spiritual gifts" which denotes those qualities which give evidence of the indwelling presence of the Holy Spirit in a man: they are "manifestations of the Spirit" (cf. 1 Cor. 12:7). "Faith" in the sense of 1 Cor. 12:9 is one such gift; Christian charity is another, and the greatest of them all (1 Cor. 13:13). But natural gifts as well as spiritual gifts in this more restricted sense are bestowed by the Spirit of God, and a natural gift is a spiritual gift when it is used in God's service. Paul, for example, devoted to his apostolic ministry not only those spiritual endowments which he received from his conversion onwards, but also the rich heritage and qualities which he already possessed, for these were bestowed on him in advance by God who had set him apart for his life's work even before he was born into the world (Gal. 1:15).

Would you for all practical purposes discount the possibility of the genuine exercise of the gift of tongues at the present day?

No; if I did so, I should be guilty of ignorant dogmatism. (This would not necessarily be true of someone else who knew more about the subject than I do.) But some people are born to doubt, and I am one of them. In face of such phenomena it is wise to obey the apostolic injunction: "test everything; hold fast what is good" (1 Thess. 5:21). The test of edification must be applied to glossolalic utterances as much as to utterances in normal speech; and as for knowing when an ecstatic utterance conveys a message from God and when it does not, two apostles have already supplied the criterion—in 1 Cor. 12:3 and 1 John 4:1-3.

God the Father

THE EXISTENCE OF GOD

"It often seems to people who are not religious as if there was no conceivable event or series of events the occurrence of which would be admitted by sophisticated religious people to be a sufficient reason for conceding 'There wasn't a God after all'." Do you think there is any substance in this complaint by a well-known Professor of Philosophy?

There is probably considerable substance in it if it means that believers in God are unlikely to give up their belief in God through the force of any conceivable argument or through the logic of any conceivable event or events. I can think of no event which, objectively viewed, might seem more calculated to make a believer give up his belief in God than our Lord's dereliction on the cross. They said, "He trusted in God . . .", as much as to say, "Much good His trust in God is doing Him now!" But if our Lord's trust in God survived that event— if, as is true, that event is to manʸ believers the ultimate demonstration both of His own Deity and of the truth of all His teaching about the Father—then it is difficult to imagine any other event that would lead a believer to conclude that, after all, there was no God. If the existence of God was something to be established by a chain of logical or practical reasoning, then we should have to concede, even if only theoretically, that the demonstration of a flaw in the process of reasoning would imperil the validity of our conclusion that He existed. But the fact is, God is at the *beginning* of every chain of reasoning; He is the ground of all thinking as well as (in Paul Tillich's words) the ground of all being. Mr. A (let us say) is a believer in God; Mr. B is not. But God's existence is no more dependent on Mr. A's belief in Him that it is on Mr. B's unbelief. Mr. A could not believe in God unless God were there antecedently to be believed in; but equally Mr. B could not *disbelieve* in God unless God were there antecedently to be disbelieved in. The unbeliever no doubt thinks it very unfair of the believer to argue in this "Heads I win; tails you lose" fashion; but since God is God, the position cannot be otherwise.

THE "DEATH" OF GOD

What is the meaning of modern theological talk about the "death of God", sometimes expressed in book-titles like God Is No More *and so forth?*

All that these statements really mean is that the consciousness of God is absent from the minds of many men and women in the world today. If God were nothing more than an idea in people's minds, then His survival would indeed be very doubtful. But when we are bidden to come to terms with this state of affairs, and present the Christian faith to our contemporaries in language which does not call for any awareness of God, we must demur. One writer, who speaks of "the concrete actuality of God's withdrawal from our time", says: "To speak the name of God in a time of this withdrawal is nothing

less than blasphemy . . . We do not allow God to be God when we pronounce his name in his absence." But he can be refuted out of his own mouth. For elsewhere in the article from which I quote he compares our present predicament to the Babylonian exile, a catastrophe in which "Israel lost everything which was the source of order and meaning to an ancient people"; yet "a new form of faith was born out of that crisis." Precisely, and that new form of faith was born because the God of Israel proved by His presence and activity that (unlike the gods of Israel's neighbours) He did not depend for His existence on His people; it was they who entirely depended on Him. The heathen might say in contempt, "Where is their God now?"—but their God showed quite plainly where He was by so directing the course of history that His people's fortunes were restored and the wondering heathen were compelled to say, "The LORD has done great things for them." So, in a day when God is absent from the world-view of so many, it is for His people to know and proclaim His presence and power, that all together may be compelled to confess that He is the living and true God.

THE NAMES AND TITLES OF GOD

Do you regard the Hebrew divine name 'Elohim *as suggesting the Trinity, or simply as a plural of excellency?*

I should say that those who find in 'Elohim *an adumbration of the Trinity are reading a later revelation back into the word. According to H. L. Ellison, "The plural will have been used from patriarchal times partly as a mark of respect—"the plural of majesty"—partly because the true God sums up in Himself all the divine powers, implied by the word itself" (The Bible Student, Bangalore, October 1953).

Gospel

Is there any difference between the gospel

preached by our Lord, by Paul, and by the angel of Rev. 14:6?

There is no difference so far as the essence of the gospel is concerned; what differences may be discerned are differences of emphasis and application. For example it is natural that differences of this latter kind should be found between the gospel as preached by our Lord, or by His disciples in His name (Luke 9:1-6), *before* His death and resurrection, and the gospel as preached by the apostles and others *after* His death and resurrection. Again, while Paul and the Jerusalem apostles preached the same gospel (1 Cor. 15:11), there would be differences of emphasis and application between Paul's presentation of it to Gentiles (cf. Rom. 2:16; 16:25) and their presentation of the same gospel to Jews. But I agree heartily with C. F. Hogg that "there is but one gospel, however variously it is described." In the same context he said of the eternal gospel of Rev. 14:6 that "here the word 'eternal' is sufficient in itself above all dispensational considerations, and suggesting that it is so called because it partakes of the timelessness of God Himself. Conversely, it would be incongruous to speak of a temporary message, given for an occasion, as 'an eternal gospel'." He pointed out that the angelic message of Rev. 14:7 can scarcely be the content of the "eternal gospel" of verse 6 (*What saith the Scripture?* p. 72f.).

Harvest Festivals

What should be our attitude to Harvest Festival Services where fruit, vegetables, and the like are brought or sent to the church meeting-place for subsequent distribution to those in need?

It is only our artificial urban and industrial outlook that makes us think there is anything odd about such a procedure. There are parts of the world where the regular Sunday offering is brought in the form of farm or dairy produce. It is wholly desirable that our indebtedness to God for His kind provision in such matters should be brought vividly to our attention on so appropriate an occasion; it is an indebtedness, of course, shared by Christians and non-Christians alike. And as for the subsequent disposal of the produce, what is given to the poor is reckoned by the Lord as lent to Himself (cf. Prov. 19:17).

Do not the vegetable gifts, etc., brought to church at Harvest Festival Services smack rather of Cain's offering?

Not unless those who bring them do so in the same spirit as animated Cain when he brought his offering to God. Each of the two offerings in Gen. 4 was a thank-offering (Heb. *minchāh*), and it was as proper for Cain, the farmer, to bring the first-fruits of his corn as it was for Abel, the shepherd, to bring the first-fruits of his flock.

Further to a point raised in the answer to these questions, is it the duty of all mankind to present first-fruits to God?

I believe it is. Whatever form such presentation may take, it is a proper acknowledgment of God's mercies and of our common dependence on Him for life and breath and all things. Professor Wilhelm Schmidt, of Vienna, whose researches into religious origins led him to the conclusion that primeval man practised a monotheistic worship, held that first-fruits were the most primitive form of sacrifice as a permanent institution. But no offering could be acceptable to God if the offerer's heart was full of rebellion against Him, nor could it be regarded as a substitute for righteousness and mercy. God's first call to men is to repent and be reconciled to Himself (Acts 17:30; 2 Cor. 5:20).

Healing

Is not divine healing Scriptural?

Of course it is. God is still, as He was in the wilderness days, "the LORD your healer" (Ex. 15:26). But bodily healing, though it was at times a concomitant of the apostolic preaching, was not an essential element in it; and while God is often pleased to answer His children's prayer by removing an infirmity, at other times He accomplishes His purposes in their lives by means of the infirmity, and answers their prayer by giving them added grace to bear it. Paul's narrative in 2 Cor. 12:7-10 has an important bearing on this question, and will repay careful consideration. See pp. 43f.

Please comment on the remark of Dr. G. Campbell Morgan, in The Corinthian Letters of Paul, p. 153, that he had personally met people in Britain today who possessed the gift of healing, and believed that they were not the only ones.

I have no doubt that he had met such people, and that there are several at the present time who have this gift. In a number of cases it may well be accompanied by a sense of vocation which leads those who have it to take the appropriate professional qualifications so that they may be able to exercise it more effectively. Others, I understand, possess and exercise the gift without the professional qualifications. My own knowledge of such people is second-hand, but it would be very foolish of me to say dogmatically that because (unlike Dr. Campbell Morgan) I have not met them personally there are no such people. (See also p. 207.)

Heaven

Would you agree with a well-known Anglican clergyman who is reported to have said that he expected to meet atheists in heaven?

Yes—by then they will be ex-atheists, of course. Another Anglican clergyman has recently reminded us that there will be no bishops in heaven, by which he did not mean that no bishop can get to heaven, but that when he gets there he will no longer be a bishop. As for the remark to which you refer, it was, I understand, an off-the-cuff reply to an inquisitive reporter. But I suspect that the atheists whom the speaker had in mind are people who ought to be atheists in the sense that the god in whom they disbelieve is one who ought to be disbelieved in. To disbelieve in a false god may be a first step on the road to belief in the true God. The tragedy is that some people who believe in a false god imagine that it is the true God that they believe in, and do incalculable harm both to the reputation of our heavenly Father and to the faith of others. It is important to try to ascertain the definition of terms that people use. The late Dr. Cyril Joad (a one-time atheist, incidentally, whom we may expect to meet in heaven) used to cause a good deal of amusement on brains trusts by his gambit, "It all depends what you mean by . . ."; but it is an essential condition for profitable discussion. The early Christians, it may be remembered, were widely known as atheists because they disbelieved in the gods that most other people worshipped; their belief in the invisible God was not reckoned to them for theism.

Hebrew Words and Phrases

Why is the Hebrew word for "heaven" (shamayim), used in Gen. 1:1 and elsewhere, in the dual number?

It only looks like a dual; it is really a plural form (see any up-to-date Hebrew Lexicon, such as Brown-Driver-Briggs or Köhler-Baumgartner). According to the *Hebrew Grammar* of Gesenius-Kautzsch (Eng. trans., p. 417), *shamayim* ("heaven") and *mayim* ("water") belong, like *panim* ("face," "surface"), to the class of "plurals of *local extension* to denote localities in general, but especially level surfaces (the *surface*-plural), since in them the idea of a whole composed of innumerable separate parts or points is most evident."

What is meant by such couplets as "blood and blood" in Deut. 17:8 and 2 Chron. 19:10?

210

A controversy between "blood and blood" might be one between two parties to a blood-feud, or one where it was necessary to decide whether a death was the result of accidental manslaughter or wilful murder. A controversy between "stroke and stroke" (Deut. 17:8) would be one involving the question of compensation for bodily injuries.

Should the Hebrew word nephesh *always be translated "soul"?*

It should always be translated in accordance with the context. While the context often requires the meaning "soul" or "life-stuff", it does not always do so. How, for example, are we to translate Num. 6:6, "he shall not go near a dead *nephesh*"? Probably by "a dead *person.*" In Psa. 69:1, again, it means "neck" or "throat"; the psalmist, sinking in deep mire where there is no foothold, calls out: "Save me, O God! for the waters have come up to my neck" (so R.S.V. and similarly N.E.B.; cf. Jonah 2:5). It probably has this meaning also in Psa. 105:18, where Joseph's *nephesh* is said to have entered into iron. Here A.V. and R.V. take the expression "his *nephesh*" to be an emphatic form meaning "he", while the well-known Prayer Book rendering, "the iron entered into his soul" (cf. Coverdale, "the iron pierced his heart"), reverses subject and object. Here again R.S.V. appears to have got the right sense: "his *neck* was put in a collar of iron" (similarly N.E.B.). We get a completely different meaning in Psa. 35:25, where the psalmist's enemies are pictured as exulting over his discomfiture with the words: "Aha! our *nephesh*!"—i.e. "we have got our *desire*" (R.V. "Aha, so would we have it"). A word whose range of meaning is so wide that it can embrace both "neck" and "desire" cannot be rendered uniformly by a single term in English.

In many commentaries one reads that in Holy Scripture the Hebrew term "forty" lends itself to the sense of "many" rather than the literal number. If this is so, how can one reconcile such passages as Jer. 29:10 and Ezek. 4:6?

Sometimes the term "forty" is doubtless used as a round number, as (e.g.) when "forty years" is used as the equivalent of a generation. At other times the number is evidently exact; this is so in the case of the wilderness wanderings of the Israelites, where the 40 years' period is made up of 2 years plus 38 years, and in the case of David's reign, during which Hebron was his capital for 7½ years and Jerusalem for 33 years. As for the passages to which you refer, the 70 years of Jer. 29:10 (cf. Jer. 25:11ff.) are variously reckoned from Nebuchadrezzar's overlordship over Judah after the battle of Carchemish in 605 B.C. to the liberating decree of Cyrus, or from the destruction of the temple in 587/6 B.C. to the erection of the second temple in the reign of Darius I. The 40 years of Judah's iniquity, which Ezekiel was to bear symbolically for 40 days (Ezek. 4:6), must be taken together with the 390 years of the northern kingdom's iniquity; the sum of 430 years would be practically the time that had elapsed since the beginning of the monarchy, while the 430 days of Ezekiel's symbolical bearing of the iniquity of Israel and Judah together would correspond to the time that siege conditions obtained during Jerusalem's last days (making allowance for the temporary raising of the Chaldaean siege through the intervention of the Egyptian army).

Is there any technical reason for translating the Hebrew word bashal *(usually rendered "boil" or "seethe") by the verb "roast" in Deut. 16:7 and 2 Chron. 35:13?*

While the basic meaning of *bashal* is "boil" (except where it means "ripen," as in Gen. 40:10; Joel 3:13), there are signs that it came to be used at times in the more general sense of "cook"; when that is so, boiling will be indicated by

211

adding the words "with water" (cf. Exodus 12:9, A.V., "nor sodden at all with water"), and roasting will be indicated by adding the words "with fire", as in 2 Chron. 35:13. This last verse is specially interesting, for the same verb *bashal* is used both of "roasting the passover with fire" and of "boiling the (other) holy offerings in pots, in cauldrons, and in pans." Not only the A.V. and R.V., but even the R.S.V., render the former of the two occurrences of *bashal* by "roasted" here; and it is difficult to see what alternative they had, unless they had chosen the non-committal word "cooked" (as N.E.B. does). Sometimes, again, *bashal* is used where the form of cooking is evidently baking; as in Num. 11:8 and 2 Sam. 13:8. The fact that *bashal* is used in this wider sense as well as in the more precise sense of "boil" should warn us not to overpress the contrast between the roasting (Heb. *salah*) of the passover lamb in Ex. 12:9 and its being boiled (Heb. *bashal*) in Deut. 16:7 (R.V. marg., R.S.V., N.E.B.). In 1 Sam. 2:13, 15, *bashal* means quite specifically "boil", for the contrast is emphasized between boiled flesh and flesh to roast. In each place where the verb occurs, then, the context will indicate whether it has the narrower or the wider sense.

Heresy

What kinds of teaching may properly be called heretical? Some people denounce as heresy any teaching which disagrees with their own, or which is contrary to "the tradition of the elders."

In the New Testament a heretic is a factious person, a partisan, rather than one who holds false doctrine. But the latter sense soon became the regular one. Historically, a heretic is one who refuses the Christian faith formulated in the ecumenical creeds and confessions; or, to give a definition more acceptable to many readers of *The Harvester*, he is one who does not adhere to the apostolic

teaching preserved in the New Testament. But I ought to distinguish carefully between one who rejects the apostolic teaching itself and one who rejects my interpretation of the apostolic teaching. And certainly we must not call a man a heretic simply because he departs from the teaching or practice that has become traditional in our ecclesiastical circle; if we do, we are making it more difficult for Christians to receive and impart the fresh light which God continually causes to break forth from His Word. We may be thankful, indeed, that we are generally encouraged to study the Bible for ourselves and make known the results of our study whether they are in strict conformity with "tradition" or not. But all this means that we should be very careful in our use of the term heresy. True, it sometimes has a technical, neutral sense, and there are some people and groups who would welcome it as a positive compliment; but with regard to its common, pejorative sense, perhaps we should take Mr. Harold St. John's advice; "the word might be applied to such a movement as 'Christian Science,' *provided the speaker were in a very humble frame of mind.*" (See also pp. 165f.)

Holy Shroud

Can you comment on a recent report, ascribed to the International Foundation for the Holy Shroud of Turin, according to which our Lord's heart was still beating when He was taken down from the cross, since the body whose marks appear on the shroud continued to bleed after it was wrapped in the shroud?

I might take this report more seriously if I thought there was any reason to connect the Turin shroud with our Lord's body. But I can see no reason to think that a shroud first known in the fourteenth century A.D. had anything to do with His body. One positive argument against thinking so is that our Lord's head was covered separately with a napkin (John

20:7), whereas the Turin shroud bears the impress or likeness of a whole body, including the head. And if there is any substance in the report which you mention, that is another and even more positive counter-argument, for our Lord was dead before His body was removed from the cross. This is not a question of theological presupposition regarding Biblical inspiration and the like: it is a straightforward question of preferring the explicit evidence of a first-century witness to the ambiguous evidence of a fourteenth-century witness— if "witness" is an appropriate designation to use of the Turin shroud, for it is difficult to ascertain to what it testifies. Are the marks on it bloodstains and the like, caused by contact with a crucified body, or are they made by a painter's brush, or (as has been affirmed more than once) have they the nature of a photographic negative? The best treatment of the subject known to me is the article "Suaire" in the *Dictionnaire d'Archéologie Chrétienne et de Liturgie* (a French Catholic encyclopaedia), by Dom Henri Leclercq, who sums up the findings of a historical inquiry as follows: "The piece of material preserved at Turin is a product executed towards the middle of the 14th century, a product to which its later fame assigns an honourable place in the history of pious mystifications. The discussion of these latter is not the province of Christian archaeology."

Holy Spirit

Is it correct to speak of being "filled with Holy Spirit" or being "guided by Holy Spirit", omitting the definite article? It is said, by way of justifying such a mode of speech, that the article is missing in the original Greek.

Sometimes it is missing, and sometimes it is present; but its absence or presence is largely due to the canons of Greek usage and not to theological considerations. The rules for the use of the definite article in Greek are not the same as those for its use in English, and an attempt to reproduce Greek usage literally in English can only result in bad, or even misleading, English. There is no biblical doctrine that cannot be expressed in plain, grammatical English. The late John Brown of Greenock and Edinburgh (whom some of our readers in Scotland may remember) used to say: "Excellent Greek may be execrable English, and excellent English execrable Greek." To speak of being "filled with Holy Spirit" and the like might give the unintended impression that it is not a Divine Person, but a divine force or influence, that is being spoken of.

An argument frequently used to support the personality of the Holy Spirit is that the masculine pronoun ekeinos is used of Him in John 14:26; 15:26; 16:8, 13, 14, although the Greek word for "spirit" is neuter. But may not the masculine pronoun be intended to agree with the masculine pronoun paraklētos?

No doubt it is, but the conclusion of the argument is not weakened thereby; *paraklētos* is a personal noun, meaning "advocate" or "counsellor", and together with the repeated *ekeinos* which stands in agreement with it, it underlines the personality of the Spirit.

Is there any historical evidence that the Holy Spirit was worshipped in apostolic days, or is there any such evidence in the catacombs of Rome?

There is, I should say, no evidence that He was *worshipped* in apostolic days, although He was invoked in worship ("Come, Holy Spirit"). Invocation of the Spirit has Scriptural precedent, as when Ezekiel prophesized at the command of God: "Come, from the four winds, O breath, and breathe upon these slain, that they may live" (Ezek. 37:9). Such invocation of the Spirit is attested in the catacomb inscriptions and other early Christian monuments; but we must not regard the catacomb inscriptions as authoritative, or we might find ourselves obliged to adopt the invocation of departed saints!

HIS INDWELLING

It is commonly said that the Holy Spirit takes up residence in a believer immediately he is converted. Where is the Scripture to substantiate this?

Those who make the statement to which you refer would perhaps find it substantiated in Rom. 8:9, "Any one who does not have the Spirit of Christ does not belong to him." If having the Spirit of Christ is tantamount to being indwelt by the Spirit of Christ, it would seem to follow that anyone not so indwelt has not been converted. Since it is the Spirit alone who brings men into living relation with Christ, there can be no such relation with Christ apart from the Spirit. I know there are some Bible teachers who would have something to say in reply to this, but you may find it a satisfactory answer. (See pp. 166f.)

In a leaflet entitled The Baptism with the Holy Spirit, *it is stated that "when you receive the baptism with the Holy Spirit, you will speak in another tongue through the supernatural utterance of the Holy Spirit (Acts 2:4)." Would you please comment on this statement?*

I recognize the leaflet which you quote, and hold the writer in high esteem. But there are three comments that come to mind as I consider this statement. First, if we are to use New Testament language with precision, the baptism with (or "in") the Holy Spirit does not appear to be an inward personal experience so much as the act of Christ by which believers are incorporated "into one body" (1 Cor. 12:13). The risen Lord's promise to the apostles, "before many days you shall be baptized with ('in') the Holy Spirit" (Acts 1:5) was certainly fulfilled on the day of Pentecost, but their inward experience, which coincided with the Lord's

act, is expressed in Acts 2:4 thus: "they were all *filled* with the Holy Spirit." So I should prefer to say, "when you are filled with the Spirit," instead of "when you receive the baptism with the Holy Spirit." However, you may think that this is mere quibbling over words. Second, although the apostles "began to speak in other tongues" when they were filled with the Spirit on that occasion, it is not implied that all who were filled with the Spirit would receive the same manifestation. At the end of Peter's address, he assured his hearers that if they repented and were baptized in the name of Jesus Christ for the forgiveness of their sins they would "receive the gift of the Holy Spirit" (Acts 2:38); but it is outrunning the evidence to suppose that they would all thereupon speak with tongues, or that all in fact did so. On two other specified occasions in Acts the reception of the Spirit was accompanied by the gift of tongues (cf. 10:44-46; 19:6); but it cannot be inferred from these passages that this gift invariably accompanied the reception of the Spirit. In fact, where the gifts of the Spirit are enumerated in 1 Corinthians (12:8-11, 28f.), it is clearly said that they are variously apportioned among believers, so that not all have gifts of healings, not all speak with tongues, not all interpret, and so forth. In face of this it is hazardous to affirm that even in New Testament days the gift of tongues was invariably given, at least initially, as a sign of the indwelling or filling by the Spirit. Whereas the gifts of the Spirit were apportioned variously, the graces making up the fruit of the Spirit (Gal. 5:22f.) are found together, and it may be added that the fruit of the Spirit is an even surer token of His presence in one's life than the gifts are: the gifts can be counterfeited, but not the fruit. Third, the writer whose statement you quote goes on to refer to his own experience, and does so in Scriptural terms. When he received this gift, he tells us, he himself was edified, which is exactly what Paul says of it in

1 Cor. 14:4. Others who have had a similar experience bear the same testimony. But in this as in other respects we must beware of treating our own experience as a standard for others. If a man has received blessing in one particular way, let him thank God for it, but let him remember that his brother may receive comparable blessing in quite a different way. The experience in question is a minority one: inquiry would show, I think, that the majority of Christians today—Spirit-sealed, Spirit-baptized, Spirit-indwelt and Spirit-filled Christians—have not received the gift of tongues. And this is evidently in accordance with the mind of the Spirit, since He distributes His gifts "to each one individually as he wills" (1 Cor. 12:11). See pp. 154f., 207.

IHS

What is the significance of the latters IHC or IHS embroidered on bookmarks in pulpit Bibles and on other articles of church equipment?

The letters IHC or IHS represent an abbreviation of the Greek form of "Jesus" (IHCOYC), frequently found in early Greek and Latin manuscripts. A later explanation regards them as the initials of three Latin words, *Iesus Hominum Salvator*, "Jesus the Saviour of Men"; but this is not their original significance.

Immortality

Is it Scriptural to speak of the immortality of the soul?

Not if its *inherent* immortality is meant. The phrase "immortality of the soul" can be misleading, because it tends to confound the Biblical teaching with the Platonic doctrine that the soul has immortality in itself. In the Bible, God alone has immortality in Himself (1 Tim. 6:16); all other beings who have immortality receive it from Him. That impeccably orthodox divine, the late William Hoste, wrote as follows on the unending character of the

future existence of human beings: "This is loosely described as the 'immortality of the soul': a term which is based on a misapprehension as to the meaning of death. If man had been created incapable of death, the divine warning would have been meaningless: 'In the day that thou eatest thereof, thou shalt surely die.' Man is capable of death by his very constitution, but not of ending his being. He must exist eternally either in harmony with God, which is life, or out of harmony with Him, which is death —'the second death'" (*Beyond the Grave*, p. 5). Let it be mentioned, in addition, that when "mortality" and "immortality" are mentioned in the Bible with reference to human beings, it is the body, not the soul, that is in view.

Infant Dedication

A service for child dedication is becoming increasingly popular and well received. Have we any scriptural precedent for this, and can we call upon Old Testament incidents to support it?

Since the Old Testament has not ceased to be part of Christian Scripture, we may well appeal to it in such matters just as our Lord and His apostles appealed to it in questions regarding marriage (Mark 10:6-8; Eph. 5:31; 1 Pet. 3:6). So, in relation to the question now before us, we may adduce Hannah's "lending" Samuel to the Lord "all the days of his life" (1 Sam. 1:11, 28), or the wise man's admonition to "train up (literally 'dedicate' or 'initiate') a child in the way he should go" (Prov. 22:6). But, quite apart from the question of precedent, it is a natural and fitting response to God's goodness that Christian parents should seek the fellowship of their Christian friends in thanking Him for the gift of a new child and in seeking His grace for themselves and for the child. When and where this service should take place depends on what is most convenient for all who are concerned in it. The setting of such domestic events in the context of church fellowship is equally and appropriately recognized in Christian marriage and Christian funerals.

Inspiration

It has been stated that, when Paul speaks of every Scripture as being inspired of God (2 Tim. 3:16), he neither there nor in any other place claims that his own epistles belonged to the category of inspired Scripture. What then are we to understand by his reference in Gal. 1:11f. and 2 Cor. 12:7 to revelations which he received? What is the difference between inspiration and revelation?

In 2 Tim. 3:16 divine inspiration is predicated of the sacred writings which Timothy had known from his childhood— i.e. the Old Testament Scriptures. Of course, the principle there stated need not be restricted to these. The other passages you mention do not refer to Paul's writings; Gal. 1:11f. refers to the revelation of the gospel which he received directly from Christ when first he was called to be an apostle; 2 Cor. 12:7 refers to revelations he received on the occasion when he was rapt to the third heaven. The former revelation finds expression in several of his epistles, but not so the latter revelations, for they were not to be expressed in words. Revelation denotes God's unfolding of Himself and His truth to men; inspiration is one of the ways in which He does so.

Dean Alford apparently regards the Evangelists' variation in reporting the wording of Pilate's "accusation" placed on the cross as proof abundant of what he calls "the suicidal theory of verbal inspiration." Would you comment on this?

No reasonable view of Biblical inspiration insists that all reports are verbatim reports. For example, as I have suggested elsewhere, the reports of speeches which we find in the Acts of the Apostles are probably reliable summaries of what was said rather than full transcripts. If the Evangelists give the general purport of Pilate's "title" we need ask for no more— although it has been suggested that the wording in the three languages may have differed somewhat and that these differing versions may be reproduced respectively by Matthew, Luke and John, while Mark gives the gist of the inscription as "The King of the Jews." But when people speak or write about "verbal inspiration", whether with approval or with disapproval, it is necessary to discover what they understand by the phrase. In a note on Paul's description of the apostolic doctrine as "words . . . which the Holy Spirit teaches" (1 Cor. 2:13), Bishop Lightfoot says: "the notion of verbal inspiration in a certain sense is involved in the very conception of an inspiration at all, because words are at once the instruments of carrying on and the means of expressing ideas so that the words must both lead and follow the thought." He goes on to say, however: "But the passage gives no countenance to the popular doctrine of verbal inspiration, whether right or wrong" (*Notes on Epistles of St. Paul*, 1895, p. 180). By "the popular doctrine of verbal inspiration" he probably meant much the same thing as Alford had in mind when he spoke of "the suicidal theory of verbal inspiration"—perhaps a mechanical dictation theory. If the expression "verbal inspiration" is used to denote the idea of 1 Cor. 2:13, that is all right. But in practice it has become a shibboleth by which some people try to test other people's orthodoxy, and for that reason is better avoided. It is best to remain content with such a simple statement as that of 2 Pet. 1:21, which says of the biblical writers: "men they were, but impelled by the Holy Spirit, they spoke the words of God" (N.E.B.). It is because of that fact that the written record of their words can be described as "inspired by God" (2 Tim. 3:16). The whole subject is one where the repetition of clichés is too often a substitute for rational thinking.

Is it the original text of Scripture, or the versions which we use, that should be described as inspired?

While our ultimate appeal must be to the purest ascertainable text of the original languages of Scripture (and even a statement like that begs more questions than is always realized), it is true that, by the "singular providence of God" (as the *Westminster Confession of Faith* puts it), the work of transmission and translation has been carried out with such care that God's saving revelation is accessible to any man who reads or hears the Bible in his own tongue. The Bible is not like the Qur'an, which (I am told) loses its virtue when translated from Arabic into another language. The Bible does not lose its inspiration and authority by being translated.

Can you give a definition of biblical inspiration which will pass every test?

One might make a tentative approach to the definition for which you ask by saying that Biblical inspiration is that special control exercised by the Spirit of God over the speakers or writers of Holy Scripture, by reason of which their words adequately convey the Word of God. I believe that a definition along these lines would pass most tests, although the detailed application of any one test to the definition would afford material for many supplementary questions.

I recently came across the statement: "The New Testament was not written for the most part in literary Greek— some of it (Revelation especially) is not even grammatical!" If the latter statement is correct, does it not strike a deadly blow at "verbal inspiration"?

No; question of grammar and questions of inspiration are quite distinct. Some parts of the New Testament are written in good literary Greek—e.g. Hebrews, 1 Peter and Luke-Acts (except when Luke for sufficient reasons adopts a different style from his own natural one). Some parts are written in more colloquial Greek, and other parts are intermediate in character. At one time New Testament Greek was thought by some to be a special language of the Holy Ghost; when, towards the end of the last century, parallels to New Testament Greek began to be discovered, it appeared that the "words . . . which the Spirit teaches" were largely spoken or written in the language of the common people. The various speakers and writers in the New Testament use the Greek forms and constructions which come most naturally to them; this does not affect their inspiration one whit. Neither is the inspiration of Revelation affected one whit by its exceptional grammar. The writer of Revelation shows himself to be quite familiar with ordinary grammatical usage, but he deviates from it systematically and deliberately for certain reasons which the student may try to discover. There is, indeed, sufficient coherence in the idiosyncratic grammar of Revelation for R. H. Charles to devote to its study a considerable section of the introduction to his commentary on that book.

In discussing the situations in which some of the books of the Bible came to be written (e.g. in your Expanded Paraphrase of the Epistles of Paul) *do you find any difficulty in relating these circumstances to the doctrine of inspiration?*

No; for one thing, our reconstruction of the circumstances is often hypothetical (this is true of much of the discussion in the book you mention), whereas the inspiration of the writings is spiritually discerned. For another thing, no matter what the writers' circumstances and methods of operation were, these have been overruled and used by the Spirit of God to achieve His own purpose.

Questions of structure, date and authorship of the documents do not affect their inspiration. For (in the words of Bishop Handley Moule) "He who chose the writers of the Holy Scriptures, many men scattered over many ages, used them each in his surroundings and in his character, yet so as to harmonize them all in the Book which, while many, is one. He used them with the sovereign skill of Deity. And that skilful use meant that He used their whole being, which He had made, and their whole circumstances, which He had ordered. . . . He can take a human personality, made in His own image, pregnant, formative, causative, in all its living thought, sensibility, and will, and can throw it freely upon its task of thinking and expression—and behold the product will be His; His matter, His thought, His exposition, His Word, 'living and abiding for ever'" (*The Epistle to the Romans*, 1893, p. 7f.).

Jacob and Israel

Could you state the significance of the names "Jacob" and "Israel" as used in the Old Testament? They are frequently used alternately (e.g., Psa. 14:7; Isa. 9:8; 10:20-22; 14:1, 2, etc.), although the mysterious wrestler said to Jacob: "Your name shall no more be called Jacob, but Israel" (Gen. 32:28).

Where the names Jacob and Israel are used in deliberate contrast to each other, then their respective significance is in view. Jacob is the man who tried to help God to achieve His purpose, scheming and supplanting and striving only to find himself at the end faced by a desperate situation of his own contriving from which none but God could deliver him; Israel is the man who learned to give up striving and wrestling, who clung to God in naked faith and received his fullest blessing from God when he was no longer able to do anything but weep and cling (cf. Hosea 12:3-5). But in the poetical passages of the Old Testament (and of the New, for

that matter) we have to reckon with the figure of speech called parallelism, which often involves the repetition of the identical thought in different words. In this connexion Jacob and Israel are often used in two parallel clauses as alternate synonyms for the man or the nation, without any emphasis being laid on the original distinction between the two names; e.g.,

"He has not beheld misfortune in Jacob,
Nor has he seen trouble in Israel: . . .
For there is no enchantment against Jacob,
No divination against Israel" (Num. 23:21, 23).

Judas

Do you think Judas was present at the institution of the Lord's Supper?

If Luke 22:15-21 reproduces the original sequence of our Lord's words on that occasion, then Judas was certainly present. But Luke's order here is perhaps not the time-order, and it seems more probable to me that Judas was present when our Lord broke the bread and gave it to His disciples, but had left the room before the blessing and distribution of the cup "after supper." In any case it is a salutary and solemnizing thought that my bodily presence at the Lord's Table and my partaking of the bread will not of itself guarantee that I cherish no treasonable thoughts against Christ in my heart.

Judgment

At the judgment seat of Christ, what will be the position of one who, while certainly converted, backslides very deeply into sin, influencing others for evil and bringing dishonour to the Lord's name? Will he simply lose his reward, or receive some positive punishment?

Is there any good reason to believe that the alleged conversion of such a person was genuine? The test of reality is continuance. But if his conversion was genuine

—and in the circumstances that is something which only God knows—he comes within the range of certain very solemn warnings of the New Testament. On one of these, Col. 3:25, the late C. F. Hogg and W. E. Vine wrote as follows: "He that 'knoweth how to deliver the godly out of temptation, and to keep the unrighteous under punishment unto the day of judgment' (2 Pet. 2:9), knows also how to direct and to use the working of His law of sowing and reaping in the case of His children also. The attempt to alleviate the text of some of its weight by suggesting that the law operates only in this life, fails, for there is nothing in the text or context to lead the reader to think other than that while the sowing is here, the reaping is hereafter" (*Touching the Coming of the Lord*, 1919, p. 85). The warnings to believers in the New Testament are for our health, and we ignore or deflect or minimize them at our peril.

Where will the judgment-seat of Christ be set up?

If the word "where" implies some particular location in space, I have no answer to this question. Otherwise, the answer is surely that the judgment seat of Christ is set up where the soul, stripped of all subterfuge and camouflage, finds itself directly confronted by the "kind but searching glance" of Him with whom we have to do, and humbly and gratefully embraces His all-righteous and all-merciful verdict.

When will the judgment seat of Christ be set up?

On the day which is variously called "the day of our Lord Jesus Christ" (1 Cor. 1:8), "the day of the Lord (Jesus)" (1 Cor. 5:5), "the day of our Lord Jesus" (2 Cor. 1:14), "the day of Jesus Christ" (Phil. 1:6), "the day of Christ" (Phil. 1:10; 2:16), and so forth. That is the day when the Lord will perfect the good work which He has begun in His people, when He will review and reward their service, when He will "bring to light the things now hidden in darkness, and will disclose the purposes of the heart" (1 Cor. 4:5; cf. Rom. 2:16). And since it is clear that all this takes place "before our Lord Jesus at his coming" (1 Thess. 2:19), it follows that it is at the Lord's advent that His people appear before His judgment seat.

Justification

We sometimes hear it stated that "God sees the believer as perfect in Christ." Is there definite Scriptural evidence for this claim?

I do not remember hearing a statement made in exactly these words. But I expect that whoever made the statement had the believer's justification in mind; in that case, Scriptural support could be found in 2 Cor. 5:21, "so that in him we might become the righteousness of God." Again in Rom. 8:30 we have the statement: "those whom he justified he also glorified", where the glory which awaits the justified (i.e., their complete conformity to Christ on the day of His appearing) is viewed as being so settled in the purpose of God that it can be expressed in the past tense, as though it had already taken place. But it would certainly be a help if people would express their meaning more precisely and lucidly.

Does Scripture clearly show that we should distinguish between the believer's "standing" and his "state", to use terminology favoured by some teachers?

While this terminology does not occur in Scripture, those who use it (if I understand them rightly) mean by a believer's "standing" his righteous status in God's sight as a justified sinner, and by his "state" the stage which he has reached in sanctification or growth in grace. The distinction is thus quite a Scriptural and practical one.

The Roman Catholic Bible has "justice" where our versions have "righteousness," and Young's Concordance also gives "justice" as an alternative word. An Anglican minister also substituted "justice" for "righteousness" when he quoted Matt. 6:33 in a recent broadcast. Surely these two words are neither synonymous nor interchangeable; does not the change of words render meaningless such verses as Rom. 5:17 and Phil. 3:9?

The English language uses both these words where Greek has only one—*dikaiosynē*. In English "righteousness' and "justice" are synonymous but not entirely interchangeable; that is to say, there is a large area of common meaning, but there are certain contexts in which the one is more suitable than the other. There is no difference between the righteousness of God whereby He declares the sinner righteous and His justice whereby He justifies the sinner. The Roman Catholic Bible has "justice" uniformly because it is based on the Latin Vulgate, which translates Greek *dikaiosyne* by *iustitia*—the proper Latin word to use for this purpose. To our ears "righteousness" may seem more appropriate than "justice" in Rom. 5:17 and Phil. 3:9, but if we had been accustomed to use the noun "justice" in the same sense as the verb "justify"—that is to say, to use it of the status of a man whom God has declared "just" in His sight—we should find nothing inappropriate in it. As for Matt. 6:33, where righteousness in practice is meant, the minister to whom you refer was probably quoting from the New English Bible.

If we accept the doctrine of justification by faith, set out in Romans, as being apostolic and therefore inspired, must we conclude that Jas. 2:21, which teaches justification by words, is not apostolic, but tainted with Judaism, in view of Gal. 2:11-16 and Acts 21:18-26? If a believer comes to that conclusion, has
an assembly or an individual believer any scriptural ground for refusing him fellowship on that ground?

The conclusion which you refer to would be unavoidable if James's doctrine of justification by works were in direct contradiction to the Pauline (and not only Pauline) doctrine of justification by faith. But it is by no means a necessary conclusion. Jas. 2:21 uses neither "justify" nor "faith" in exactly the same sense as Paul. As for "faith", James uses this term in two senses. There is the sense in which faith is necessary in order to make prayer effective (Jas. 1:6; 5:15; cf. 2:1, 5); and there is the sense in which faith is a purely mental assent to truth, such as demons may render, without being anything bettered thereby (Jas. 2:19). It is this latter kind of faith which James describes as "dead"; and Paul would have agreed with him. The faith which, according to Paul, is indispensable for right relations with God is a personal and confident trust in God, not barrenly intellectual but spiritually dynamic—"faith working through love" (Gal. 5:6). As for the verb "to justify", James is not thinking, as Paul is, in terms of the question: "How can man be just with God?" What James is concerned to show when he speaks of justification in this passage is rather that a man's works reveal the quality of his faith; in other words, his claim to have faith is not justified until he shows his faith by means of his works. Paul is countering legalism, while James is attacking antinomianism. But if a Christian reader prefers the conclusion which you mention, a difference of interpretation should be no barrier to fellowship. You would not propose, I imagine, to excommunicate Martin Luther for his depreciation of the Epistle of James!

When people speak of justification "by faith alone, apart from works", is the addition of the adverb "alone" justified?

220

This question was addressed 450 years ago to Luther, when he translated Rom. 3:28, "So we reckon that man becomes righteous without the works of the law, through faith alone." It was pointed out to him that there is no word in the Greek corresponding to "alone", but he replied that although Greek idiom did not require it, good German did. (We may compare R.S.V. at Rom. 11:20, "you stand fast *only* by faith", and N.E.B. at Gal. 2:16, "but *only* through faith in Christ Jesus", where the words I have italicized are epexegetic additions, calculated to bring the sense out more clearly in English.) But Luther was moved by considerations of gospel truth even more than by considerations of German idiom; he had in mind a perversion of the gospel which taught that men might be justified before God by works of a legal character and was at pains to give it no loophole in his Bible translation. His addition of "alone" was a way of underlining and emphasizing the phrase "without the works of the law." When we speak of salvation as procured through faith alone, that is what we mean; it is another way of saying "not of works" (Eph. 2:9). Faith alone justifies, but the faith that justifies is not alone; it is followed by those "good works, which God prepared beforehand, that we should walk in them" (Eph. 2:10).

Kingdom of God/Heaven

Is it consistent with a true interpretation of the contents of the gospels to differentiate between the expressions "the kingdom of heaven" and "the kingdom of God," assigning one to the Jew and the other to the Church?

I think not. In a number of places where Matthew has "the kingdom of heaven" the other Synoptists have "the kingdom of God" (compare, for example, Matt. 19:14 with Mark 10:14 and Luke 18:16). We may take it that our Lord used an Aramaic expression which could be rendered indifferently by either phrase;

Matthew for the most part prefers to render it by "the kingdom of heaven," the other Evangelists by "the kingdom of God." We may compare the two synonymous statements in Dan. 4: "the Most High rules" (vv. 17, 25, 32) and "Heaven rules" (v. 26). The distinctions which have been discerned between the "kingdom of God" and the "kingdom of heaven" arise from Matthew's distinctive perspective on the kingdom.

From Luke 16:16 and Acts 28:31 I deduce that the kingdom of God and/or heaven (Matt. 19:23, 24; Mark 10:23, 24; Luke 18:24, 25) and the church of Matt. 16:18 are the same. Am I correct?

While the kingdom of God and the kingdom of heaven are identical, I should not agree that the kingdom is identical with the church of Matt. 16:18. The church is a community of human beings; the kingdom is the rule of God in the life of men. There is indeed a close relation between the two, for the church is (or ought to be) the community in which the rule of God is most completely accepted and manifested. Or, to put it otherwise, the kingdom is the new order of God's dealings with mankind proclaimed in advance by John the Baptist, inaugurated by our Lord and entered by believers. According to Luke 16:16 John marks the end of the preceding order (described here in terms of "the law and the prophets"); "since then the good news of the kingdom of God is preached." Our Lord preached this good news and taught His disciples to do so, and this they did, both before and after His death and resurrection. You mention Acts 28:31, where "preaching the kingdom of God and teaching about the Lord Jesus Christ" are conjoined in Paul's ministry in Rome; some years earlier, Paul himself summed up his Ephesian ministry as "testifying to the gospel of the grace of God" and "preaching the kingdom" (Acts 20:24, 25). The gospel of the kingdom was subject to limitations during

221

our Lord's ministry before His passion (cf. Luke 12:50); once He had suffered and triumphed it was unleashed "with power" (Mark 9:1); but it was essentially the same gospel. The church consists of those who obey the gospel and so become heirs of the kingdom. Old Testament believers who, apart from us, could not attain perfection (Heb. 11:40), in resurrection are fellow-heirs with us of the unshakable kingdom of Heb. 12:28—that well-founded city and "better country" to which Abraham and others looked forward (Heb. 11:10, 16)—and fellow-members of the glorified church.

Laying on of Hands

What was the significance of the laying on of hands in apostolic days? Should it be practised today?

It appears to have been, for the most part, a sign of fellowship or solidarity. By this action the twelve apostles manifested their fellowship with the seven men appointed to be almoners in the primitive Jerusalem church (Acts 6:6), Peter and John welcomed the Samaritan believers (formerly despised as half-castes) into the Spirit-baptized fellowship of the people of God (Acts 8:17), Ananias of Damascus similarly welcomed Saul of Tarsus (Acts 9:17), the leaders of the church at Antioch expressed their fellowship with Barnabas and Saul when they set out on their joint missionary tour of Cyprus and Asia Minor (Acts 13:3), and so forth. The same action is very fittingly used for the same purpose today on such occasions as the appointment of elders and other ministers, the commendation and sending forth of missionaries, and the like.

The Lord's Prayer

On what grounds do some evangelical Christians omit any use of the Lord's Prayer? As our Lord expressly instructed His disciples "When you pray, say . . .",

it is difficult to understand why it is never used.

In some quarters its non-use may be due to an exaggerated dispensationalism which regards our Lord's teaching in the Synoptic Gospels as not intended for the "church age." Others may fear that its repeated use may make it little more than a "vain repetition" if people get into the way of reciting it without thinking of the meaning of the words; but this danger attaches to the use of any form of words. By dint of constant repetition we can build up our own forms of prayer which, if we are not careful, can be recited without thought; and our own forms are not so good as the form of words which our Lord taught His disciples. There is, of course, no obligation to repeat the identical words every time; we can regard the Lord's Prayer as a model prayer—"Pray then like this" (Matt. 6:9)—showing us what the range of our prayers should be. "It contains, as recorded by Matthew (R.V.), fifty-five words, can be repeated in less than half a minute, contains petitions which range from the common bread-and-butter needs of our breakfast tables to the ultimate achievement of the age-long purposes of God; puts God's glory first, our needs second, does not rule out material matters as too trifling to pray about, yet insists on the supremacy of the spiritual, and emphasizes the basic condition of the disciples' enjoyment of the Father's forgiveness" (C. F. Hogg and J. B. Watson, *On the Sermon on the Mount*, 1947, p. 65). But as a prayer for Christians to pray aloud together, when as children they address their heavenly Father, could it ever be surpassed? I remember that, in my undergraduate days in Cambridge, a young Anglican clergyman expounded an ultra-dispensational line to a CICCU group in my rooms in college and deprecated the use of the Lord's Prayer. "But", said I, "you use it everytime you conduct a church service." "Yes", said he, "but I spiritualize it." He did not explain how one "spiritualizes" the Lord's

Prayer, and I have never understood what he meant. Happily, a few years later he learned a more excellent way. '

The Lord's Supper

While it is fully recognized that the bread and wine in the Lord's Supper are symbols of the body and blood of Christ, it is clear that our Lord said "This is my body" and "This is my blood" (Matt. 26:26, 28), and also "he who eats my flesh and drinks my blood has eternal life" (John 6:54). How can we explain these Scriptures to people who believe that the elements are corporally charged into the body and blood of Christ?

When our Lord instituted the Lord's Supper on the night of His betrayal, it was impossible for His disciples to understand His words, "This is my body . . . this is my blood", in any other than a symbolical sense. He was present in body with them; they could see, hear, and touch Him; how could they have understood Him to mean His physical body? The paterfamilias at every passover meal used similar language when he lifted a plate of unleavened bread and said, "This is the bread of affliction which our ancestors ate in the land of Egypt." The participants knew that it was not the *same* bread as their fathers had eaten so many centuries before, but that it *represented* that bread. As for John 6:54 and its context, our Lord Himself explained that these words were to be understood spiritually, as against some hearers who were inclined (v. 52) to take them in a crassly material sense: "It is the spirit that gives life, the flesh is of no avail; the words that I have spoken to you are spirit and life" (v. 63). In both places the natural meaning of the language is made clear by the context.

Is it strictly correct to speak of the "real presence" of Christ in the Lord's Supper?

Certainly; like many other expressions that we use which are not found in Scripture, this one conveys a Scriptural truth, and one moreover which is repeatedly verified in Christian experience—that in the giving and taking of the bread and the cup Christ communicates Himself to the believing soul. If the phrase has been misused to imply that Christ is localized in the elements in a bodily manner, that is no reason for avoiding its proper use, as occasion may require. No believer need be deterred from praying, with Charles Wesley:

> "To every faithful soul appear,
> And show Thy real presence here."

Is Sunday morning the right time to take communion?

If there were one particular "right time", there would have been a clear direction on the point in Holy Scripture. It appears from Acts 2:46 that the believers in the primitive Church of Jerusalem broke bread "day by day"; and I suppose that at one time or another, I myself (in common, no doubt, with many of my readers) have broken bread on all seven days of the week. We know from Acts 20:7 that on a certain "first day of the week" (perhaps April 17, A.D. 57) the Christians in Troas met for the breaking of bread, and Paul and his fellow-travellers were present on that occasion. It may well be that they were accustomed to meet for that purpose regularly on the first day of the week, although that is not expressly stated. Certainly the choice of the first day for the purpose became an early, regular and widespread practice. As I read Acts 20:7-11, they met on Sunday night, and because of exceptional circumstances it was Monday morning before they broke bread. (The N.E.B., however, has a different interpretation). Let us realize that the important questions are not *when* we break the bread, or *where* we do it, but *with what attitude of heart.*

Is there any New Testament basis for the

223

view that unless a believer is baptized by immersion in water he cannot break bread?

Baptism and the breaking of bread are both outward acts, ordained by our Lord, in which believers manifest their response of faith to God's grace bestowed upon them in Christ. The Scriptural and normal order is that baptism takes place once and for all at the beginning of the Christian life; the breaking of bread is repeated frequently in the course of the Christian life. But this does not mean that the former is an indispensable prerequisite of the latter. There may be reasons of health or age against baptizing certain believers according to the mode indicated in the question; these would be no bar to their breaking bread. And there are other believers who conscientiously believe that they have been Scripturally baptized, although their baptism did not take the form of immersion in water. A few years ago an Anglican bishop of my acquaintance invited delegates to a youth conference to participate in a communion service provided they were baptized members of a Christian church. When it was pointed out to him that some of the delegates belonged to the Salvation Army or the Society of Friends, he amended his invitation to include "all who consider themselves to have been baptized." I ought not to make it a condition of fellowship (in the breaking of bread or in any other way) that my brethren and sisters accept the same interpretation of the Scriptural doctrine and mode of baptism as I do myself, even if mine were the right one.

Is it permissible for believers to observe the Lord's Supper if they are not members of a properly constituted church and meeting as such? For example, may they do so if they are away from home and there is no opportunity to join with members of another local church in this memorial ordinance?

When our Lord instituted this memorial ordinance, He said nothing about His disciples' continuing to remember Him thus *as members of a local church*; nor did His apostles lay down any such rule. Naturally the breaking of bread will normally take place within the fellowship of a local church; but there is no Scriptural regulation confining it to such a fellowship. Unfortunately there is a type of ecclesiasticism which cannot tolerate the simplicity of New Testament liberty, but must ever be introducing its own legislation and restrictive glosses. It is found in many streams of Christian tradition, and takes various forms; but we should pray to be delivered from it wherever and however it may appear. One of the most memorable communion services in which I ever participated was held in Jerusalem with a party of pilgrims (representing a greater variety of Christian tradition than I dare specify here), on what is probably to be identified with the "place called The Pavement" where Pilate passed sentence on our Lord. It was a memorable occasion not only because of the place but because the procedure was so "untraditional."

It is contended by some people known to us that nobody should be allowed to take communion unless they are "in fellowship" and bring a letter confirming that they are so, or else give a good reason for not bringing one. The reason given for for this contention is that, failing such precautions, someone may get up to minister and teach unsound doctrine. Will this contention stand the test of the New Testament?

No, of course not. There is no question of our "allowing" any Christian to break bread; the invitation to do so comes from the Lord, and it is a pleasure and a privilege to welcome His people who desire to join us in accepting His invitation, irrespective of their denominational labels, whether they come armed with a letter or not. (The question of discipline within the local church is not at issue here.) This, indeed, is the normal practice of the people called Open Brethren; one might even go further and say that it is one of the fundamental reasons for the rise and continuance of the Brethren movement. But it cannot be too often emphasized that, while every Christian has a place at the Lord's Table by divine right, not every Christian has a right to minister the Word there. And the fear expressed by the friends referred to in your question would not exist if it were clearly understood that the elders of the church are responsible to see to it that the church receives wholesome ministry, and it is for them to encourage or to restrain ministry accordingly. If we give the impression that at our communion services any one is free to minister—provided one is a man and not a woman!—we have ourselves to thank for the difficulties in which we are landed.

In some of our churches one brother gives thanks for the bread and another for the cup; elsewhere one and the same brother gives thanks for both. Is not the latter practice preferable, seeing that it is a single act of worship and should not be divided?

This argument would suggest that one person should conduct the whole meeting, seeing that it is all a single act of worship. The point is that it is an act of worship by the whole church, and those members who take a vocal or active part in the worship, e.g. by giving thanks or by breaking the bread and pouring the cup, do so on behalf of the whole church. There is absolutely no issue of principle involved in the question you raise. It is frequently a matter of local custom or convenience, but it should not be allowed to harden into a rule which would limit spiritual freedom. The New Testament is remarkably sparing of procedural legislation for the observance of the Lord's Supper; but what the New Testament lacks has been more than amply supplied by our traditions.

If the Lord's Supper superseded the Passover, should we not restrict its celebration to once a year?

There was a specific direction in Old Testament times, repeated a number of times, for the annual celebration of the Passover. No such direction is given for the Lord's Supper in the New Testament, and as far back as our information carries us, it is clear that early Christians kept it once a week (if not indeed more frequently), even if the Easter communion was a special occasion, as it still is in some Christian traditions. An annual celebration would have been kept on the anniversary of the Passion or Resurrection, or on the Sunday nearest to one or another of these anniversaries; but the first day of the week on which there was a meeting at Troas for the breaking of bread (Acts 20:7) was at least a week later than that. A weekly celebration is probably indicated.

Why should we not use individual communion cups at the breaking of bread?

I have on several occasions taken communion in places where individual cups were used, but it seems to me that their use may tend to obscure the sense of fellowship uniting those who partake in the "communion of the blood of Christ" (1 Cor. 10:16), declaring their joint "interest in the Saviour's blood." I have wondered at times why many Christians who are such sticklers for an adequate supply of water in baptism, lest the significance of that sacrament should be obscured, appear to be much less concerned about the possibility of obscuring part of the significance of the other gospel sacrament. The use of three or four cups where there is a large company of communicants is not on the same footing, because in that case many do actually partake of the same cup. (Even so, some prefer to use one cup only and refill it as occasion requires.) The use of individual cups is sometimes defended on hygienic grounds, but where real wine is used this consideration has less cogency, except in those areas where local public health regulations enforce their use. However, the question of individual cups (like the question of the composition of the wine itself) relates to the externalities of the ordinance, and excessive concentration on the externalities may obscure our appreciation of the inward and spiritual significance more than the mere use of individual cups can do.

In your previous answer you make a parenthetical allusion to "the question of the composition of the wine itself." This question has been a leading topic in recent discussion here, and I should like to have your comments on it.

As I indicated in my parenthetical allusion to the matter, this question relates to one of the externalities of the communion service. In my judgment, whether the wine used is fermented or unfermented is usually of no great importance. Many of us can no doubt testify that they have attended some places where fermented wine was used and others where unfermented wine was used, and that (if we noticed the difference at all) it did not affect our remembrance, communion and worship in the slighest degree. What *is* appalling, however, is to find Christians, whom one would otherwise regard as spiritually mature, insisting that the wine *must* be fermented or that it *must* be unfermented, to a point where fellowship is threatened and the purpose of the holy ordinance obscured. (The same considerations apply to the use of leavened or unleavened bread in communion).

In a situation where no men were available, would it be right for Christian women to take the Lord's Supper together?

Let me call in J. N. Darby to answer this question—not because he was J. N. Darby, but because on this point I believe him to be on the right lines. Darby was no feminist: "I think it is a little out of place," he said, "for a woman even to raise a hymn; but I do not object, if she do it modestly." But he went on: "If three women were on a desert island, I do not see why they should not break bread together, if they did it privately. A man and his wife being alone, I see no objection to their breaking bread, if they themselves feel free and are disposed" (*Collected Writings*, XXVI, p. 429). The operative sentence here is the one about the desert island. If the island were really a desert one, the three women could hardly break bread in any other way than "privately." I would simply add that there are other desert islands than those which are entirely surrounded by water.

Marriage and Divorce

Is it permissible for a Christian woman who has divorced her husband for adultery, to marry again?

When Paul was asked certain questions in this field, and could quote a commandment of the Lord, he was happy; that put an end to all controversy. Where he could quote no commandment of the Lord, he gave his own judgment, "by way of permission, not of commandment" (1 Cor. 7:6). My judgment is not so good as Paul's, and I am hesitant about publicizing it at all in matters of this kind. However, there is no call for my judgment in the present instance, for the Lord's ruling in Mark 10:12 seems to answer this question conclusively in the negative, unless it can be shown that the kind of case you mention forms an exception to His ruling.

In Deut. 24:2 a woman who has been put away by her husband can marry again. In Mark 10:12, if she puts away her husband and marries another, she commits adultery. The woman in Deut. 24:2 is the guilty party; the woman in Mark 10:12 is not the guilty party. Is there not an inconsistency here?

The woman in Deut. 24:2 was not necessarily the guilty party. There was a wide variety of circumstances which might constitute "some unseemly thing" in the sense of Deut. 24:1. As late as our Lord's time the leading rabbinical schools differed quite radically on the interpretation of this passage. If the woman was the guilty party in the sense that she was guilty of unchastity, then under the Old Testament law she had committed a capital offence and would not survive to become another man's wife (cf. Deut. 22:13-27); if therefore she did marry another man after her divorce, that would indicate that she was not guilty of any offence of which the law took cognizance. And our Lord's ruling against divorce, on the basis of the creation ordinance, provided in effect a protection for women who might otherwise be arbitrarily divorced, without opportunity of redress. As for Mark 10:12, we must remember that under Jewish law a wife could not divorce her husband. Under Roman law, however, she could; and our Lord may have had some particular case in mind. Some of the ladies of the Herod family, being Roman citizens, availed themselves of their rights under Roman law to divorce their husbands, and quite recently there had been a notorious case of this— the case of Herodias, who divorced her husband Herod Philip so as to marry his brother the tetrarch of Galilee. In that case the woman was the guilty party, from the standpoint of Jewish law. There is thus no inconsistency.

Further to this question, could not the modern difficulties about divorce and remarriage be avoided if the church leaders made a "no divorce" rule binding, in the sense of Matt. 18:18? Would not such protect the children?

The elders might certainly, in keeping with their responsibilities and in fellowship with the church membership, make such a rule binding. But this would not necessarily be a final solution. A really difficult case might arise, and the rule might be broken. What then? If the elders felt that some measure of discipline was called for, it would have to be applied with delicacy and discretion; otherwise the parties involved would probably leave that church and seek fellowship where it would be granted them. Scriptural standards ought to be maintained, but their maintenance in the secular and ecclesiastical situation in which we are placed today calls for quite extraordinary wisdom on the part of responsible leaders, as they endeavour to reach a right judgment on each case as it arises.

Should a Christian who marries a divorced person (the innocent party) be debarred from communion?

The circumstances which require exclusion from the Lord's Table, according to the New Testament, are few and well defined; I do not recall that the situation you mention is included among them.

Millennium

Are we right in expecting a millennium?

My own judgment on this vexed question, from which many Bible students more competent than myself would dissent, is that Scripture encourages us to believe that on this earth, where He was rejected and crucified, Jesus will ultimately receive universal and joyful recognition as Lord and King. This is simply to say that I do not believe we are deluding ourselves when we sing such hymns as "Jesus shall reign," but rather that these express the teaching of Scripture. If this is what is meant by a millennium, then my answer to your question is "Yes."

Please say a few words in clarification of the essential features of amillennialism,

227

and its relation to premillennialism and postmillennialism.

All these terms have to do with the interpretation of the millennium or "thousand years" of Rev. 20:1-7, during which Satan is bound in the abyss and the faithful confessors and martyrs come to life and reign with Christ (whether in heaven or on earth is not stated here). The premillennial interpretation regards the advent of Christ as taking place before this period (hence the prefix pre-); the amillennial and postmillennial interpretations regard the advent as taking place after it. The premillennial and postmillennial interpretations share the view that the millennium is to be realized on earth at a time yet future; the amillennial interpretation identifies it with the present reign of Christ at the right hand of God (1 Cor. 15:25), where by faith His people are raised and seated with Him (Eph. 2:6; Col. 3:1). The term "amillennial" is thus strictly a misnomer; the amillennialist does not deny the millennium of Rev. 20 but interprets it as being present, not future. The premillennial and amillennial interpretations were both held in the early Christian centuries; the postmillennial interpretation as we now know it was held by some Puritan exegetes in the seventeenth century; it envisages the millennium as the final and most glorious age of the church, resulting from the world-wide dissemination and acceptance of the gospel. But the first proponents of this view preferred to base it on Rom. 11:11-32. As for the binding of Satan in Rev. 20:1-3, premillennialists and postmillennialists think of this as future, whereas amillennialists prefer to identify it with the binding of the strong man through our Lord's ministry (Matt. 12:29; Mark 3:27). If I may interpose a personal observation, it seems plain to me that the binding of Satan in the abyss in Rev. 20:1-3 is later than his being thrown down to earth in Rev. 12:9, and that (in the light of Luke 10:18) it is his being thrown down to earth that is the immediate consequence of our Lord's ministry. John in the Revelation views Satan as unbound and raging on earth at the time of writing, and at that same time the souls of the martyrs are still awaiting their vindication (Rev. 6:9-11); not until the tale of martyrs is complete do they receive their vindication and enthronement (Rev. 20:4). It will no doubt be said, and said quite truly, that in these few words I have oversimplified the three lines of interpretation referred to in the question, especially as each of them, in practice, involves other features than the interpretation of Rev. 20. But (largely on this same ground) it may also be true that each of these three lines of interpretation, taken by itself, oversimplifies the Biblical data. If we are content to follow the relevant passages of Scripture as they come, we can dispense with interpretative labels; I for my part would not care to wear any of them.

Ministry

Is there any scriptural foundation for an "any man" ministry? If not, what are the principles of the New Testament concerning "the ministry"?

The answer to your first question is "No, certainly not." And the answer to your second question is to be found in such places as Rom. 12:6-8; 1 Cor. 12:4-11, 28f.; Eph. 4:7-16. The teaching of these and other relevant Scripture is that Christians are responsible to cultivate the various ministries for which they are gifted. The particular ministry which you have in mind is the ministry of the Word; those who are qualified to engage in this ministry have a responsibility to exercise this gift for the glory of God and the edification of their fellows, and the other members of the church have a responsibility to give them full opportunity for its exercise.

Some Christians condemn "one man ministry" in the homeland, but practise it on

*the foreign mission field. Is it really
unscriptural? What is wrong with having
a full-time pastor in the Scriptural
sense of that word?*

To answer your last question first,
there is nothing wrong with it; who said
there was? A full-time pastor is as Scripturally justified as a full-time evangelist; and
many local churches are spiritually declin-
ing for lack of adequate pastoral ministry.
The "one man ministry" which is deprecated is the system in which one man is
charged with performing not only the
ministry for which he is gifted, but all the
other ministries for which he is not gifted.
Of course, both in this country and
overseas it may happen that a man is
obliged to discharge various forms of
ministry for which he is not qualified
simply because there is no one available
who is so qualified. My own experience
does not enable me to judge whether this
is more in evidence on the foreign mission
field than it is in the homeland, but if so,
it is a question of available resources and
not a distinction of principle.

Modernism

What is Modernism?

The term might be defined in a technical
way, by reference to the movement in the
Roman Catholic Church associated with
the names of Alfred Loisy and George
Tyrell, or to the Modern Churchmen's
Union in the Church of England. But as
more popularly used (and I think it is the
popular use that the questioner has in
mind), Modernism is a name given to that
trend of thought which (among other
things) tends to regard our Lord rather
as the finest flowering of humanity than
as the incarnate Saviour, tends to regard
His redemptive work rather as a supreme
example of self-sacrificial love than as a
divinely provided satisfaction for sin,
and tends to regard the Bible rather as a
record of man's quest for God than as the
record of God's self-revelation to man.

Nazarenes

Who are the Nazarenes?

If your question relates to the Church
of the Nazarene, this is the largest contemporary organization of those who are
sometimes called "Holiness People", because of the emphasis which they lay on
John Wesley's doctrine of sanctification.
The Church of the Nazarene represents a
merger over many years of several per-
fectionist movements and groups in the
U.S.A. and in this country; within recent
years it has incorporated the Calvary
Holiness Church, well known and highly
respected in some northern cities of
England. An authoritative account of the
tenets and history of the Church of the
Nazarene in Britain is *In the Steps of John
Wesley*, by Dr. Jack Ford (Kansas City,
1968). If, on the other hand, you have in
mind the Nazarenes of Eastern Europe,
they are located mainly in the Danube
valley and the Balkan lands. You will find
a sympathetic account of them in E. H.
Broadbent's *The Pilgrim Church* (1931),
p. 329ff. He had first-hand acquaintance
with them, and won their confidence to a
point where they were willing to look on
him as one who was "not far from the
kingdom of God"! Their movement is
traced back to the conversion and testimony of a Swiss preacher, S. H. Fröhlich,
in 1828. The Nazarenes are simple and
inoffensive people, practising New Testament principles of Christian worship and
non-conformity to the world. "They
live so quietly, so much to themselves, that
they would hardly ever be heard of except
for their constant conflict with the various
Governments, due to their absolute refusal
to bear arms." Their movement has been
carried by emigration to America. It may
be worth pointing out that in Semitic
languages (Arabic, Hebrew, etc.), to this
day Christians as a whole are generally
described as "Nazarenes."

Nebuchadnezzar

Why is the great Babylonian king's name

spelt sometimes Nebuchadnezzar and sometimes Nebuchadrezzar, and in some versions Nabochodonosor?

The spelling Nebuchadrezzar represents the consonants of the Babylonian form (Nabu-kudurri-uzur) more accurately; the spelling Nebuchadnezzar represents the pronunciation which became current among the Jews (perhaps because they found it easier); Nabochodonosor is the form which the name takes in the Greek Bible, and preserves the original vowels better than the other forms do.

Open Brethren and Spiritual Liberty

I recently saw a letter signed by the leader of a Bible Teaching Conference, in the course of which he said: "One of the things that attracts many of us to the Christian Brethren is its breadth, not its narrowness." Do you think this is generally true?

My own experience certainly confirms that of the writer whom you quote. In the course of my academic peregrinations, as student and teacher, over the past forty years and more, I have been for shorter or longer periods a member of seven or eight churches of "Open Brethren", and have visited many other in both hemispheres. In them I have regularly found an atmosphere of spiritual and intellectual liberty so congenial and indeed exhilarating that I doubt if it could be surpassed elsewhere. The acknowledgment of the paramount authority of Scripture has been united with a readiness to receive whatever fresh light God might yet have to break forth from His Word. Neither in biblical study and exposition, nor in my collaboration with people of other traditions and viewpoints have I been conscious of any inhibition on the part of my brethren; on the contrary, I have uniformly enjoyed their fellowship and encouragement. In my professional life I am naturally dedicated to the principle of academic freedom, and I have no sense of tension between the atmosphere of free enquiry in which my university work is conducted and the atmosphere in which I share the worship and service of the local church to which I belong. No doubt there are exceptions to what I believe to be the general rule among Open Brethren; occasionally one hears of a local church which is subjected, in matters of doctrine and practice alike, to the dictates of one man or one family or one clique. Such a situation is deplorable, but happily not typical; in fact, one sometimes hears of this sort of thing in other circles. It is a failing of human nature in general, not of Brethren in particular.

In the answer to the last question, you say that you have no sense of tension between the atmosphere of free enquiry into Biblical learning proper to a secular university and the atmosphere of a local church. Is there not a difference between the specific commitment which is fundamental to the latter and the specific lack of commitment which is fundamental to the former.

I did not say that the atmosphere was the same in the one place as in the other, but that there was no sense of tension between the two. Besides, I should not agree with your reference to a "specific lack of commitment" in the academic atmosphere of free enquiry; there is a specific commitment to follow truth wherever it may lead. And for a Christian who believes Christ to be truth incarnate and knows the whole world to be God's world there can be no inhibitions in the pursuit of learning or any fear lest "inconvenient" facts should come to light. He has learned that the universe is a rational universe because God is its Creator; he knows that all truth is God's truth and must therefore ultimately be revealed as self-consistent, however difficult it may be for us with our partial vision to see it so at present. I think of one whom many of us used to know as an elder statesman of the Inter-Varsity Fellowship, the Rev. G. T. Manley. In

1893 Mr. Manley gained the coveted distinction of Senior Wranglership in the University of Cambridge; that is to say, he headed the list of honours graduates in Mathematics. (Bertrand Russell appeared in the same list.) Not long before he achieved this success, Mr. Manley was converted through a CICCU sermon. In the correspondence on "Fundamentalism" which appeared in the columns of *The Times* in August, 1955, Mr. Manley recalled that when he was converted as an undergraduate he "felt a new responsibility for thinking out the foundations upon which the Christian faith rested" and found that "a true conversion is rather a stimulus to study than a check upon it." His testimony is true, and can be amply corroborated by the experience of others. Just as, in the ethical realm, the service of God is perfect freedom, so in the intellectual realm the knowledge of God is perfect freedom.

In your pamphlet Who are the Brethren? *(Pickering and Inglis, 1961), you say that no single line of prophetic interpretation is held or imposed among the churches of Open Brethren. But is there not a tendency for those who hold a majority view (whichever direction the majority view may take in any given assembly or area) to discourage the expression of a minority view?*

No doubt there is such a tendency; it is not confined to any one community in particular. The tolerance of minority views (not to speak of a Voltairean determination to defend to the death the other man's right to express them) does not come naturally to any one; it is a delicate plant of late growth, and can very quickly be killed. Of course there are faults on either side. I have heard a speaker, about to deal with some aspect of biblical interpretation, say that he does not wish to be controversial, and then defend a partisan viewpoint with such warmth as to make it plain that, in

his judgment, the charge of being controversial lies against those who differ from him. On the other hand, some proponents of minority views get the idea that the teaching of these views is a sacred trust which they must at all costs discharge, and so they press them in season, out of season (and especially out of season), until their hearers long for a change. But my experience confirms me in the belief that what I said is true, and I believe there is more Christian tolerance, and a greater willingness to give an unbiased consideration, in the light of Scripture, to new or minority views, among Open Brethren than there is in many circles which at first blush might be thought to be more liberal. Much depends, however, on the way in which a speaker or writer puts an interpretation across. If people immediately get the impression that he thinks they are all wrong and he is right, he is unlikely to win or influence them.

A well-known writer has suggested that among the churches to which most readers of The Harvester *belong there is a nebulous but powerful "establishment" from whose line it is perilous to deviate. Do you think this is so, and in that case can you identify its members?*

The term "the establishment" appears to have been first given by Henry Fairlie to a group of people in public life whose authority is not constitutionally defined but who nevertheless between them effectively condition the climate of public opinion. Among the churches to which you refer an analogous situation can be more clearly recognized on a regional level. Thus, while lip-service might be paid to the independence of the local church, it has frequently been found in the past that the churches in one region have taken a well-defined line on such matters as "reception", prophetic interpretation, attitude to trade unionism and co-operative societies, female hair-style, and so forth. An individual member or church that deviated from the regional line in one of these respects would be regarded, albeit with tolerant good humour, as being out of step. When one inquires into the reason for this, it will sometimes be found that a couple of generations before there was a gifted leader in that region who held and voiced decided views on some of these matters; the younger men of his day, who later became leaders in their turn, grew up as his disciples, and so a climate of opinion was engendered which, to most members of the churches in that region, was as natural as the air they breathed. It is difficult to reproduce the same situation on a country-wide scale, because where spiritual liberty is enjoyed there will be numerous cross-currents. Yet the writer whom you mention shows how such a situation could come about, and he writes from his own experience. The members of such an "establishment" would be, for example, the conveners of influential conferences, members of influential committees, editors of influential periodicals—and possibly, for aught I know, people who answer questions in these periodicals. But since conferences, committees and periodicals do not all take the same line—indeed, some of them (conferences particularly) give the appearance of taking deliberately opposed lines—the danger of having one overall climate of opinion imposed is not very great. Moreover, some *potential* members of such an "establishment" are by temperament and practice as anti-establishment as the writer to whom you refer, and they find that, when they resist or ignore the pressure to conform to the prevalent climate of opinion, life goes on much the same as ever, only more so—just as *his* nonconformity has enabled him to influence the thinking of others in a degree which would not otherwise have been possible.

Parables

Is there no allegorical element in any of the gospel parables?

There may be in some; in one or two (e.g. the Parable of the Vineyard) it is fairly plain. But in general it is best to take the parables as parables, stories told in order to drive home one particular point. To try to allegorize the several features of a parable lands one sometimes in unnecessary complications—as, for example, when the interpretation of the Parable of the Ten Virgins is made to depend on the answers given to such questions as "Who is the bridegroom?" "Who is the bride (who does not figure in the normal text of the parable)?" "Who are the wise virgins?" "Who are the foolish virgins?" "What are the lamps?" "What is the oil?" And even "What is the wick that sucks up the oil?" I know that answers have been given to all these questions, just as (to take another example) allegorical identifications have been offered in the Parable of the Good Samaritan for the priest, the Levite, the Samaritan, the Samaritan's beast, the victim, the thieves, the innkeeper, the inn and the two pence—not to mention Jerusalem and Jericho and the road between them. But all this is irrelevant. The point of the latter parable is "Go and do likewise" as surely as the point of the former is "Keep awake for you know neither the day nor the hour."

Pentecostalism

Can you suggest why there has been a revival of interest in "Pentecostal" activities? What might it be a reaction from?

I am not the best person to answer this question, as the recent revival of interest in these activities is known to me only by hearsay; I have not come into personal contact with it. But the analogy of similar revivals at other periods in Christian history suggests that it might be a reaction from over-organization and too much intellectualism in the life of the church. Whether this is actually so in the present situation those with direct experience of it may be able to say.

232

Prayer

It is frequently emphasized that the more people there are who pray for a certain blessing, the more likely is the desired answer. Although I have been a Christian for many years, I do not understand why this should be so.

I think some speakers and writers express themselves unwisely on these matters. Our Lord does emphasize the importance of fellowship in prayer, but He gives the most emphatic assurance to two of His people who agree on earth as touching anything that they shall ask (Matt. 18:19). The 1859 revival has been traced back to a prayer-meeting of four young men in an Antrim village. We are, of course, glad to see great multitudes united in prayer—glad especially for their sakes—but we should not imagine that God is more impressed by the prayers of ten thousand than He is by the prayers of ten.

Is any point of principle involved in the question whether God should be publicly addressed as "Thou" or "You"?

No, none. The fact that people who use the pronoun "you" in the singular for most purposes continue to address God as "Thou" is an accident arising out of a development of pronominal usage within the English language. At one time (as still in some English dialects) "thou" was used for all purposes as the pronoun of the second person singular; when the plural "you" began to encroach on its province, "you" was regarded as the polite form and "thou" remained as the familiar form. In Biblical language no distinction at all is made in this respect between the form used for addressing God and that used for addressing anyone else. Does anyone seriously consider, that God Himself is at all concerned about a matter of this kind? When our Lord addressed God, and taught His followers to address Him, by the term for "Father" habitually employed in the affectionate informality of the family circle, I expect a number of people felt it mildly irreverent to hear God being called "Abba." What is important is that children of the heavenly Father should speak to Him in language which comes naturally and spontaneously, and not in language which they feel to be artificial and stilted. By use and won't I myself use "Thou" when praying both publicly and privately; but there are some people who would get all tied up if they tried to do so, because they don't know the proper verbal forms which go with "Thou." It ill becomes us to criticize our brothers and sisters for the way in which they talk to the Father of us all.

Preaching

As I compare the booklet God's Way of Salvation, *by the late Alexander Marshall with much gospel preaching that I hear today, I am struck by the difference between the two. That booklet emphasizes believing on the Lord Jesus as the One who died and bore our sins; much gospel preaching today says we must pray to be saved and ask the Lord to come into our hearts. Which is right?*

Undoubtedly the gospel as Alexander Marshall sets it forth in *God's Way of Salvation* is the New Testament gospel. The glory of the New Testament gospel is that it encourages us to place all our trust in the work of Christ and the word of God. These are things which never change, and are not at all affected by our moods or feelings or inward experiences. A subjective presentation of the gospel, on the other hand, encourages me to look back to something I have done, and in times of doubt or depression I may well wonder whether I did it right, whether my confession of faith was genuine, whether I really gave my heart to the Saviour or not. How much better to say,

"My hope is built on nothing less
Than Jesus' blood and righteousness; . . .
His oath, His covenant, His blood
Support me in the 'whelming flood."

233

What are the essential points which should be covered in preaching the gospel?

There is only one essential point, and that is that "Christ Jesus came into the world to save sinners"; but it can be presented in a wide variety of ways. Preachers—and especially young preachers—should be advised that it is neither desirable nor practicable to cover the whole "plan of salvation" or declare "the whole counsel of God" in a single short address. This may underline the importance of consecutive ministry, in which different aspects of the gospel can be dealt with systematically. A preacher will also ask himself (if he is wise) what particular presentation of the message is likely to be of most help to the particular group of people whom he is to address. If he makes his preaching truly expository, he will run no risk of always harping on one string, yet he will never miss the essential point. For the Scriptures, amid their infinite variety, testify of Christ, and the preacher's aim is to show his hearers their need of Christ, and Christ's all-sufficiency to meet that need.

Should we not more carefully note the kind of "gospel" our Lord Jesus Christ, the great Sower, preached in His earthly ministry—e.g. in the Sermon on the Mount?

This question reminds me of a remark I once heard made in a broadcast talk by my Manchester predecessor, the late T. W. Manson, to the effect that the Sermon on the Mount is nowadays "a very popular substitute for the gospel." (Not that he was depreciating the Sermon on the Mount; on the contrary, he was expounding it.) The Sermon on the Mount is not called the gospel. The gospel which our Lord proclaimed, especially to "the poor" (Matt. 11:5; Luke 4:18), was the good news that the kingdom of God had drawn near, that the acceptable year of the Lord had arrived, that the salvation so long foretold was at hand. The apostles later carried forward His joyful message by proclaiming that this salvation had been secured for mankind by His death and resurrection. In the Sermon on the Mount He laid down the rule of practice for His followers, the only firm foundation for life. If even the righteous requirements of the law could not be fulfilled except by the power of the Spirit (Rom. 8:4), still less could the higher standard of the Sermon be attained apart from His power. And the way to receive the Spirit is fairly clearly indicated in Acts 15:7-9; Gal. 3:2; Eph. 1:13.

Should a preacher attack persons by name in the course of his address?

No, if by attacking persons you really mean attacking persons. But it may sometimes be necessary to refute in public views expressed by certain persons, and even to name these persons as holding the views in question. For example, say that Mr. Smith, an eloquent and persuasive preacher, comes to my town, and some of the people from my place of worship are attracted by his ministry. Good and well; until I learn that Mr. Smith holds and propagates doctrines which in my judgment are subersive of Biblical Christianity. Then I may think it wise in the course of my own ministry to say why I regard these doctrines as pernicious, and it might even be advisable to add that these are the doctrines which Mr. Smith maintains. If I do that, some people will accuse me of attacking Mr. Smith, and some will go so far as to say that I am jealous because Mr. Smith is attracting bigger audiences than I do. (Let me hasten to add that the situation I have sketched is wholly imaginary, and that, so far as I remember, I have never publicly named anyone in this way!) But of course I am not attacking Mr. Smith; I am simply trying to show that Mr. Smith's views are unscriptural. And Mr. Smith is perfectly free to return the compliment and refute my views. This sort of thing can be done in perfect courtesy. What is intolerable is indulgence in personal denigration—a practice more restrained in this country than in some others because our laws of slander and libel are fortunately stricter. I well remember being greatly shocked in my late teens when a Scots preacher (long since with God) referred publicly to an eminent Christian scholar as having "spat in the face of Christ." It was the only occasion in my life when I felt like walking out of a public meeting in protest, though I did not do so. Even if the charge had been justified (instead of being absurdly baseless), it would have been grossly discourteous to express it in such terms. I do not know if I have touched the kind of situation my questioner has in mind, but I hope some of my remarks may be helpful.

Predestination

Considering that predestination, with reference to man, is mentioned so seldom in the New Testament, and also having in mind Rom. 11:33f., do you agree that any pronouncement on the subject should be brief and guarded?

Yes, of course; and I imagine that no reasonable person would disagree. But I should insist still more that any pronouncement on the subject should be in accordance with the teaching of Scripture. And the teaching is that God has predestinated His people to be holy (Eph. 1:4), to be related to Him as sons (Eph. 1:5) and to be conformed to the image of His Son (Rom. 8:29). If to the idea of predestination you add that of election, you may find the teaching of Scripture to be that some are elect in order that through them others may be blessed. When God chose Abraham He certainly had this purpose in mind (Gen. 12:3b); and what was true of Abraham is true also of Abraham's spiritual seed. This is rather different from a widespread impression which has it that some are elect and the rest without more ado consigned to perdition. It is a good thing to refresh our minds every so often by going back to the Scriptures and see what they really teach.

Please elaborate your statement that we "may find the teaching of Scripture to be that some are elect in order that others through them may be blessed."

Here are a few scriptures to consider. In Matt. 25:34-40 those who are addressed by the Son of Man as "blessed of my Father" and enter into life are clearly distinguished from "these my brethren." In Rev. 21:24 "the nations shall walk amidst the light of" the New Jerusalem, which symbolizes the community of the elect. And in Eph. 1:9f.; 3:8ff., the church (consisting of those who, according to Ch. 1:4, were chosen in Christ before the world's foundation) is presented not only as God's masterpiece of reconciliation but also as His pilot scheme for the reconciled universe of the future. Both in this world and in the world to come, it appears, the elect of God are the vehicles of His blessing to others. See pp. 196f.

Regeneration

When a well-known religious writer of our day says "I belong by nature to the 'once-born' rather than to the 'twice-born' type", does he mean that he is unregenerate?

No; in the next sentence he says: "I have never really doubted the fundamental truth of the Christian faith." He uses the terms "once-born" and "twice-born" to denote two different types of experience in psychological and not in theological terms. The psychological use of these two terms goes back to F. W. Newman, *The Soul: Her Sorrows and her Aspirations* (1849) and was popularized by William James in his *Varieties of Religious Experience* (1902). This use has little or nothing to do with the New Testament teaching about regeneration. A "once-born" type in this psychological sense may be regenerate, and a "twice-born" type may be unregenerate. It is surprising that a generally well-informed reviewer in an evangelical weekly should have taken the statement quoted in your question as an admission by the writer that he is not "born again" in the sense of John 3:3; it shows how careful writers should be to avoid being misunderstood even by intelligent readers.

Resurrection

What (if anything) comes out of the grave at the Christian's resurrection? Scarcely, I suppose, "our house which is from heaven." If, as we may suppose, the apostle Paul has been with Christ in heaven for nearly two thousand years, will he go back to a grave in Rome in order to be raised from the dead at the Second Coming?

This is the sort of question that makes me wonder why I ever consented to be responsible for *The Harvester* question page; however I answer it, I am bound to get into trouble in some quarter! Certainly Paul's conscious self does not go back from being "with Christ" to be raised from a grave in Rome. What happens at the resurrection is that Paul's conscious self receives the "body of glory" of which he wrote in Phil. 3:21—an organ of communication with the changed environment and of service under the new conditions of the resurrection age. What relation this body of glory bears to the body which was entombed on the Ostian Way is a question which Paul himself could answer only by analogy—the analogy of the seed sown and the full ear of grain that springs up in 1 Cor. 15:35-49 ("what you sow is not the body which is to be, but a bare kernel"), or the analogy of a new house or a new garment replacing the old (2 Cor. 5:1-10). See p. 101.

Revival

From time to time in the history of the Christian Church there have been out-pourings of the Holy Spirit which resulted in a great number of conversions and the awakening and enduing with power of many Christians. In view of these past incidents and the present indifference to the gospel, should we (a) expect revival in our time—or is the day too far gone? (b) pray for revival?

We should expect it, pray for it, work for it, and make room for it in our own individual and corporate lives, so that it may not come and find us unprepared. Revival is, of course, a reawakening to fresh power and activity of the spiritual life that is already present in the people of God; the conversion of unbelievers is a result of it, but is not the revival itself. The story of similar movements of the Spirit of God in the past is an encouragement to faith: what He has done before He can do again. The secret of the achievement of William Carey (the bicentenary of whose birth we celebrated some years ago) is available to every Christian: "Expect great things from God; attempt great things for God." What is wanted is men who will make themselves as conversant in detail with the need of the world today as Carey made himself with the need of the world in the late eighteenth century, and put themselves at God's disposal for the meeting of that need. But we can become so spiritually dormant that God works and we fail to notice it. Dr. Edwin Orr, who knows more about the history of spiritual awakenings than anyone else I know, holds that our generation has already witnessed a great revival in many parts of the world—beginning in 1948—but the only area in the British Isles to experience it to any marked degree was the Island of Lewis. But it was during that movement that Dr. Billy Graham underwent the spiritual awakening that has enabled him to accomplish so much for the Kingdom of God. Yet there is no reason why God should not revive His people again within the present generation.

Roman Catholicism

Is the pamphlet entitled The Divine Authority of the Holy Scriptures, *attributed to Bishop Strossmayer, a genuine report of his speech at the Vatican Council of 1870?*

Evidently not. The arguments of the pamphlet are good Protestant arguments, but not such as a Roman Catholic bishop would have used in 1870. J. G. Strossmayer, Bishop of Bosnia and Sirmia, was a faithful Roman Catholic, although he disagreed with the Ultramontane school. The burden of his speech at the Council (extracts from which are quoted by Lord Acton in his *History of Freedom*) was that no Pope could on his own authority assume the functions of an ecumenical council (which the Pope virtually did as a result of the infallibility decree of 1870), and that even at an ecumenical council matters of faith should be settled by moral unanimity and not by a majority vote. His speech was punctuated by disorderly interruptions. He did not at first sign the infallibility decree, but submitted later.

What is a Requiem High Mass?

"Mass" is a name popularly given to the Holy Communion by Roman Catholics, Lutherans and some others; the term is apparently derived from the words of dismissal at the end of the service. Among Roman Catholics High Mass is a more elaborate form of the service than Low Mass; Low Mass is *said* whereas High Mass is *sung*, with instrumental accompaniment and certain other adjuncts such as the use of incense. Requiem Mass is the service (High or Low) conducted with a special view to the repose of the soul of one who has died in the faith; it includes features specially appropriate to this purpose (such as the *Dies Irae*) and receives its name from the first word in the prayer: "Rest (Latin *requiem*) eternal grant unto him, O Lord; and let light perpetual shine upon him."

Do not the healings which take place at Lourdes confirm the doctrine of the Immaculate Conception of Mary?

The point underlying your question is that, according to the received account of the origin of the Lourdes cult, the Mother of our Lord appeared to Bernadette Soubirous and said to her: "I am the Immaculate Conception." As this took place in 1858, it was felt to add confirmation to the dogma that Mary was conceived without inheriting the taint of original sin, which had been promulgated four years earlier. As for the healings which take place at Lourdes, it must be remembered that, of the thousands who visit the shrines, very few are officially stated to be cured (the cure of nervous complaints is not reckoned as miraculous). My Roman Catholic informants tell me that the majority of those who are helped by a visit do not return cured, but are enabled to bear their afflictions with more grace and patience than before. In any case, it is illogical to argue from the fact of cures to the truth of the dogma associated with the place where the cures take place. There are many ancient inscriptions at Epidaurus in Greece, testifying to miraculous cures experienced by visitors to the temple of Asklepios there. Some at least of these cures were no doubt genuine, but no one today would suppose that they therefore confirm the local cult-legend of Asklepios. Similar phenomena can be paralleled from sacred sites of many religions. But we have a surer rule of faith by which we may test anything that is offered for our acceptance as Christian dogma. (See also pp. 209f.)

Sacrifices

Is it safe to say that blood-sacrifice in Old Testament times had no more than temporary value (restoring to commonwealth status) unless mixed with faith? And if so, were not Abel, Noah, Abraham and David, all of whom brought blood-sacrifices, saved through the obedience of faith?

The answer to both questions is "Yes." The great prophets had constantly to warn their fellow-countrymen against the prevalent fallacy that the outward performance of the prescribed sacrificial ritual had any value in God's sight unless it was the spontaneous expression, of a loyal and obedient heart. If it was not, it was an abomination to Him. So strongly did the prophets press this home that many of their more recent interpreters (and some of their more ancient ones) have mistakenly supposed their attack on mere sacrifice to be an attack on sacrifice as such. The sacrifices offered by the Old Testament characters whom you have mentioned, and by others who might be added, were the visible token of their inward faith, but it was not their sacrificial work but their faith in God which it manifested that saved them. And when sacrifice was not available their faith saved them none the less. That Old Testament believers were justified by faith as much as we are is evident from Rom. 4 and Heb. 11.

If the penalty for a wilful (high-handed) sin was "cutting off" under the Levitical law, could there have been any sacrificial provision for sins other than unintentional ones?

There does appear to have been special sacrificial provision, by means of sin-offering or "reparation-offering," for a limited class of conscious sins as well as those committed unwittingly (cf. Lev. 5:1ff.; 6:1ff.). But in general it is true to say that there was no sacrificial provision for individuals who sinned "with a high hand" (Num. 15:30), although there were periodical sacrifices for the removal of corporate sin and defilement, such as the sin-offering of the Day of Atonement (Lev. 16) and the ritual of the red heifer (Num. 19). The only recourse for an individual who sinned with a high hand—especially by committing murder, adultery or blasphemy (which included perjury)—

was to cast himself in repentance upon the mercy of God. In his sin against Uriah and his wife, David was guilty of all three (for indirect blasphemy cf. 2 Sam. 12:14); but when he made repentant confession to God and sought His pardon and cleansing, he received through Nathan the assurance of divine forgiveness: "The LORD also has put away your sin; you shall not die" (2 Sam. 12:13). Even under the régime of law, God showed Himself a God of grace.

Salvation

Is there Scriptural warrant for the view that one can be "saved today and lost tomorrow"?

No; the expression is a contradiction in terms, if we use the word "saved" in its Scriptural sense. We must remember, of course, on the one hand, that some may appear or claim to be saved who are not truly so (think of the seed that fell among thorns and on stony ground); and, on the other hand, that some genuine believers "shall be saved, yet so as through fire" (1 Cor. 3:15).

What is meant by the "final perseverance of the saints"?

This is a phrase which conveys the Scriptural truth that genuine believers "by God's power are guarded through faith for a salvation ready to be revealed in the last time" (1 Pet. 1:5). It is founded on our Lord's assurance that His sheep "shall never perish" (John 10:28). It reminds us, too, that continuance in the faith proves the reality of our confession; it is the saints who persevere to the end. The doctrine has found classic expression in English hymnody in Toplady's great hymn, "A debtor to mercy alone."

Sanctification

What is the difference between santification and holiness?

In the A.V. there is no clear difference between the two terms, for they appear

238

as alternative renderings of the same Greek word (*hagiasmos*). The R.V., however, translates *hagiasmos* uniformly by "sanctification," reserving "holiness" as the rendering of *hosiotēs, hagiotēs* and *hagiōsynē*. When this distinction is observed, we may say that sanctification is God's bestowal of holiness upon His people, and that in two senses: (*a*) when He sets them apart for Himself, making them "saints" in the sense in which this term is used of all believers; (*b*) when His Holy Spirit accomplishes His gracious work within us, "whereby we are renewed in the whole man after the image of God, and are enabled more and more to die unto sin, and live unto righteousness."

What is meant by a "clean heart"?

In the New Testament parallels to this Old Testament expression (Psa. 51:10) we read of hearts which God has cleansed by faith, such as the hearts of Cornelius and his friends who believed the gospel when they heard it proclaimed by Peter and received the Holy Spirit in consequence (Acts 15:9); we read of "hearts sprinkled clean from an evil conscience" (Heb. 10:22). So, in this New-Testament age, a clean heart will be the heart of a believer in Christ who has experienced the cleansing efficacy of His sacrificial death and allows the indwelling Holy Spirit to perform His sanctifying work in his life. Such is the heart for which Charles Wesley prays in the hymn "O for a heart to praise my God"—

A heart in every thought renewed,
 And full of love divine;
Perfect, and right, and pure, and good,
 A copy, Lord, of Thine.

How far should we expect conversion to change a man's nature? I have in mind a professing Christian of over thirty years' standing whose ungovernable temper has spoiled his own life and other people's. When this seems to be inherited from one's parents, can conversion alter it?

If you can get hold of a little book by C. S. Lewis entitled *Beyond Personality*, please read carefully the tenth chapter, which he calls "Nice People or New Men." There are in it some very salutary thoughts for "nice people" (those, for example, who are naturally gifted with placid and equable temperaments) and some encouraging words for the "nasty people" who have such a wretched machine to learn to drive. But, strong as the influence of heredity may be, thirty years of Christianity should make some change for the better. There are many well-known cases of people who had all the disadvantages that poor heredity and early environment could bring, and yet have surmounted them all triumphantly, thanks to the gospel; unfortunately, these are counterbalanced by cases of people who have made shipwreck in spite of every natural advantage. It is easy to sit in judgment on such an unpleasant and public besetting sin as an uncontrolled temper, when some Christians may indulge in other, less obtrusive, sins which are equally ruinous. But if there is no sign of victory over a habitual sin of one kind or the other throughout a long period, a professing Christian ought seriously to consider if he has ever genuinely experienced the grace of God. When Christ saves a man, "He breaks the power of cancelled sin."

Saul

Why is King Saul not included in Heb. 11? Would he correspond to a believer today who backslides?

Plainly the reason why King Saul is not included in the survey of Old Testament characters in Heb. 11 is that he could not be described as a man of faith. The tragedy of Saul's life is that, great as his qualities were, they were not equal to the responsibilities of kingship in Israel. So long as he acted as military leader under the general direction of Samuel, his role was one for which he was admirably fitted, and he achieved marked success. But when he asserted his independence of Samuel, whom he knew to be God's mouthpiece, he found that he had outstripped his own capacity; hence the melancholia which darkened his latter days. Had he not been a fundamentally religious man, his spiritual failure would not have preyed on his mind as it did. "If he had been a hard-mouthed creature like Jehoiakim who sat with his toes at the brazier and slit the prophet Jeremiah's roll and tossed it into the fire, he would merely have hardened his heart and gone his own way" (A. C. Welch). He may indeed correspond to a believer to-day who backslides, but to one who backslides as a result of attempting a work for God to which he has not been called, and going down beneath the weight of the consequent spiritual defeat.

Did not King Saul show something of the mind of Christ in advance of his time by sparing the Amalekite king?

We may be very sure that it was not from humanitarian or compassionate motives that Saul spared Agag's life. He had no compunction about wiping out Agag's subjects, regardless of age or sex, although their bloodguiltiness was less than Agag's. It is more likely that, being a king himself, Saul had the idea that a king deserved more considerate treatment than commoners. When Samuel charged him with disobedience to the divine command, it never occurred to Saul to plead humanitarian principles in extenuation.

Science and Faith

Can you conceive of any scientific discovery being made in the future which would seriously affect the validity of the Christian faith?

No; and this is not because I lack sufficient imagination. All future discoveries must be related to that which we already know, and must be interpreted in the light of it. Christian faith is not primarily a matter of intellectual reasoning (though it includes this element); in that case it could be undermined if future discovery proved one link in the chain of argument to be fallacious. Christian faith is primarily a matter of the knowledge and love of God in terms of a personal relationship. Your experience of God over the years is something possessing independent validity, which cannot be undone by some discovery that anyone can make. Or, if you think of the historic events on which the Christian faith is based—the incarnation, ministry, death and resurrection of Christ—it is difficult to imagine what future discoveries could overthrow the evidence on which we accept them, although they might enable us to view it in a fresh light. What we want to bear in mind is that the world is God's creation, and every possible scientific discovery that can be made will be a discovery about the world that God created or the way in which He has created and sustains it, and will give us further cause to appreciate His wisdom and power. Even if the discoveries are as revolutionary as the synthesizing of life in the laboratory or the existence of rational life on other planets, the Christian will take them in his stride. At one time it was argued by some that the Christian faith would be undermined if it were found that human beings lived in the Antipodes, but when visitors from the northern hemisphere made contact with the inhabitants of Australia and New Zealand no one appears to have become an infidel in consequence. Future discoveries may upset our theories but they will only increase our knowledge, and they certainly cannot undo what we already know. See p. 190.

Sectarianism

What is a sect?

A party, something designedly smaller than the whole. It has been said that when two or more congregations or local churches combine to act together ecclesiastically, and recognize a bond between them such as does not exist between *all* such churches or congregations, a sect is formed. C. F. Hogg used to say that a sect is formed when we put a limiting adjective before the word "Christians" or any other word that embraces all the people of God, in order to distinguish some of them ecclesiastically from others. Of course a church may be technically in a sectarian connexion and be completely free of a sectarian spirit, and *vice versa*. A simple way of finding out whether a church is sectarian or not is to inquire whether it imposes any conditions for admitting believers to its fellowship over and above those which Christ has required for receiving them to fellowship with Himself.

Were sectarian barriers between Christians so impenetrable in the early part of the nineteenth century as is frequently asserted?

They were indeed more rigid than they are today. But the situation should not be exaggerated. The story of the Walkerites who, according to W. B. Neatby's information, refused to unite with Thomas Kelly's followers because the latter would not commit themselves to the statement that John Wesley was in hell, reflects a degree of bigotry which would be extreme in any generation. We should remember that the British and Foreign Bible Society was based, right from its foundation in 1804, on interdenominational co-operation. And from the year 1842 there survives a letter by Robert Murray McCheyne (included in his *Memoir and Remains* by Andrew Bonar) on "Communion with Brethren of Other Denominations," which sets forth what probably most readers of *The Harvester* would acknowledge to be the Scriptural position on this matter.

Sin

Are not idle gossip and slandering worse sins than theft?

We do not consider ourselves competent to arrange such sins as these in ascending or descending order of heinousness. Certainly idle gossip and slander are every bit as sinful as theft, and are to be judged no less severely. But your question has been answered in the affirmative in words far more eloquent than this column has at its command:

"Who steals my purse steals trash; 'tis
                              something, nothing;
'Twas mine, 'tis his, and has been slave
                              to thousands;
But he that filches from me my good name
Robs me of that which not enriches him,
And makes me poor indeed."

Is it true that the Christian dogma of original sin, on which the whole evangelical scheme rests, is out of accord with the facts of human life?

I should have thought tha nothing is more completely in accord with the facts as we know them. It is a dogma which hardly needs divine revelation for its acceptance; it could be inferred from our daily newspapers. There is a radical disease that affects all mankind and leaves no area of human life completely uninfected. If we recall the atrocities of the Nazi extermination camps during World War II, we have to reckon with the fact that these horrors were actually perpetrated, and that the people responsible for them were people very much like ourselves, northern Europeans, heirs of centuries-old Christian civilization, who yet could be conditioned to a point where they committed or connived at such atrocities with no particular sense that they were doing wrong, and no thought of assessing their conduct by the elementary rule of "Do as you would be done by." I can understand this problem a little in the light of the biblical teaching about original sin; it would be horribly inexplicable otherwise.

Spirits

Is it possible for a house, once used for

seances, to continue to be inhabited by an evil spirit? I have returned to a house once so used and at times I seem to have a consciousness of this. Is it only imagination? If not, what can one do about it?

I have no experience of this sort of thing, but it would be foolish to dismiss such an undesirable presence as impossible. Even if it is only your imagination, you want to get rid of it. I should suggest that a few of the elders of your church or other Christian friends should be invited to hold a service of prayer in the room affected, asking God in the name of Jesus (before which "devils fear and fly") to banish any evil influence which may survive from the former misuse of the place, and to make the presence and power of Christ very real in the house and in those who live there. Suitable passages of the Bible might be read, and a suitable hymn sung—perhaps the one that begins:

"Spirit divine, attend our prayers,
And make this house Thy home."

It is important, however, that those present at such a service—call it a service of exorcism if you will—should be in earnest about the matter and not treat it as a stunt.

Sunday

Why do Christians observe Sunday as the Lord's day instead of Saturday (the Jewish sabbath)? The only verse I know is Acts 20:7. Are there any other Scriptures showing that the early Christians observed the first day of the week? Is it true that the Emperor Constantine, at the instance of the Bishop of Rome, changed the day from Saturday to Sunday?

Let us get Constantine out of the way first. He did not change one day to another; he enacted that the first day of the week should be a public holiday. Before that, neither Saturday nor Sunday was a holiday for Gentiles (whether Christians or pagans) throughout the Empire. But for generations before the time of Constantine, Christians had come together for worship on the first day of the week, meeting early in the morning before they went to work or late in the evening after their work was done. In the order of creation, one day's rest after six days work is good for men, animals and machinery alike, but it makes no difference where one begins to count the days. Under the Jewish law, the reservation of one day in seven for God was an acknowledgment that the whole week was His, just as the setting aside of a tithe of one's income was an acknowledgment that the whole income was His. But in Christianity the whole matter is set upon a new footing. Whether it be time or property that is given to God, the essence of the giving lies in its being spontaneous and cheerful, not reluctant or constrained. There is no suggestion at all that the observance of the sabbath was enjoined by the apostles on their Gentile converts. On the contrary, we find such words as these: "One man esteems one day as better than another, while another man esteems all days (alike). Let every one be fully convinced in his own mind. He who observes the day, observes it in honour of the Lord" (Rom. 14:5f.). "Let no one pass judgment on you . . . with regard to . . . a sabbath" (Col. 2:16). The very fewness of the references to the first day, to which you draw attention, indicates how little disposed the apostles were to replace the old sabbath law by a new one. Few as the references to the first day are, however, the references to the seventh day in the apostolic age are fewer still. But if we ask on which day Christians did meet for worship in the apostolic and sub-apostolic age, the few indications that we have (e.g. Acts 20:7; 1 Cor. 16:2; and possibly Rev. 1:10, with Didache 14:1) all point to the first day of the week, and we need not look far for a reason for that when we consider that our Lord's resurrection took place on that day. An interesting study of the subject is Willy Rordorf's *Sunday* (London, 1968).

Synagogue

Is there any Scriptural (i.e. Old Testament) authority for the synagogue? If so, where is it to be found? If not, bearing in mind that our Lord regularly attended the synagogue (Luke 4:16; John 18:20) and ostensibly approved of it, what authority have some of our stricter friends for asserting that certain "man-made" institutions do not likewise meet with our Lord's approval?

A synagogue is simply a meeting, or "gathering together," and the coming together of the people of God for prayer and the study of His Word was surely so manifestly in line with His will that it hardly required explicit Scriptural authorization. The Jerusalem temple was the place where sacrificial worship was carried on, but it was only on high days and holy days that the ordinary Israelite could make the journey thither. The local fellowship of the synagogues therefore was something that, from the Babylonian exile onwards, supplied a real spiritual need. Express authorization, if such were necessary, might be found in a passage like Psa. 50:5. The Lord's approval of His people's coming together for these purposes is shown by Mal. 3:16. An actual reference to synagogues has been traced in Psa. 74:8 (cf. A.V. and R.V.), and this is probably right, although some commentators interpret the passage otherwise; another synagogue-reference has sometimes been seen in "the place Casiphia" (Ezra 8:17). As for "man-made" institutions of the present day, while I do not think the analogy with the synagogue has much relevance, it is wise not to be too free with such epithets, especially if they are used in a disparaging sense.

Tabernacle

Was the gateway of the wilderness tabernacle three or four spaces wide (assuming each "space," i.e., the distance between two adjacent pillars, to have been five cubits)?

It depends largely on how we count the pillars. If no pillar is counted twice, so that there were sixty pillars in all, then the space between each two adjacent pillars (on average, at least) was five cubits and the twenty cubits of the gateway (Exod. 27:16) would be equivalent to four spaces. It is possible, however, that the corner pillars are counted twice—that, for example, the south-west pillar is reckoned both as one of the twenty on the south side and as one of the ten on the west side. In that case the gateway would be more like three spaces wide. Some models of the tabernacle follow the one method of reckoning, some follow the other. You should consult the article "Tabernacle" by Dr. D. W. Gooding in the I.V.F. *New Bible Dictionary*; on p. 1233 he discusses the two alternative methods of reckoning mentioned above, but points out that the second one "gives very awkward measurements for the spaces between the pillars."

Tithing

Is it true that a free-will offering can be given to God only after we have already given Him one-tenth of our income? Is the tenth the same for a single person as for one with a family?

First of all, whether we give God one-tenth or nine-tenths of our income, it remains true that we give Him but His own. Then we should remember that in Israel the tithe was an income-tax for the maintenance of the theocratic state. No hard-and-fast regulations are laid down in the New Testament which would yield a cut-and-dried answer to the second part of the question, but it is clearly taught that the proportion of our giving should be, "every man according to his ability." Other things being equal, a single man earning (say) £5,000 a year will be able to give more than a man who has to support a family on the same income. Each Christian must come to a conscientious decision on this subject before God, and

243

not be content to submit to the dogmatic statements of others; and it will be surprising if grace does not impel him to give a larger proportion than ever the law demanded.

Should tithing be on the gross income before taxation or on the net amount actually received?

Anyone who suggested that it should be on the gross income before taxation should be asked to deal with the situation where the taxation amounts to more than nine-tenths of the whole! But the Christian life is not controlled by detailed rules of this kind, which would only have the effect of diminishing the necessity of personal exercize in the matter. What the New Testament teaches on the subject is that a Christian's giving should be regular, systematic and liberal; that he should not ask, "What am I required to give?" but "How much can I give?" and then "How much more can I give?"

Can contributions to worthwhile "secular" causes (e.g., Oxfam) be correctly made out of one's regular tithe, or should the tithe be devoted to specific Christian work carried on by known Christian organizations or individuals?

One of the specific directions for the expenditure of the tithe (Deut. 14:28-29) provides that it shall be shared with the disinherited, the sojourner, the fatherless and the widow. The relief of poverty was one of the purposes for which the tithe was instituted. Apart from any question of the tithe, there is the principle enunciated in Prov. 19:17, "He who is kind to the poor lends to the Lord, and he will repay him for his deed"—which formed the text for Dean Swift's famous one-sentence charity sermon: "If you like the security, down with the dust!" Such charitable causes as you have in mind are most appropriate recipients for your tithe; but in practice it does not matter much whether the help you give them comes out

of your tithe or out of your remaining income. The Lord will reckon it as lent to Him in either case. If you follow the practice of some of our American friends and give your entire tithe to your local church, the church may decide to make a donation to Oxfam or a similar cause, and part of your tithe will go there after all. (Let me add that the view that one's whole tithe should be paid over to the local church, sometimes based on the identification of the local church with the "storehouse" of Mal. 3:10, is not one that I should necessarily endorse.)

Typology

Have we any authority for using Old Testament characters, such as Joseph, as "types" of Christ?

I should say "illustrations" rather than "types." It has often been pointed out that the only Old Testament character who is expressly called a "type" of Christ in the New Testament is Adam (Rom. 5:14). But where an Old Testament character or incident offers itself as an apt illustration of the gospel, the preacher may feel quite free to use it, even if it is not so used in the New Testament. He will not, however, feel himself obliged to find a gospel analogy in every detail. The deception which Joseph practised on his brothers in the matter of his cup (Gen. 44:2ff.) could scarcely be applied in this way. (Incidentally, this deception, even if it was practised for a desirable purpose, is overlooked by those who describe Joseph as one of the few "flawless" figures of Scriptures.) I suppose that a certain analogy between Joseph's career and Christ's is implied, though not expressed, in the course of Stephen's narrative (Acts 7:9-14). I should use such incidents as the healing of Naaman (2 Kings 5), the call of Isaiah (Isa. 6) and the cleansing of Joshua (Zech. 3) with great confidence as illustrations of certain aspects of the gospel, again without pressing every detail or allegorizing the narratives.

Should we look at Solomon's temple in minute detail and draw from it prophecies concerning Christ?

Here again, if certain features of Solomon's temple lend themselves, without forcing, as illustrations of the new temple which consists of the household of faith, good and well. But in the New Testament it is the mobile tent of wilderness days, and not the static edifice built by Solomon, that is presented as "a parable for the time now present" (Heb. 9:9); in fact a contrast between the two is suggested in Stephen's speech, where the former is viewed as more appropriate for a pilgrim people than the latter (Acts 7:44-50).

Would you comment on a statement to the effect that much popular typological teaching about the Mosaic tabernacle is the product of an unrestrained imagination?

When I listen to the exposition of Scripture, I like to be able to weigh the evidence and decide in my own mind whether this is in fact what is meant by the Scripture which is being expounded. But in much tabernacle typology to which I have listened there is no means of controlling what is offered as the spiritual significance of this part or that of the building or its furniture. For example, in Ex. 26:26ff. mention is made of five bars which were to run horizontally round the north, south and west sides of the tabernacle. One interpreter tells me that the middle bar "in the midst of the boards" was hidden from sight and denotes the deity of Christ, while the other four represent the quadrilateral of Acts 2:42—the apostles' teaching and fellowship, the breaking of bread and the prayers. But another interpreter tells me that the boards, which form the framework of the sanctuary, represent our Lord's sufferings on the cross, while the bars represent "the God-given faith of the true church that enables the sanctuary to be

supported upon the redemptive sufferings of Christ"; they are five, because five is the number of grace; they ran round three sides, because three times five means heavenly grace; while the middle one "may well represent Christ, the Man from heaven, whose faith ran from end to end of His life and supports the sanctuary of God formed by His people." There is nothing wrong with the doctrine in either case, but neither interpreter explains why the five bars have the significance which he attaches to them. If I were to enlarge the scope of my research, no doubt I should find other interpreters explaining the bars otherwise. How am I to know which, if any, of their interpretations is the right one? I have some idea of the basic principles of Bible interpretation, but none of these principles will help me here. So I go back to the Epistle to the Hebrews, and content myself with the reflection that, whatever significance may be attached to the individual details, the whole structure, furniture and ceremonial of the tabernacle served as the Holy Spirit's parable or object-lesson to show the inadequacy of an order "according to which gifts and sacrifices are offered which cannot perfect the conscience of the worshipper, but deal only with food and drink and various ablutions, regulations for the body imposed until the time of reformation" (Heb. 9:9f.). Interpretation of the tabernacle will be more solidly based and the more spiritually helpful in accordance as it rests upon the teaching of the Epistle to the Hebrews, where the relation between the earthly and the heavenly sanctuary is presented as much in terms of contrast as in terms of comparison.

In the light of Ex. 7:10-12 and Num. 21:8f. would it be right to think of the serpent as a type of Christ?

No: Ex. 7:10-12 is irrelevant, and when our Lord in John 3:14f. refers to the brazen serpent of Num. 21 He is using the incident as an illustration, not as a "type." The only point of comparison between the brazen serpent and the Son of Man is that both were "lifted up." There was no healing virtue in the serpent itself, nor any special sacredness (see 2 Kings 18:4); it was modelled, in fact, on the very creatures that had wrought such deadly havoc. The bitten Israelites were cured by obeying God's command. But there is an infinite wealth of healing virtue in the Saviour who was lifted up on the cross.

It seems to me that the detailed exposition of the Levitical sacrifices, spiritualized so as to refer to our Lord, involves considerable reading into the Old Testament text. Should not the fact that they are not treated in this way in the New Testament make us cautious about expounding them thus?

No doubt the ritual details have sometimes been interpreted in a manner which draws largely upon the interpreter's imagination. But the spiritualization of these sacrifices goes back to Old Testament times. Thus in Hos. 14:2 the repentant Israelites, realizing what kind of sacrifice is truly acceptable to God say: "so will we render as bullocks the offering of our lips" (echoed in Heb. 13:15, where the Septuagint text is followed). In Psa. 40:6-8 (quoted and applied in Heb. 10:5ff.) it is stated that God does not take pleasure in the four main varieties of sacrifice but in the obedience of a heart which delights to do His will. And this principle is supremely illustrated in the devotion of the Suffering Servant, who spontaneously yields up his life as a guilt-offering to make the many righteous (Isa. 53:10f.). Already in the Old Testament, then, we find anticipated the New Testament doctrine of acceptable sacrifice, exemplified primarily in the perfect self-offering of Christ, and then in the "living sacrifice" which is the believer's "reasonable service" or "spiritual worship" (Rom. 12:1). If the Levitical offerings are sanely expounded in such a way as to bring out these lessons, good and well. But when they are thus expounded, their limitations will be borne in mind; their typical teaching is one of contrast more than comparison, "for it is impossible that the blood of bulls and goats should take away sins" (Heb. 10:4).

Universalism

It is urged by believers in the ultimate reconciliation of all men to God that any other view is a reflection on God's power or else on His love. Have you any comment on this?

The doctrine of ultimate universal reconciliation is so obviously one that every Christian would wish to believe if he could, that the fact that many Christians find it impossible to accept it suggests that it is beset with serious difficulties. We know that God has pledged His word to bless and save all those who repent of their sin. There never was, and never will be, a sincere act of repentance for sin against God anywhere in His universe without an immediate response of His forgiving grace. But what if some will not repent? Are there not those who by deliberate persistence in rebellion against the known will of God render themselves incapable of repentance, and would refuse God's mercy even if it were thrust upon them? I say "even if it were thrust upon them"; but in fact God does not violate the personalities of those whom He has endowed with moral responsibility. He desires freely consenting servants and worshippers, not reluctant or mechanical slaves. If men choose irrevocably to follow their own way instead of His—if they say, like Milton's Satan, "Better to rule in hell than serve in heaven"—they may do so, but God has warned them of the consequences of their wretched choice. "In the long run, the answer to all those who object to the doctrine of hell is itself a question: 'What are you asking God to do?' To, wipe out their past sins, and, at all costs, to give them a fresh start, smoothing every difficulty and offering every miraculous help? But He has done so, on Calvary. To forgive them? They will not be forgiven. To leave them alone? Alas, I am afraid that is what He does" (C. S. Lewis, *The Problem of Pain*, p. 116).

Women and the Church's Ministry

Is there any evidence known to you, scriptural or otherwise, to show that women exercised the gift of an evangelist (Eph. 4:11) in the early days of the Church?

I cannot recall any such evidence to mind, so far as the public exercise of this gift is concerned. This relates, of course, to the specific gift (cf. also Acts 21:8; 2 Tim. 4:5), and not to every Christian's permanent duty of public and private witness. Chrysostom uses a feminine noun meaning "evangelist" with reference to the woman of Samaria (John 4:29, 39, 42), for example, but something more official than this is implied in the question, I think.

If women's ministry is excluded in mixed gatherings, why do those brethren who exclude it read books by such women as Ada Habershon?

It would be more appropriate that those brethren should be asked this question directly. But, in so far as I can interpret their thoughts on the matter, I suggest that their answer—and an eminently reasonable and scriptural one—would be that they find the writings of Miss Habershon (and other women who might be named) helpful in the understanding of Scripture and in the promotion of spiritual life. But if once this principle is conceded, where is it going to lead?

Can you recommend some work which treats the question of the ministry of women in a helpful way?

Yes, one of the best works known to me on the subject is *The Ordination of Women to the Priesthood*, by Margaret E. Thrall (SCM Press, 1958). As the title indicates, Dr. Thrall writes more directly for the Anglican situation; but when the necessary translations and adjustments are made, in terminology and so forth, her treatment will be found relevant far beyond that situation. That is because she takes quite seriously the biblical teaching on the subject and does not ignore it or try to get round it. No treatment of the subject will be theologically satisfactory which does not do justice to the place of woman in creation and grace. Too often her Christian status has been understood as though it were simply a continuation of subjection to the "rule" of Gen. 3:16. On this H. L. Ellison has an important remark to make in *The Message of the O.T.* (The Paternoster Press, 1969, p. 20): "the misunderstanding of the judgment on Eve . . . has lived on in the Church. Her love for her husband was to be turned to 'desire'. This is a rare word, found only three times, and its use in Gen. 4:7 indicates something of the wild drive involved in it. Her husband would take advantage of it to rule over her. There is nothing in the Hebrew to suggest either a command or something seemly in a woman's being ruled by her husband. The ruling in place of partnership is a sign of the Fall." The new creation does not abrogate the order of the first creation, so long as temporal existence persists, but the reign of grace undoes the effect of the fall, and restores woman's proper "authority", of which in 1 Cor. 11:10 her veil was the symbol. Wearing that symbol of authority she had liberty to pray or prophesy in meetings of the church. (See p. 95.)

Worship

In view of the references in the New Testament to the singing of psalms, should not some provision be made for this means of praise by Christian people?

Are not the hundred and fifty Psalms implied in these references?

No doubt the references to "psalms" in the New Testament do include the Old Testament Psalter, but possibly other hymns of praise as well. But there is provision made in most Christian groups for singing suitable parts of the Old Testament Psalter. In my native country of Scotland we have traditionally had the whole metrical Psalter bound in at the end of the Bible. Even in England, most hymn-books have a selection of versions of the Psalms, though they are not always recognized as such. For example, do we remember that when we sing "Jesus shall reign" or "Hail to the Lord's anointed" we are singing a version of Psa. 72, that "Praise, my soul, the King of heaven" is a version of Psa. 103, "O worship the King" of Psa. 104, and that "O God our help in ages past" is a version of Psa. 90? I should not care to restrict congregational praise to the hundred and fifty Psalms, as do some Christians for whom I have a specially high esteem; but I should prefer to do that than to have to sing some of the ditties that pass for Christian praise in this generation.

Since our worship ought to be offered to the Father (cf. John 4:21-24; Col. 1:12; Heb. 13:15), why are so few hymns in certain collections addressed to Him, the majority being addressed to the Son? Is not the Father thereby robbed?

I do not suppose it possible that the Father can be robbed because His children give too much glory to the Son: it is His will "that all may honour the Son, even as they honour the Father" (John 5:23). None of us can ever honour the Son so highly as the Father Himself has honoured Him, and when we bow the knee in Jesus' name and confess that He is Lord, we glorify the Father in so doing (Phil. 2:9-11). In one of the earliest descriptions of a meeting of Christians after New Testament times (that reported by the younger

Pliny about A.D. 112), we are told how "they came together on a fixed day before sunrise and recited an antiphonal hymn of praise to Christ as God." But, when that has been said, it remains true that worship is properly offered to the Father through the Son in the power of the Spirit. If you ask on what principles the compilers of certain hymnbooks have made their selections, I can only reply that life is full of mysteries, and that is one of them. But English hymnody abounds with immortal compositions which have served successive generations of Christians as vehicles of true worship and praise to God the Father, and there are several hymnbooks which contain a high proportion of these.

Would you accept the implications of the remark attributed to General Booth: "Why should the devil have all the good tunes?" Is it desirable to sing sacred words to secular tunes?

The devil has no good tunes, just as he has no title to anything else that is good. He may steal them; he cannot compose them. Everything that is good comes from God. It is desirable to sing sacred words to appropriate tunes; drawing the frontiers between sacred and secular tunes would be a difficult task. I was brought up in an environment where "I heard the voice of Jesus say" was sung to "The Auld Hoose," "O Christ, what burdens bowed Thy head" to "The Rowan Tree," "I am waiting for the dawning" to "Just before the battle, mother" and "Faint not, Christian, though the road . . ." to "Killarney" (it will be gathered that we used *The Believer's Hymn Book* but did not confine ourselves to the tunes printed in the music edition). Some of these settings were more suitable than others, but no one found anything undesirable about any of them.

Further to the previous question, is there not a danger that the associations of some "secular" tunes might take some people's

minds off the meaning of the "sacred" words they were invited to sing to them? And is there not an even greater danger, as Sir Robert Anderson used to argue, of using words in Christian praise which (to whatever tune they are sung) are more appropriate to the music hall than to the worship of God?

The first danger which you suggest is conceivable; I have never been put off by such associations myself, but this may be because I know the "sacred" words to several of the tunes I mentioned better than the "secular" words. For example, I know only the first line of the song "Just before the battle, mother," but when I hear the tune I think either of "I am waiting for the dawning" or of "When we reach our peaceful dwelling." The tunes, as I emphasized, must be appropriate, and for people who would be put off by them they would *not* be appropriate. As for the second danger you mention—yes, of course. I am insufficiently acquainted with modern hymnology to judge it in this regard, but long exposure to popular hymns of the later 19th and earlier 20th centuries has forced certain conclusions on me. If I may venture on a quotation of a kind rarely found in the pages of *The Harvester*, there was a very popular ditty in the earlier 19th century which ran something like this:

"She's all my fancy painted her;
   She's lovely, she's divine;
But her heart it is another's
   And she never can be mine.
Yet loved I as man never loved,
   A love without decay;
And my heart, my heart is breaking
   For the love of Alice Grey."

(Readers of Dickens may recall how Dick Swiveller parodies the second stanza in *The Old Curiosity Shop*.) Why do I quote this here? Simply because one index of its popularity is the way in which its phraseology or cadences influenced expressions in "sacred songs" composed in the decades following its heyday. If I had

unlimited money, and nothing better to do with it, I think I might pay someone to pursue a course of research in order to discover how frequently and how pervasively snatches of this short sentimental composition were echoed in popular hymns, especially in expressing a believer's feelings towards the Lord. The results of such a survey would be impressive, but not edifying. How Christians whose tastes should have been conditioned by Watts and Wesley—or, for the matter of that, by Darby, J. G. Deck and Sir Edward Denny—could tolerate this sort of thing for so long is difficult to understand.

Some of our teachers deprecate what they feel to be undue concentration in Christian worship on the physical aspect of the Lord's sufferings, either in hymns or in meditation. What do you think about this?

It is perhaps best to observe the proportion and reserve which we find in the New Testament itself. No doubt it was unnecessary for the New Testament writers to instruct their readers in the details of death by crucifixion; nevertheless, the last thing that the Evangelists aim at in their passion narratives is the eliciting of pity for the sufferings of the Crucified One. I know that much Christian piety has been nourished by concentration on the wounds of Christ, but in this regard the frontier between pure adoration and morbid sentimentalism is dangerously thin. Much hymnody on this subject has passed right over from the former to the latter; I had better not to be too specific, as I should inevitably be found criticizing some people's favourite hymns. But I will mention two hymns: Charles Wesley's *O love divine! What hast thou done?* (as originally given, and not in the denatured corruption found in certain collections) and F. W. Faber's *O come and mourn with me awhile!* Both deal with the passion of our Lord; each has as its refrain an adaptation of a well-known sentence of

Ignatius (albeit not in the Ignatian sense): in the former, "My Lord, my Love is crucified", and in the latter, "Jesus, our Love, is crucified." It is a good exercise to compare the two, and to discover why Wesley's is so superbly effective, not a foot wrong, not a word out of place, and why the latter—well, why the latter could be described by Sir Robert Anderson as displaying "the mawkish irreverence of the love-song, combined with the revolting materialism of 'the religion of the shambles'" (*The Buddha of Christendom*, p. 311). I cannot agree entirely with Sir Robert's description, for I will not charge anything with irreverence if it is not irreverently intended; but the whole composition, however viewed, is wide open to criticism. Unless this kind of thing is done right, it is better not done at all.

What is the "well-known sentence of Ignatius" and the "Ignatian sense" to which reference is made in the answer to the last question?

In his letter to the Roman church, written on his way to Rome to be exposed to the beasts in the arena, Ignatius says "My love (*erōs*) has been crucified" (7:2). A long-standing interpretation of these words takes them to refer to Christ, as the Beloved of his soul (hence their use in hymns by Zinzendorf, Wesley, Faber and others); but their context makes it much more probable that Ignatius, in imminent and eager expectation of a martyr's death, means that all his earthly and temporal desires have been crucified with Christ (in the sense of Gal. 5:24; 6:14). "My *erōs* has been crucified," he says, "and there is in me no fire of love for material things . . . I have no delight in corruptible food or the pleasures of this life. I desire the 'bread of God' which is the flesh of Jesus Christ . . . and His blood, which is love (*agapē*) incorruptible."

Writing

How far back in history was writing practised?

Writing is known to have been practised at least as early as 3000 B.C. About that date we have evidence for the use both of the cuneiform scripts of Mesopotamia and Elam and of the hieroglyphic script of Egypt.

In what sort of script did Moses probably write?

Most probably in an early form of the North Semitic alphabet, which came into use two or three centuries before the time of Moses.

INDEX OF SUBJECTS TREATED

ABBA, 233
Abiding in Christ, 71f., 133
Abomination of Desolation, 34, 58f., 59
Adultery, 43, 69f.
Affluent Society, 56
Albury Conferences, 199
Allegory, 47, 52f., 61, 232
Almoners, 77, 79
Amillennialism, 228
Angels, 78, 79, 95, 121, 138
Anger, 106f.
Anointing, 126f.
Antichrist, 113, 139, 140, 153f.
Antinomianism, 113, 131, 220
Apocalypse, 136
Apocrypha, 150f.
Apostasy, 72, 102, 121f., 124f., 134, 154
Apostles, 75, 77, 89, 105, 106, 141, 142
    Authority, 91, 180
    Teaching, 234
Apostolic Age, 76, 97
Apostolic Council, 41, 49, 80
Apostolic Succession, 154
Arian Controversy, 24
Atonement, 44f., 229

BACKSLIDING, 240
Baptism:
    Jewish, 67
    John's, 67
    Essene, 67
    Christian, 65, 67, 78, 86, 97, 102, 108, 109, 171
Baptismal Regeneration, 75f., 83ff., 127f.
Beast, Number of, 140, 154
Beatific Vision, 125f.
Bible:
    Authority of Text, 176
    Interpretation, 6, 30f., 58, 66, 101, 113, 117
    Translation, 36, 39, 68, 90, 93, 160, 211, 221
Biblical Criticism:
    And Inspiration, 217f.
    Higher, 156
    Lower, 156, 158
Binding & Loosing, 48
Birth
Blasphemy, 46f., 66, 72, 91, 113
Body of Christ, 65, 96, 172
Book of Life, 110
Breaking of Bread, 76, 82, 83
Brethren:
    History, 126, 163ff.
    Raison d'être, 225
    Letter of Ten, 164f.
    Assemblies & Pastors, 184f., 229
    Function of Trustees, 185
    Discipline, 165, 227
    Remuneration of workers, 186
    Stated ministry, 187, 225, 228, 234
    Doctrine, 165f.
Bride of Christ, 141

CALENDARS, 168
Calvary Holiness Church, 229
Canticles, Book of, 26
Capital Punishment, 9, 10, 59, 70, 77, 204
Catechumens, 171
Celibacy, 93
Cherubim, 18
Children of God, 67, 133
Christians, 62, 79, 146
    Hellenistic, 77, 79, 81
    Jewish, 80f.
Christology, 24
Christophanies, 6
Chronology, Biblical, 169f.
Church:
    ekklēsia, 48, 49, 52, 76, 115f., 196
    Local independency, 180f.
    Leadership, 115, 117, 183
    Membership, 181, 188, 220, 222, 241
    And the Kingdom of God, 221f.
    And the New Creation, 172, 235
    And the Canon of Scripture, 170f.
Church Unity, 103, 105
    New Testament principle, 181, 195, 241
    Darbyite principle, 118, 194f.
Church of the Nazarenes, 229
Circumcision, 67, 104, 108
Cities of Refuge, 17
"Clean Groundism", 195
Collection, The, 79, 80, 103, 181
Confession, 189
Consecration, 88
Conversion, 50f., 80, 239
Council of Jehovah, 4f.
Council of Trent, 47
Covenant/*diathēkē*, 123
Creation, 2, 22, 190, 193
    instrumentality of Christ, 191
    ex nihilo, 125
Credal formuli, 25, 106, 190
Cremation, 35
Crucifixion, 64f., 65, 178f., 191
Cup of Blessing, 93f.

DAVIDIC KINGSHIP, 17, 25, 60, 80, 120f., 140
Day of Atonement, 11f., 122, 123
Deaconesses, 184
Deacons, 77, 79, 115, 182, 185
Dead Sea Scrolls, 14, 21f., 65, 77, 141f., 147ff., 158
Death, 22, 30f., 85f., 96, 180
    spiritual death, 86f., 104
    Christians and death, 88, 101, 104, 109, 129
Decalogue, 70, 81
Demon-possession, 42, 44, 191
Didaché, 100, 106, 242
Discipleship, 51, 53, 54
Dispensationalism, 80, 154, 191, 222
Divorce, 54, 193, 226f., 91f.
Docetism, 133f.

Doctrine, 192, 193, 234
    Danger of clichés, 216
    Theologizing from Scripture, 71, 76, 83, 125, 171, 176, 196
    Federal Theology, 205f.
    Covenant Theology, 205

EASTER, 194
Ecumenism, 194f.
Eldership, 79f., 115, 117, 168
    Qualification, 184
    Totalitarianism, 181
    Teaching office, 182
    Retirement, 183f.
Election, 79, 87, 114, 196f., 197f., 235
Epilepsy, 42
Eschatology, 42, 53, 148
    Realized, 117f., 198
    Inaugurated, 199
Eternal Life, 22, 52, 61f., 85, 87, 202
Eternity, 2, 202, 203
Eucharist, 4, 57, 64f.
Evangelicalism, 164f., 203f., 205
Excommunication, 90f., 204
Exile, 28, 29, 36, 243
Exodus, 7ff., 28, 170
Exorcism, 241f.

FAITH, 48, 56, 75f., 80, 85, 86, 204, 220, 240
Fall, 206, 247
Fate, 205
Fatherhood, 105
Feasts, Jewish, 69, 70
Fellowship, 76, 80f., 96, 181, 224
First-born, 13, 25, 108
First-fruits, 209
Flesh, 86, 116
Flood, 55, 169
Forgiveness, 13f., 48, 51f., 76, 206
Fornication, 43, 80f.
Freedom, 231
Fry MS, 199
Fulfilment, 75, 87, 89, 94
Fundamentalism, 206, 230

GENETICS, 6f.
Gentiles, 39, 48, 59f., 64, 65, 67f., 70, 80f., 85, 87, 89, 111, 127, 139, 201
Gifts, spiritual, 62, 78, 80, 96f., 97f., 106, 207
Glossolalia, 97f., 207, 214f.
Golden Calf, 10, 18
Gospel, 44, 46f., 50, 53, 58, 148, 208, 221f., 233
Guilt, 86

HANNUKAH, 70
Head Coverings, 94f.
Healing, 127, 209f., 237
Heaven, 210
Heavenly Voice, 45
Hell, 51
Heresy, 192, 199, 212
Holiness, 86, 103, 125, 194, 238f.
Holy Shroud, 212f.
Holy Spirit, 5, 10, 40, 46f., 53, 62, 65, 69, 73, 75, 78, 83, 89, 161, 166f., 214
Hope, 131, 198

IDOLATRY, 10, 18, 80, 113
Immortality, 86, 215

Infant Dedication, 215f.
Inspiration, 216, 217f.
Insufflation, 73
Irreverence, 250

JUDGMENT, 40, 44, 46, 50, 54, 56, 60, 61, 68, 86, 90, 101f., 103, 127, 218f., 205.
Justification, 86, 89, 125, 198, 219ff.

KEYS OF THE KINGDOM, 50
Kingdom of God, 43f., 46, 47, 50f., 55f., 58, 63, 67f., 139, 147, 199, 221f.
Kingdom of Heaven, 46, 47, 50f., 221

LAWS AND THE CHRISTIAN, 5, 16, 51, 81, 86, 101
Laying on of Hands, 116, 121, 222
Letters of Commendation, 100f., 224f.
Lord's Day, 88
Lord's Prayer, 43, 222f.
Lord's Supper, 62f., 95f., 100, 218, 223, 225, 227

MAN, 3, 5, 15, 86, 205f., 222
Many, The, 86, 197
Maranatha, 100, 142
Mass, 237
Memorial, 95
Messiah, 22, 27f., 28, 37, 48, 64, 120f., 140, 149
Millenium, 141, 227f.
Moabite Stone, 19
Modernism, 229
Mystery, 89, 139

NATURAL REVALATION, 205
Nature, 85, 90
New Creation, 65, 190, 205
New English Bible, 21f., 39, 48f., 89, 160
"New Lumpism", 195

OLD TESTAMENT USAGE, 41, 215

PAPACY, 152, 153, 237
Parables, 46, 47, 52f., 54, 57, 61, 70, 176f., 232
Passover, 8f., 63, 65, 75, 144, 194, 212, 223, 225
Pater Noster, 146
Pentecost, Day of, 48, 53, 154
Pentecostalism, 232
Perseverence of the Saints, 51, 71f., 88f., 125, 218f., 238
Polygamy, 115
Postmillenialism, 228
Prayer, 71, 232
Preaching, 233f.
Predestination, 235
Premillenialism, 228
Prophecy, 97f., 99, 116, 130, 136
Psalm Titles, 21f.

REGENERATION, 49, 66, 235
Remembrance, 95
Remnant, 148
Repentance, 76
Reprobation, 87
Resurrection, 31, 60, 63, 70, 125, 142, 236
    Resurrection Body, 100f., 142, 235f.
    Present Experience, 86, 109
Revelation, 205, 216
Revised Version, 159f., 161
Revised Standard Version, 27, 85, 89, 160, 162

Revival, 236
Righteousness, 85, 220

SABBATARIANISM, 242
Sacrifice, 14, 32f., 44, 238, 246
St. Thomas, Gospel of, 151f.
Salvation, 51, 52, 56, 72, 75f., 80, 85, 114, 221, 238
    Of God, 90f., 101, 103, 125, 157
Sanctification, 125, 238f.
Schism, 194
Science and Faith, 240
Scofield Reference Bible, 4, 11, 17, 27, 80, 111
Second Advent, 100, 199
Second Death, 30, 50, 215
Secret Mark, 151
Secret Rapture, 199f., 200
Sectarianism, 240f.
Separatism, 118, 131, 194
Septuagint, 41, 44, 157, 162f.
Sermon on the Mount, 42, 234
Sickness, 43, 127
Sin, 11, 44, 85f., 88, 238f., 241
    Original sin, 23, 86, 241
    Mortal sin, 134

Sukkah, 69
Sunday, 82, 223, 242
Synagogues, 50, 94f., 114, 243

TEACHER OF RIGHTEOUSNESS, 148f.
Temple, 54, 70, 71, 77, 124, 243
    New Temple, 105, 124
Temptation, 40, 44, 51, 121, 126, 137
Time, 2, 190
Tithing, 243f.
Tribulation The, 54f., 138f.
Trinity, 2, 26, 65, 106, 134
Truth, 134, 148, 193, 205, 230, 240
Typology, 12, 47, 110, 244ff.

UNIVERSALISM, 202, 246f.

WESTMINSTER CONFESSION OF FAITH, 192, 205, 217
—— Shorter Catechism, 9, 172, 192f., 205f.
Women, 51, 95, 99, 115, 116f., 184, 226, 247
Worldliness, 50, 189
Worship, 107, 173, 247ff.

INDEX OF PERSONS AND PLACES

AARON, 10, 11, 41
Abiathar, 17f.
Abner, 17
Abraham, 15, 25, 49, 70, 145, 169, 235
Absalom, 17
Achan, 15
Acton, *Lord*, 237
Adam, 4, 73, 197, 205f., 244
Adonis, 34
Agabus, 97
Ahab, 19, 39
Aland, K., 158
Albright, W. F., 150, 170
Alexander, 113
Alexander the Great, 157
Alexander, W. M., 191
Alexandria, 86
   & Christianity, 151
Alford, *Dean*, 112, 216
Alfred the Great, 81
Allegro, J. M., 150
Amenophis, 8
Amusin, I. D., 149
Ananias, 50, 83f.
Ananias son of Nedebaeus, 84
Anathoth, 18
Anderson, *Sir* Robert, 9, 156, 249f.
Andronicus, 106
Antioch, 64, 79, 80, 103
Antiochus Epiphanes, 34f., 70, 140, 157
Apis, 10
Apollos, 82, 101
Aquila, 27, 82
Armenians, 35
Arndt-Gingrich, 61f.
Assyrians, 28, 29, 31, 35, 99, 178
Athaliah, 39
Athenians, 39
Augustine, 47, 190
Augustus, 141
Azariah, 20
Azazel, 11f.

BABEL, 6
Babylon, 19, 28, 30f., 31, 36
   Symbolized, 152f.
Banks, F. A., 167
Barkokhba, 146
Barnabus, 79f., 103, 106, 119
Barrett, C. K., 66
Barth, Karl, 155f.
Beasley-Murray, G. R., 31
Beek, M. A., 8
Belial, 156
Ben-Gurion, D., 8f.
Bengel, J. A., 85
Bennet, W. H., 165

Berkhof, L., 205
Berkouwer, G. C., 155
Bernard, T. D., 58
Bethel, 18
Bethlehem, 25
Bezalel, 10
Black, M., 147, 158
Blaiklock, E. M., 136
Bonner, A., 241
Booth, *General*, 248
Borland, Andrew, 108
Bowyer, W., 128
Bozrah, 29
Broadbent, E. H., 229
Brown, C., 156
Brown, J., 213
Brown-Driver-Briggs, 210
Brownlee, W. H., 150
Bruce, F. F., 64, 83, 102, 148, 150, 158, 170, 171, 190, 204, 206, 217, 228, 231
Bunyan, J., 119
Burns, R., 197, 241
Burrows, M., 150
Butler, S., 164
Butler Stoney, J., 119

CABLE & FRENCH, 163f.
Cadman Colwell, E., 66
Caesarea, 80
Caiaphas, 84, 90
Cain, 4, 134, 209
Calvin, J., 102, 113f., 197f., 205
Campbell Morgan, G., 3, 210
Capernaum, 42, 45
Cardale, E., 199
Carey, W., 236
Carpocrites, 151
Caven, *Earl of*, 164
Cephas, 48
Chadwick, 99
Chapman, R. C., 185f., 187
Charles, R. H., 217
Christ:
   Incarnation, 66, 72, 148, 158, 173
   Dual Nature, 50, 172, 173
     Humanity, 72, 116, 133
     Divinity, 68, 72, 109, 150, 162, 173, 207f.
   Death, 65, 72, 77, 133, 144, 165
     As sacrifice, 44, 46, 94, 95, 125
   Resurrection, 127, 179f.
   Ascension, 10, 106, 116
   Lordship, 40, 110, 139, 141
   Cosmic Rôle, 24f., 121, 172
   Second Coming, 13, 22, 49, 56f., 57, 62, 136, 200

   Parousia, 57, 63, 200
   Day of Christ, 51, 110, 219
Christie, W. M., 42
Chrysostom, 104, 111, 115, 159, 247
Church of the Holy Sepulchre, 144f.
Clark, R. E. D., 9
Claudius, 141
Clement of Alexandria, 34, 151
Cleopas, 65
Clermont-Ganneau, 153
Coad, F. R., 164, 165, 188
Cocceius, J., 205
Constantine, 158, 159, 242
Cornelius, 48, 50, 56, 78, 80, 85, 166
Craik, H., 165, 188
Cross, F. M., 150
Cyrus, 29, 79

DAN, 18
Daniel, 29, 33
Darby, J. N., 22, 61, 111, 165, 166, 194, 200, 226, 249
—— Bible Translation, 63, 78, 83, 94, 115, 116, 117, 118, 121, 134, 173
Darbyites, 199
Darwin, C., 207
David, 16ff. pass., 20, 41, 79, 145f., 238
Davidson, A. B., 122
Deck, J. G., 249
Delitzsch, F., 15, 123
Demas, 118
Denney, E., 131, 249
Dickens, C., 249
Didymus, 151
Driver, G. R., 65
——, S. R., 17, 23
Drummond, H., 199

EDEN, 31f.
Edersheim, A., 12, 69
Edom, 29, 87
Eerdman, B. D., 23
Egypt, 7f, 29
Elihu, 16, 29
Elijah, 38, 46, 50, 64, 67, 83, 125, 153
Elisha, 78, 83, 125
Ellicott, C. J., 160f.
Ellison, H. L., 20, 21, 30, 35, 208, 247
Enoch, 128
Epiphanius, 134
Erasmus, 134, 159
Esau, 87, 134
Essenes, 147, 149
Ethbaal II, 32

Ethiopia, 29
Ethiopian Eunoch, 78
Euphrates, 15
Eusebius, 152, 158
Eutychus, 82f.
Ezra, 27, 29

FABER, F. W., 249f.
Farquharson, J., 35
Fenton, F., 161
Fertile Crescent, 32
Fisher, W., 197
Flinders Petrie, 9
Foakes-Jackson, F. J., 171
Ford, J., 229
Fröhlich, S. H., 229
Fuller, T., 170

GABRIEL, 67
Gadarenes, 45
Gaebelein, F., 192
Gaius, 141, 152
Galatia, South, 80
Galba, 141
Galilee, Lake of, 41, 44
Gaster, T. H., 148
Gehenna, 30, 50
Geldenhuys, N., 62
Gergasenes, 44
Gesenius-Kautzch, 210
Gethsemane, 44, 79
Gilgamesh Epic, 169
Gitta, 77
Gnostics, 5f., 151
Godet, 40
Gog, 32
Goliath, 17
Gooding, D. W., 243
Goodspeed, E. J., 71, 94, 115, 116, 128
Gordon, S. D., 192
Gosse, P. H. & E., 163ff.
Graham, Billy, 204, 236
Grant, F. C., 162
——, F. W., 165
Grant, R. M. & Freedman, D. N., 152
Green, M., 56
Griesbach, J. J., 158
Groves, A. N., 126, 195
Guillaume, A., 65
Gyges, 32

HABERSHON, A., 247
Hades, 22
Hadrian, 145
Hall, P., 199
Hammond, T. C., 48
Haran, 15
Hargrove, C., 164
Harris, J. C., 164
Harrison, R. K., 23
Hart, H.St.J., 178
Hebron, 17
Hegesippus, 175
Herculaneum, 146f.
Herod Agrippa I, 146
Herod Antipas, 45, 46, 64
Herod Philip, 227

Herod the Great, 35, 146, 168
Herodias, 55, 227
Hillel, 55, 67
Hippolytus, 34
Hiram, 18
Hodge, C., 95, 96
Hogg, C. F., 42, 103, 111, 112, 170, 186, 209, 241
Hogg-Watson, 222
Hooke, S. H., 116
Hort, F. G. A., 76, 158f., 161
——, G., 7
Hoste, W., 179, 215
Housman, A. E., 156
Howard, W. F., 79
Hughes, A., 33
Hyksos, 8
Hyland, T. M., 168
Hymenaeus, 113, 117

IBNU'l-FARID, 26
Ignatius, 137, 250
Inge, Dean, 62
Irenaeus, 34, 139
Irving, E., 199
Isaac, 25, 70
Israel, the Nation, 6, 87
Israel, son of Isaac, 218
Isserlin, B. S. J., 24

JACOB, 6f., 13, 14, 87f., 218
Jairus's daughter, 45f., 83
James, brother of Jesus, 79, 80, 144, 175
James, son of Alphaeus, 45
James, W., 235
Jehovah's Witnesses, 30, 66, 108
Jephthah, 15f.
Jeremias, J., 144
Jerome, 47, 104, 150
Jerusalem, 27, 29, 59, 79f., 144f., 145f., 146
Fall of, 57f., 59, 64, 127
the spiritual, 141
Jesse, 16
Jesus, 40, 45, 54
Historical, 144, 148, 149f.
Birth of, 25, 39f., 40, 66, 168, 169
Virginal conception, 40, 162
'almah, 27f., 39f.
bethulah, 27f.
parthenos, 27, 39, 92
Geneologies, 37f., 39, 60
Physique, 175
Languages used, 175f.
Family, 47, 174, 175
Sinlessness, 121, 176
Baptism, 46, 67
Temptations, 41
Gethsemane, 179
Trial, 64, 178
Descent into Hell, 191
Sufferings, 178, 249
High Priesthood, 121ff., 131f., 177, 183f.
Agrapha, 83, 151
Titles of
Lamb, The, 110

Light of the World, The, 66, 195
Mediator, The, 48, 190
Son of David, 80, 120
Son of God, 24f., 47, 68, 69, 171f., 174
monogenēs, 24f.
Son of Man, 41, 46, 53, 60, 61, 63, 68, 140
Word of God, 66
Jews, 70, 80, 85, 87f., 147
Jezebel, 39
Joab, 17, 18
Joad, C., 210
Job, 21, 29
John the Baptist, 46, 50, 67, 97, 221
Johnson, A. R., 3
Joram, 39
Joseph, father of Jesus, 40, 47, 61
Joseph, son of Jacob, 13
Josephus, 8, 35, 53, 144f., 168
Joshua, the High Priest, 37
R. Judah ben Tema, 40, 91
Judah, tribe of, 18
Judas Iscariot, 51, 63, 68, 71, 75, 218
Judas Maccabaeus, 70, 146
Junias, 106
Jupiter Capitolinus, 34
Justin Martyr, 77

KAHLE, P. E., 169
Kelly, J. N. D., 190
Kelly, T., 241
——, W., 35, 75, 110ff., 138, 166, 200
Kenites, 147
Kenyon, K., 144f.
Kidron, 71
Kilpatrick, G. D., 158
Kirkpatrick, D., 177
Kitchen, K., 7
Kittel, G., 21
Knox, R. A., 116, 162
Köhler-Baumgartner, 210

LAMSA, G. M., 163
Lang, G. H., 43, 123, 200
Langdon, S. H., 169
Lazarus, 44, 62
Leclercq, H., 213
Levi, son of Alphaeus, 45
Lewis, C. S., 23, 239, 247
Lightfoot, J. B., 109, 216
Lincoln, W., 164
Lloyd, S., 162
Loisy, A., 229
Lucifer, 28
Luke, 64
Luther, M., 153, 220
Lysimachus of Alexandria, 8

MACKINTOSH, C. H., 166, 176
McKnight, W. J., 58
Machen, J. G., 60
Magog, 32
Manean, 64
Manasseh, 12f.

Manetho, 8
Manley, G. T., 230f.
Manson, T. W., 46, 70, 184, 234
Margoliouth, D. S., 26
Mark, John, 119, 151
Markham, E., 204
Marshall, A., 233
Martha, 62, 101
Mary, mother of Jesus, 40, 47, 60, 140, 174, 237
Matthew, 45
Matthias, 75, 142
Mauro, P., 35
Mayor, J. B., 135
Melkart, 32
Melchizedek, 6, 122
Merenptah, 8
Mesha, 19
Metzger, B. M., 66, 158
Michael, *Bishop*, 150
Miller, A., 180
Milton, 3, 246
Mixture, R. L., 190
Moab, 19
Moffatt, J., 71, 78, 91, 94, 114, 116, 128, 162, 177
Moltmann, J., 198
Montanists, 152
Montefiore, H. W., 197
Montgomery, J., 160
Moriah, 145
Morris, L., 95
Morton Smith, 151
Moses, 7ff., 41, 139, 149, 250
Moule, C. F. D., 66
——, H., 104, 162, 218
Moulton, J. H., 79, 160
Mudditt, B. H., 183
Müller, G., 165, 187
Murray McCheyne, R., 241

Nag Hammadi, 151
Napata, 29
Nazareth, 40, 47, 147
Nazarenes, 229
Nazirites, 82, 94
Neatby, W. B., 195, 241
Nebuchadnezzar, 229f.
Nehemiah, 27, 29
Nero, 141, 152
Nestle, E., 158
Nevius, J. L., 191
Newberry Bible, 115
Newman, F. W., 126, 235
——, J. H., 202
Newton, B. W., 49, 85, 116, 137, 163, 165, 199, 205
Nicodemus, 67, 68
Nicolaitans, 137
Nicolas, 137
Nile River, 29
Ninevah, 129
Noah, 5, 60f.
Norlie, 23
North, C. R., 30

Ockenga, H. J., 203
Oded, 20
Og, 13
Omri, 19, 77

Origen, 25, 144
Orlinsky, H. M., 27
Orr, E., 236
——, J., 207
Osarsiph, 8
Otho, 141
Otto, R., 207
Oxyrhynchus, 151

Papias, 152
Parker, T. H. L., 156
Parrot, A., 6
Parthians, 35, 141
Paul: 46f., 47, 49, 59, 71, 75, 77, 78, 79f., 83, 84, 86, 142
    Persecutor, 103
    Tent maker, 111
    Authority, 90, 103
    Missionary, 81, 82, 89
    Message, 102, 205
    Sufferings, 109f.
    "Trophies" of, 152
Pearce Hubbard, 145
Persians, 37
Peter, 48f., 50, 53, 68, 78, 79, 80, 85, 152f.
Petra, 29
Pharoah, 7, 87
Pharisees, 69f., 77, 150, 168
Philetus, 117
Philip, apostle, 77
——, evangelist, 77f.
Phillips, J. B., 96, 160
Philo, 122
Pilate, 43, 56, 64, 72, 77, 90, 144, 216
Pliny the Younger, 248
Polycarp, 117
Pompeii, 146
Powell, J. E., 197
Powell Davies, A., 150
Priscillian, 134

Qumran, 21f., 77, 147ff., 151
Quodvultdeus, 140

Rahab, 39
Rackham, R. B., 77
Ramsey, W., 83
Ras Shamra, 27
Rechabites, 147
Redpath, H. A., 31
Rendle Short, A., 6f., 191
Rendel Harris, J., 128
R. Resh Lakish, 31
Robertson, M., 77
Robinson, J. A., 105
Rogers, E. E. W., 184
Romans, 56, 59f., 77, 112, 146
Rordorf, W., 242
Rowden, H. H., 126
Rowley, H. H., 67, 150
Rupp, G., 177
Ryrie, C. C., 192

Sadducees, 150
St. John, H., 62, 183, 212
Salkinson, 15
Salmon ben Nahshon, 39
——, G., 140

Salome, 174
Samaria, 77
Samaritans, 35, 78
Sanhedrin, 76f., 91
Saphira, 50
Satan, 3f., 4f., 21, 28, 31f., 41, 68, 90f., 117, 180, 228
    The Devil, 106f., 248
    The Evil One, 43
Sauer, E., 72
Saul, 239f.
Schmidt, W., 209
Schonfield, H. J., 87
Scroggie, W. G., 2, 23, 155
Scythians, 32
Sebaste, 77
"Septima", 165
Severian, 111
Shammai, 51, 67
Shekhinah, 116
Sheol, 22, 28
Simon Magus, 77, 121
Simon [Leper], 57
—— [Sorcerer], 167
Simpson, E. K., 116
Solomon, 18, 120f.
Soltau, H. W., 12, 163f.
Spurgeon, C. H., 198
Stafford Wright, J., 191
Stauffer, E., 72
Stephen, 77, 79, 169
    Speech of, 244f.
Stibbs, A. M., 129
Streeter, B. H., 188
Strong, L., 163f.
Strossmayer, J. G., 237
Stuart, C. E., 165
Sudan, 28
Sukenik, 153
Susanna, 29
Swete, H. B., 132, 142
Swift, *Dean*, 244
Symeon: See Peter
Syrophoenician woman, 48

Tacitus, 8
Tammuz, 34
Taylor, James Jnr., 195
Temple, W., 71
Tertullian, 34, 205
Theophilus, 171
Thrall, M. E., 247
Tiberius, 141
Tillich, P., 208
Timothy, 113, 116
Tirhakah, 29
Titius Justus, 81
Titus, Paul's friend, 103
——, Emperor, 141, 168
Toplady, 238
Torrey, C. C., 44, 62
Tracy, J., 53
Transjordan, 13, 23
Tregelles, S. P., 35, 116, 137, 187, 199
Troas, 82
Turner, C. H., 164
——, N., 66
Tweedy, 200

INDEX OF PERSONS AND PLACES

Tyndale, W., 196
Tyre, 31f., 32
Tyrell, G., 229
Tyrranus, 81f.

Underwood, A. C., 198
Unger, M. F., 191
Ur, 15, 169
Uzziah, 27, 35

Vespasian, 141
Vine, W. E., 89, 103f.
Vitellius, 141
Von Soden, 162

Warfield, B. B., 201
Watson, J. B., 43, 181

Watts, I., 160, 249
Weiser, A., 24
Welch, A. C., 240
Wesley, C., 65, 131f., 177, 223, 249f.
——, J., 229, 241
Westcott, B. F., 71, 104, 120, 123, 124, 158, 171
Weymouth, R. F., 70, 86, 94, 116, 142
Wigram, G. V., 187, 199
Wikgren, A., 158
Wilder, A. N., 178
Williams, C. B., 49
Williams, K., 116
Wilson, E., 150
Winer, G. B., 160

Wiseman, D. J.169,
Woolley, L., 169
Wuest, K., 161

Yarmuk, 44
Young, R., 15, 16, 160, 220

Zachaeus, 56f.
Zacharias, son of Jehoida, 53
Zadok, 18
Zechariah, 67
Zerubbabel, 37
Zeus, 34
Zimmerli, W., 31
Zinzendorf, *Count*, 250
Zophar, 21
Zwingli, 95f.

INDEX OF SCRIPTURE REFERENCES

Bold figures indicate the main treatment of the passage quoted

OLD TESTAMENT

Genesis:
1:1 **2**, 108, 161, 210
1:2 72
1:26 **2**
1:28 2
2:7 **2**, 73
2:19 3
3:1 **3**
3:14f. **3f.**
3:16 247
4:3f. 209
4:7 **4**, 247
4:8 163
4:14 204
4:26 **4**
6:1–4 127
6:2 **4f.**
6:3 **5**
6:4 17
7:11 5
8:3 **5**
9:1 2
9:3 **5**
9:25 6
11:1–9 **6**
11:26f. 169
12:3 235
13:13 60
14:18–20 **6**, 122
15:1–18 124
15:6 49
15:13 170
15:16 170
16:12 204
17:14 204
21:33 202
22:2 25, 144, 145
22:8 70
30:37–42 **6f.**
37:3 73
40:10 211
46:27 14
48:5 13
48:14f. 13
48:22 13
49:10 **7**

Exodus
3:14 72
3:18 **7**
7–12 **7f.**
7:10–12 245
12:9 212
12:13 **8**
12:15 **9**, 47
12:22 **9f.**
12:33–15:19 **8**
12:37 8
12:40 170
14–15 **9**
14:1ff. **9**
15:26 210
19:1 7
20:7 **9**
21–23 81
22:2f. **10**
24:3–8 124
24:8 125
25:16 123
25:20 31
25:21 123
28:3 10
28:31–35 12
31:3 **10**
31:14f. **9**, 204
32:4f. **10**
35:31 10
40:34 116

Leviticus:
1–3 **10f.**
4:2 **11**
4:3 122
4:22ff. **11**
5:1–6 11
5:11–13 124
5:17 11
11:1–47 6
11:6 **11**
16 **11f.**, 124
17:10 204
18 43
18:5 52

Numbers:
6:1–21 82
6:6 211
7:1 124
10:7 15
10:9 15
11:8 212
14:27 60
16:46 124
17:10 123
19:19 **12**
20:8–11 123
20:10 42
21:6 **3**
21:8f. 245f.
23:21 218
28–29 11
31:16 137
31:50 124
32 13
32:33 **12f.**
33:3 9

Deuteronomy:
1:35 60
3:13–15 13
6:16 42
11:14 **13**
14:3–20 6
14:28f. 244
16:7 212
17:8 210f.
21:22f. 178
22:20f. 43
23:1–3 **13f.**
24:1f. 55, 226f.
32:8 **14**, 163
32:9 14
33 139
33:2 37
33:15 203

Joshua:
6:20 **15**
7:24f **15**
9:23 6

10:1   145
10:5   145
10:23   145
12:10   145f.
17:2   13
20:7   17
22   13
24:2f.   **15**

JUDGES:
1:8   145
1:28   6
5:4f.   37
5:11   16
5:12   106
5:16   23
11:31   **15**
11:39   **15**
11:40   **16**

RUTH:
4:6   **16**

1 SAMUEL:
1:3   7
1:11   215
1:28   215
2:13   212
2:15   212
3   **16**
4:21   16
13:14   79
13:21   **16**
16:10ff.   **16**
17:4   **4**
30:17   28

2 SAMUEL:
2:18–23   17
3:27   17
3:33f.   **17**
4:1   17
5:7–9   145
7:14   120
12:14   234
12:22   92
13:8   212
14:21ff.   **17**
18:5   16
18:29   16
18:32   16
26:19   204

1 KINGS:
2:5   17
2:27   17f.
4:2–19   **18**
6:1   170
6:22   123
6:23   **18**
7:13   **18**
8:9   123
10:19   **19**
12:28   **18**
17:21   83
17:22   125
19:2   50
19:10   50
19:14   50
21:10   21
21:13   21

2 KINGS:
3:4ff.   **19**
4:34f.   83, 125
6:17   78
17:5   35
18:4   246
19:9   29
20:18   33
24:8   **19**
24, 15   **19**

1 CHRONICLES:
2:13–15   16
5:1   13
12:28   16
24   137
27:18   16
29:20   173

2 CHRONICLES:
2:7   18
2:13ff.   18
3:1   145
15:1–8   **20**
19:10   210f.
24:30   53
26:16ff.   35
28:19   **19f.**
35:13   212
36:9   19

EZRA:
8:17   243

ESTHER:
4:14   92

JOB:
1:6   4f.
1:11   **21**
2:5   **21**
2:9   **21**
3:9   28
11:17   28
27:5f.   21
27:13ff.   **21**
28   21
32:6ff.   29
38:12   28
41:18   28

PSALMS:
2:7   120, 171f.
2:9   140
2:11   **22**
4:4   106
8:1   16
14:7   88
16:10   **22,** 36
19:1   **22**
22   179
23:6   **22**
24:7   203
24:9   203
33:6   125
33:9   125
35:25   211
40:6–8   246
40:6   158
45   **23**
50:5   243
51   14

51:5   **23**
53:6   88
68:13   **23**
68:18   106
69:1   211
72   160
73:24   180
74:8   243
77:5   203
79:9   **24**
89:20   79
89:27   25
90   248
90:2   203
91:11f.   41
95:10   60
102:25–27   203
103   248
104   248
104:4   121
105:18   211
110:3   28
110:4   6
118:22   76
125:1   203
137:5   **24**
139:8   180
149:5–9   140

PROVERBS:
8:22ff.   **24f.,** 108
11:30   **25**
19:17   209
22:6   215

ECCLESIASTES:
8:10   **26**
12:1   **26**

CANTICLES:
8:6   38

ISAIAH:
1:18   205
1:26   **27**
6:1   **27**
6:2   3
6:9f.   176f.
7:14   **27f., 39f.**
8:1   37
8:2   53
9:6   **28**
9:7   202
10:3   127
11:2   10, 136
11:15   **28**
14:12   **28**
14:21ff.   **28**
18:1   **28**
19:23–25   28
21:8   147
25:1   **29f.**
27:9   88
27:13   60
28:11f.   98, 99
28:16   157
28:21   129
28:29   28
29:2   **29**
33:21   69

34:4   138
34:6   **29**
37:9   29
39:7   33
40:2   36
40:3   67
41:4   72
44:28   29, 79
45:13   29
51:1f.   49
52:1   29
52:7   29
52:13–53:12   **30**
53:2   175
53:4   44
53:7   110
53:10f.   246
53:10   **30**
53:11   147
53:12   **30**, 44, 63, 109
54:1   29
55:1–3   69, 121
55:3   121
57:15   190
59:20f.   87f.
61:1f.   41, 46, 161
63:1   29
64:1   1

JEREMIAH:
8:6   139
18:2f.   64
19:1–13   64
20:19   111
23:5   37
25:11ff.   211
26:15   36
26:19   36
29:10   211
31:31–34   88, 94
32:6-15   64
33:15   37
51:39   **30f.**
51:57   **30f.**

LAMENTATIONS:
3:4   **31**

EZEKIEL:
1:3   19
1:5ff.   137
1:10   **31**

4:6   211
8:14   34
10:1ff.   137
10:14f.   **31**
13:10   77
21:27   7
27:13   32
28:11ff.   31f.
32:26   32
36:2   203
36:25–27   67f.
37:9   68, 213
37:10   68
37:14   68
38:2   32
38:6   32
43ff.   **32f.**
45:15   32
45:17   32
45:20   32
47:1ff.   69

DANIEL:
1:3   **33**
1:7   **33**
2   139
2:44   **33**, 139, 202
7   139, 140
7:14   139
7:17   **33**
7:22   140
7:27   140
9:24–27   168
9:27   33f.
10:13   14
10:20   14
11:31   34
11:37   **34**
11:44   **34f.**
12:11   34

HOSEA:
6:3   13
6:7   206
10:12   148
12:3–5   218
14:2   246

JOEL:
2:14   92
2:23   148
2:31   75, 138
3:13   211

3:15   138
3:18   69

AMOS:
1:1   **35**
6:10   **35**
9:1   35
9:10   80
9:11   80
9:12   87

JONAH:
2:2–9   35
2:5   211
3:9   92, 129
4:2   129f.

MICAH:
3:12   **36**
5:2   **36**
5:3   27
7:14   36

HABAKKUK:
2:12ff.   **36f.**
3:2   13
3:3   **37**
3:6   203

HAGGAI:
2:7   **37**

ZECHARIAH:
1:1   53
4:2–10   136
6:11   37
6:12   **37**, 72
9:9   72
11:13   63
12:7ff.   **38**
12:10   72
13:1   38
13:5   **38**
14:5   35
14:8   69

MALACHI:
1:2f.   87
1:11   114
3:2   38
3:10   244
3:16   243
4:1   38
4:5f.   **38**, 67

THE NEW TESTAMENT

MATTHEW:
1:2–16   41
1:8   **39**
1:12f.   37
1:15   **39**
1:23   27, 28, 29
1:25   46
2:1ff.   35
2:11   173
2:12   79
2:13   61
2:16   169
2:17   64

2:22   79
3:11   **40**, 97
3:12   46
4:1–11   41
4:5   61
4:6   **41**
4:8   61
4:14   **64**
4:24   42
5–7   **42**
5:1   42
5:8   125
5:16   127
5:22   **42**

5:25   54
5:32   **42**, 54f.
5:33ff.   9
5:34   **43**
5:41   42
6:9   222
6:10   **43**
6:13   **44**
6:19–21   53
6:33   220
7:2   113
7:11   53
7:28   42
8:5ff.   48

8:17 **44,** 64
8:28 **45**
9:9 **45**
9:24 **45**
9:38 **46**
10:9–11 175
11:3 **46**
11:5 234
11:11 **46**
11:14 38, 67
11:27 41, 174
12:17 64
12:28 43, 198
12:29 228
12:31f. **46f.**
12:40 35
13:11–17 176
13:33 **47**
13:37ff. **46**
13:45f. **47**
13:55f. **47,** 174
14:15–33 **47f.**
15:21–28 **48f.**
16:18 **48f.,** 50, 152, 221
16:19 **49,** 73
16:22–28 **46f.**
16:28 **50**
17:10–13 38
17:12 **50**
17:14–18 42
18:1–4 **50f.**
18:7–9 **51**
18:10 79
18:15 **51**
18:17 **52**
18:18 **49,** 73
18:19 233
19:9 42, **50f.,** 54f.
19:2† **55f.**
19:28 27
20:16 57
20:20ff. 148
20:25–28 51
21:18–22 56
21:19 **56**
22:14 57
23:35 **53**
24 138
24:3ff. **57**
24:8 57
24:14 **58**
24:15 **54**
24:15–28 **58**
24:28 56
24:29 **60,** 138
24:30 56
24:31 **60**
24:34 **60**
24:37–39 **60,** 61
24:40f. **60f.**
24:46 56
25:1 **61**
25:31ff. **61f.,** 235
25:46 **61f.**
26:6 **62**
26:28f. **62,** 197
26:29 **63**
26:41 44
26:47 178

26:50 **63**
26:52 **63**
26:64 64
27:9 **63f.**
27:11 **64**
27:36 **64**
27:45 **64**
27:46 **65**
27:56 174, 175
28:16ff. 41
28:19f. **65,** 80, 134, 155

Mark:
1:2f. 64
1:8 154
1:11 171, 172
1:15 33
2:14 **45**
3:27 228
3:28f. **46f.**
4:11f. 176f.
4:26–29 47
5:1 **45**
5:39 **45**
6:3 **47,** 174
6:35–52 **47f.**
7:24–30 **48**
8:14–21 46
8:33 68
9:1 **50,** 222
9:7 116, 171
9:13 **50**
9:42–48 **51**
10:6–8 215
10:12 54, 226, 227
10:25 **55f.**
10:27 56
10:35ff. 151
11:12–24 **56**
11:14 56
11:20–24 **59**
13 138
13:4ff. 57
13:8 **57f.**
13:10 **58**
13:14 **58**
13:14–23 **59**
13:18 **59**
13:25 **60**
13:29 130
13:30 **60**
14:3 **62,** 153
14:24f. 62, **190,** 197
14:25 **63**
14:55–59 77
14:62 72
15:2 **64**
15:8 57
15:33 **64**
15:34f. **64**
15:40 174, 175
16:9–20 155
16:16 155

Luke:
1:4 171
1:15 161
1:17 67
1:26f. 40
1:33 202

1:35 171, 174
1:66 19
1:70 203
2:7 **40**
2:12 **40**
2:33 **40**
2:36 126
2:42 **40**
3:16 **40,** 97
3:17 46
3:21f. 46, 171f.
3:22 171, 172
3:23 40
3:23–38 40
3:27 37
3:31 38
4:1–12 **41**
4:10 41
4:16–19 175
4:18ff. 41
4:18 161, 234
4:25–27 48
5:10 25f.
5:27 **45**
6:13 71, 196
6:17 41
6:17–49 **42**
7:2ff. 48
7:19 **46**
7:28 **46**
8:3 175
8:10 176
8:12–17 **47f.**
8:19 **47**
8:26 **45**
8:31 139
8:49 83
8:52 **45**
8:53 45f., **61**
9:1–6 209
9:23–26 54
9:27 50
10:1 **52**
10:2 **46**
10:17 **52**
10:18 228
10:20 110
10:22 41
10:28 **52**
10:34 **52f.**
11:2 **43**
11:44 **44**
11:13 **53**
11:20 198
11:51 **53**
12:10 **46f.**
12:32 140
12:33 **53**
12:50 222
12:58f. **53f.**
13:20f. **47**
13:21 45
14:33 **54**
16:9 **54**
16:16 221
16:18 55
17:1f. **51**
17:26f. **60**
17:34–36 **60f.**

17:37 **56**
18:13 206
18:25 **55f.**
19:8 **56f.**
19:41–44 53f.
19:44 127
21 138
21:7ff. **57**
21:12 **57**
21:20 58
21:20–24 **59**
21:24 **59**
21:25f. **60**
21:32 **60**
21:36 59
22:15–21 218
22:18 63
22:20 58, 62f., 197
22:29f. 140
22:30 27
22:31f. 132, 177
22:36 **63**
22:53 4
22:70 64
23:3 **64**
23:7–12 **64**
23:28–31 59
23:30 138
23:35 **64f.**
24:25 **65**

JOHN:
1:1 25, **66**
1:3 191
1:9 **66**, 132
1:13 **66**
1:14 24, 116, 175
1:18 24, 171
1:21 **67**
1:29 45, 132
1:32–35 46, **67**, 134
1:43 67
1:45 40
2:1 175
3:3, 5 **50, 67f.**
3:8 **68**
3:13 **68**
3:16 24, 132
3:18 24, 198
3:19–21 66
3:34 136
3:35 73
4:14 69
4:29 247
4:39 247
4:42 247
5:19–21 68
5:19 68
5:20 73
5:22 68
5:23 173, 248
5:25 68, 118, 198
5:26 **68**
5:27 68
5:30 **68**
6:1–14 **47f.**
6:39–44 101
6:54 101, 223
6:70 **68**, 71

7:16 68
7:37ff. **69**
7:39 10
8:6f. **69f.**
8:12 66
8:24 72
8:28 68, 72
8:31f. 51
8:55 **70**
8:56 49, **70**
9:4f. 66
9:38 166, 173
9:39–41 66
10:16 **70**
10:18 4
10:22 **70**
11:11 45
11:24 101
12:32 198
12:35f. 66
13:2 68
13:8 **70f.**
13:23 73
13:27 68
13:31ff. **71**
13:36 71
14:3 61, **71**
14:9 174
14:13f. **71**
14:31 71
15:4 **71f.**
15:6 **71f.**
15:12 133
16:5 71
16:7 154
17 177
17:4 177
17:6ff. 132
17:24 **72**
18:1 71
18:5 **72**
18:11 179
18:33–37 64
18:36 43
19:2–3 178
19:5 **72**
19:14 178
19:16 61
19:25 174, 175
19:26 73
19:31–34 191
19:31 177f.
19:34 **72,** 133
20:7 212
20:22 **73**
20:23 **49**
20:25 191
21:7 73
21:20 73
21:15–17 73

ACTS:
1:5 97, 214
1:9 116
1:15–26 **75**
1:22 106
1:22 106
2:4 214
2:14 75

2:16 75
2:25–31 22
2:20 **75**
2:27 36
2:33 10, 97, 154
2:36 126
2:38 **75f.**, 84, 154, 155, 166f.,
   214
2:42 **76**
2:44f. **76**
2:46 223
3:17 90
3:19 201
3:21 201, 203
4:11 **76f.**
4:13 98
4:27 64
4:36 106
6:1–6 182, 185
6:2 75
6:5 **77,** 137
6:13f. 77
7:2–50 79, 244
7:58 **77**
8:5 **77**
8:12–17 155
8:16 65, **78,** 167
8:17 121, 167
8:26 **78**
8:32 **78,** 110
9:15 196
10:2 56
10:3 78
10:9ff. 47
10:22 79
10:34f. 85
10:38 172
10:44–48 155, 167, 214
11:14 85
11:26 62, **79**
11:28 97
11:29f. 103
11:30 **79**
12 145
12:7 **78**
12:9 78
12:15 **79**
12:25 103
13:1 65, 189
13:10 69
13:13 119
13:17 196
13:22 **79**
13:33 171f.
13:34 121
13:35 36
13:46 48, 50
13:48 110
13:50 49
14:23 **79f.,** 183
15:14 **80,** 197
15:17 87
15:20 43
15:23–29 50, 81
15:29 43, **80**
16:24 178
16:34 **81**
17:2 187
17:4 **81**

17:7   112
17:17   187
17:28   68
17:30   209
17:31   56
18:4   187
18:5   **82**
18:7   81
18:8   **82**
18:18   94
18:19–19:8   187
18:24   **82**
18:27   101
19:5f.   65, 167
19:5   59
19:6   121, 167, 214
19:9   82, 187
19:29–41
20:7   **82,** 223, 225
20:8   **82f.**
20:9f.   **82**
20:11   **83**
20:24f.   58
20:35   **83**
21:8   247
21:10f.   97
21:23–26   82
21:24   94
21:25   43
21:28   77
22:16   **83,** 108, 154
23:5   **84**
24:6   77
26:6ff.   **82**
26:7   126
28:13f.   146
28:28   47
28:31   58, 221

ROMANS:
1:2   89
1:4   127, 171, 172
1:9   43
1:20   22, 202
1:25   113, 203
2:4   87, 131
2:5–7   **85**
2:14   **85**
2:15   85
2:16   209, 219
3:19–30   85
3:21   89
3:28   220f.
3:30   **85**
4:3   118
4:13ff.   192
5:10   104
5:12   **85f.**
5:12–21   138, 206
5:14   192, 244
5:15   102, 197
5:17   220
5:18   **86,** 176, 197
5:19   176, 197
5:20   192
6:2–11   104, 128, 202
6:2f.   155
6:3f.   **86**
6:11   129

7:10   86
7:14   **86**
7:25   86
8   167
8:2   **86**
8:9   214
8:11   127, 129
8:13   **86f.**
8:19ff.   121
8:18–22   172
8:20   170
8:23   101
8:28–30   57
8:29   25, 196, 235
8:30   219
8:34   177
8:37   87
9:1   43
9:13   **87**
9:22   **87,** 196
9:31   85
9:33   157f.
10:4   32
10:5   52, 85
10:7   139
10:11   157f.
10:15   29
10:18   22
11:11–32   228
11:25–27   58, **87f.,** 201
12:1   **87,** 246
13:4   112
14:1   **88**
14:5   242
14:6   194
14:8   **88**
14:15   **88f.**
15:8–12   89
15:16   **89**
16:1f.   101, 184
16:7   106
16:25–27   **89**
16:25   203
16:26   202

1 CORINTHIANS:
1:8   219
1:9   167
1:12   **89**
1:13   89
1:30   176
2:7   203
2:8   **89f.**
2:13   216
2:14   **90**
2:16   **90**
3:3   97
3:16   167
3:17   91
4:3   **90**
4:5   219
5:1   43, 100
5:2   113
5:3–5   50
5:4f.   73
5:5   **90f.,** 102, 134, 219
5:7   194
6:2f.   140
6:4   **91**

6:11   84
6:12f.   81
6:13–20   100
6:14   **109f.,** 200
6:19   167
7:6   226
7:7   **91**
7:15   **91f.**
7:16   92
7:19   104
7:21   **92**
7:25ff.   **92**
7:36ff.   **92**
8:1   98
8:11   **88f.**
9:1   106
10:4   **93**
10:14–22   96
10:16f.   **93f.,** 96
11:3   172
11:4   **94**
11:5ff.   **94,** 99
11:6   **94**
11:7   2
11:10   **95,** 247
11:15   **95**
11:16   100
11:17–34   96
11:17   94
11:24   62, **95f.**
11:25   93
11:26   63
11:29   **96**
11:30   102, 127, 134
11:31   **90**
12:3   65, 207
12:4–6   134
12:7   207
12:8ff.   **96f.,** 214
12:9   207
12:10   **97**
12:11   215
12:13   **97,** 155, 214
12:28f.   214
12:31   53, **97**
13:2   97
13:5   119
13:8   **97**
13:13   207
14   **98**
14:1   53, **97**
14:2ff.   **98**
14:4   214f.
14:16   **98**
14:18   98
14:21   98
14:22   **98**
14:26   **99**
14:34   **99**
14:36   **99**
15   201
15:8   106
15:11   209
15:14   179
15:20   194
15:22   138
15:23–28   131
15:23   110
15:25   141, 228

15:29 155
15:32 110
15:35–49 236
15:45 127
15:48 131
15:51 200
15:52 60, **100**
16:22 **100**

2 CORINTHIANS:
1:14 219
2:5–11 50, **100**
3:1 **100**f.
3:7–18 206
3:17 127
4:10ff. 110
4:14 200
5:1–10 201, 236
5:8 **101**
5:10 **101**f.
5:14 **102**
5:17 172
5:20 **102**, 209
5:21 176, 219
6:1 102
6:15 156
6:17 **103**
8:19 79f.
9:15 **103**
10:7 89
11:3 3
11:10f. 43
11:31 43
12:1 100
12:7–10 209f.
12:7 216
12:8 71
12:19 43
12:21 100
13:8 148
13:14 134

GALATIANS:
1:3 103
1:5 203
1:11f. 216
1:15 207
1:20 43
1:23 103
2:3 **103**
2:10 **103**
2:11–16 193f.
2:18 **103**
3:6ff. 192
3:8 49
3:13 176, 178
3:17 169f.
3:19 122, 192
3:27 65, 155
4:26f. 29
5:6 104, 220
5:22 107, 214
5:24 250
6:5 **103**f.
6:6 117
6:8 87
6:14 54, 250
6:15 104

EPHESIANS:
1:4 196, 235

1:9f. 131, 235
1:10 106
1:13 167
1:22f. 172
2:1–7 104
2:1 **104**
2:5 **104**
2:8 **104**
2:9f. 221
2:10 172
2:13–22 80
2:20 48, **89**, 105, 106
2:21 **105**
2:22 124
3:5 89, 105
3:8ff. 235
3:15 **105**
3:19 **105**f.
3:21 203
4:4–6 134
4:5 **105**, 154, 155
4:8 **106**
4:11 89, 105, 106
4:27 **106**f.
4:30 111
5:9 **107**
5:15 **107**
5:18 **107**
5:19 **107**
5:24 **107**f.
5:25 197
5:26 **108**
5:31 215
6:12 90

PHILIPPIANS:
1:6 219
1:10 219
1:21–24 201
1:21 **109**
1:23 101
1:28 104
2:6f. **109**
2:10f. 173
2:12 200
2:16 219
3:3 30
3:9 176, 220
3:11 **109**
3:20 200
3:21 236
4:3 **110**

COLOSSIANS:
1:15 25, **108**
1:16 191
1:18 25
2:10 172
2:11f. **108**
2:12 155
2:14 113
2:15 90, 106, 127
2:16 **108**, 109, 242
3:1 228
3:3 **109**
3:25 218f.

1 THESSALONIANS:
1:9 65, 82
2:19 219

4 201
4:13–17 101
4:15 200
4:16 15, 110
4:17 200
5:8f. 131
5:10 45, **110**
5:14 **110**f.
5:19 **111**
5:21 207
5:23 131

2 THESSALONIANS:
1:7 61
2:1 200
2:4 59, 113
2:6f. **111**ff.
2:11 **113**
3:6 111
3:7 111
3:11 111

1 TIMOTHY:
1:18 116
1:20 91, **113**
2:1–5 **113**f.
2:5 49
2:6 197
2:8 **114**
2:9 **114**
2:20 91
3:1 **115**
3:2 **115**, 117
3:8–13 **115**
3:11 68
3:15 **115**f.
3:16 **116**, 173
4:4f. 5, 81
4:12 **116**
4:14 113, **116**
5:3–16 **116**
5:9 115
5:17 **117**
5:18 185
6:3–5 131
6:16 215

2 TIMOTHY:
1:6 116
1:10 180
1:18 **113**
2:2 154, 182
2:6 **117**
2:17f. 113, **117**f.
2:19–21 **118**
3:1–8 131
3:13 131
3:3 68
3:8–13 184
3:16 216
4:5 247
4:10 **118**f.
4:11 **119**

TITUS:
1:6 115
2:13 68, 131, 162, 173

HEBREWS:
1:2 125, 171, 190, 191
1:4 **120**

1:5 **120,** 171f.
1:6 24f.
1:7 **121**
2:9 **121**
2:14 4
2:15 180
2:17 131
3:6 124
3:10 60
4:15 **121,** 132
5:5 172
5:7 179
6:2 **121**
6:4 121f.
6:13 49
7:1–10 6
7:3 **122,** 124
7:16 202
7:22 **122**
7:25 132, 177
7:27 **122**
8:13 206
9:1–5 **122f.**
9:4 **123**
9:12 12, 126
9:13ff. 94
9:14 134
9:16f. **123f.**
9:18–20 125
9:23 **124**
9:25 126
9:28 44
10:4 14
10:5ff. 158, 246
10:12 **124**
10:15ff. 94
10:22 **124**
10:26ff. **124f.**
10:29 **125**
10:30 102
10:37 201
11:3 **125,** 190
11:4 134
11:10 222
11:16 222
11:17 24f.
11:19 70
11:35 **125**
11:40 222
12:14 **125**
12:23 128
12:24 **126**
13:6 130
13:15 246

JAMES:
1:1 **126**
1:2 **126**
1:5f. 53, 220
1:18 172
2:1 220
2:5 220
2:19 220
2:21 220
3:6 **126**
3:15 90
4:15 187
5:14 **126f.**
5:15 220

1 PETER:
1:1f. 196
1:5 128
1:9f. 128
1:18 124
1:19 110
2:2 128
2:5 124
2:6 157f.
2:8 196
2:9 219
2:12 **127**
2:24 44, 176
3:6 215
3:18ff. **127f.**
4:1–3 **129**
4:6 **129**
5:13 152

2 PETER:
1:1 162
1:11 202
1:19 **130**
1:20 **130**
1:21 216
2:1ff. **130f.**
2:4 127
3:10ff. **131**
3:14 131
3:15 **131**

1 JOHN:
1:7 134
2:1 **131f.,** 133
2:2 **132**
2:9–11 **132**
2:15 132f.
2:19 134
3:8 **133**
3:9 **133**
3:11f. 134
3:12 132
4:1–3 207
4:9 24, 171
4:20 **133**
5:3 133
5:6 **133f.**
5:7 134
5:8 **133f.**
5:18 25

3 JOHN:
4 **134**
9f. **134**
12 101

JUDE:
5 **93**
6 5, 202
7 203
8 127
11 **134**
22f **135**
25 203

REVELATION:
1:3 **136**
1:4 **136**
1:5 25
1:19 136
2–3 **136**
2:4 **137**

2:6 **137**
2:7 **137**
2:12–17 137
2:26f. 140
3:1 136
3:14 108
3:18 137
4:4 **137**
4:5 136
4:6ff. 31
5:6 136
5:9 **137f.**
6 57, 58
6:6 **138**
6:8 **138**
6:9 141
6:11 142
6:13 60, **138**
6:16 138
6:17ff. **138f.**
7:5–8 **139**
7:9–17 142
8:2 136
9:1 **139**
10:7 **139**
11:2f. 34, 60
11:15 **139,** 202
12:1–6 **139f.**
12:4 54, 60
12:9 3, 228
12:10 5
12:11 142
12:14 34
13:1 **140**
13:5 34
13:7 140
13:8 110
13:18 **140**
14:1–5 142
14:4 39, 142
14:6f. 209
15:2 142
16 138
16:12 **141**
17:3ff. **141**
17:8 110
17:10 **141**
19:7f. **141**
19:10 142
19:11ff. 29
20:1–7 228
20:2 69
20:3ff. **141**
20:4 **141f.**
20:10 **142**
20:12 110
20:15 110
21 141
21:3 172
21:14 **142**
21:24 172, 235
21:26 37
21:27 110
22:1ff. 69
22:9 136
22:10 **136**
22:17 **142**
22:18 159
22:20 100